Rabbi Abraham Ibn Ezra's

Commentary On The Book of Psalms

ACADEMIC
STUDIES
PRESS

The Reference Library of Jewish Intellectual History

Abraham Ibn Ezra's

COMMENTARY

On The First Book of Psalms:

CHAPTER 1-41

Translated and Annotated by
H. Norman Strickman

Boston
2009

Library of Congress Cataloging-in-Publication Data
Ibn Ezra, Abraham ben Meïr, 1092-1167.
 Rabbi Abraham Ibn Ezra's commentary on the first two books of Psalms / translated
and annotated by H. Norman Strickman.
    p. cm. -- (The reference library of Jewish intellectual history)
 Includes bibliographical references and index.
 ISBN 978-1-934843-30-7
 1. Bible. O.T. Psalms--Commentaries--Early works to 1800. I. Strickman, H. Nor-
man, 1940- II. Title.

BS1429.I24 2009
223'.2077--dc22

                          2009008078

Book design by Olga Grabovsky

Published by Academic Studies Press in 2009

28 Montfern Avenue
Brighton, MA 02135, USA
press@academicstudiespress.com
www.academicstudiespress.com

CONTENTS

INTRODUCTION

Abraham ibn Ezra — his life and works

LIFE

Rabbi Abraham ben Meir ibn Ezra was one of the outstanding personalities produced by medieval Andalusian Jewry. He was a noted poet, mathematician, astrologer, grammarian, and philosopher. Above all, Ibn Ezra was one of the greatest Bible commentators of all time.

Ibn Ezra was born in 1092 C.E. in Tudela, Spain, and died in 1164.[1] His place of death is unknown. London,[2] Calahorra,[3] Rome,[4] and the Land of Israel[5] have been suggested as the place of his demise.

Little is known of Ibn Ezra's family life. He alluded to five sons,[6] but only one, Isaac, is known by name.[7] The latter was a poet of note who spent most of his life in the Near East. Isaac is reported to have converted to Islam while in Babylonia.[8] He later returned

1. According to a statement found in several codices, Ibn Ezra (henceforth I.E.) died on Monday, the first day of 1 Adar 4927 (January 23, 1167) at the age of seventy-five. If this date is accepted, then I.E. was born in 1092. See M. Friedlander, *The Commentary of Ibn Ezra on Isaiah*, (London: 1873) p. xxvii n. 54. However, H. Graetz believes that I.E. was born between 1088 and 1089. See H. Graetz, *Divre Yeme Yisra'el* (translated by S. P. Rabinowitz) Vol. 4, (Warsaw: 1916) p. 212. Also see J.L. Fleisher, *Be-Ezu Shanah Met Rabbenu Avraham ibn Ezra* in *R. Avraham ibn Ezra, Kovetz Ma'amarim Al Toledatav Vi-Yetzirotav*, (Tzion, Tel Aviv: 1970) pp. 5-16.

2. E. Z. Melammed, *Mefareshe Ha- Mikra*, Jerusalem: 1978), Volume 2, p. 520.

3. Abraham Zacuto, *Sefer Ha-Yuchasin* (London: 1857).

4. See L. Zunz, *Die Monatstage des Kalenderjares* (Berlin: 1872). Quoted in Friedlander p. xxvi, note 53.

5. Naphtali ben Menachem. *Mechkere Rabbenu Avraham ibn Ezra*. (Sinai 10, Israel: 1942) pp. 266-287.

6. See I.E. on Exodus 2: 1.

7. For Isaac's biography see *Yitzhak ibn Ezra Shirim*, Ed. Menahem H. Schmeltzer (New York: 1979), pp. 9-11; and Sarah Katz, *Fair Verses of the Jewish Adalusian Poets* (Heb.), (Jerusalem: 1997) pp. 101-126.

8. Ibid.

to Judaism.[9] A heartrending lament by Ibn Ezra[10] reveals that Isaac predeceased his father. Ibn Ezra's wife died before 1140[11] and he never remarried.

While in Spain Ibn Ezra was primarily known as a poet. He later reminisced:

> In days of old in my youth;
> I composed poems;
> I placed them as pearls;
> On the necks of the Hebrews.[12]

Ibn Ezra was on very friendly terms with the great poet and philosopher Rabbi Judah Ha-Levi. In his commentary on Scripture he quotes conversations on biblical and philosophic topics in which he engaged in with the great poet.[13] It is also worthy of note that Ibn Ezra's son Isaac accompanied Rabbi Judah Ha-Levi on his journey to Egypt.[14]

Some sources claim that Ibn Ezra and Rabbi Judah Ha-Levi were cousins, the sons of two sisters. Other traditions claim that Ibn Ezra married Rabbi Judah Ha-Levi's daughter. However, there are no contemporary records that substantiate these traditions. Hence historians gave them no credence.[15]

Ibn Ezra was on such intimate terms with Judah Ha-Levi that after the latter's death he imagined the great poet inviting him to join him in the next word. He pictures Judah as telling him:

> Though sweet my slumber, my strong love for thee
> Bids me arise and seek thy presence, friend!
> The heavenly angels yearn to hear thy song,
> And ask thee now to join their holy ranks.
> Come; let our spirits chant in unison,
> While in the dust our wearied bodies rest.

---

9. See Chapter 3 of Al-Charizi's *Tahkemoni*. Quoted in *Ha-Shirah Ha-Ivrit Bi-Sefarad U-Ve-Provance*, Chaim Shirman (Jerusalem and Tel Aviv: 1956) p. 112. J. L. Fleisher disputes this. See his, *Eleh Toledot Yitzhak ben Avraham* in *Apiryon*, Year 5, No.1. This is also disputed by David Kahana. See his *Rabbi Avraham ibn Ezra*, vol. 2, (Warsaw: 1922), pp. 78-81. According to Kahana, Isaac's patron converted to Islam and the apostasy was mistakenly attributed to Isaac.

10. David Goldstein, *The Jewish Poets of Spain*, (London, 1965), p. 161.

11. *Ibn Ezra Al Ha-Torah*, Vol. 1, edited by Asher Weiser, (Jerusalem: 1976) p. 9.

12. See Kahana Vol. 1, p.22.

13. See Ibn Ezra's commentary on Ex. 20:1; Num. 27:3; Deut. 33:5; 29:19; Zech. 8:6; Dan. 9:2.

14. See Schmeltzer p. 10.

15. See Joseph Cohen, *Haguto Ha-Filosofit Shel Rabbenu Avraham ibn Ezra*, (Israel: 1996) p. 57-58.

Though Ibn Ezra loved and admired Rabbi Judah Ha-Levi he unsurprisingly turned down the invitation. He mused:

> Return, my brother Judah, to the rest,
> For God permits me not to follow thee.
> A happy lot may still be mine on earth;
> For Heaven's manna I'm not yet prepared,
> And though my grief be bitter for thy death
> I cannot go where thou would'st beckon me. [16]

Ibn Ezra also counted among his close friends Rabbi Moses ibn Ezra[17] (c. 1055- c. After 1135) and Rabbi Joseph ibn Tzadik (c. 1095-1149). Rabbi Moses was a prominent poet from a powerful family with connections to the court of Granada. He was brought up in wealth and culture. Rabbi Moses composed both secular and liturgical poetry.

Rabbi Joseph ibn Tzadik was a *dayyan,*[18] philosopher and poet. His work *Olam Katan*[19] was praised by Maimonides and is alluded to in Ibn Ezra's commentary on the Pentateuch.[20]

Abraham ibn Ezra lived in Spain until 1140 C.E.[21] He then left his homeland and lived as an itinerant scholar until his death. It was during this period that most of his books were written. His travels included Italy, France and England.[22] His journeys might also have taken him to Egypt and other places in North Africa.[23]

It is not certain as to why Ibn Ezra left Spain. We do not know what motivated him to leave his friends and family and wander across the face of Europe. In his introduction to his commentary on *Lamentations*, Ibn Ezra writes that he left Spain *because of the fury of the oppressor* (chamat ha-metzik).[24] In his introduction to *Koheleth*, which he wrote in Rome, Ibn Ezra notes that he came to

---

16. Friedlander p. xv.

17. The two were not related.

18. A religious judge.

19. The Microcosm.

20. See I.E. on Gen. 1:26: "May God's name be blessed. He commenced with the macrocosm and concluded with the microcosm."

21. Ibid.

22. Melammed, pp. 519-520.

23. Norman Golb, *History and Culture of the Jews of Rouen in the Middle Ages* (Heb), (Tel Aviv: 1976), p. 45.

24. Ibn Ezra borrowed the phrase *chamat ha-metzik* from Is. 51:13.

that city with "an affrighted soul."[25] He goes on to implore God for a change in fortune, for up to now he has been like *a terebinth whose leaves wither.*[26] In one of his poems Ibn Ezra alludes to a tragedy that befell his family. He writes:

> The wandering troops gathered against me.
> They camped round about my heart.
> They did not take up their journey.
> They fought mightily with me.
> I trembled, lest I die before they die.
> They took hold of my neck to afflict me in their anger.
> They shattered my house and its guardians moved.
> My children cried...
> My troubles were as great as the sand of the sea.
> How could the seas pass over me without my troubles drowning?
> How can rivers of tears descend from my eyes,
> Over the flames of my heart without extinguishing them?
> The flesh of my body is consumed.
> My mind has become dumb.
> I ask people who were plagued.
> They do no know nor did they hear of any such sufferings as mine...
> What can I now do?
> There is no strength in my hands.
> I am occupied.
> Therefore my words are confused.[27]

We do not know when the above occurred. If it took place shortly before Ibn Ezra's exit from Spain then we can safely assume that this persecution precipitated Ibn Ezra's departure

There are those who tie Ibn Ezra's departure from Spain to the Almohades' invasion.[28] However, the Almohades invasion took place in 1145, while Ibn Ezra left Spain some five years earlier.

Some suggest that Ibn Ezra's poverty was the reason for his leaving his homeland.[29] Concerning his poverty wrote:

> I cannot become rich; the fates are against me;
> Were I a dealer in shrouds, no man would ever die,

---

25. See Ps. 6:4.

26. See Isaiah 1:30

27. Kahana, Vol. 2, p. 36. My Transation.

28. Kahana Vol. 2, p. 10.

29. Friedlander, p. xiv.

4

Ill-starred was my birth, unpropitious the planets;
Were I a seller of candles, the sun would never set.[30]

In a similar vein he complains:

I come in the morn,
To the house of the nobly born.
They say he rode away.
I come again at the end of the day,
But he is not at his best, and needs rest.
He is either sleeping or riding afar-
Woe to the man who is born without a star.[31]

In another poem he complains about his threadbare cloak.

Like to a sieve is that old cloak of mine,
A sieve that wheat and barley might refine.
I spread it tent-like in the mid of night,
And view through it the stars in endless line;
The Moon, Orion, and the Pleiades,
And countless constellations through it shine.

I am weary counting all its numerous holes,
Jagged and cleft like a saw in their design.
The threads with which my cloak is patched exceed
The warp and weft by more than nine times nine;
And should a fly fall in its mazy web,
He's speedily despair and to death resign...
O God, exchange it for a cloak of praise,
But make its seams much stronger, Power divine![32]

In Spain Ibn Ezra was known primarily as a poet. However, he also was a master of Hebrew grammar, Sephardic biblical exegesis, astrology, mathematics and philosophy. The latter were generally unknown by the inhabitants of Italy, Franco-Germany and England. Thus Rabbi Judah ibn Tibbon (c. 1120- 1190) writes:

"The Jews living in exile in France and in all the borders of Edom do not know Arabic. Books written in Arabic are like sealed books to them. They can not approach them until they are translated into the Hebrew tongue...[this was so] until the wise man Rabbi Abraham ben Ezra came

---

30. Friedlander, p. xiv.

31. Meyer Waxman, *A History of Jewish Literature*, (New Jersey: 1960), Volume 1, p. 234.

32. Harry H. Fine, *Gems of Hebrew Verse*. Boston: 1940.

to their country and helped them...with regard to this by composing short compositions..."[33]

Ibn Ezra mastered these sciences and parleyed his expertise into a source of sustenance. The question is, was this planned in advance, or did Ibn Ezra see an opportunity and seize it?

Ibn Ezra arrived in Rome in 1140. He there composed his first works of Biblical exegesis, a commentary on the Scroll of Koheleth[34] and a commentary on the book of Job.[35] He also translated the grammatical works of Judah Hayuj from Arabic to Hebrew and wrote a grammatical work called the *Moznayim* (The Balance).[36]

Ibn Ezra left Rome after spending a number of fruitful years there. The reason for his departure is unknown. He may have been motivated by a need to travel and to experience new vistas.

It is hard to establish Ibn Ezra's exact itinerary after leaving Rome. Graetz believes that he went to the city of Solerno[37] where he found a patron by the name of Elyakim[38] who supplied all of his needs.[39]

According to Graetz, Ibn Ezra encountered some opposition in Solerno. A well-respected Rabbi of Greek origin[40] criticized Ibn Ezra's work. He accused Ibn Ezra's of promoting heretical ideas. Ibn Ezra responded by labeling his opponent "a Greek grasshopper." He charged him and his supporters with libeling the Spanish scholars[41] by casting aspersions on their religious beliefs.

Ibn Ezra also spent some time in Mantova where in the fall of 1145 he composed the *Sefer Ha-Tzachot*,[42] a work dealing with Hebrew grammar and meter.

---

33. See Wilinsky, M. *Sefer Ha-Rikmah Le-Rabbenu ibn Janah, Be-Targumo Shel Rabbenu Yehudah ibn Tibbon*, (Jerusalem: 1964) p. 4.

34. See I.E.'s introduction to his commentary on Koheleth. According to Graetz, I.E. composed his commentary on all of the Five Scrolls in Rome. See *Geschichte*, VI, p. 371.

35. See I.E.'s introduction to his commentary on *Job*. Also see Graetz, *Divre Yeme Yisra'el*, VI, p. 371.

36. Graetz. *Divre Yeme Yisra'el*, VI, p. 371.

37. Some dispute Graetz's assertion. See Golb, p. 45; note 118. If the incident that follows did not take place in Solarno, then it occurred in some other European city, for Ibn Ezra speaks of the incident.

38. Elyakim like Ibn Ezra was of Sephardic origin.

39. Graetz. *Divre Yeme Yisra'el*, VI, p. 371-2.

40. Graetz gives his name as Shimiy.

41. Ibn Ezra refers to them as "faithful children."

42. Levin, *Yalkut Ibn Ezra*, 379-396.

Ibn Ezra then betook himself to Lucca where he completed a commentary on Isaiah;[43] a commentary on the early prophets; a commentary on the Pentateuch;[44] a defense of Saadiah Gaon's Biblical exegeses from the criticism of Menachem ben Saruk;[45]and possibly a work on Astronomy.[46]

Ibn Ezra's commentary on the Bible was a major contribution to biblical exegesis. It is based on the rules of Hebrew grammar and focuses on the plain meaning of the text. In the introduction to his commentary on the Pentateuch, Ibn Ezra wrote: "I will not show favoritism to anyone when it comes to interpreting the Torah. I will, to the utmost of my ability try to understand grammatically every word and then do my best to explain it."[47]

Although Ibn Ezra held that, generally speaking, the Bible is to be taken at face value, he made an exception for those verses that contradict reason. He thus believed that all verses that refer to God in human terms are not to be taken literally but are to be interpreted metaphorically. I.E. stressed "that the Torah spoke in the language of man, for it was given to humans who speak and hear."[48]

Ibn Ezra respectfully differed with the Rabbis of the Talmud in instances in which he believed that their interpretations contradicted the literal meaning of the text. However, in cases that had halakhic relevance, Ibn Ezra maintained that the law transmitted by the Rabbis was true in itself, but that the Sages had used the biblical verse under discussion as a means of formulating the laws. Ibn Ezra thus maintained, contrary to the rabbinic sages, that *be fruitful, and multiply* (Genesis 1:28) is not a command but a blessing, and that the Sages merely used this verse as a mode for the transmission of a law passed on to them.[49]

Commenting on Exodus 23:2, Ibn Ezra noted that the Rabbis interpreted *achare rabbim le-hattot* (after a multitude to pervert justice) to mean that legal disputes are to be solved in accordance with the majority opinion of a court of law,[50] after which he argued that this is not the literal meaning of the verse. Ibn

---

43. In the spring of 1146.

44. The short commentary.

45. The *Sefat Yeter.* Edited by G.H. Lippman. 1843.

46. Later known as the *Tabulae Pisanea.* However, these may have been composed in Pizza. See Golb, p. 45; note 119.

47. *Ibn Ezra's Commentary on The Pentateuch, Genesis;* translated and annotated by H. Norman Strickman and Arthur Silver, (New York: 1988) p. 17.

48. See I.E on Gen. 1:26.

49. I. E. on Gen. 1:28.

50. San. 2a.

Ezra then said that the Sages used this text as a sign by which to remember the above noted halakhah.

In some cases, Ibn Ezra claimed that a law that the Talmud derives from a biblical verse is really rabbinic in origin. For example, Exodus 23:19 reads, *Thou shalt not seethe a kid in its mother's milk.* According to the Rabbis, this verse prohibits the cooking of any kosher meat and milk.[51] Ibn Ezra insisted that the Pentateuch prohibits only the cooking of a kid in its mother's milk and that the other prohibitions are rabbinic.[52]

When Ibn Ezra offered an interpretation of a verse that differed with the halakhah, he usually added a note to the effect that the halakhah is to be followed because it is independent of the verse or because one is obligated to follow the rabbinic interpretations since "the minds of the sages were greater than our minds." Ibn Ezra did not want his literal approach to undermine the halakhah or to serve as a support for anti-halakhic sectarians.

Ibn Ezra was infuriated when shown a commentary on the Bible with a view that reckoned the beginning of the biblical day with the morning, not the night before as maintained by halakhah. Ibn Ezra feared that this commentary might cause the Sabbath to be desecrated by suggesting that work might be permitted on the eve of the Sabbath. He wrote a book entitled The *Sabbath Epistle* to refute the notion that the Sabbath begins in the morning. Ibn Ezra cursed the author of the aforementioned commentary with the imprecation, "May the hand of him who wrote this wither, and may his eyes be darkened[53].

Ibn Ezra's commentaries influenced all subsequent major Bible commentators. Indeed, he is quoted in the commentaries of Abraham Maimonides, Nahmanides, Bahya ben Asher, Levi ben Gershom, and Abravanel as well as other exegetes, philosophers, and scholars. Maimonides is reported to have charged his son not to pay attention to any Bible commentaries other than those of Ibn Ezra.[54]

51. See Hullin 113b.

52. See I.E. on Ex. 23:19.

53. See "Sefer Ha-Shabbat," in *Yalkut Ibn Ezra.* Ed. Israel Levin (New York and Tel Aviv: 1985). See also Graetz, p. 228.

54. The authenticity of Maimonides' charge has been challenged. See Y. L. Krinsky, *Chumash Im Pirush Mechokeke Yehudah* (New York: 1975), p. 18. Also see Rabbi Jacob Emden's *Mitpachat Sefarim,* Chap. 9, p. 71.

COMMENTARY ON THE BOOK OF PSALMS

Ibn Ezra wrote two commentaries to the book of Psalms. One survives only in fragments.[55] The other completed on the 15th day of Elul in the Hebrew year 4916 (September 2, 1156) in the city of Rouen in Northern France survives in full and is the standard commentary of I.E. which is printed in the Rabbinic Bible. [56]

According to Ibn Ezra the purpose of human life is to observe God's law; know and love God;[57] and share one's knowledge of God with other human beings. He believes that the person who is "always conscious of God and His deeds and wonders, and informs people of God's glory... is one of those who *turn the many to righteousness* (Dan. 12:3).[58] The latter is the primary purpose of the book of psalms, for "the secret of all psalms is (contained in) the statement, *I will extoll Thee, my God, O King* (Ps. 145:1); *Bless the Lord, ye angels of His* (Ps.103: 20); *O magnify the Lord with me* (ibid 34:4)."[59]

Ibn Ezra believes that the book of Psalms contains hymns composed by King David and various other authors. He maintains that all of the latter, with the exception of the composer of Ps. 90, were contemporaries of King David. He took issue with Rabbi Saadiah Gaon who believed that King David wrote the entire book of Psalms.[60]

Ibn Ezra believes that many of the psalms were composed to be chanted to the tune of popular songs. He claims that the name of the song to which the psalm was to be chanted is indicated by a word in the opening sentence of the psalm. Examples of the latter are *la-menatze'ach al ha-gittit* (For the Leader; upon the Gittith) (Ps. 8:1); and *la-menatze'ach al ha-sheminit* (For the Leader; on the Sheminith) (Ps.12: 1). According to Ibn Ezra the former was to be sung to the tune of a song opening with the words "The Gittite boasts"[61] and the latter to a song opening with the words "On the Sheminith."[62]

---

55. The fragment consists of I.E.'s introduction to Psalms and his commentary to Ps. 1 and Ps 2 1-5. See Uriel Simon, *Four Approaches to the Book of Psalms: From Saadiah Gaon to Abraham ibn Ezra*; translated by Lenn J. Schramm (New York: 1991) pp. 308-333.

56. Ibid. P. 146. Simon believes that I.E. possibly wrote this commentary in less than ten months.

57. See *The Secret of the Torah: A Translation of Ibn Ezra's Yesod Mora Ve-Sod Ha-Torah*; translated and annotated by H. Norman Strickman, (New Jersey: 1995), pp. 10; 142; 143, 176-179.

58. Ibid. 108.

59. Ibid. P. 179-180.

60. Simon 177-182.

61. I.E. on Ps. 8:1.

62. *I.E. on Ps. 12:1.*

Ibn Ezra is of the opinion that the book of Psalms is a prophetic work. He believes that many of its compositions deal with future events. He differs with Rabbi Moses ibn Giqatilah[63] who believed that the psalms were non- prophetic compositions.[64]

Aside from being a Bible commentator, Ibn Ezra was also a philosopher of note. His philosophical views are expressed in his Biblical commentaries, his poetry and his short treatises, especially his *Yesod Mora* which was one of the first philosophic works to be written in Hebrew.

Ibn Ezra was essentially a Neo-Platonist and was greatly influenced by Solomon ibn Gabirol the Spanish poet and philosopher. Ibn Ezra divided the universe into three worlds: the upper world of the "intelligences" or angels, the intermediate world of the heavenly spheres,[65] and the lower sublunary world, the corporeal world of creation and decay.[66] He believed that the Biblical account of creation only applied to the sublunary world.[67]

Ibn Ezra taught that God is one and that all things exist by virtue of Him.[68] The Lord is incorporeal and has no likeness or form.[69] Hence God is not subject to human feelings or corporeal accidents.[70]

Ibn Ezra believed that God does not come directly into contact with the material world and that the sub lunar world was not created directly by God but by angels termed *Elohim* by Scripture. He thus interpreted the word *Elohim* in the first chapter of Genesis as meaning God acting through the angels.[71]

Ibn Ezra held that man has three souls: vegetative, animal and rational.[72] The latter alone is immortal.[73]

Ibn Ezra believed that man's rational soul comes from the upper world, and that immortality is achieved by developing one's soul. He writes:

'Man's soul is unique. When given by God, it is like a tablet set before a scribe. When God's writing, which consists of the categorical knowledge of the

---

63. A noted tenth century Spanish grammarian and Bible commentator.

64. Simon, p. 189.

65. See I.E. on Ps. 19:

66. I.*E. on Ex. 3:15*

67. I.E. on Gen. 1:2.

68. Ibid. 1:26.

69. Ibid.

70. I.E. on Ps.2: 4.

71. *I.E. on Gen. 1:1.*

72. *See The Secret of he Torah*, page 96 (Yesod Mora, Chap. 8)

73. Ibid. p. 173.

things made out of the four elements,[74] the knowledge of the spheres, the throne of glory, the secret of the chariot,[75] and the knowledge of the Most High, is inscribed on the tablet, the soul cleaves to God the Glorious while it is yet in man and also afterward when its power is removed from the body which is its place here on earth."[76]

According to Ibn Ezra the wicked are left entirely to the fates that the stars determine for them. However, their ultimate punishment is the destruction of their souls.[77]

Ibn Ezra stresses the importance of the Land of Israel of Israel. He explains that "Scripture tells of the purchase of the field of Machpelah to teach us of the superiority of the Land of Israel over all the countries, both for the living and for the dead."[78] He notes that God's Divine presence rests in the Land of Israel and that the sanctity of the Land of Israel is like that of Mt. Sinai at the time of the revelation.[79]

Ibn Ezra explains that the Temple was built on Mount Moriah because, "There are places upon the earth that receive power from above (Ps. 24:2)."

He further notes:

> "Divine Manifestation varies in accordance with the natural makeup of the recipient and in accordance with the upper power that is above the receiver. Therefore, the place of the holy temple [Mount Mariah] was chosen."[80]

Ibn Ezra's commentary on Psalms is part of the important intellectual bequest that this great medieval scholar left behind. It along with the other works produced by the great minds of Israel is part of the great "inheritance of congregation of Jacob."

The translation of the Book Psalms employed in this work is that of the Jewish Publication Society 1917. The text of I.E.'s commentary of Psalms that serves as the basis of this translation is the version that is printed in the *Mikra'ot Gedolot* editions of the Bible. That text contains many obvious errors. I tried to correct

---

74. The four elements were believed to be eternal and unchanging. Like God, man must attain eternal knowledge. Hence I.E. speaks of knowledge of the categories rather than knowledge of the particulars.

75. Seen by Ezekiel. See Ezekiel, Chapter 1.

76. *The Secret of the Torah* p. 143.

77. I.E. on Ps.1: 6 and 49:13. See Radak on Ps. 49:13. The latter is an elaboration of I.E's comment on this verse.

78. I.E. on Gen. 23:19.

79. I.E. on Ps. 68:17.

80. I.E. on Ex. 25:38.

many of these mistakes by comparing the *Mikra'ot Gedolot* text with the version printed in the *Ha-Keter* edition of I.E.'s commentary on Psalms. I also found J. Filwarg's[81] emendations very helpful.

In order to make the translation readable it was occasionally necessary to insert words that are not in the Hebrew text of Ibn Ezra. I did not always place these insertions in brackets, for they are clearly implied in the text and the brackets would serve to distract the reader. At other times when I felt that the insertions were in essence real additions to the text I inserted the words in brackets. However, I tried the keep the latter to a minimum.

I hope, God willing, to translate and annotate all of I.E.'s commentary to the book of Psalms. My original plan was to publish a volume every six months and to finish the entire project in two years. However, my teaching schedule did not allow me the leisure to follow this schedule. I now hope to complete the project, God willing, in about three years.

I want to express my deepest appreciation to all those whose generous contributions made the publication of these volumes possible. May Ha-Shem bestow His blessings upon them so that they can continue in their support of Torah.

I offer my deepest thanks to:

Ari & Deborah Brand

Moshe and Lori Eidlisz

Yossi & Amy Golshan

Reuben & Carol Greenberg

Aryeh & Michelle Jacobson

Harris & Avital Leitner

Avi & Hindy Norensberg

Avi & Yael Saperstein

Asher & Mimi Silverberg

Zalmy & Beila Steiner

Yaakov & Chani Ugowitz

When I started to work on this translation I lost my beloved mother, Ida Strickman. She was a pious and God fearing woman. She brought me up to the study of Torah and love of Judaism. I miss her and will never forget her. I dedicate this volume to her blessed memory.

---

81. *Bene Reshef*, Piotrakow: 1900

TO THE BOOK OF PSALMS

I WILL PRAISE GOD WHOSE SMALLEST ACT IS GREATER THAN ALL THE GREAT ACTS PUT TOGETHER.

BY THE BREATH OF HIS MOUTH THE SPHERES[1] TURN AND THE HEAVENLY HOSTS RUN UPON THEIR TRACKS.

ALL THE CONSTELLATIONS DO HIS WILL.

HIS ACTS ARE WONDROUS AND REVEALED.

I WILL DESCRIBE HIS GLORY IN PRECIOUS WORDS THAT[2] CANNOT BE WEIGHED AGAINST GOLD.

IT IS THE JOY OF MY HEART TO IMPLORE MY ROCK.

MY ENTIRE DESIRE IS TO PREPARE PRAYERS TO OFFER TO HIM.

I DEDICATE[3] THIS COMMENTARY ON THE BOOK OF PSALMS TO[4] HIS NAME.

HE WILL HELP ME[5] BEGIN AND FINISH THIS WORK.

The word of Abraham the son of Meir ibn Ezra the Spaniard:

The book[6] of psalms consists of hymns. The poet or the composer's name is written at the beginning of the psalm. However, there are many psalms that are not ascribed

---

1. The heavenly spheres which circle the earth and in which the planets and stars were believed to be embedded. See I.E. on Ps. 8:4.

2. Lit., "for they."

3. Lit., "I compose."

4. Lit., "in."

5. Lit. "He is my help."

6. Lit. "This book."

to a specific poet. The first psalm; the second psalm; the psalm opening with the words, *O Thou that dwellest in the covert of the Most High* (Ps. 91: 1), and the psalm following it,[7] are examples of the latter.

There is a great controversy among the commentaries.

Some say that David wrote the entire book of Psalms and that David was a prophet.[8] The verse *according to the commandment of David the man of God* (Neh. 12:24) proves this, for we do not find such an expression[9] used in Scripture except in regard to a prophet. Furthermore, David, in his "last words" said: *The spirit of the Lord spoke by me* (11 Sam. 23:2). *Spoke by me* is similar to *spoke with me* (Zech. 1:9). Furthermore, David said: *and His word was upon my tongue* (11 Sam. 23:2).[10]

We also find the name Jeduthan joined with David in a Psalm.[11] The reason for this is as follows: David composed this psalm. He then gave this psalm to Jeduthun to play because Jeduthan was one of the choirmasters.[12]

The same is the case with *Of Solomon. Give the king Thy judgments, O God* (Ps. 72:1). It is a prophecy by David regarding his son. Similarly, *A prayer of Moses, the man of God* (Ps. 90:1) was composed by David. He gave this psalm to the descendants of Moses, Shebual and his sons.[13] Similarly, all the psalms of Asaf and the sons of Korah were [composed by David and] handed over to one of the sons of Heman the grandson of Samuel,[14] who was a descendent of Korah, as is stated in the book of Chronicles.[15]

By the rivers of Babylon (Ps. 137:1) and *O God, the heathen are come into Thine inheritance* (Ps. 79:1) are David's prophecies, which David uttered regarding the future. It is like; *A son shall be born unto the house of David, Josiah by name* (1 Kings 13:2).[16]

There are others who say that the Book of Psalms does not contain any prophecies concerning the future.[17] It is because of this that the ancients placed it [among

---

7. Ps. 92.

8. This is the opinion of Rabbi Saadiah Gaon. See Uriel Simon, *Four Approaches to the Book of Psalms,* (New York: 1991), p. 1-42.

9. Man of God.

10. These statements indicate prophetic utterances.

11. *For Jeduthun. A Psalm of David* (Ps. 62:1).

12. Ibid.

13. See 1 Chron. 23: 15-17. David gave this psalm to the descendants of Moses to chant and play in the Temple.

14. For use in the Temple service.

15. 1 Chron. 6:18.

16. Which is a prophetic statement.

17. This is the opinion of Rabbi Moses ibn Giqatilah. See Simon, *Four Approaches to the Book of*

the Writings]¹⁸ with Job and the scrolls.¹⁹ The fact that we find the words *miz-mor* (psalm) *shir* (song) and *tefillah* (prayer) in it²⁰ proves this.²¹ They say that *By the rivers of Babylon* (Ps. 137) was composed by one of the poets in Babylonia. They similarly say that every psalm *of the sons of Korah* was composed by one of the poets of the sons of Heman who lived in Babylonia. Their words pertain to the exile. We do not find such a thing in David's psalms.²²

They say that also Asaph is the name of a poet who lived in Babylonia. They maintain that he is not to be identified with the Asaph who was a choirmaster in the days of David.

Ethan the Ezrahite similarly composed a psalm²³ when the kingdom of David was destroyed in the days of Zedekiah.²⁴

The composers of the book²⁵ of Psalms did not did not know the name of the authors of those psalms which do not have a name attached to them. The same is the case with the psalms of the sons of Korah. They were written by one of Korah's descendents. However, they²⁶ did not know his name.

The psalm, *Happy is they that are upright in the way* (Ps. 119:1) was composed by one of the young men of Israel who was honored by one of the Babylonian kings.²⁷ *Wherewithal shall a young man keep his way pure* (ibid. V. 9);²⁸ *I am small²⁹ and despised* (ibid. v. 141), and *Even though princes sit and talk against me,*³⁰ (ibid. 23) are proof of this.

Psalms, p. 113.

18. The *ketuvim*, the third part of the Bible.

19. Among the *ketubim*, the writings.

20. The five Scrolls: Kohelet, Ruth; Songs of Songs; Lamentations and Esther.

21. Songs and prayers are not prophecies.

22. David does not speak of the exile.

23. Ps. 89.

24. For the psalm speaks of Israel's devastation.

25. Lit. "This book."

26. The editors of the Book of Psalms. I.E. identifies them as the men of the great assembly. See I.E.'s Introduction to the "First Recension" in *Four Approaches to the Book of Psalms*, p. 314.

27. The reference appears to refer to one of the young men mentioned in the book of Daniel. See Daniel 1:1-4.

28. See Dan. 1: 8.

29. The commentaries take this to mean, young.

30. The commentaries take the reference to be to the princes who are jealous of the honor given to the Judean young man. See Dan. 3:8.

However, my mind inclines towards the words of the ancients of blessed memory.[31] They taught that the entire book of Psalms was written under the influence of the Holy Spirit.[32] Why are they[33] amazed at the word song?[34] The song of *Ha'azinu*[35] (Deut. 32:1) clearly shows that the term song can refer to a prophecy.

A prayer of Habakkuk (Hab. 3:1) likewise shows that the term prayer may apply to a prophecy. Habakkuk also uttered a prophetic prayer on behalf of the righteous, namely *How long, O Lord, shall I cry* (ibid. 1:2). We similarly find Isaiah saying, *O Lord, why Thou dost make us to err from Thy ways* (Is. 63:17).[36]

All psalms that begin with the name of David[37] were written by David or by one of the poets who prophesied concerning David. They are like *[A Psalm] Of Solomon. Give the king Thy Judgments, O God* (72:1) [38] which was composed by one of the poets regarding Solomon.

A Prayer of Moses (Ps. 90:1) was composed by Moses.

A Psalm of Asaf was also [not authored by David.] A man called Asaf who lived in the days of David composed it. Scripture tells us that Asaph *prophesied according to the direction of the king*[39] (1 Chron. 25:2).

The psalms of the songs of Korah were composed by the sons of Heman[40] the poet. All of them lived during the time of David.[41] Scripture tells us that Heman was *the seer of the king* (ibid. v. 5).

The psalm reading *of Solomon* (Ps. 127.1) was composed by someone who prophesied concerning Solomon or about the messiah his son.[42] The messiah is referred to as Solomon in the same manner as the messiah is called David in *and David my servant shall be their prince forever* (Ez. 37:25). The latter is similar to *Therefore fear thou not, O Jacob My servant, saith the Lord* (Jer. 30:10; 46:27).[43]

---

31. The Rabbis of the Talmud.

32. It is a prophetic work.

33. Those who maintain that Book of Psalms is not a prophetic work.

34. Placed at the beginning of certain psalms. This indicates to the above commentaries that the Book of Psalms is not prophetic.

35. Composed by Moses.

36. This too was a prayer.

37. Psalms that begin with *A psalm of David* or the like.

38. Which was not written by Solomon. See I.E. on Ps. 72:1.

39. David.

40. Who were descendents of Korah. They are listed in 1 Chron. 25:4.

41. Ibid. Verse 5.

42. His descendent.

43. Jacob in Jeremiah does not refer to Jacob the patriarch, but to his children the people of Israel.

It is possible that those psalms that do not have a particular name at their beginning were not composed by David. On the other hand David might have composed them. They might be similar to the psalm *O give thanks unto the Lord, call upon His name* (105:1). The name of David does not appear in it. However, David wrote this psalm. It is clearly stated in Chronicles that David composed this psalm in honor of the ark,[44] and gave it to Asaf the poet.[45]

Why are the commentaries[46] amazed that the words *The Prophecy of David* does not appear at the beginning of the Book of Psalms when there is no doubt among the Israelites that our master Moses composed the book of Genesis even though it does not open with *And the Lord spoke unto Moses*, for this[47] is the tradition which our holy fathers of blessed memory received.

Similarly David in Ezekiel 37:25 does not refer to King David, but to the messiah his descendent.

44. Lit., "over the ark."

45. See 1 Chron. 16:7.

46. Who claim that Psalms is not prophetic.

47. That Moses is the author of the Genesis.

CHAPTER 1

1. HAPPY IS THE MAN THAT HATH NOT WALKED IN THE COUNSEL OF THE WICKED, NOR STOOD IN THE WAY OF SINNERS, NOR SAT IN THE SEAT OF THE SCORNFUL.

HAPPY IS THE MAN. Our Rabbis of blessed memory said that standing in the way of sinners is a greater transgression than walking in the counsel of the wicked and that sitting in the seat of the scornful is worse then either standing in the way of sinners or walking [in the counsel of the wicked][1]. Now if this so, then scorners[2] are worse than sinners.[3] Rabbi Moses Ha-Kohen[4] says the reverse.[5] He says that *ve-lo amad* (nor stood) means, and did not even stand.[6]

In my opinion, the term wicked *(resha'im)* refers to those who are in constant flux.[7] Compare, *But the wicked* (resha'im) *are like the troubled sea; For it cannot rest* (Is. 57:20). Similarly, and *withersoever he[8] turned himself, he unsettled them* (yarshi'a)[9] *(1 Sam. 14:47)*. Likewise, and *When He gives quietness, who then can disturb* (yarshi'a)[10] *(Job. 34: 29)*. It is for this reason that *walked* is mentioned with the *wicked* (resha'im). Our clause refers

---

1. In other words our verse deals with a progression of evil behavior. See *Avodah Zarah* 18b.

2. Mentioned at the end of our verse.

3. Who are mentioned in the first part of our verse.

4. Rabbi Moses ben Samuel Giqatila, an eleventh century Bible commentator. I.E. Ezra quotes him very often in his commentary on Psalms.

5. According to Rabbi Moses Ha-Kohen the verse starts with the most serious offence and concludes with the least serious.

6. Our verse is to be understood as follows: Happy is the man who has not walked in the counsel of the wicked (the major offense), nor even stood in the way of sinners (a lesser offence) nor even sat in the seat of the scornful (a lesser offence).

7. Hence Scripture speaks of walking in the council of the wicked.

8. King Saul.

9. Translated according to I.E.

10. Translated according to I.E. See I.E. on Job 34:29.

to a person who is enticed into following the counsel of someone who is wicked and is seduced to follow a path that he is unacquainted with.

Chata'im (sinners) are worse than *resha'im* (wicked). It is because of this that Scripture speaks of *the way of sinners.* It does so because sinners are in the habit of walking in an evil way.[11]

Sitting [in the seat of the scornful] is worse than *standing [in the way of sinners].* This is the opinion of the Rabbis.[12]

The word *letzim* (scorners) comes from the same root as the word *melitz* (interpreter) in *for the interpreter was between them* (Gen. 42:23). The *melitz* reveals the secret of Reuben[13] to Simeon.[14] The *letzim* are the opposite of the *anavim* (humble). We thus read: *If it concerns the scorners* (letzim) *He scorns them* (Prov. 3:34). The verse then goes on to say, *But to the humble* (anavim) *He gives grace* (ibid). The *anavim* are ashamed to speak ill or to ascribe fault or to reveal secrets.

The *shema*[15] (Deut. 6: 4-9) speaks of the four positions of the human body. They are: [Sitting, walking, lying down and rising up. We thus read: *when thou sittest in thy house, and when thou walkest by the way, and when thou liest down, and when thou risest up* (Deut. 6:7).]

When thou walkest is the opposite of *when thou sittest,* for moving is the opposite of resting. *And when thou liest* is the opposite of *and when thou risest up* (ibid).[16]

Sat in our verse[17] corresponds to *when thou sittest.* Similarly, *walked* corresponds to *when thou walkest.* Likewise, *stood*[18] corresponds to *when thou risest.*[19] Lying down is not mentioned in our verse because most of the time a person is asleep when he is lying down.[20] According to the rules of Hebrew grammar a letter is prefixed to a verb to indicate the imperfect. A *yod* placed before the third person perfect[21] changes the verb into a third

---

11. Literally, "in this way."

12. See note 1.

13. The *melitz* interprets the words of Reuben. Secret here does not refer to something which one wants to keep hidden.

14. Reuben and Simeon are hypothetical names. The point is that the *letz* reveals personal secrets.

15. The Shema, like our psalm, speaks of the positions of the body. I.E. elaborates on the four positions of the human body in Chapter 10 of his *Yesod Mora.* See *The Secret ot the Torah, A Translation of Abraham Ibn Ezra's Yesod Mora Ve-Sod Ha-Torah;* translated and annotated by H. Norman Strickman, (New Jersey: 1995) pp. 139-142.

16. *And when thou risest up* is the fourth position of the human body.

17. Literally, "in Psalms."

18. In our verse.

19. Lit. "Also *walked* corresponds to *when you rise.*"

20. Hence there is no need to mention it in our verse.

21. A *pa'al.* Comp. *Katav,* he wrote.

person imperfect.²² The perfect and imperfect are used to indicate the present form.²³ Compare, *And the posts of the door were moved* (va-yanu'u)²⁴...*and the house will be filled*²⁵ *with smoke* (yimmale)²⁶ (Is. 6:4). The same applies to *halakh* (walked)²⁷... and to *yehege* (doth he meditate) in and *in His law doth he meditate* (v. 2).²⁸ [The meaning of the latter is:] He²⁹ is not interested in nor does he desire the vanities of this world. On the contrary all of his delight is in the Torah of God, to fulfill the commandments.

[2 BUT HIS DELIGHT IS IN THE LAW OF THE LORD; AND IN HIS LAW DOTH HE MEDITATE DAY AND NIGHT.]

The Torah shows a person the right way.³⁰ Hence the term Torah.³¹

The word *yehegeh* (meditate) means, to contemplate.³² Compare, *And the meditation of my heart* (ve-hagut) *shall be understanding* (Ps. 49:4). It also refers to the utterance of the lips as in, *And my tongue shall speak* (tehegeh) *of Your righteousness* (Ps. 35:28).³³

Scripture reads: *And in His law doth he meditate* (V. 2). It does not read: "And in it doth he meditate."³⁴ The former reading is more poetic. Look, Scripture employs the word Israel five times in one verse.³⁵

Scripture mentions day and night in the Shema, in correspondence to the four positions of the body.³⁶

---

22. A *yifal*. Comp. *Yikhtov*, he will write.

23. When they speak of one event.

24. *Va-yanu'u* is a perfect.

25. Translated lit.

26. *Yimmale* is an imperfect. According to I.E. the verse should be rendered: *And the posts of the door were moving.... and the house was filling with smoke.* See Friedlander on Is. 1:24.

27. *Halakh* should be rendered as a present form. According to I.E. our verse should be rendered: *Happy is the man who walks not in the counsel of the wicked, And stands not in the way of sinners, Nor sits where the scorners sit.*

28. *Yehege* is a future form. Hence I.E.'s comment.

29. The righteous person.

30. Or, directs a person on the right way.

31. Which means teaching, direction and instruction.

32. Lit., "to meditations of the heart."

33. Thus, according to I.E., *And in His law doth he meditate day and night* means, he contemplates on and speaks of God's law day and night

34. When a noun is employed, normal usage requires that the noun be next referred to by a pronoun. Why then does Scripture repeat the word *Torah*?

35. Num. 1:19. See I.E. on Ex. 34:4.

36. Sitting and walking take place mainly during the day. Lying down to sleep and rising from sleep take

3. AND HE SHALL BE LIKE A TREE PLANTED BY STREAMS OF WATER, THAT BRINGETH FORTH ITS FRUIT IN ITS SEASON, AND WHOSE LEAF DOTH NOT WITHER; AND IN WHATSOEVER HE DOETH HE SHALL PROSPER.

BROOKS OF WATER. The word *palge* (brooks) is related to the word *pallag* (divide) in *divide (pallag) their tongue* (Ps. 55:10). *By brooks of water* means, by one of the brooks.[37] It is similar to *Into the innermost parts* (yarkete) *of the ship* (Jonah 1:5);[38] *And was buried in the cities of Gilead*[39] (Judges 12:7)[40] and, *the foal of asses*[41] (Zech. 9:9).[42] Some say that *its fruit* refers to the children of one's youth.[43]

AND WHOSE LEAF DOES NOT WITHER. His wealth shall be preserved for as long as he lives, for *Wisdom is good with an inheritance* (Ecc. 7:11).

AND IN WHATSOEVER HE DOETH HE SHALL PROSPER. The reference is to the person who is compared to a tree. Others say that *And whatsoever he doesth he shall prosper*[44] refers to the tree. If a branch will be taken from the tree and planted, it will prosper. Others say that the reference is to its leaf.[45] It is similar to *and the leaf thereof for healing* (Ezk. 47:12).
According to my opinion:

---

place at night (before sunrise). See Jonah Filwarg's *Bene Reshef* (Pietrekov: 1900) on Ps. 1:1.

37. A tree normally grows by a brook of water. Why then does the Psalm speak of brooks? Hence I.E. comment that *by brooks* means, by *a* brook.

38. Wherein *yarkete* (parts) is to be understood as one of the parts, for Jonah did not lay down *in the innermost parts of the ships* he rather lay down in *one* of the innermost parts of the ship.

39. Translated literally.

40. Wherein the meaning of *cities* is, one of the cities, for Jeptah was not buried in the cities of Gilead.

41. Translated literally.

42. *Of asses* should be understood as of an ass.

43. In other words *piryo* (its fruit) refers to the righteous person rather than to the tree. It should be noted that if this is the case then *piryo* should be rendered, *his fruit*.

44. According to this opinion *ve-khol asher ya'aseh yatzli'ach* (And whatsoever *he* doeth shall prosper) means, and whatsoever *it* does shall prosper.

45. When used for medicinal purposes.

[1] *Its fruit* refers to the rational soul.[46] It will be satiated with God's Torah. It will know its creator and His everlasting deeds.[47] The rational soul will cleave to the[48] upper world[49] when it leaves the body. The soul when separating from its body can be compared to a ripe fruit on a tree, which separates from the tree. The fruit no longer has a need for the tree, for the tree was created for the fruit.[50]

[2] *And whose leaf does not whither* refers to the memory of the righteous. Compare, *The memory of the righteous shall be for a blessing* (Prov.10: 7).

[3] *And in whatsoever he doeth he shall prosper* refers to wealth, children[51] and honor.

4. NOT SO THE WICKED; BUT THEY ARE LIKE THE CHAFF WHICH THE WIND DRIVETH AWAY.

LIKE THE CHAFF. *Motz* (chaff) refers to the thin part of the straw. Compare, *As the chaff* (ka-motz) *that is driven by the wind out of the threshing-floor* (Hos.13: 3). Note the following: The soul of the righteous is compared to grain, for[52] the grain [unlike the chaff] endures. However, the wicked are like straw before the wind.

5. THEREFORE THE WICKED SHALL NOT STAND IN THE JUDGMENT, NOR SINNERS IN THE CONGREAGATION OF THE RIGHTEOUS.

THEREFORE. Scripture notes that the souls of the wicked will be destroyed and the memory of their children will be blotted out in this world. Hence Scripture reads: *lo ya-kumu* (shall not stand). The latter means shall not last.

The word *ba-mishpat* (in the judgment) is similar in meaning to the word *be-mishpat* (into the judgment) in *For God shall bring every work into the judgment* (Ecc. 12:14). The *bet* in the word *ba-mishpat* is vocalized with a *pattach* to indicate that the definite article is

---

46. Lit. "The wise soul." Heb. *Ha-neshamah ha-chakhamah*. According to I.E. there are three souls in the human body, a rational soul, an animal soul and a vegetable soul. See Chapter 7 of the *Yesod Mora; The Secret of the Torah p. 96.*

47. The reference is to the various categories into which all created things fall. The categories are eternal while the particulars are in flux. The soul gains immortality by obtaining knowledge of that which is eternal. See Chapter 1 of the *Yesod Mora; The Secret of the Torah p. 33.*

48. Lit., "its."

49. The place of its origin.

50. The body was similarly created to serve the soul. When the soul no longer has any need of the body it discards it.

51. Or sons.

52. Literally, "which."

missing.[53] It is similar to the word *ba-shamayim* (in the heavens).[54] Compare, "O Lord, in the heavens (ba-shamayim) is Thy loving kindness."[55]
The judgment refers to a day set aside as a day of judgment for all.[56] It may also relate to the judgment following an individual's death.[57]

[IN THE CONGREGATION OF THE RIGHTEOUS.] When the righteous gather together it is well with all of them.[58] The opposite is true when the wicked gather together.

6. FOR THE LORD KNOWS[59] THE WAY OF THE RIGHTEOUS; BUT THE WAY OF THE WICKED SHALL PERISH.

FOR THE LORD KNOWS. There is no doubt that the revered God knows the whole[60] and the particulars.[61]
The whole is the soul of all life[62] that animates all created beings.[63] The particulars refer to each one of the species. The particulars also refer to each and every individual creature of the specie, for they are all the work of His hands. However, the knowledge of each individual be he righteous or wicked is by way of the whole.[64]

---

53. A *heh* vocalized with a *pattach*. Thus *ba-mishpat* is short for *be-ha-mishpat*.

54. The word *ba-shamayim* is vocalized with a *pattach* beneath the *bet* because it is short for *be-ha-shamyim*. In other words the *pattach* beneath the *bet* compensates for the missing direct object (the *heh*).

55. Ps. 36:6. It should be noted that Ps. 36:6 reads: *Adonai be-ha-ha-shamayim chasdekha* (O Lord in the heavens is Thy loving kindness). It is possible that I.E. intended to quote Ps.103: 19 which reads *ba-shamayim,* and accidentally quoted Ps. 36:6 omitting the *heh.* See I.E.'s comment on Ps. 36:6 where he notes that in contradistinction to Ps. 103:19, which reads *ba-shamyim,* Ps. 36: 6 reads *be-ha-shamayim.*

56. A day set aside for the judgment of all people upon earth. The reference is to *Rosh Ha-Shanah.* See I.E. on Ex. 33:34. I.E.'s point is that Scripture reads *ba-mishpat* (the *bet* vocalized with a vowel indicating the definite article) because it refers to a specific judgment,

57. Literally, "the judgment of each individual following that person's death."

58. Hence the wicked are excluded from their company.

59. Translated lit. Heb., *yode'a.*

60. Heb., *kelalim,* the various eternal categories into which things fall. According to I.E. God's mind is permanent and unchanging. Hence His knowledge consists of that which is permanent.

61. *For the Lord knows the way of the righteous* might be taken to imply that God does not know the way of the wicked. Hence I.E.'s comment.

62. Heb., *nefesh kol chai.* See Job.

63. The reference appears to be to the cosmic or world soul from which each and every individual soul is derived.

64. This comment has caused a certain amount of discomfort among students of I.E., for I.E. seems to imply that God knows the particular individual only as implied in the whole. See: I. Husik, *A History of Mediaeval Jewish Philosophy,* Jewish Publication Society, (Phila. 1940) p. 193; I.E.'s comments on Gen

God is eternally cognizant of the known[65] sciences.[66]

God knows the souls of the righteous, because they are everlasting and eternal.[67] The Lord also[68] knows that the souls of the wicked will perish. The meaning of *But the way of the wicked shall perish* thus is: The way of the wicked leads to destruction. Now if the souls of the wicked will perish then the souls of the scornful[69] will certainly be destroyed.[70] It is also possible that the word *wicked* includes *sinners* and *scorners.*

18:21 and Nahmanides' ad loc retort; J.L. Krinsky (*Chumash Me-chokeke Yehudah*, Reinman Seforim Center Inc. N.Y. 1975) on Gen. 18:21; Rabbi Hasdai Cresces' *Or Adonai*, Chapter 2; and Rabbi Abraham Yitzchak Kook's *Orot Ha-Kodesh, Musar Ha-Kodesh* Vol. 11 (Jerusalem: 1990), p. 439.

65. The sciences that we are aware of.

66. Heb. *Ummanut.* The term refers to both the arts and the sciences. God knows the scientific laws, which govern the world, for these laws are eternal. See *Umamnut* in Jacob Klatzkin's *Otzar Ha-Munachim Ha-Filosofiyim* (Berlin: 1928), Vol. 1, p. 55.

67. Lit., "because they last and exist forever."

68. In addition to knowing the souls of the righteous.

69. "The scornful" is probably short for the sinners and the scornful. See next note.

70. Verse 1 speaks of the wicked, the sinners and the scornful. However, our verse implies that only the wicked will be punished. Hence I.E.'s comment.

CHAPTER 2

1. WHY ARE THE NATIONS IN AN UPROAR? AND WHY DO THE PEOPLES MUTTER IN VAIN?

WHY ARE THE NATIONS IN AN UPROAR? It appears to me that this psalm was written by one of the poets in honor of David.[1] He composed it on the day of David's anointment. The Psalm therefore reads: *This day have I begotten thee* (v. 7). It is also possible that our Psalm refers to the messiah.[2]

The word *rageshu* (uproar) means, gather.[3] The word *rigshat* (gathering) in *From the gathering of the workers of iniquity* (Ps. 64:3)[4] is similar.

The *lamed* in the word *le'ummim* (peoples) is a root letter.[5] Compare, *u-le'om mi-le'om ye'ematz* (and one people shall be stronger than the other people) (Gen.25: 13).

MUTTER IN VAIN. *Yehegu* (mutter*)* is to be rendered, speak.[6] *Yehegu* is similar to the word *yehegeh* (speak) in *Neither shall my tongue speak deceit* (Job. 27:4).

The nations say, *Let us break their bands asunder* (v. 3).

2. THE KINGS OF THE EARTH STAND UP, AND THE RULERS TAKE COUNSEL TOGETHER, AGAINST THE LORD, AND AGAINST HIS ANOINTED.

STAND UP. The kings and the rulers stand up together with the nations and take counsel.

---

1. Lit., "concerning David."

2. This is the opinion of some Talmudic *aggadot*. See *Sukkah* 52b. Also see Rashi: "Our Rabbis interpreted this as referring to the king messiah. However, according to the plain meaning of the text it appears proper to interpret it as referring to David."

3. So too Radak. Others render storm or rage.

4. Translated according to I.E. Others render, tumult or rage.

5. Its root is *lamed, alef, mem*.

6. The word *yehegeh* can refer to thought or speech (See I.E. on Ps. 1:1). Hence I.E.'s comment.

The word *nosedu*[7] (take counsel) comes from the same root as *sod* (secret).[8] It is like the word *yerivai* (those that strive with me)[9] in *Strive O Lord, with those that strive with me* (Ps. 35:1). *Yerivai* is related to the word *rav* (strive) (Jud.11: 25). It is one of those words that drop its middle root letter. Its root is *resh, yod, bet*. The root of *sod* is similarly *samekh, yod, dalet*. The *yod* of the word *yerivai* was switched.[10] The noun which *yerivai* describes is omitted.[11]

It is also possible that the word *nosedu* is to be connected to the word *yesod* (foundation).[12] If we accept the opinions of those who say that this psalm was composed by a poet in honor of David or that David prophesied about himself,[13] then we must explain our verse as speaking of the many nations that Scripture tells us were under David's hand.

However, our verse is better explained in accordance with those who say that our chapter deals with the messiah. The meaning of *Against the Lord* is that the nations reject the discipline of the rational mind, which God has placed in every human being.[14]

AND AGAINST HIS ANOINTED. They do not cringe before him. They do not accept his authority and offer him tribute.[15]

3. LET US BREAK THEIR BANDS ASUNDER AND CAST AWAY THEIR CORDS FROM US.

LET US BREAK THEIR BANDS ASUNDER. *Mosrotemo* (their bands) comes from the same root as *moser* (band). Also the word *avotemo* (cords) means ropes. It refers to thick cords. Both parts of our verse say the same thing in different words. It is poetic to do so.[16] Compare:

---

7. Which comes from the root *yod, samekh, dalet*.

8. So too Rashi. The root of *sod* is *samekh, yod/vav, dalet*.

9. Its root is *yod, resh, bet*.

10. In other words the root *yod, resh, bet*, is a variant of the root *resh, yod, bet*. The root *yod, samekh, dalet* is similarly a variant of the root *samekh, yod, dalet*.

11. Lit. "It lacks an adjective." The noun which *yerivai* governs is missing. Ps. 35:1, which literally reads, "Strive, O Lord with who strive with me" should be interpreted as if written, Strive, O Lord, with *the men* that strive with me. So Filwarg.

12. From the root *yod, samekh, dalet*. In this case the phrase *nosedu yachad* (take counsel together) is to be rendered, "they form one foundation" that is they unite and form an alliance."

13. If David is the author of this Psalm.

14. According to I.E. it is possible for the human mind to discover the basic laws of the Torah, for these laws are rational laws. See Chapter 5 of I.E.'s *Yesod Mora; The Secret of the Torah*, p. 75. I.E. believes that all people are obligated to abide by these laws.

15. Lit., "to offer him tribute."

16. Moderns refer to this aspect of Biblical poetry as synonymous parallelism.

How shall I curse, [whom God has not cursed?]
And how shall I bring wrath, [upon whom the Lord has no wrath?
(Num. 23:8).]

4. HE THAT SITTETH IN HEAVEN LAUGHETH, THE LORD HATH THEM IN DERISION.

HE THAT SITTETH. Scripture reads: *He that sitteth in heaven.* It says this, because it earlier said, *The kings of the earth stand up.* It contrasts *He that sitteth in heaven,* which is located[17] above all human beings, with the kings of the earth.[18]
The Gaon[19] says that the meaning of *laugheth* is that God will make them objects of laughter and scorn.[20]
The following is the real meaning of *laugheth*:
God created all matter i.e. substance. He also created the forms.[21] The forms consist of the accidents, all which man makes or the images of living creatures, which he can conceive. God whose name alone is exalted is above being made out of matter.[22] He is certainly beyond the accidents.[23] It is only because the one who speaks[24] is human, and likewise the one who hears, that the Torah spoke in the language of men so that the one who hears will understand.[25] They[26] thus attributed human form to the earth. Hence we read: *And the earth opened her mouth* (Num. 16:32); *from the thighs of the earth* (Jer. 25:32; 31:8; 50:41).[27]

---

17. Lit., "that are." The Hebrew word for heaven (shamayim) is in the plural.

18. It contrasts God who sits in heaven with the kings who live on the lowly earth.

19. Rabbi Saadiah Gaon.

20. Rabbi Saadiah Gaon was bothered by the image of God sitting in heaven and laughing.

21. The form that matter takes.

22. Lit. "And his name alone is exalted from being matter."

23. God is unchangeable.

24. Heb. *Ha-medabber.*

25. I.E. employs a similar expression in chapter 12 of His *Yesod Mora* and in his commentary on Gen. 1:26. The clause may be explained to mean that the Torah was given to people who speak and hear. Indeed this is how I rendered it in my translation of I.E.'s commentary on Genesis. However, from a similar comment in Deut. 5: 5 it appears the term *ha-medabber* refers to Moses. In this case we should interpret: For Moses who spoke and Israel who heard were human.

26. The prophets.

27. I.E. makes a similar point in Gen. 1:26. He there writes: "A human being cannot speak of things above or below him without employing human terminology. Hence Scripture uses such terms as *the mouth of the earth* (Num 16:30) [and] *the hand of the Jordan* (Num. 13:29)." I.E.'s point is that *He that sitteth in heaven laughteth* is a metaphor.

[THE LORD HATH THEM IN DERISION.] The word *lamo* (them) means, at them.[28] The verb *yilag* (mock) is always connected to the object by a *lamed*. Compare, *yalagu li* (mock me) (Ps. 22:8). The meaning of *ve-oyevenu yilagu lamo* (and our enemies mock themselves) (Ps. 80:7) is therefore,[29] as I shall explain, a euphemism.[30]

5. THEN WILL HE SPEAK UNTO THEM IN HIS WRATH, AND AFFRIGHT THEM IN HIS SORE DISPLEASURE.

THEN. Some say that *yedabber* (will He speak) means, he will destroy. Compare, *and destroyed* (va-tedabber) *all the royal seed* (11 Chron. 22:10). *Tedabber* in the latter refers to death. Compare, *Ho, your plagues* (devarekha), *O death. Devarekha* is similar to *va-tedabber* (destroyed)[31] in *and destroyed all the royal seed* (11 Chron. 22: 10). The latter is clearly indicated in the Book of Kings. (11 Kings 11:1).[32] *Va-tedabber* is related to the word *dever* (pestilence) in *a very grievous pestilence* (Ex. 9:3)

The above noted commentaries interpret the word *elemo* (unto them) as meaning, the mighty.[33] Compare, *ele ha-aretz* (the chief men of the land) in *and the chief men of the land carried he* (11 Kings 24:15). However, their interpretation is incorrect, for *ele ha-aretz* is similar to *abbire ha-bashan* (strong bulls of Bashan)[34] (Ps. 22:13).[35] Furthermore[36] *ele* is spelled with a *yod*,[37] for it[38] comes from the same root as *eyal* (strength) in *that has no strength* (Ps. 88:5).[39]

The correct interpretation[40] is as follows:

---

28. I.E. renders *Adonai yilag lamo* (The lord hath them in derision): The Lord laughs at them.

29. Being that *lamo* means at them.

30. "At themselves" is a euphemism for, at God. See I.E. on Ps. 80:7. Thus Ps. 80:7 should be understood as *And our enemies laugh at God.*

31. Both words come from the same root. Their root is, *dalet, bet, resh.*

32. Lit. "For it is written in another book." I.E.'s point is that whereas 11 Chron. 22: 10 reads *va-tedabber et kol zera ha-mamlakha*, a parallel verse in 11 Kings 11:1 reads: *va-te'abbed* (and destroyed) *et kol zera ha-mamlakhah.* We thus see that *va-tedabber* means, and destroyed.

33. According to this interpretation our clause should be rendered: Then will He destroy their mighty ones.

34. The word "*Bulls*" is a metaphor for the chiefs or mighty men.

35. I.E.'s point is that *ele ha-ha-aretz* means the bulls of the land, not the mighty ones of the land. Hence the word *elemo* cannot be rendered their strong ones.

36. Lit., "also." According to Filwarg this is another interpretation. I.E. now says even if *ele* means mighty or strong it does not imply that *elemo* has a similar meaning.

37. Whereas *elemo* is spelled without a *yod*. Hence it cannot be compared to the word *ele* in *ele ha-aretz.*

38. *Ele.*

39. Translated according to I.E.

40. Of *yeddaber* and *elemo.*

Yedabber is to be taken according to its plain meaning.[41] *Elemo*[42] means *at them* and *alemo*[43] means *on them*.

Gods speaks to them thus: *Why do the nations gather?*[44]

6. TRULY IT IS I THAT HAVE ESTABLISHED MY KING UPON ZION, MY HOLY MOUNTAIN.

TRULY IT IS I THAT HAVE ESTABLISHED. *Nasakhti* (established) should be defined, I have crowned. *Malki* means,[45] the one who is my prince (*nesikhi*).[46] We thus read that the five kings of Midian (Num 31:8) were the princes (*nesikhe*) of Sihon (Joshua 13:21).[47]

Note the following: Sometimes the superior is connected to the inferior.[48] At other times the reverse is the case.[49] Compare, *Thou art my King, O God* (Ps.44: 5); *Truly it is I that*[50] *have appointed My king*, *The Lord is his inheritance* (Deut. 10:9; 18:2); and *Yet they are Thy people and Thine inheritance* (Deut. 9: 29). *To bow before the king, the Lord of hosts* (Zech. 14:16; 17)[51] which like *All kings shall prostrate themselves before him* (Ps. 72:11) refers to the messiah is similar;[52] for if the reference[53] was to God then the *lamed* of *le-melekh* (before the king) would have a *pattach* beneath it.[54]

---

41. It means, *will He speak.*

42. Spelled with an *alef.*

43. Spelled with an *ayin.* The point is, just as *alemo* means on them, *elemo* means at them (Filwarg). No one disputes that *alemo* means on them. Hence I.E.'s analogy.

44. Verse 1. Translated according to I.E.

45. *My king* means, My king who is My prince.

46. Our verse reads: *Va-ani nasakhti malki* (Truly it is I that have appointed my king). We would expect *va-ani himlakhti malki* or *va-ani nasakhti nesikhi,* for in such cases Hebrew employs verbs and nouns from the same root. Hence I.E. points out that the import of *va-ani nasakhti malki* is, I have appointed My king who is My prince.

47. We thus see that the nouns *melekh* and *nasikh* are related. Similarly the verbs *nasakh* and *himlikh.* Thus a king may be referred to as a prince.

48. At times God says to a Human being, "you are My king."

49. At other times man says to God, "*You* are my king."

50. God.

51. Translated according to I.E. I.E. interprets this clause: *to bow before the king of the Lord of hosts.*

52. In that the less important (the messiah) is connected to the more important (the Lord of Hosts).

53. The clause *before the king* in Zech.

54. The *pattach* beneath the *lamed* would indicate the definite article, the reference being the Lord of hosts that follows.

7. I WILL TELL OF THE DECREE: THE LORD SAID UNTO ME: THOU ART MY SON, THIS DAY HAVE I BEGOTTEN THEE.

I WILL TELL. These are the words of David regarding his prophecy[55] or the words of the poet speaking on behalf of David. *Asapperah el chok* (I will relate the decree) means, I will issue a decree that what I now say should be told. In other words, I will order that it be related that *The Lord said unto me: Thou art My son*, that is, God told me, *"serve the Lord as a son honors his father.*[56]

THIS DAY HAVE I BEGOTTEN THEE. This is similar to *Of the Rock that begot you; you were unmindful* (Deut. 32:18).[57]

8. ASK OF ME, AND I WILL GIVE THE NATIONS FOR THINE INHERITANCE, AND THE ENDS OF THE EARTH FOR THY POSESSION.

ASK. It is customary for a father to leave an inheritance[58] for his son. Scripture therefore reads *nations for thine inheritance.*

AND THE ENDS OF THE EARTH. *Afse* (ends of) is related to[59] the word *afes* (gone) in *for our money is all gone* (Gen. 47:15). It refers to places that have no inhabitants.[60]

9. THOU SHALT BREAK THEM WITH A ROD OF IRON; THOU SHALT DASH THEM IN PIECES LIKE A POTTER'S VESSEL.

THOU SHALL BREAK THEM. *Tero'em*[61] means, *You shall break them.* The *ayin*[62] should have received a *dagesh*[63] *like the kaf* in *tesokkem* (you will cover them)[64] and the *bet* in *tesobbem* (you will surround them).[65] However, it does not, for it is a guttural.

---

55. What God told him, viz. *Thou art My son* etc.

56. Compare, Mal. 1:6.

57. *Begot you* means, created you. Similarly, *begotten thee*. See I.E. on Deut. 32:18.

58. Lit. "To cause his son to inherit."

59. Lit. "Comes from the same root as."

60. Lit. "Cut off from inhabitants."

61. From the root *resh, ayin, ayin.*

62. In *tero'em.*

63. To compensate for one of the missing *ayins*, for *tero'em* is spelled with one *ayin*.

64. From the root *sin, kaf, kaf. Tesokkem* is spelled with only one *kaf*. The *dagesh* compensates for the missing letter.

65. From the root *samekh, bet, bet. Tesobbem* is spelled with only one *bet*. The *dagesh* compensates for the

WITH A ROD OF IRON. The sword will break them.[66] Our verse is in contrast to *Why do the nations gather* (v. 1)?[67]

10. NOW THEREFORE, O YE KINGS, BE WISE; BE ADMONISHED, YE JUDGES OF THE EARTH.

NOW THEREFORE, O YE KINGS. *Ye kings* refers to the kings of the earth.
Be wise rather than take counsel against the Lord.
Be admonished rather then say, *Let us break their bands asunder.*

YE JUDGES OF THE EARTH. The reference is to *the rulers* (in v. 2).

11. SERVE THE LORD WITH FEAR, AND REJOICE WITH TREMBLING.

Serve *the Lord with fear* rather than say,[68] *Let us break their bands asunder.*

SERVE. Serving God[69] means fearing God and not violating His commands.

AND REJOICE. When joy comes, do not forget to tremble because of the fear of God. Some say that the word *gilu* (rejoice)[70] means, and you will rejoice.[71] They compare *gilu* to the word *mut* (die)[72] in *and die in the mount* (Deut. 32:50)[73] and to *peru u-revu* (be fruitful and multiply) (Gen.1: 22).[74] The latter was a blessing given to the fish of the sea.[75] *And rejoice with trembling* means, you will rejoice if you tremble before the Lord.

---

missing letter.
66. The *rod of iron* refers to the sword.
67. See I.E. on verse 1.
68. Lit.," in reverse of their words."
69. Lit., "service of God".
70. Which is in the imperative.
71. In other words *gilu* is to be interpreted as an imperfect.
72. Which is an imperative but is to be rendered as an imperfect, for a person cannot determine the time of his natural demise. See I.E. on Gen. 1:22.
73. Which is to be rendered, and you will die on the mount. See above note.
74. Which though in the imperative are to be interpreted as imperfects, for commands were not directed to animals.
75. According to I.E, Gen. 1:22 is to be interpreted, may you be fruitful and may you multiply.

12. DO HOMAGE IN PURITY (*NASHEKU BAR*), LEST HE BE ANGRY, AND YE PERISH IN THE WAY, WHEN HIS WRATH IS SPEEDILY KINDLED. HAPPY ARE ALL THEY THAT TAKE REFUGE IN HIM.

DO HOMAGE IN PURITY. Note the following: *Serve the Lord* (v. 11) is in contrast to *Against the Lord* (v. 1). *Nasheku bar*[76] (do homage in purity) is in contrast to *and against His anointed* (v. 1).

The meaning of *bar* (purity) in our verse is similar to the meaning of *beri* (my son)[77] in *What, my son? and what, O son of my womb* (Prov. 31:2). Scripture similarly reads, *Thou art My son* (v. 7).

It is customary among the nations of the world for one to place his hand[78] under the hand of the king as the brothers of Solomon did.[79] It is similarly customary for[80] slaves to place their hands under their master's thigh,[81] or[82] to kiss the king.[83] This custom is practiced in India this very day.

[LEST HE BE ANGRY.] The reference is to God who is mentioned in the previous verse. [84] This is so even though the name of God is some distance from this clause. Compare, *The earth swallowed them* (Ex. 15:12). The latter does not refer to *Who is like unto Thee, O Lord among the mighty* (ibid. v. 11).[85] It refers to *The enemy [who] said [I will pursue, I will overtake...my hand shall destroy them]* (ibid v. 9).[86] Similarly, *and they will set up the tabernacle before they come* (Num. 10:21)[87] does not refer to what immediately precedes it.

Others say that the word *nasheku* (do homage) is connected to the word *neshek* (arm). *Nashku bar* means, arm yourself with a pure weapon.[88] Thus *bar* (purity) is similar to the word *bare*

---

76. Scripture reads *var*. *Var* is the word *bar* minus the *dagesh* in the *bet*. The *dagesh* is omitted because the *bet* follows a *vav*. This word will henceforth be referred to as *bar*.

77. In other words *bar* means son, for *beri* is the word *bar* with the first person pronominal suffix.

78. Lit., "to place their hands."

79. See 1 Chron. 29:24.

80. Lit., "or for."

81. See I.E.'s comment on Gen 24:2.

82. The reference is apparently to any of the king's subjects.

83. In other words the meaning of *nasheku bar* (do homage in purity) is, kiss the king (the son).

84. Literally, the first verse.

85. Which precedes it.

86. Which is some distance from it.

87. Translated lit. *And they will set up* refers to the sons of Gerson and the sons of Merari mentioned in verse 17. See I.E. on Num. 10:21.

88. Cf. Rashi: "Arm yourself with purity of heart."

(pure) in *to such as are pure in heart* (Ps. 73:1). Our verse should have read: *nasheku bor.*[89] Alternatively, it should be interpreted as if reading: *nasheku ha-bar* (take[90] the pure)[91] or *nasheku keli ha-bar* (take the pure weapon). [92]

AND YOU PERISH IN THE WAY. *Ve-tovedu derekh* (and you perish in the way) means, and you perish with regard to the way.[93] It is similar to *ke-elah novelet aleha* (a terebinth whose leaf fades) (Is. 1:30),[94] for the terebinth itself does not fade. It is only its leaves that fade. The verb [95] is intransitive.[96]
Rabbi Moses Ha-Kohen says that *derekh* (way) is similar to the word *midrakh* (tread) in *for the sole of the foot to tread on* (Deut. 2:5).[97] However this interpretation is farfetched, for it does not make sense.

WHEN HIS WRATH IS SPEEDLY KINDLED. [98] *Yivar* (kindled) is a transitive verb.[99] Compare, *tivar* (burneth) in *As the fire that burns the forest* (Ps. 83:15). It[100] is used in the sense of a devouring fire.[101] The act of destruction[102] is missing. There is no need to mention it[103] for (God's) fierce anger is compared to fire.[104]

---

89. The Hebrew word for purity comes from the root *bet, resh, resh*. Nouns from such double roots are vocalized with a *cholam*. Compare *chok*, from the root *chet, kof, kof* (Filwarg). Thus our verse should have read *nashku bor*.

90. I.E.'s paraphrase of *arm yourselves with*.

91. Take the pure thing (Filwarg).

92. The point is that *bar* is short for *ha-bar* or *kli ha-bar*. In this case *bar* is an adjective and is properly vocalized with a *pattach*. Compare *bar levav* (Ps. 24:4).

93. Our verse reads: *ve-tovedu derekh*. This literally means, and you perish the way. Hence I.E.'s interpretation.

94. Which literally means, *as a terebinth fades its leaves*. I.E. interprets this to mean, as a terebinth fades with regard to its leaves, that is when its leaves fall.

95. Lit. *For it is an intransitive verb.*

96. According to I.E., *ve-tovedu derekh* (and ye perish in the way) means, and you are lost with regard to the way, that is, you will not be able to find the correct path (Filwarg).

97. According to this interpretation, *ve-tovedu derekh* apparently mean, and you lose your footsteps.

98. Hebrew, *ki yivar ki-me'at appo*. See next note.

99. Hence *ki yivar ki-me'at appo* (When suddenly his wrath is kindled) should be rendered, When His wrath suddenly burns or devours.

100. In other words *yivar* is transitive. It means to burn others, to devour, to consume.

101. See Deut. 4:24, 9:3.

102. That which God's wrath shall consume is not mentioned in our verse.

103. For it is understood.

104. According to I.E. our clause should be interpreted: When God's wrath suddenly consumes you.

CHAPTER 3

1. A PSALM OF DAVID, WHEN HE FLED FROM ABSALOM HIS SON.

A PSALM OF DAVID, WHEN HE FLED. Rabbi Saadiah Gaon wanted to connect the Psalms to each other.[1] He explained that this Psalm follows *Why are the nations in an uproar?* (2:1) because David said that what befell Absolam will befall these nations. Now a commentator cannot connect the psalms in this manner.[2]

This Psalm, which deals with Absalom's rebellion, was placed[3] in the first Book of Psalms. Now[4] there are five Books of Psalms.[5] Hence, one should not be amazed if we find in Book Five of Psalms a prayer uttered by David in a cave[6] long before the rebellion of Absalom.[7] The Psalm is prophetic. David prophesied that he would prevail over his enemies.[8]

> *And he answered me out of His holy mountain* (v. 5)[9] is similar to Jonah's supplication: *And my prayer came in unto Thee* (Jonah 2:8).[10]

---

1. Rabbi Saadiah Gaon believes that the psalms are thematically connected.

2. If Saadiah's interpretation was correct then Ps. 3 would have preceded Ps. 2.

3. Lit., "is written."

4. Lit., "for."

5. Psalms consists of five books. Book 1: Ps.1-41; Book 2: 42-72; Book 3: 73-89; Book 4: 90-106; Book 5: 107- 150.

6. The reference is to Ps. 142, which contains a prayer offered by David when he fled from King Saul.

7. The Psalms in the various books are not in chronological order. Hence a psalm in a later book may have preceded a psalm recorded in an earlier book.

8. Hence the use of term psalm is not out of place.

9. This was stated prophetically, for God did not as of yet answer David's prayer.

10. Jonah spoke prophetically, for God had not yet answered his prayer.

2. LORD, HOW MANY ARE MINE ADVERSARIES BECOME! MANY ARE THEY THAT RISE UP AGAINST ME.

LORD, HOW MANY. In the holy tongue the term *mah* (how)[11] can be used with reference to something very important and in regard to something that is insignificant. Compare *How* (mah) *manifold are Thy works, O Lord* (Ps.104: 24); *What* (mah) *is man, that Thou art mindful of him* (ibid. 8:5).
Mah (how) is here used in the sense of wonder.[12]
The Israelites were divided into three groups.[13] Some like the people of Benjamin were adversaries of David.[14] Others rose up against David. This group consisted of Absolam.[15] Amasah,[16] and other relatives of David.[17] Another group[18] said that David fell and would not arise again.[19]

3. MANY THERE ARE THAT SAY OF MY SOUL; THERE IS NO SALVATION FOR HIM IN GOD. SELAH.

OF MY SOUL. *Le-nafshi* means, of my soul.[20] The *lamed* here is similar to the *lamed* in *and Pharaoh will say of the children* (le-vene) *of Israel* (Ex. 14:3)[21] and the *lamed* in *say of me* (li):[22] *He is my brother* (Gen. 20:13).

---

11. Or, what.

12. It introduces a question. *Mah* literally means, what. Hence I.E.'s comment that here it means, how.

13. The term *many* (rabbu, rabbim) is employed three times by David. This indicates to I.E. that David had three types of enemies (Filwarg).

14. Saul, the king who David displaced, came from the tribe of Benjamin.

15. Lit. "David's son."

16. See 11 Sam. 17:25.

17. David's relatives did not hate David. They wanted to seize power for their own personal reasons (Filwarg).

18. Mentioned in verse 3.

19. They were opportunists. Hence they joined the rebellion.

20. The *lamed* usually has the meaning of, to. Here it has the meaning of, because, concerning, or of. Thus *le-nafshi* does not mean to my soul but *of my soul.*

21. Not to the children of Israel. See note 20.

22. Not to me. See note 20.

SALVATION. The word *yeshuatah* (salvation) has two letters that are feminine endings.[23] This is poetic. Compare, *ematah* (dread) (Ex.15: 16)[24] and *ba-tzaratah* (in distress) (Ps. 120:1).[25] Scripture uses the term *lo*[26](for him) with reference to the word *nefesh* (soul).[27] It similarly reads, *le-hafik nefesh ra'ev*[28] (to make empty the soul of the hungry) (Is. 32: 6).

[SELAH.] Many explain the word *selah* to mean forever. However, this is incorrect.[29] The one who translated the Book of Psalms for non-Jews[30] said that the word *selah* is not an ordinary word.[31] It indicates a certain tone. The fact that this word is not found elsewhere in Scripture with the exception of the three times that it is found in the prayer of Habakkuk,[32] which like certain psalms has the words *Upon Shigionoth*[33] in it, like a *Shiggaion of David* (Ps. 7:1)[34] does, is proof of this. Habakkuk concludes with the words: *For the Leader. With my string music* (Hab. 3:19).[35]

How can[36] the meaning of *selah* be forever when Scripture states: *I proved thee at the waters of Meribah. Selah* (Ps. 81:8)?[37] Scripture also states in one place:[38] *[God cometh from Teman] And the Holy One from mount Paran. Selah* (Habakkuk 3:3).[39]- However some say

---

23. The *heh* and the *tav*. One letter would suffice. Indeed the usual form of the word is *yeshu'ah*.

24. The usual form of the word is *emah*.

25. See note 23. The usual form of the word *tzaratah* is *tzarah*. The printed texts read *ba-tzaratam*. The latter is an obvious error.

26. *Lo* is masculine.

27. *Nefesh* is a feminine. Hence the term used should have been *lah* (for her).

28. *Ra'ev* is masculine. In view of the fact that *nefesh* is feminine Scripture should have used the term *re'evah*. I.E. points out that Scripture is occasionally inconsistent in this type of grammatical usage. He does not explain why.

29. I.E. will soon explain why.

30. The reference is to Jerome (d. 512) who translated the Bible into Latin.

31. Lit. "The word *selah* has no meaning."

32. Hab. 3:3, 9, 13.

33. Hab. 3:1. For I.E.'s interpretation of a *Shigaion* see his comments on Ps. 7:1.

34. Hab. 3:1 reads: *A prayer of Habakkuk the prophet. Upon Shigionoth.* Ps 7:1 reads: *Shiggaion of David, which he sang unto the Lord, concerning Cush a Benjamite.*

35. Comp. Ps. 6:1. This is additional proof that Habakkuk's prayer is a psalm like composition.

36. So Filwarg. The printed texts read: "Behold, the meaning of *seleh* is forever." This reading is contradicted by what follows.

37. For in this case the verse means, I proved thee at the waters of meribah forever. However, God did not prove Israel **forever** at the waters of meribah. Hence the word *selah* cannot mean forever.

38. Lit., "it was also once written."

39. God does not always come from mount Paran. Hence we have additional proof that *selah* cannot mean forever.

---

that the word *Selah*[40] refers back to the Holy One.[41]- Scripture further states: *Uncovering the foundation even unto the neck. Selah* (Hab. 3:13).[42]

The correct interpretation of *Selah* is, it is so or thus it is. This explanation is true and correct.

4. BUT THOU, O LORD, ART A SHIELD ABOUT ME; MY GLORY, AND THE LIFTER UP OF MY HEAD.

BUT THOU, O LORD, ART A SHIELD. The word *magen* (shield)[43] is a noun. It is not a verb, for if it was then it would be vocalized like the word *mesev* (turn back)[44] in *Behold, I will turn back* (Jer. 21:3).[45]

Scripture reads: *a shield*. It says this, because David did not enter into the battle.[46]

Scripture reads: *My glory*. It says this, because whoever is victorious is honored.

5. WITH MY VOICE I CALL UNTO THE LORD, AND HE ANSWERETH ME OUT OF HIS HOLY MOUNTAIN. SELAH.

WITH MY VOICE. I will not enter the battle,[47] but will raise my voice in prayer.

OUT OF HIS HOLY MOUNTAIN. The mountain[48] is called the holy mountain,[49] because the ark was in Zion. This[50] was before the incident of Araunah the Jebusite.[51]

---

40. In Hab. 3:3.

41. *Selah* describes God. According to this interpretation our verse should be understood as saying, And the Holy One who is eternal (selah) from mount Paran. Thus this verse cannot be used as an argument against those who maintain that *selah* means forever.

42. This verse is additional proof that *selah* does not mean forever.

43. From the root *gimel, nun, nun*.

44. From the root *samekh, bet, bet*.

45. For this is the way double roots in the *hifil* are vocalized.

46. Against Absalom. See 11 Sam. 18 1-4.

47. See note 46.

48. Mt. Zion.

49. Even though the temple had not yet been erected.

50. Absalom's rebellion.

51. David bought the site where the temple would ultimately be built from Araunah the Jebusite. The purchase is described in 11 Sam. 24: 22-24. Absalom's rebellion is described in 11 Sam 15-18.

6. I LAY ME DOWN, AND I SLEEP; I AWAKE, FOR THE LORD SUSTAINETH ME.

I LAY ME DOWN. I lay me down securely and sleep the night before the battle.[52] Some say that a person is like one who sleeps when his star falls and like one who is awake when his star arises to do him good.[53]

7. I AM NOT AFRAID OF TEN THOUSANDS OF PEOPLE, THAT HAVE SET THEMSELVES AGAINST ME ROUND ABOUT.

THAT HAVE SET THEMSELVES AGAINST ME. *Shatu* (set themselves) is similar to *shot shatu ha-sha'arah* (set themselves in array at the gate) (Is. 22:7). It means, they battled.[54] Others say that our text is to be interpreted as if written, *shatu ha-shatat*.[55] The latter means, they set the nets.[56] Scripture therefore reads: *round about.*

8. ARISE, O LORD; SAVE ME, O MY GOD; FOR THOU HAST SMITTEN ALL MINE ENEMIES UPON THE CHEEK, THOU HAST BROKEN THE TEETH OF THE WICKED.

ARISE, O LORD. Note that a verbal noun[57] follows every Hebrew perfect or imperfect verb even though the noun is not always written.[58] Thus *u-verakh ve-lo ashivennah* (and when He hath blessed, I cannot call it back) (Num. 23:20) is to be interpreted as if written, *u-varakh berakhah ve-lo ashivenah* (and when He hath blessed a blessing, I cannot call it back). The same applies to *But in the multitude of those who counsel, counsel is established* (Prov. 15:22)[59] and to *For Thou hast smitten all mine enemies with a cheek blow* (makkat lechi).[60]

52. With Absalom.

53. Thus *I sleep* refers to the time that David's star was unfavorably positioned and *I awake* to the time that his star was favorably positioned.

54. Thus *set themselves* means, set themselves in battle.

55. Our verse literally reads, "That have set (shatu) against me round about." I.E. apparently believes that the verb *shatu* implies the noun *shatot*. See I.E. on the next verse.

56. See I.E. on Ps. 11:3.

57. The term used by I.E. is *shem ha-po'al*. The reference here is to a noun derived from a verb.

58. In this case it is implied in the verb.

59. Prov. 15:22 literally reads: *But in the multitude of those who counsel, it is established.* According to I.E. the verb *yo'atzim* (to counsel) implies the noun *etzah* (counsel).

60. V. 8 literally reads: *For Thou hast smitten* (hikkita) *all mine enemies cheek* (lechi). According to I.E. the noun *makkat* is implied in the verb *hikkita*. Hence his interpretation.

On the other hand it is possible that the word *lechi*[61] lacks a *bet* as in the case of the word *bet* (house of) in *that was found in the house of the Lord* (2 Kings 12:11)[62] and *sheshet* (six)[63] in for *in six days the Lord made heaven and earth* (Ex. 20:11).[64] Our verse thus should be read as if written, *ba-lechi* (upon the cheek).

Thou hast broken the teeth of the wicked (v. 8) is in contrast to *Many are there that say of my soul; [There is no salvation for him in God]* (v. 2). It will then become clear to all that *Salvation belongeth unto the Lord* (v.9) and that[65] God helps those Whom He loves.[66]

[9. SALVATION BELONGETH UNTO THE LORD; THY BLESSING BE UPON THY PEOPLE. SELAH.]

Upon Thy people (v. 9) refers to those who fought[67] on behalf of David. They [68] and not those who aid a son to rebel against his father are truly the people of God. Note, David prayed that God bless them so that none of them be killed[69] in the battle. On the other hand David might have prophesied this.[70]

---

61. In other words *lechi* should be interpreted as if written *ba- lechi*, the meaning of which is, upon the cheek.

62. The clause literally reads: That was found house of the Lord. With the *bet* it reads: *That was found in the house of the Lord.*

63. The word *sheshet* is to be read as if written, *be-sheshet.*

64. With out the bet the clause reads: For six days the Lord made heaven and earth. With the bet it reads: For in six days the Lord made heaven and earth.

65. Lit., "for."

66. Lit., "those whom He takes pleasure in."

67. lit., "fight."

68. Lit., "for they."

69. Lit., "missing."

70. What is recorded in our verse.

CHAPTER 4

1. FOR THE LEADER; WITH STRING MUSIC; A PSALM OF DAVID.

FOR THE LEADER; WITH STRING MUSIC. The Gaon[1] said that David composed this poem and gave it to one of the musicians to perpetually play it.[2] According to the Gaon *la-menatze'ach* (for the leader) means, forever (la-netzach).

Others say that *mena'tze'ach* refers to the individual who is in charge of the musicians.[3] Compare, *u-menatzchim alehem* (oversee them) (11 Chron. 2:1). This interpretation is correct.

The lamed of *la-menatze'ah* has been vocalized with a *pattach* because it refers to a specifically known individual.[4]

The word *neginot* (string music) indicates that this psalm had two tunes.[5]

Others say that *neginot* is the name of a musical instrument.[6]

According to my opinion Israel had songs and poems with various tunes.[7] The tune to which our psalm was to be performed opened with the word *be-niginot*. Observe, the tune of the psalm was written along with it.[8] The same applies to such

---

1. Rabbi Saadiah Gaon.

2. Rabbi Saadiah Gaon connects the word *la-menatze'ach* with the word *netzach* (forever). According to Rabbi Saadiah Gaon this poem was assigned to a specific musician.

3. In other words, *la-mentatze'ach* means, for the choirmaster.

4. The *pattach* beneath the *lamed* indicates the direct object, for *la* is equivalent *le-ha*.

5. *Niginot* is in the plural. This interpretation renders *neginot* as tunes. It believes that our verse is to be rendered: *For the leader, a psalm of David to be performed to two tunes.*

6. According to this interpretation our verse should be rendered: *For the leader, a psalm of David to be played upon neginot.*

7. Prior to the composition of the Book of Psalms.

8. The word *be-niginot* indicates the melody of the psalm.

terms as: *la-ma'alot;*[9] *ha-ma'a lot;*[10] *al alamot;*[11] *al ayelet ha-shachar;*[12] *al yonat elem*[13] and *machalat.*[14]

2. ANSWER ME WHEN I CALL, O GOD OF MY RIGHTEOUSNESS, THOU WHO DIDST SET ME FREE WHEN I WAS IN DISTRESS; BE GRACIOUS UNTO ME, AND HEAR MY PRAYER.

WHEN I CALL. *O God of my righteousness* means, You are the first cause in the revelation of my righteousness.[15]
Ba-tzar (in distress) is a noun.[16] Compare, *ba-tzar li* (in my distress) (Ps. 18:7).[17]

3. O YE SONS OF MEN, HOW LONG SHALL MY GLORY BE PUT TO SHAME, IN THAT YE LOVE VANITY, AND SEEK FALSEHOOD. SELAH

SONS OF MEN. Rabbi Moses Ha-Kohen says that this psalm deals with the same issue that the previous psalm does.[18]
David addresses the *Sons of Men,*[19] because men are haughty when they are young.
He asks them: How long shall you put my glory to shame? That which you desire shall not come to pass. It will not come into being because in reality you seek after falsehood.
Rabbi Moses Ha-Kohen is of the opinion that David addresses Absalom's helpers.[20]

9. Ps. 128.

10. Ps. 120.

11. Ps. 46.

12. Ps. 22:1.

13. Ps. 56:1.

14. Ps. 53:1. I.E.'s point is that the psalms were performed to the tunes of pre-existent songs. The opening word of the song that a given psalm was to be performed to was inserted in the first line of the psalm. See, *Four Approaches to the Book of Psalms*, pp. 233-234.

15. In other words, *God of righteousness* means, God who reveals my righteousness. I.E. speaks of God as being the first cause in revealing David's righteousness because he believed that God does not act directly in human affairs. See *Ibn Ezra's Commentary on the Pentateuch*, Vol. 1 page xii. Also see I.E.'s comment on Gen 1:1 and the notes thereto.

16. What I.E. means is that *tzar* is a noun.

17. Wherein *tzar* is a noun.

18. It deals with Absalom's rebellion.

19. *Sons of* (bene) means, young.

20. Those who support Absalom.

4. BUT KNOW THAT THE LORD HATH SET APART THE GODLY MAN AS HIS OWN; THE LORD WILL HEAR WHEN I CALL UNTO HIM.

BUT KNOW THAT THE LORD HATH SET APART. [*Hiflah Adonai* means, God has set apart.] Compare, *asher yafleh Adonai* (that the Lord sets apart) (Ex. 11:7).[21]
God has set apart and made known the identity of His godly man, for the Lord will hear when he[22] calls to Him.

5. TREMBLE, AND SIN NOT; COMMUNE WITH YOUR OWN HEART UPON YOUR BED, AND BE STILL. SELAH

TREMBLE. The word *rigzu* (tremble) means, fear. Compare, *al tirgezu ba-darekh* (fear not in the way) (Gen 45:24).[23]
David said, "fear God," because the King[24] inquires after his shame. David said this because his enemies did not honor him. On the contrary, they shamed him and spread lies about him.[25]

[COMMUNE WITH YOUR OWN HEART UPON YOUR BED, AND BE STILL. SELAH.] Some say that this means, do not allow the falsehood that you thought in your heart to leave your mouths. However this is incorrect.[26]
Scripture writes, *And speaks truth in his heart* (Ps. 15:2).[27] It likewise reads: *A heart that deviseth wicked thoughts* (Prov. 6:18).
The thought of the heart is what is most important. The tongue is only the intermediary between the heart and those who hear.[28]
Others say the meaning of our verse is, when you are in your beds at night and are not distracted by human affairs let your minds contemplate this.[29] Furthermore, do not speak falsehood during the day. This is the meaning of *and be still. Selah.*

---

21. *Hiflah* and *yafleh* came from the same root (*peh, lamed, heh*) and have similar meanings.
22. The godly man.
23. Translated according to I.E.
24. God.
25. Lit. "And spoke falsehood concerning him."
26. For Scripture seems to be tolerating evil thoughts.
27. It does not say and speaketh truth with his lips.
28. The tongue verbalizes one's thought.
29. To tremble and refrain from sinning.

6. OFFER THE SACRIFICES OF RIGHTEOUSNESS AND PUT YOUR TRUST IN THE LORD.[30]

OFFER THE SACRIFICES OF RIGHTEOUSNESS. The reference is to peace offerings[31] whose organs [32] are not offered[33] to atone for guilt.[34] It does not refer to offerings brought for the commission of a sin[35] or for some illegitimate notion that arises in one's heart,[36] that is, in one's thoughts.[37] *Then You will delight in the sacrifices of righteousness, burnt offering and whole offering* (Ps. 51: 21)[38] does not refute the aforementioned,[39] for the verse is to be read as if written, *and burnt offering.*[40] Compare, *re'uven shimon* (Ruben and Simeon) (1 Chron. 2:1).[41] *Offer the sacrifices of righteousness* means, forsake vanity and give thanks to God for favoring you.[42]

7. MANY THERE ARE THAT SAY: OH THAT WE COULD SEE SOME GOOD! LORD, LIFT THOU UP THE LIGHT OF THY COUNTENANCE UPON US.

MANY THERE ARE. David now goes back and quotes the words of those who pursue falsehood and vanity.[43] He says, "When I and my men were in distress those who seek after falsehood said regarding me and my men, *Oh that we could see some good.*"[44]

---

30. Heb. *Zivche tzedek.*

31. Heb. *Shelamim.*

32. Hebrew, *emurim.* The portion of the sacrifice offered on the altar.

33. On the altar.

34. As are those of the *asham* sacrifice. For the *asham* sacrifice, see Lev. 5: 14-26; 14:12; 19:20-22; Num. 5:5-8.

35. As are those of a *chattat.* For the *chattat* sacrifice see Lev. 4:1-35.

36. As are those of an *olah,* a burnt offering. For the *olah* sacrifice see Lev. 1: 1-17. According to the Rabbis the *olah* was brought to atone for evil thoughts that arise (oleh) in one's heart. See *Va-Yikra Rabbah* 7:3 and I.E. on Lev. 1:4.

37. In other words by *heart* the Rabbis mean, thoughts.

38. Translated lit.

39. That *sacrifices of righteousness* refers to peace offerings and not to sin offerings.

40. The word *olah* (burnt-offering) is to be interpreted as if written, *ve-olah* (and a burnt offering). Thus *burnt-offering and whole offering* do not refer back to *sacrifices of righteousness* but deals with additional offerings.

41. 1 Chron. 2 reads: *re'uven, shimon* (Reuben, Simon). However, the context requires *re'uven ve-shimon.* We thus see that Scripture occasionally omits a connective *vav.* However, the text is to be interpreted as if it contained a connective *vav.*

42. Lit. "For giving his pleasantness to you." See Ps. 90:17.

43. See v. 3.

44. The destruction of David.

43

Some say that the word *nesah* (lift Thou up) comes from a stem that drops its final root letter. Its stem is *nun, samekh, [heh]*. *Nesah* should have been vocalized like *re'eh* (see)[45] and *aseh* (make)[46] in the verse, *and see and make them*[47] (Ex. 25:40).[48] However, it is vocalized like *ve-eshah* (and I will occupy myself)[49] in *And I will occupy myself with Your statutes* (Ps. 119:117).

In reality [50] the *heh* is like an *alef* and the *samekh* like a *sin*.[51]

Some verbs, namely verbs consisting of two letters such as *kam* (arose)[52] and *shav* (returned),[53] are classified as letters that drop their middle stem letter.[54] Now in the imperative all such words are pronounced, like *kum* (get up) and *shuv* (return).[55] The middle letter[56], which corresponds to the second letter of normal verbs, is dropped[57]. However, the correct interpretation is, the *heh*,[58] is in place of an *alef* and the *samekh*[59] in place of a *sin*. *Nesah* (lift up) is similar to *yissah* (lift up) in *The Lord lift up His face*

---

45. From the root *resh, alef, heh*.

46. From the root *ayin, sin, heh*.

47. Translated literally.

48. *Nesah* (shevah, kametz) should have been vocalized *neseh* (sheva tzereh), for that is how words ending in a *heh* are vocalized in the first person male imperative.

49. From the root, *shin, ayin, heh*. *Ve-eshah* should have been vocalized *ve-esheh* (segol beneath the ayin), for that is how words coming from roots ending in a *heh* are vocalized in the imperfect. We thus see that Scripture occasionally uses a *kametz* when the rules of grammar call for a *tzereh* or a *segol*.

50. This note appears to be misplaced here, for I.E. later repeats and elaborates upon the points he here makes. Filwarg believed it to be a scribal error. It is also possible that I.E. started making a point, digressed and then returned to his original point. On the other hand this note might be a gloss that that was inserted into the text.

51. Scripture occasionally interchanges these letters. Thus *nesah* spelled *nun, sin, heh* is a variant of *nesah* (lift up) spelled *nun, samekh, alef*. Words ending in an *alef* are vocalized with a *kametz* in the first person male imperative. Compare, *kera* (read). Hence the vocalization *nesah* and the meaning, lift up.

52. Spelled, *kof, mem*.

53. Spelled *shin, vav*.

54. *Ayin vavs*. Literally, "letters whose middle root letters are silent." Some commentator's connected the word *nesah* to the root *nun, vav, samekh* from which the word *nes* banner is derived. They interpret the word *nesah* to mean, raise.

55. *Kum* is spelled *kov, vav mem*, and *shuv* is spelled *shin, vav, bet*. In other words if *nesah* came from the root *nun, vav, samekh* our verse should have read *nus* and not *nesah*.

56. The *vav*.

57. In the perfect.

58. In *nesah* in our verse.

59. In *nesah* in our verse.

to you (Num. 6:26) and to *nissah*[60] (lift up) in *If one lift up*[61] *a word to you, will you be weary* (Job 4:2).[62]

8. THOU HAST PUT GLADNESS IN MY HEART, MORE THAN WHEN THEIR CORN AND THEIR WINE INCREASE.

THOU HAST PUT. They desire that we not see good. However, I was happy when I saw that they prospered.[63] *You have put gladness in my heart* means; You gave me a good heart, so that I would desire good for all.

Rabbi Judah ben Balaam explains that *me'et deganam ve-tirosham rabbu* (more than when their grain and their wine increase) is to be inverted.[64]

However, in reality *me'et deganam ve-tirosham rabbu* means, from the time that their grain and wine increase.[65] There is no reason to invert words that were spoken under the influence of the Holy Spirit.

9. IN PEACE, WILL I BOTH LAY MYSELF DOWN AND SLEEP; FOR THOU, LORD, MAKEST ME TO DWELL ALONE IN SAFETY.[66]

IN PEACE. Without fear. *Yachdav*[67](altogether) refers to the many.[68] He will be among them.[69]

---

60. Spelled *nun, samakh, heh.* According to I.E., this word too is a variant of the root *nun, sin, alef* and means to lift up.

61. That is, utter.

62. Translated according to I.E.

63. According to I.E. the meaning of our verse is as follows: You put gladness in my heart when their grain and wine increase.

64. *Me'et deganam ve-tirosham rabbu* (more than when their grain and their wine increase) literally means, when their grain and wine increase. This is to be interpreted as, when <u>my</u> grain and <u>my</u> wine increase. Rabbi Judah interprets thus because he believes that David would not say, Thou hast put gladness in <u>my</u> heart when <u>their</u> grain and wine increase.

65. For the verse tells us that David rejoiced when the people who now are his enemies prospered.

66. Heb. *Be-shalom.*

67. Lit., together. Hence I.E.'s comments.

68. Mentioned in verse 7 (Many there are...). Even though "the many" sought David's harm, David did not seek their misfortune. See Radak.

69. Our clause is to be understood as, all of us will enjoy peace together.

The word *badad* (alone) has the same meaning with or without a *lamed*.[70] The same is the case with the word *la-vetach* (in safety).[71] Scripture also employs *betach* (in safety). Observe, Scripture reads, *Adonai badad yanchenu* (Deut. 32: 12). The correct meaning of the latter is: The Lord alone did lead him (Deut. 32:12).[72] This is also the meaning of *attah Adonai le-vadad* (for You, Lord…alone).[73]

On the other hand the meaning of our verse might be, whether they were together with me,[74] or I was alone,[75] that is by myself,[76] You cause me to dwell [in safety.[77]]

---

70. *Badad* and *le-vadad* both mean, alone. Our verse reads, *le-vadad*.

71. In our verse.

72. *Adonai badad yanchennu* might be translated as; The Lord did lead him alone. In other words, no other nation accompanied Israel. Hence I.E.'s comment.

73. *Attah Adonai le-vadad, la-vetach toshiveni* means, for Thou, Lord alone, makest me dwell in safety.

74. I.E.'s interpretation of *yachdav* (both) in the first part of the verse

75. Heb. *le-vadad*. According to this interpretation *le-vadad* refers to David, not to God.

76. Heb. *Le-vadi*.

77. According to this opinion our verse means, in peace will I lay me down and sleep whether with others (yachdav) or alone (le-vadad), because You O Lord cause me to dwell in safety.

CHAPTER 5

1. FOR THE LEADER; UPON THE NEHILOTH. A PSALM OF DAVID.

FOR THE LEADER; UPON (EL) THE NEHILOTH. The word *el*[1] has the same meaning as *al* (upon).[2] Compare the word *al* (to) in *and prayed to* (al) *the Lord* (1 Sam. 1:10).[3] The reverse is the case in *For* (el) *this child I prayed* (ibid. v. 27).[4] The *alef* does not interchange with an *ayin*.[5] Only the *alef, heh, vav, yod* interchange.
The *sin and samekh* likewise interchange because they are close in origin.[6]
The word *Nechilot* is taken from the opening of a poem.[7] It possibly comes from the same root as the word *yinchalu* (shall take possession) in *shall take possession... for you* (Num. 34:17).[8] It follows the paradigm of the word *akhilah* (meal) in *of that meal* (1 Kings 19:8).[9]

2. GIVE EAR TO MY WORDS, O LORD, CONSIDER MY MEDITATION.

GIVE EAR TO MY WORDS. *Ha'azinah* (give ear) is connected to the word *oznayim* (ears).[10] Compare, *Incline Thine ear* (oznekha) (Ps.88: 3).

---

1. The word *el* usually has the meaning of *to*.

2. That is, the word *el* occasionally has the meaning of *al*. I.E. comments thus because our verse reads, *el ha-nechilot*. If we would translate *el* as meaning "to", then *el ha-nechilot* would be rendered, to the *nechilot*.

3. Wherein *al* is used with the meaning of "to."

4. Here the word *el* is used in the sense of "for."

5. If it did, then we could say that *el* is a variant of *al* and *al* a variant of *el*, for *el* is spelled *alef lamed* and *al, ayin lamed*.

6. The *sin* and *samekh* are both dentals.

7. This psalm had the same tune as that of a song beginning with the word *nechilot*. See I.E. on Ps. 4:1.

8. Its root is *nun, chet, lamed*.

9. The root *alef, kaf, lamed* gives us the word *akhilah*, the plural of which is *akhilot*. The root *nun, chet, lamed* similarly gives us the word *nechilah*, the plural of which is *nechilot*.

10. The verb *ha'azinah* (give ear) is derived from the word *ozen* (ear).

CONSIDER. *Binah* (consider)[11] is an imperative.[12] It is like *simah*[13] (give) in, *Give now* (Job 17:3).

MY MEDITATION. The middle stem letter has been doubled in *hagigi* (my meditation). Its root is *heh, gimel, alef*.[14] Compare, *zenuneha* (her adulteries) (Hos. 2:4).[15]

David said *consider* to God. He spoke as people normally do. [16] The same applies to *and know my heart* (Ps. 139:23) and *To my word... give ear.*

Give ear to my words, O Lord, consider my meditation means, make it clear to all that you accepted my prayer; for there is no doubt that God who is all,[17] knows all and has no need for ears. Compare,[18] *He that planted the ear, shall He not hear?* (Ibid. 94:9).[19]

3. HEARKEN TO THE VOICE OF MY CRY, MY KING, AND MY GOD; FOR UNTO THEE DO I PRAY.

HEARKEN (HAKSHIVAH). Verbs coming from the stem *kof, shin, bet*[20] are always followed by a *lamed*.[21] It is therefore incorrect to say *mi yakshiveni* (who will listen to me).[22]

[MY KING.] The meaning of *my king* is, I have no king to cry out to, but You alone.[23]

4. O LORD, IN THE MORNING SHALT THOU HEAR MY VOICE; IN THE MORNING WILL I ORDER MY PRAYER UNTO THEE, AND WILL LOOK FORWARD.

---

11. From the root *bet, yod, nun*.

12. The usual imperative form of this verb is *bin*. *Binah* is usually found as a noun meaning, understanding. Hence I.E.'s comment.

13. An imperative from the root, *sin, yod, mem*.

14. This appears to be a scribal error. Our text should read, *heh, gimel, heh*. See Filwarg and *Ha-Keter*.

15. The root of *zenuneha* is *zayin, nun, heh*. The middle root letter is doubled in *zenuneha*.

16. God is omniscient. There is no reason to ask him to consider. Hence I.E.'s comment. See I.E. on Ps. 2:4.

17. Lit. "The all."

18. Lit., "after the manner of."

19. See I.E. on Ps. 94:9.

20. The root of *hakshivah*.

21. As is the case in our verse, viz., *hakshivah le-kol* (hearken to the voice).

22. For in this case the root is not connected to a *lamed* or to a word with a *lamed* prefixed to it.

23. Lit., "The meaning of *my king* is, I have no king that I should cry out to him but You alone."

O LORD, IN THE MORNING. *Boker* (morning)[24] means, every morning. Compare, *chadashim la-bekarim*[25] (new every morning) (Lam. 3:23).

The object[26] is missing in the clause *e'erakh lekha va-atzappeh* (will I order unto Thee, and will look forward).[27] It should be read as if written, *e'erakh lekha tefilati va-atzappeh* (I will order my prayer unto Thee and look forward). I have already noted that verbs[28] imply nouns. Compare, *u-verakh ve-lo ashivennah* (when He has blessed, I cannot call it back) (Num. 23:20),[29] and *u-verov yo'atzim takum* (But in the multitude of counseling it is established)[30] (Prov. 15:22) wherein *takum* is in the imperfect. The previous verse should be read as if written, *For unto Thee do I pray my prayer*.[31]

The word *lekha* (unto Thee) in the phrase *boker e'erakh lekha* (in the morning will I order my prayer unto Thee) applies to this clause and to the word that follows.[32] The latter is to be read as if written, *and will look forward unto Thee*.[33] Compare, *A gift in secret pacifieth anger...* (Prov. 21:14).[34]

5. FOR THOU ART NOT A GOD THAT HATH PLEASURE IN WICKEDNESS; EVIL SHALL NOT SOJOURN WITH THEE.

FOR THOU ART NOT A GOD (El) THAT HATH PLEASURE IN WICKEDNESS. Its meaning is, You God Who have the power[35] to do good takes no delight in wickedness. The psalmist stated this because he had earlier[36] called[37] God, *my king*.[38]

---

24. Our verse literally reads: *O Lord, morning shalt You hear my voice.* I.E. interprets this to mean: *O Lord, every morning shall You hear my voice.*

25. We thus see that *morning* sometimes means *every morning.*

26. My prayer.

27. This is the literal meaning of this clause.

28. In the perfect and imperfect. See I.E. on Ps. 3:8.

29. Ibid.

30. Translated lit. See I.E. on Ps. 3:8 and the notes thereto.

31. Verse 3 reads: *ki elekha etpallal.* According to I.E., the noun *tefilati* (my prayer) is implied in the verb *etpallal* (do I pray). It is to this prayer that our verse refers.

32. The nomenclature used by I.E. for this is, *moshekhet atzmah va-acheret immah.*

33. *Va-atzappeh* (and will hope) is to be read as if written, *va-atzappeh lekha* (and will hope in you).

34. The verse reads: *A gift in secret pacifieth anger, and a present in the bosom strong wrath.* According to I.E. this should be interpreted as if written: *A gift in secret pacifieth anger, and a present in the bosom pacifieth strong wrath.* We thus see that at times a word written earlier also refers to what follows.

35. The name *El* is used for the Deity in our verse. *El* indicates power. Hence I.E.'s comment.

36. In verse 3.

37. Lit., "mentioned."

38. See I.E.'s note on verse 3.

EVIL SHALL NOT SOJOURN WITH THEE. *Yegurkha* means, *sojourn with Thee.*[39] Compare, *Yishkvennah* (shall lie with her) (Deut. 28:30).[40] The same is the case with the word *gedelani* (grew up with me)[41] in, *grew up with me as with a father* (Job. 31:18).

Ra (evil) means, an evil person.[42] It is not a noun. The next clause, which reads, The boasters - that is, the scoffers- *shall not stand in Thy sight*, as is the case with people,[43] is proof of this.[44]

6. THE BOASTERS SHALL NOT STAND IN THY SIGHT; THOU HATEST ALL WORKERS OF INIQUITY.

THE BOASTERS SHALL NOT STAND IN THY SIGHT. Its meaning is that boasters shall not strand before you like servants who stand over their king.[45]

7. THOU DESTROYEST THEM THAT SPEAK FALSEHOOD; THE LORD ABHORRETH THE MAN OF BLOOD AND DECEIT.

THOU DESTROYEST… THE MAN OF BLOOD AND DECEIT. The reference is to a talebearer. Compare, *Their tongue is a sharpened arrow, It speaketh deceit* (Jer. 9:7).

THE LORD ABHORRETH. God is the subject.[46] Its meaning is that the man of blood and deceit[47] is abhorred and abominated in the eyes of God.

---

39. According to the rules of grammar *yegurkha* should be rendered, sojourn Thee, for *yegurkha* is a compound of the verb *yegur* (sojourn) plus the pronoun *otekha* (you). Hence I.E.'s comment.

40. *Yishkevennah* is a compound of *yishkav* and *otah*. The word thus literally means, "shall lie her." However, the latter does not make any sense. Hence it is to be rendered, lie with her. It is thus analogous to *yegurkha*.

41. *Gedalani* is a compound of *gadal* (raised up) and *oti* (me). *Gedalani* literally means, "grew up me." However, *gedalani* should be rendered: grew up with me.

42. According to I.E. *lo yegurkha ra* (evil shall not sojourn with Thee) means, evil people shall not sojourn with Thee. In other words evil is short for evil people. Thus *ra* is an adjective.

43. Human beings tolerate evil people. God does not.

44. That *ra* means an evil person, for the next verse continues the thread of thought of this verse.

45. They will not stand in the presence of God.

46. Our verse literally reads: The man of blood and deceit abohorreth the Lord. Hence I.E. comments that it is God who does the abhorring. In other words our text is to be interpreted as follows: *The Lord abohorreth the man of blood and deceit.*

47. Lit., he.

8. BUT AS FOR ME, IN THE ABUNDANCE OF THY LOVING KINDNESS WILL I COME INTO THY HOUSE; I WILL BOW DOWN TOWARD THY HOLY TEMPLE IN THE FEAR OF THEE.

BUT AS FOR ME. David now goes back to what he said at the beginning, namely *O Lord, in the morning Thou shalt hear my voice* (v. 4). David notes that he comes to the house of God. However, unlike those who bring the first fruits[48] of the earth concerning whom it is written, *and thou shalt bow before the Lord thy God* (Deut 26:10),[49] he does not have a gift with him when he bows in God's temple.

The following is the meaning of our clause: I have no gift. I come only to give thanks for the loving kindness which You God have shown me.

[IN THE FEAR OF THEE.] Its meaning is, I have nothing to offer You when I come to bow before You, except for my fear of You.

The word *yiratekha* (fear of Thee) is similar to the word *yirato* (His fear) in *and that His fear may be before you, that ye sin not* (Ex. 20:18). *Yirato* (His fear) means, people[50] will fear the Lord.[51]

9. O LORD, LEAD ME IN THY RIGHTEOUSNESS BECAUSE OF THEM THAT LIE IN WAIT FOR ME; MAKE THY WAY STRAIGHT BEFORE MY FACE.

O LORD, LEAD ME IN THY RIGHTEOUSNESS. I open my prayer with the supplication that You lead me in Your righteous ways.

BECAUSE OF THEM THAT LIE IN WAIT FOR ME. For I fear that my feet will slip and that You will punish me and then those who lie in wait for me will rejoice.

Shorerai (them that lie in wait for me) comes from the same root as the word *ashurennu* (I behold him)[52] in *I behold him, but not neigh* (Num. 24:17). Compare, *oyen* (eyed) in

---

48. Deut. 26:1-11.

49. Translated literally.

50. Lit., "others."

51. Not that the Lord will fear people, for Scripture goes on to say, *that ye sin not*. I.E.'s point is that the word *yiratekha* can either mean, your fear or fear of Thee. He points out that here like in Ex. 20 18 it refers to fear of the Lord.

52. Its root is *shin, vav, resh.* Its meaning is, to look or gaze.

and Saul eyed David (1 Sam. 18:9). *Shorerai* (them that lie in wait for me) means, those who look forward to an evil day.[53]

The word *hayshar* (make straight) is similar to the word *haytze* (bring forth) in *bring forth with thee* (Gen. 8:17).[54]

10. FOR THERE IS NO SINCERITY IN THEIR MOUTH; THEIR INWARD PART IS A YAWNING GULF, THEIR THROAT IS AN OPEN SEPULCHRE; THEY MAKE SMOOTH THEIR TONGUE.

FOR THERE IS NO SINCERITY IN THEIR MOUTH. There is no sincerity in the mouth of each one of them.[55] Compare, *Rachel weeping for her children: She refuseth to be comforted for her children, because he is not* (Jer. 31:15).[56] *Nekhonah* (sincerity) is an adjective describing *millah* (word) or *dibberah* (statement).[57] But *the rich man answers impudent* (Prov. 18:23)[58] and *his food fat* (Hab. 1:16)[59] are similar.

THEIR INWARD PART. The reference is to the heart, which is hidden.[60]

A YAWNING GULF. The word *havvot* (a yawning gulf) is related to the word *hoveh* (wouldest be) in *and thou wouldest be their king* (Neh. 6:6). They[61] think evil thoughts and hope that they come to pass and come to be.[62]

---

53. Lit., "who look at an evil day." People who look forward to a day that evil shall befall me. See Radak. I.E. interprets *and Saul eyed David*, similarly.

54. The root of *hayshar* is *yod, shin, resh*. The root of *haytza* is *yod, tzadi, alef*. Both words are in the *hifil*. In such cases the *yod* ordinarily changes to a *vav*. However, it doesn't do so here. Hence I.E.'s comment. I.E. makes the very same point in his notes on Gen. 8:17. It should be noted that the *ketiv* spells both words with a *vav*.

55. The text literally reads: *in his mouth* (pihu). Hence I.E.'s comment.

56. Translated literally. According to I.E., the meaning of Jer. 31:15 is as follows: *She refuseth to be comforted for her children because each one of them is not*. In I.E.'s opinion, whenever Scripture speaks of a plural and then employs a singular, the reference is to each one of the singular. See I.E on Gen. 49.22.

57. Neither *millah* nor *dibberah* is in the text. What I.E. means is that the verse should be read as if one of these words were in the text. Our verse literally reads: *For there is no honest in his mouth*. According to I.E. this should be read as if written, *For there is no honest word in his mouth*. The latter is to be interpreted, For there is no honest word in each one of their mouths.

58. Translated lit. According to I.E., Prov. 18:23 should be rendered: But the rich man answers [with] impudent words. Thus *impudent* modifies "words" even though the latter is not in the text.

59. Translated according to I.E.. *And his food fat is* short for, and his food a fat lamb (Filwarg). Here too "fat" modifies lamb even though lamb is not in the text.

60. The heart is hidden beneath the chest wall.

61. Lit., "for they."

62. According to I.E. *kirbam havvot* (their inward part is a yawning gulf) means, they think evil thoughts

AN OPEN SEPULCHRE. Harm at hand.

THEY MAKE SMOOTH THEIR TONGUE. *Yachalikun* (they make smooth) is related to the work *chalak* (smooth)[63] in *and I am a smooth man* (Gen. 27:11). Both words are related to *chelek ke-chelek* (like portions) (Deut. 18:8). A smooth surface is referred to as *chalak* because all its parts are equal.[64]

11. HOLD THEM GUILTY, O GOD, LET THEM FALL BY THEIR OWN COUNSELS; CAST THEM DOWN IN THE MULTITUDE OF THEIR TRANSGRESSIONS; FOR THEY HAVE REBELLED AGAINST THEE.

HOLD THEM GUILTY. The *alef* in *ha'ashimem* (hold them guilty) is a root letter.[65] On the other hand it might interchange with the *yod*[66] of *tishammenah* (shall be desolate) (Ezek. 6:6).[67] Compare, *tesham* (be desolate)[68] in *and that the land be not desolate* (Gen. 47:20). *Let them fall* by their own counsel[69] means; their counsel shall cast them down.

12. SO SHALL ALL THOSE THAT TAKE REFUGE IN THEE REJOICE, THEY SHALL EVER SHOUT FOR JOY, AND THOU SHALT SHELTER THEM; LET THEM ALSO THAT LOVE THY NAME EXULT IN THEE.

SO SHALL… REJOICE …AND THOU SHALT SHELTER THEM. Scripture reads: *shelter them*. It so reads, because it earlier said *those that take refuge in Thee* (v. 7).

---

in their inward part, i.e. in their heart.

63. Both words come from the same root (*chet, lamed, kof*) and have similar meanings.

64. Similarly, when something is smooth all of its parts feel the same. I.E. makes a similar point in his comments on Gen. 27:11.

65. The root of *ha'ashimem* is *alef, shin, mem*. Words from this root have the meaning of guilty.

66. Reading *be-yod* rather than *ke-yod*. Filwarg; *Ha-Keter*.

67. The root of *tishammenah* is *yod, shin, mem*. Similarly *ha'ashimem*, for the *alef* and the *yod* interchange. According to this interpretation the meaning of *ha'ashimem* is, make them desolate.

68. According to I.E. *tesham* comes from the root *yod, shin, mem*. See I.E. on Gen. 47:20 and the notes thereto.

69. *Mi-mo'atzotehem* literally means, from their counsels. Hence I.E. comment.

Tasekh (Shelter) comes from a double root.[70] The *samekh*, like the *lamed* in *ve-hakel*[71] (so shall they make it easier) in *so shall they make it easier for thee* (Ex.18: 22), does not have a *dagesh* in it.[72]

13. FOR THOU DOST BLESS THE RIGHTEOUS; O LORD, THOU DOST ENCOMPASS HIM WITH FAVOR AS WITH A SHIELD.

FOR THOU DOST BLESS THE RIGHTEOUS. This verse is connected to the previous verse.[73] For those who love Your name shall rejoice in You[74] when they see that You cast aside the wicked and bless the righteous.[75]

Some say that *tatrennu* (Thou dost encompass him) is a *kal*. It is like the word *oterim* (compassed) in *and his men compassed David* (1 Sam. 23:26).[76]

However, in reality *tatrennu* is a *hifil*.[77] It is like the word *yashrennu* in *the king will enrich him* (yashrennu) (1 Sam. 17:25). *Yashrennu* means, he will enrich him.[78] *Tatrennu* has two objects. However, in reality the main object of *tatrennu* is God's favor; for the Holy One Blessed is He encompasses the righteous with His favor.[79] Now the righteous who is compassed by God's favor is partially the object 's to *tatrennu*.[80] However, in reality God's favor alone is the object of *tatrenu*.[81]

---

70. Its root is *samekh, kaf, kaf.*

71. From the root *kof, lamed, lamed.*

72. A *dagesh* is usually placed in the first root letter of a word coming from a double root when one of the double letters is missing. Thus the word *yiddemu* (they are still) (Ex. 15:16) which comes from the root *dalet, mem, mem* has a *dagesh* in the *dalet*. Hence I.E. points out that this is not always the case. See Filwarg.

73. Both verses should be read as one verse.

74. I.E.'s paraphrase of the previous verse.

75. As implied and stated in our verse.

76. If *tatrennu* is a *kal*, a simple active form, then *ratzon tatrennu* means, favor encompasses him or favor will encompass him.

77. In the second person.

78. Hence it is in the *hifil*. I.E. comments thus, because *yashrennu* is a *kal* form. See Filwarg.

79. The meaning of *tatrennu ratzaon* (Thou dost encompass him favor) thus is; You cause favor to encompass him.

80. Thus *tatrennu ratzon* can be translated as; You cause him to be encompassed with favor.

81. The second interpretation being secondary.

CHAPTER 6

1. FOR THE LEADER; WITH STRING MUSIC; ON THE SHEMINITH. A PSALM OF DAVID.

FOR THE LEADER; WITH STRING MUSIC; ON THE SHEMINITH. Some say that the *Sheminith* was an instrument with eight strings.[1] It is also possible that *Sheminith* refers to a song[2] that had eight tunes. Scripture therefore reads, *be-niginot* (with string-music).[3] This psalm was to be performed according to the eighth tune.[4]

2. O LORD, REBUKE ME NOT IN THINE ANGER, NEITHER CHASTEN ME IN THY WRATH.

O LORD. It appears to me that David composed this psalm when he was sick. He later recovered from his illness. It is also possible that this psalm was written as a prophecy concerning Israel who in exile are like those who are sick.
If we accept the first interpretation then David [in addition to praying] also prophesied that he would be healed. Jonah did the same in his prayer. Compare, *Yet I will look again toward Thy holy temple* (Jonah 2:5).[5]
God chastens for sin with His diseases. Compare, *With rebukes dost Thou chasten man for iniquity* (Ps. 39:12).

BE GRACIOUS UNTO ME, O LORD, FOR I LANGUISH AWAY; HEAL ME, O LORD, FOR MY BONES ARE AFFRIGHTED.

1. See I.E. on Ps. 4:1 and the notes thereto.

2. Lit., "or there was a song."

3. Lit., "with tunes."

4. Of that particular song. According to I.E. our verse should be rendered: *For the leader; to be performed according to a song that has* [many] *tunes;* [employing the] *eighth tune, a psalm of David.*

5. Jonah said this while he still in the belly of the fish.

BE GRACIOUS UNTO ME, O LORD. Rabbi Moses Ha-Kohen notes that the word *umlal* (languish) is vocalized with a *pattach*. He therefore says that this indicates that the word is not an adjective[6] but is a deficient verb.[7] Compare, *ve-neshar ani* (and I was left) (Ezk. 9:8). The latter should have read, *ve-nisharti*.[8] It is similar to *ra'ah* (hath seen)[9] in *I am the man that hath seen affliction* (Lam. 3:1) and to *yosif* (I will add)[10] in *I will add unto thy days* (Is. 38:5). Rabbi Moses is correct.

FOR MY BONES ARE AFFRIGHTED. The bones, which are the foundation of the body, do not feel anything.[11] My bones seemed to experience pain because of the severity of the illness. Observe, the bones stand for the body.[12]

4. MY SOUL ALSO IS SORE AFFRIGHTED; AND THOU, O LORD HOW LONG?

MY SOUL. My soul, which is tied to the body, is more *affrighted* than my body.[13] Scripture therefore reads, *me'od* (sore).

HOW LONG? How long shall my soul, which does not have the strength to bear its suffering, be terrified?

5. RETURN, O LORD, DELIVER MY SOUL; SAVE ME FOR THY MERCY'S SAKE.

RETURN, O LORD. Return from Your fierce anger[14] and *for Thy mercy's sake* save me from my illness. David did not pray like Hezekiah did.[15]

---

6. If *umlal* were an adjective then it would have been vocalized with a *kametz*.

7. It is lacking the first person perfect suffix. In other words *umlal* is short for *umlalti*. *Umlalti* literally means; I languished. The *lamed* of *umlalti* is vocalized with a *pattach*.

8. In other words *ve-neshar* is short for *ve-nisharti*.

9. *Ra'ah* is short for *ra'iti*. It too is thus a defective verb.

10. *Yosif* literally means, he will add. However, the context requires, I will add. Hence *yosif* is to be interpreted as if written, *osif*.

11. I.E. makes the same point in his comments on Gen. 3:18.

12. *My bones are affrighted* means, my body is affrighted. I.E. comments thus, because he believes that bones have no sensation.

13. Lit., "the body."

14. Lit. "He should return from his fierce anger."

15. When King Hezekiah was ill, he asked God to remember his many good deeds (See Is. 38: 1-3). However, David threw himself upon God's mercies.

Death[16] will be very difficult for me because I will not be able to mention You with my lips,[17] nor will I be able to publicly praise You.[18]

[6. FOR IN DEATH THERE IS NO REMEMBRANCE OF THEE; IN THE NETHER WORLD WHO WILL GIVE THEE THANKS?]

7. I AM WEARY WITH MY GROANING; EVERY NIGHT MAKE I MY BED TO SWIM; I MELT AWAY MY COUCH WITH MY TEARS.

I AM WEARY. David tells of the severity of his illness and of his great[19] groaning. The word *ascheh* (I swim) is similar in meaning to *ha-socheh* (he that swimmeth) and *li-sechot* (to swim) in *As he that swimmeth spreadeth forth his hands to swim* (Is. 25:11).[20] *Mittati* (my bed) is the object of *ascheh* (I swim). *Ascheh… mittati* means, I make my bed to swim in the water produced by my tears.[21] The aforementioned is similar to *neither was there any breath left in me* (Dan. 10:17).[22] Some say[23] that *ascheh* (I swim) is an Aramaic word meaning, I will wash.[24]

8. MINE EYE IS DIMMED BECAUSE OF VEXATION; IT WAXETH OLD BECAUSE OF ALL MINE ADVERSARIES.

The word *asheshah* (dimmed) is related to the word *ash* (rot) in *rot shall eat them up* (Is. 50: 9).[25]

---

16. Lit ., "for my death."

17. I.E.'s paraphrase of *For in death there is no remembrance of Thee* (V. 6). According to I.E., *remembrance of Thee* means, mention of You.

18. I.E.'s paraphrase of *In the nether-world who will give Thee thanks* (v.6).

19. Lit., "many."

20. In other words, *ascheh* means, I swim.

21. Lit. "Its meaning is: from the water of my tears."

22. Daniel did not stop breathing. Hence Dan. 10:17 is not to be taken literally. The same is the case with our verse.

23. See Radak.

24. In other words, *ascheh* was borrowed from Aramaic. According to this interpretation the meaning of our verse is: I wash my bed with my tears every night.

25. Translated according to I.E. See Radak.

Scripture reads *Mine eye*[26] because David was sick when he saw that his enemies were rejoicing. The latter is the meaning of *because of vexation*. David's enemies[27] came to visit him[28] in order to avenge themselves.[29] Scripture therefore reads, *Depart from me* (v. 9). *It waxeth old* refers back to *Mine eye*. The meaning of the latter is, my eye is wasted because of my many tears.[30]

Be-khol tzorerai means, *because of all my adversaries*.[31] There are many other such instances.[32]

9. DEPART FROM ME, ALL YE WORKERS OF INIQUITY; FOR THE LORD HATH HEARD THE VOICE OF MY WEEPING.

DEPART FROM ME, ALL YE WORKERS OF INIQUITY. The *workers of iniquity* refer to David's adversaries.[33] The *workers of iniquity* stand in contrast to David and his work.[34]

10. THE LORD HATH HEARD MY SUPPLICATION; THE LORD RECEIVETH MY PRAYER.

THE LORD HATH HEARD MY SUPPLICATION. David admits that God and not the physicians healed him from his illness. God healed David because David prayed to him.

Yikkach (receiveth) means, accept.[35] Or its meaning is, the Lord will accept my prayer in place of a burnt offering.

---

26. That is, Scripture reads: *Mine eye is dimmed*.

27. Lit., "these enemies."

28. Lit., "to see."

29. By gloating at David's illness.

30. Lit., "crying." I.E. interprets our clause as follows: Mine eye waxeth old from the tears I shed because of all my adversaries.

31. The *bet* of *be-khol* has the meaning of, because. The *bet* usually indicates in. Hence I.E.'s comment.

32. Where the *bet* has the meaning of because.

33. Mentioned in the previous verse.

34. In other words, the workers of iniquity stand in contrast to David, who was a worker of righteousness.

35. The meaning of our verse is, the Lord will accept my prayer.

11. ALL MY ENEMIES SHALL BE ASHAMED AND SORE AFFRIGHTED; THEY SHALL TURN BACK, THEY SHALL BE ASHAMED SUDDENLY.

ALL MY ENEMIES SHALL BE ASHAMED AND SORE AFFRIGHTED. My enemies shall be ashamed and affrighted when they see me healthy and they themselves fall sick. *Sore affrighted*[36] is therefore in contrast to *my bones are affrighted* (v. 3) and to *My soul also is sore affrighted* (v. 4).

THEY SHALL TURN BACK. They will be sorry. [37] On the other hand, it might mean, they shall seek my peace.[38]

---

36. Which according to I.E., refers to the sickness of his enemies.

37. For their actions.

38. They shall turn back and seek my peace. Radak.

CHAPTER 7

1. SHIGGAION OF DAVID, WHICH HE SANG UNTO THE LORD, CONCERNING CUSH, A BENJAMITE.

SHIGGAION. Some say that *shiggaion* means, pleasure.[1] Compare, *tishgeh tamid* (be thou pleased always) (Prov. 5: 19). Others say that the reference is to David's error.[2] However, in my opinion the reference is to the tune of a poem that started with the word *shiggaion*.[3]

CONCERNING CUSH. This is similar to what the Spanish poets do. They write the name of a well-known poem[4] at the beginning of their poem.[5]

CONCERNING CUSH A BENJAMITE. Some say that the reference is to Saul who was exceedingly handsome.[6] They claim that our verse is similar to *for he* (Moses) *had married a Cushite women* (Num. 12:1).[7] However, I believe that it is extremely far fetched to

---

1. According to this interpretation, *shiggaion le-david* (Shiggaion of David) means, a pleasurable psalm of David.

2. From the word *shagah* to err or to sin. This is the opinion of the Rabbinic sages. See Rashi and Radak.

3. See I.E. on Ps. 4: 1.

4. A song that every one knows the tune to.

5. So that the new poem will be sung to the tune of the well-known song.

6. This is the opinion of the sages. See *Midrash Shochar Tov*. Also See Radak and Rashi.

7. According to the Rabbis the meaning of *for he* (Moses) *had married a Cushite women* is that Moses took a beautiful women (Sifre). See Rashi on Num. 12:1: "She was called the Cushite because of her beauty...in order that the evil eye should not have power (over her)..."

maintain that Scripture[8] would turn[9] a positive expression[10] into a negative one.[11] This stands the euphemism "rich of light"[12] on its head.

The sages say that David did not mention Saul in a positive way, so that the evil eye would not affect him.[13] However, the latter is very far fetched.

The proper interpretation of *Cush a Benjamite* is as follows:[14]

Cush who is mentioned in our verse was a Jew.[15] His proper name was Cush.[16] He was of the tribe of Benjamin. I say this, because it is extremely unlikely that David would say *Behold, he travaileth with iniquity* (v. 15), when speaking of Saul whom God chose [to be king over Israel].

2. O LORD MY GOD, IN THEE HAVE I TAKEN REFUGE; SAVE ME FROM ALL THEM THAT PURSUE ME, AND DELIVER ME.

O LORD MY GOD, IN THEE HAVE I TAKEN REFUGE. *Chasiti* (have I taken refuge) is an intransitive verb. It is always connected to a *bet*.[17]

3. LEST HE TEAR MY SOUL LIKE A LION, RENDING IT IN PIECES, WHILE THERE IS NONE TO DELIVER.

LEST HE TEAR. The reference is to each one of David's[18] enemies.[19] Compare, *Its branches* (banot)[20] *run* (tza'adah)[21] *over the wall* (Gen.49: 22).[22]

---

8. Lit., "they."

9. Lit., "being down."

10. Lit. "A word of praise."

11. That Scripture would call a beautiful person (Zipporah or Saul) ugly (a Cushite).

12. A Talmudic euphemism for a blind person. See *Lev. Rabba 34*. Literally, "This is the reverse of he sees much light."

13. Lit., "have power over him."

14. Lit., "The proper interpretation is."

15. Cush usually refers to Ethiopia or to an Ethiopian. Hence I.E.'s comment.

16. Cush is not a nickname.

17. Hence our verse reads, *be-kha chasiti* (in Thee have I taken refuge).

18. Lit., "his."

19. The previous verse speaks of David's enemies. Hence our verse should read, *Lest they tear*. According to I.E. when a verb in the singular governs a noun in the plural, the verb refers to each one within the plural.

20. *Banot* is a plural.

21. *Tza'adah* is a singular.

22. Its meaning is, each one of the branches run over the wall. See I.E. on Gen. 49:22.

Scripture reads *porek* (rending it in pieces), because lions break the neck (mafreket) of their prey.

WHILE THERE IS NONE TO DELIVER. Aside from You. Scripture therefore above reads, *and deliver me.*

4. O LORD MY GOD, IF I HAVE DONE THIS; IF THERE BE INIQUITY IN MY HANDS.

O LORD MY GOD, IF I HAVE DONE THIS. Its meaning is, if I have done such as this, that is, if I have torn and rended.[23]
Scripture reads: *be-khapai* (in my hands).[24] It so reads, because man employs his hands[25] when he strikes and kills.

5. IF I HAVE REQUITED HIM THAT DID EVIL UNTO ME, OR SPOILED MINE ADVERSARY UNTO EMPTINESS.

IF I HAVE REQUITED HIM THAT DID EVIL UNTO ME. *Sholemi* (him that did unto me) is a *kal*. This is so even though we do not find the word for recompense (*shil-lumim*) in the *kal* but in the *piel*.[26]
Some say[27] that *sholemi* means, he who was at peace with me.[28]
Va-achalletzah tzoreri rekam (or spoiled mine adversary unto emptiness)[29] means, how could I do evil to him who did good unto me[30] when I saved[31] those who afflict and hate

---

23. *Zot* (this) is to be interpreted as if written, *ka-zot* (such as this). In other words, our verse refers back to what is recorded in the preceding verse. However, see Rashi who explains that *if I have done this* refers to what follows.

24. Lit. , "in my palms.

25. Or palms. Lit., "these."

26. I.E.'s point is that our verse is the only place in Scripture where the root *shin, lamed, mem*, comes in the *kal* with the meaning of recompense. It usually has this meaning only in the *piel* form.

27. For the reasons pointed out in the previous note.

28. According to this interpretation, our verse should be rendered as follows: *If I have done evil to him that was at peace with me.*

29. In the context of the entire verse.

30. This interpretation explains *im gamalti sholemi ra* (if I have requited him that did evil unto me) as, how could I do evil to the one who was at peace with me?

31. Translating *va-achalletzah* (or spoiled) as, when I saved.

me without any reason? Our verse is to be so explained, because *rekam* (emptiness) means without reason.[32]

Va-achalletzah tzoreri rekam (when I saved those who afflicted me without reason[33]) is similar to, *va-ani nasakhti malki* (Truly it is that I have established My king) (Ps. 2:6).[34]

Rabbi Moses[35] says that the *vav* of *va-achalletzah* has the meaning of, but.[36] It is like the *vav* of *va-avadekha* (but...thy servants) in *but to buy food are thy servants come* (Gen. 42:10).[37] Others say that *va-achalletzah* is similar to *va-yenatzelu* (And they despoiled) in *And they despoiled* (va-yenatzelu) *the Egyptians* (Ex. 12:36).[38] However, this is very far fetched.[39]

6. LET THE ENEMY PURSUE MY SOUL, AND OVERTAKE IT, AND TREAD MY LIFE DOWN TO THE EARTH; YEA, LET HIM LAY MY GLORY IN THE DUST. SELAH.

LET THE ENEMY PURSUE MY SOUL. Some say that *yiraddof* (pursue) is a variant of *yitraddof*. However, there is no reason to say this, for there is no *dagesh* to compensate for the missing *tav*.[40] Furthermore the word should have read *yitraddef*.[41]

AND TREAD MY LIFE DOWN TO THE EARTH. By shaming me.[42]

---

32. Lit., "and this is the meaning of *rekam*".

33. Translated according to I.E.

34. The meaning of Psalm 2:6 is; how can you even think of harming David, when I have established him as My king on mount Zion? The verse here has a similar meaning (Filwarg). How can I have done evil to those who were good to me, when I didn't do any evil to those who harmed me? The *vav* in both verses thus has the meaning of when or in view of.

35. Rabbi Moses Giqatila.

36. Heb. *Rak*. Lit. Only. Rabbi Moses interprets the verse in a manner similar to that of the earlier opinion. He renders *va-achalletzah tzoreri rekam* as: Only (on the contrary) I saved those who hated me without cause.

37. Which has the meaning of only. According to I.E. Gen. 42:10 should be rendered: *only to buy food are thy servants come.*

38. It means despoiled. *Va-yenatzelu et mitzrayim* literally means, and they took away from Egypt. See I.E. on Ex. 12:36. *Va-achalletzah* similarly means, and I will take away. It usually means to take a person away from trouble, i.e. to save. However, here it means to take away someone's property. This interpretation renders our clause: Or *spoiled mine adversary unto emptiness.*

39. For the root *chalatz* always has the meaning of save. It is not found elsewhere in Scripture in the sense of despoils.

40. Of *yitradof.* Whenever a letter is dropped it is compensated for by a *dagesh.* However, a *dagesh* cannot be placed in the *resh.* Thus the *tav* would not be dropped.

41. What I.E. means is, our word should have read *yiraddef,* because the *hitpa'el* form of the root *resh, dalet, peh* is *yitraddef.*

42. Lit., "because of the shame."

YEA...MY GLORY. *My glory* (kevodi) means, my soul.[43] Compare, *let my soul* (nafshi) *not come into their council* (Gen. 49:6) and its counterpart *Unto their assembly let my glory* (glory) *not be united* (ibid.).[44] Also compare, *My heart is glad, and my glory* (kevodi), *rejoiceth* (Ps. 16:9) which is followed by *my flesh*, that is, my body[45] *also dwelleth in safety* (ibid.). Rabbi Judah ben Balaam[46] therefore[47] erred in interpreting *my glory* (kevodi) as my body. Did he not know, did he not hear, that man is a combination of body and soul and that the soul is the glorious part of man? Hence the word *kavod* (glory) refers to the soul.

What led Rabbi Judah into this difficulty was the fact that he found Scripture stating: *Let him lay my glory in the dust. Selah.* Now the soul does not go down to the dust.[48] The aforementioned verse is thus metaphoric.[49] The same is the case with *My soul cleaveth unto the dust* (Ps. 119:25).

Selah means, it was truly so.[50]

7. ARISE, O LORD, IN THINE ANGER, LIFT UP THYSELF IN INDIGNATION AGAINST MINE ADVERSARIES; YEA, AWAKE FOR ME AT THE JUDGMENT WHICH THOU HAST COMMANDED.

ARISE, O LORD, IN THINE ANGER, LIFT UP THYSELF IN INDIGNATION AGAINST MINE ADVERSARIES. Arise in Thine anger against my adversaries.[51] *Lift up Thyself* because of their anger[52]

Others say that *be-avrot tzorerai* (in indignation against mine adversaries) means, anger them so that they will be full of wrath.[53] Others say that *hinnase be-avrot tzoreai* (Lift up

---

43. Lit.," its meaning is, the soul."

44. In Gen. 49:6 *kavod* (glory) means the same as *nefesh* (soul), for parts 1 and 2 of Gen. 49:6 say the same thing in different words. The latter is termed synonymous parallelism.

45. Lit., "which is the body". I.E.'s point is that Ps. 16:9 speaks of body and soul. Hence also this verse indicates that *kavod* refers to the soul.

46. An eleventh century Spanish biblical commentator and Hebrew grammarian.

47. In view of the above.

48. Hence Rabbi Judah reasoned that *my glory* cannot refer to David's soul.

49. David didn't actually mean that his soul would rest in the dust.

50. See I.E.'s comments on Ps. 3:3.

51. Lit., "them."

52. *Be-avrot tzorerai* (in indignation against my enemies) is to be rendered, because of the anger of mine adversaries. In other words the *bet* in *be-avrot* has the meaning of, because.

53. *Lift up Thyself in indignation against mine adversaries* should be rendered: Lift up Thyself when you fill my adversaries with wrath. According to this interpretation *be-avrot* means, when You fill with wrath. This opinion explains the *bet* as meaning when.

Thyself in indignation against mine adversaries) is to be rendered: Lift Thyself up when mine adversaries are full of wrath.[54]

Rabbi Moses says *awake for me at the judgment, which Thou hast commanded* means, awake for me the judgment, which you decreed, that Saul's kingdom would be given to me.[55] Rabbi Moses interpreted our verse thus because he believed that Cush was Saul, or David was afraid to mention Saul by his known name.[56]

Ben Balaam[57] says that *awake for me* means, awake your decree to save me.[58] According to Rabbi Moses and ben Balaam[59] *urah* (awake)[60] is a transitive verb.[61] It is like the word *shav* (return), which is sometimes transitive and sometimes intransitive. However, in my opinion the word *urah* (awake) in *Yea, awake for me* is intransitive. A *kaf* is missing from the word *mishpat* (judgment).[62] Compare, *When a wild ass's colt is born a man* (Job 11:12).[63]

When the congregation of the peoples will hear of the judgment that you executed they will come from the ends of the earth [to worship You]. This is the meaning of *The congregation of the peoples compass Thee about* (v. 8).

The meaning of *And over them return Thee on high* (v. 8) is that God will return to heaven and sit upon the throne of justice. Scripture therefore immediately goes on to say: *O Lord, who ministerest judgment to the peoples* (v. 9).

It is also possible[64] that Cush had non-Jewish servants with him and that they surrounded David.[65] Attacking David is like attacking the Divine Presence,[66] for as noted at the beginning of the psalm; David served God and took refuge in Him.

---

54. This explanation interprets *be-avrot* as meaning, when they are filled with wrath.

55. In other words *awake for me the judgment which Thou hast commanded* means, put into effect the decree that You issued on my behalf.

56. Hence Cush is a pseudonym for Saul. According to the first interpretation Cush is another name for Saul, according to the second it was a code word employed by David.

57. Rabbi Judah ben Balaam. See note 46.

58. Lit., "what you decreed to save me."

59. Lit., "according to their opinion."

60. Lit., *ve-urah.*

61. For its object is the judgment. I.E. comments thus, because *urah* is usually intransitive.

62. The word *mishpat* should be read as if written, *ka-mishpat.* According to I.E. our verse should be interpreted, awake for me in accordance with the judgment (*ka-mishpat*), which You commanded.

63. According to I.E., a *kaf* should be placed in front of the word *ayir* (ass's colt). He interprets Job 11:12 as follows: Like a wild ass's colt is a man (*ke-adam*) when born.

64. Lit. "One may also say."

65. According to this interpretation, v. 8 speaks of an attack upon David by Cush and the people with him.

66. Hence v. 8 reads, *compass Thee* (God) *about;* when in reality they surrounded David.

8. AND LET THE CONGREGATION OF THE PEOPLES COMPASS THEE ABOUT, AND OVER THEM RETURN THOU ON HIGH.

THE CONGREGATION OF THE PEOPLES COMPASS THEE ABOUT. I have already explained the meaning of *the congregation of the peoples compass Thee about.*[67]
And over them return Thou on high means, raise Yourself over them and display Your might.[68]
Rabbi Moses Ha-Kohen says that *the congregation of the peoples* refers to Israel. He explains that *And over them return Thou on high* means, may God raise Israel up on high. However, his interpretation has no taste or smell.[69]

9. O LORD, WHO MINISTEREST JUDGEMENT TO THE PEOPLES, JUDGE ME, O LORD, ACCORDING TO MY RIGHTEOUSNESS, AND ACCORDING TO MINE INTEGRITY THAT IS IN ME.

O LORD, WHO MINISTEREST JUDGEMENT TO THE PEOPLES, JUDGE ME. Rabbi Moses says that *judge me* means, execute judgment upon those who oppress me. However, in my opinion David said: You O Lord who is the judge of the earth judge me according *to my righteousness,* for I did not do any evil to Cush.

10. OH THAT A FULL MEASURE OF EVIL MIGHT COME UPON THE WICKED, AND THAT THOU WOULDEST ESTABLISH THE RIGHTEOUS; FOR THE RIGHTEOUS GOD TRIETH THE HEARTS AND REINS.

OH THAT A FULL MEASURE OF EVIL MIGHT COME UPON THE WICKED. *Ra* (evil) is the subject. The word *re'sha'im* (the wicked) is the object.[70]
Some say that *yigmor na ra re'sha'im* (oh that a full measure of evil might come upon the wicked) means; may the evil[71] of the wicked be removed.

---

67. In the previous note. Lit. "I have already explained its meaning."

68. Lit.," that God should raise Himself over them and display His might."

69. It is unpalatable, for the verse reads: *And over them return Thou on high.* It does not read: *And return them on high.*

70. According to this interpretation, *yigmor na ra resha'im* (Oh that a full measure of evil might come upon the wicked) means, may evil (ra) destroy the wicked (resha'im).

71. Lit., "that the evil."

Rabbi Levi says that the *vav* prefixed to *u-bochen libbot u-khelayot* (trieth the heart and reins)[72] is superfluous. However, this is not the case. Its meaning is. You who know who is righteous and who is wicked.[73]

The reins (kelayot) allude to that which is hidden, for the reins are hidden.[74]

Scripture reads:[75] *The righteous God.* It so reads, because it earlier said[76] *establish the righteous.*[77]

11. MY SHIELD IS WITH GOD, WHO SAVETH THE UPRIGHT IN HEART.

MY SHIELD IS WITH GOD. David did not wage war.[78] He relied on God, for God saves.[79]

Scripture reads: *the upright in heart.* It so reads, because it earlier said[80] *God trieth the heart.*

12. GOD IS A RIGHTEOUS JUDGE, YEA, A GOD THAT HATH INDIGNATION EVERY DAY.

GOD IS A RIGHTEOUS JUDGE. Some say that the word *tzadik* (righteous) is the object.[81] God also[82] judges the one who angers Him every day.[83]

Every day means, God always judges.

However in my opinion the word *tzadik* (righteous) is an adjective modifying *shofet* (judge).[84] *Yea, A God that hath indignation every day* is connected to the following verse.[85]

---

72. Lit., "and trieth the heart and reins." According to Rabbi Levi, the *vav* (and) prefaced to *bochen* (trieth) should be ignored. He interprets our clause as follows: *The righteous God trieth the hearts and reins.*

73. Our clause should be interpreted as follows: *For the righteous God trieth the heart and reins.* Cf. Filwarg.

74. In the body. Lit.," like the reins, which are hidden."

75. Lit., "the meaning of."

76. Lit., "in contrast to."

77. The idea being, *the righteous God* will *establish the righteous.*

78. Against Cush.

79. Lit. "David will not wage war. He will rather rely on God, for God saves."

80. Lit., "in contrast to."

81. Reading *tzadik pa'ul* and not *tzadik po'el.* (Filwarg)

82. In addition to judging the righteous.

83. This interpretation reads our verse as follows: God Judges the righteous, God also judges the one who angers him (zo'em) every day.

84. *Shofet tzedek* thus means *a righteous judge.*

85. And not to the proceeding, as in as in the earlier interpretation

It refers to one who does not repent.[86] The word *asher* (whose) is missing in *im lo yashuv charbo yiltosh* (if a man turn not, He will whet his sword)[87] as it is in, *to show Himself strong in the behalf of them whose heart is whole* (11 Chron. 16:9).[88] Our text[89] should be interpreted as if it read: If the one whose sword is sharpened turn not. [90]

Some say that the word *El* (God) means, these. Compare, *These* (el) *were born unto the giant* (1 Chron. 20:8). They believe that the term *El* refers back to the word *wicked* mentioned above.[91]

13. IF A MAN TURN NOT, HE WILL WHET HIS SWORD, HE HATH BENT HIS BOW, AND MADE IT READY.

AND MADE IT READY. To shoot.

14. HE HATH ALSO PREPARED FOR HIM THE WEAPON OF DEATH, YEA, HIS ARROWS WHICH HE MADE SHARP.

FOR HIM. *For him* means, for himself.[92]

WEAPONS OF DEATH. Which he planned to kill others with.
Rabbi Moses said that *im lo yashuv* (If a man turn not)(v. 13) means, when a man turn not. The opposite is the case with *asher nasi yecheta* (if a ruler sinneth)[93] (Lev. 4: 22).[94]

---

86. I.E. interprets our verses as follows: *God is a righteous judge; Yea, God hath indignation every day, if a man who whets his sword does not return* (i.e. repent).

87. Lit. "If He does not turn, His sword he will make sharp."

88. The verse literally reads: *to show Himself strong in the behalf of them heart is whole.* The word *asher* (whose) has to be added to the text in order for the verse to be understood.

89. Part A of verse 13.

90. *Im lo yashuv charbo yiltosh* (if a man turn not, He will whet his sword) should be read as if written, *im lo yashuv asher charbo yiltosh* (if the one whose sword is sharp does not repent). I.E. reads Part 2 of verse 12 and part 1 of verse 13 as follows: Yea, a God that hath indignation every day, if the one whose sword is sharp does not repent.

91. In verse 10. This opinion interprets *ve-el zo'em be-khol yom* (Yea, a God that hath indignation every day) as: And upon these (the wicked), God has indignation every day.

92. The reference is to the wicked person himself. The arrows that the wicked prepare to destroy others end up killing the wicked themselves. See verse 16.

93. Translated according to I.E.

94. The point is that Scripture here uses the term *im* which usually means *if* in the sense of *when* (asher), while in Leviticus it uses the term *asher* in the sense of *if* (im).

WHICH HE MADE SHARP (*le-dokekim*). He so sharpened His sword[95] that it shines like a blazing fire.[96]

Some say that the word *le-dolekim* (sharp) is similar to the word *dalakta* (hotly pursued) in *dalakta acharai*. The latter means, *Thou hast hotly pursued after me* (Gen. 31:36). The meaning of *le-dolekim* (sharp) is, those who pursue me with the intention of killing me.[97]

WHICH HE MADE. The arrows.[98]

14. BEHOLD, HE TRAVAILETH WITH INIQUITY; YEA HE CONCEIVETH MISCHIEF, AND BRINGETH FORTH FALSEHOOD.

BEHOLD, HE TRAVAILETH WITH INIQUITY. *Yechabbel* (he travaileth) is similar to the word *chibblatekha* (in travail with thee) in thy *mother was in travail with thee* (Songs 8:5) and *chevel* (pain) in *before her pains came* (Is. 66:7).

YEA HE CONCEIVETH MISCHIEF, AND BRINGETH FORTH FALSEHOOD. Its meaning is; he starts out with vanity and ends up with nothing,[99] for all of his plans will be stopped and will not come to fruition.

15. HE HATH DIGGED A PIT, AND HOLLOWED IT, AND IS FALLEN INTO THE DITCH WHICH HE MADE.

HE HATH DIGGED A PIT. The meaning of *va-yachperehu* (and hollowed it)[100] is, he deepened it.[101]

The word *ba-shachat* (into the ditch) means, in the low place. *Shachat* follows the paradigm of *rachat* (shovel) in *Which hath been winnowed with the shovel* (Is. 30:24). *Rachat* comes from the root *resh, vav, chet*.[102]

---

95. He made his arrows for those who made their swords *blaze*.

96. *Dolekim* (sharp) comes from the root *dalet, lamed, kof*, which means to burn.

97. According to this interpretation the meaning of our verse is: *He hath also prepared for him the weapon of death, the arrows which he made for those for those who pursue me*.

98. In other words *yifal* (which He made) is connected to *chitzav* (arrows) and not to *dolekim* (sharp or blazing). See above note.

99. I.E.'s interpretation of falsehood. Rashi interprets similarly.

100. The literal meaning of *va-yachperehu* (and hollowed it) is, and dug it. Hence I.E.'s interpretation.

101. He deepened the pit that he has dug.

102. *Shachat* similarly comes from the root *shin, vav, chet*, meaning to sink down (Filwarg). Thus *shachat* means, a low place or a pit.

Others say that the word *shachat* is similar to the word *be-shachatam* (in their pit)[103] in *He was taken in their pit* (Ez. 19:8).

16. HIS MISCHIEF SHALL RETURN UPON HIS OWN HEAD, AND HIS VIOLENCE SHALL COME DOWN UPON HIS OWN PATE.

HIS MISCHIEF SHALL RETURN UPON HIS OWN HEAD, The mischief that he planned shall return upon his own head. Scripture reads: *his head.* It says this; because it goes on to mention *his pate.*[104]

Scripture reads: *shall come down.* It says this, because the decrees come from heaven.[105]

Chamaso (his violence) should be interpreted, because of his violence.[106]

17. I WILL GIVE THANKS UNTO THE LORD ACCORDING TO HIS RIGHTEOUSNESS; AND WILL SING PRAISE TO THE NAME OF THE LORD MOST HIGH.

I WILL GIVE THANKS UNTO THE LORD. For executing judgment on behalf of His righteous.

Scripture reads *Most High,* because it earlier said *shall come down.*[107]

---

103. From the root, *shin, chet, tav* meaning: A trap (Filwarg) or a pit.

104. In other words, the first half of the verse is parallel to the second part of the verse.

105. A person's fate is determined in heaven.

106. I.E. interprets our clause as follows: And because of his violence, punishment from above shall come down upon his own pate.

107. See note 104.

CHAPTER 8

1. FOR THE LEADER; UPON THE GITTITH.
A PSALM OF DAVID.

FOR THE LEADER. David handed over this psalm to the family of *Obed-edom the Gittite* (11 Sam. 6:10). *Obed-edom* was a Levite.[1] *Upon the Gittith* is similar to *for Jeduthun* (Ps. 39:1).[2] It is also possible that *upon the Gittith* refers to a poem that opened with *ha-gitit mitpa'eret* (the Gittite boasts) or something similar.[3]

Rabbi Moses says that the term *gitit* refers to an instrument belonging[4] to the family of *Obed-edom the Gittite*. However, we do not find such a form[5] used for this type of relationship.[6]

Some say that the reference is to a tune sung by those who tread (grapes) in the wine vat.[7] However, they speak nonsense.[8]

---

1. David handed over this psalm to the Levitical family of *Obed-edom the Gittite* (11 Sam. 6:10) to play and chant in the temple. *Upon the Gitteth* thus means that the duty of reciting this psalm was placed upon the family of *Obed-edom the Gittite*.

2. According to I.E., *for Jeduthun* (Ps. 39:1) means that the psalm which follows, was given to Jeduthan to play and chant in the temple. See I.E.'s introduction to Psalms.

3. In other words *upon the Gittith* means, this psalm is to be performed to the tune of a poem that opened with the word *ha-gitit*. See I.E.'s comments on Ps. 4:1.

4. Heb., *yityaches*. Rabbi Moses possibly believes that *Obed-edom* invented this instrument.

5. *Ha-gittit* (the Gittite).

6. The suffix *it* is used to relate a person to a place or to a family. Compare, *yisra'elit, shunamit*. It is not used to relate an object to a person or persons.

7. See Is. 63:2

8. Lit. "Those who speak vanity say that the reference is to a tune sung by those who tread in the wine vat."

2. O LORD, OUR LORD, HOW GLORIOUS IS THY NAME IN ALL THE EARTH! WHOSE MAJESTY IS REHEARSED ABOVE THE HEAVENS.

O LORD, OUR LORD. David opens with *O Lord, Our God* because he later says; *Thou hast made him*[9] *to have dominion over the works of Thy hands* (v. 7).[10]

HOW GLORIOUS.[11] It is a wondrous thing.[12]
The word *tenah* (rehearsed)[13] is an infinitive.[14] It is like the word *redah* (go down)[15] in *me-redah mitzrayemah* (to go down into Egypt) (Gen.46: 3). Our verse is to be interpreted as if written, *asher tet*[16] *hodekha al ha-shamayim*[17] (for you set your majesty above the heavens).[18]

3. OUT OF THE MOUTH OF BABES AND SUCKLINGS HAST THOU FOUNDED STRENGTH, BECAUSE OF THINE ADVERSARIES; THAT THOU MIGHTEST STILL THE ENEMY AND AVENGER.

OUT OF THE MOUTH OF BABES. Rabbi Moses says that *out of the mouth of babes* means, the babes themselves will praise You even though they cannot speak, for You sustain them.[19] You make them fruitful and You multiply and increase their body's height and width. However, in my opinion Scripture reads *Out of the mouth of babes,* because man is the most glorious being created in this world.[20] Now *out of the mouth of babes* refers to the

---

9. Man.

10. The point being, You who are Lord over all, gave man dominion over all creatures on earth.

11. Heb. *Mah addir.*

12. In other words *mah addir* means, how glorious. The word *mah* literally means, what. Thus *mah addir* might be explained as meaning, what glory? Hence I.E.' comment that *mah* here means, how.

13. From the root *nun, tav, nun,* meaning to give or to set.

14. I.E. comments thus, because this is not the usual form of infinitives.

15. Which is an infinitive.

16. In other words *tenah* is another way of saying *tet* (to set).

17. It reads, *asher tenah hodekha al ha-shamayim.*

18. *Tet* is the usual infinitive form for the root *nun, tav, nun,* in the *kal.* I.E. renders our verse as follows: "O Lord, our lord, how glorious is Thy name in all the earth, for you set your majesty above the heavens." See Radak.

19. The way children grow bears witness to the existence of a Creator. Thus the babes, as it were, declare that there is a God."

20. Only man has a rational soul and can speak. Human beings are the highest creation on earth. Man is

time that a child first begins to speak. Its meaning is that the power of the rational soul first appears in the body when the child begins to speak. The rational soul develops to the point where it can learn of the power of its creator by logical thinking. Indeed[21] the soul grows in strength day by day. This is the meaning of, *hast Thou founded strength*.[22] *Because of Thine adversaries* means, in order to nullify the arguments of the heretics[23] who say that there is no God.

The enemy and the avenger refer to the ones who express in word or deed their hatred of those who believe in God.[24]

4. WHEN I BEHOLD THY HEAVENS, THE WORK OF THY FINGERS, THE MOON AND THE STARS, WHICH THOU HAST ESTABLISHED.

WHEN I BEHOLD THY HEAVENS. It is known that there are seven dwelling places[25] for the lights[26] and the five moving stars.[27] The Eighth dwelling place[28] is set-aside for the great host.[29] The ninth sphere is the sphere of the constellations.[30] It moves from east to west. The tenth sphere is God's Glorious Throne.[31] Scripture therefore reads: *the work of Thy fingers* that are ten in number.

Our Psalm mentions *The moon and the stars*. It does not mention the sun because it is impossible to see the moon and the stars[32] during the day because of the light of the sun.[33]

---

referred to in Medieval Jewish philosophy as *ha-medabber*, the one who speaks.

21. Lit., "for."

22. The reference is to the strength of the soul that increases day by day.

23. Lit., "the deniers."

24. God's commandments are observed by word and by deed. See *The Secret of the Torah* p. 91 (Chap. 7 of the *Yesod Morah*).

25. In the spheres. Medieval cosmology pictured the earth as the center of the world. The earth was believed to be surrounded by ten spheres.

26. The sun and the moon. Each one of these heavenly bodies has a sphere of its own.

27. The five planets visible to ancient man, Venus, Jupiter, Mars, and Saturn. Each one of these heavenly bodies has a sphere of its own.

28. Sphere.

29. The many stars in heaven.

30. It propels the sphere of the constellations.

31. The *kisse ha-kavod*, God's glorious throne. Some of the Medieval Jewish Philosophers identified the *kisse ha-kavod* with the active intellect. See Rabbi Zerahiah Ha-Levi's introduction to his *Ma'or* in the Vilna edition of the Talmud.

32. Lit., "them."

33. Our verse would not say, when I behold the sun, the moon and the stars, for one cannot behold the

Some say that *hodekha* (Thy majesty) (v. 2) refers to the sun, for it is the great creation.[34] Now, during the day only one heavenly body is visible. However, at night a very great host is visible.[35]

5. WHAT IS MAN, THAT THOU ART MINDFUL OF HIM? AND THE SON OF MAN THAT THOU THINKEST OF HIM?

WHAT IS MAN? It is known that the moon and eleven stars are the dot in the circle of the sphere.[36] The entire earth is an undivided dot[37] with regard to the firmament.[38] However, humans are not part of the earth's mass.[39] Hence they do not receive the heavenly influence that the entire earth receives. Scripture therefore states: *What is man, that Thou art mindful of him?* The intention of the latter is to deprecate man.[40] Its import is as follows: You have creations that are greater and more glorious than man. Why then did You decide to honor man?

6. YET THOU HAST MADE HIM BUT LITTLE LOWER THAN THE ANGELS, AND HAST CROWNED HIM WITH GLORY AND HONOR.

YET THOU HAST MADE HIM BUT LITTLE LOWER THAN THE ANGELS (ELOHIM). *Elohim* means, the angels. *Except the angels* (elohin), *whose dwelling is not with flesh* (Dan. 2:11)[41] is the general proof of this.[42]

---

sun, the moon and the stars at the same time.

34. In the sky.

35. Hence our verse speaks of the night sky.

36. The reference is to the heavenly spheres. Each heavenly body is embedded in its own sphere and forms a dot on it.
The clause *and the eleven stars* presents a problem, viz. what eleven stars is I.E. referring to? It appears that the aforementioned is a copyist's error. It was inserted either consciously or unconsciously from Gen. 37:9, which speaks of Joseph's dream, which consisted of the sun and moon and eleven stars. Our sentence should read: "It is known that the moon and the stars are the dot [or dots in the case of the stars] in the circle of the sphere." I. Levin, *Yalkut Avraham ibn Ezra*, (New York-Tel Aviv 1985) p. 269.

37. Lit., "is like an undivided dot."

38. The earth is a sphere in the center of the sky. No part of it escapes the heavenly influence.

39. Lit. "Humans are apart from the earth."

40. *Mah* is used in verse 2 in the sense of wonder. Here it has a negative connotation.

41. Translated lit.

42. For *elohin* in Dan. 2:11 can only be referring to angels. *Elohin* is the Aramaic form of *elohim*.

AND HAST CROWNED HIM WITH GLORY AND HONOR. By breathing into him [43] the power of the breathe of life.[44] This soul comes from on high and is incorporeal. Hence it is immortal.

7. THOU HAST MADE HIM TO HAVE DOMINION OVER THE WORKS OF THY HANDS; THOU HAST PUT ALL THINGS UNDER HIS FEET.

THOU HAST MADE HIM TO HAVE DOMINION OVER THE WORKS OF THY HANDS. The reference is only, as Scripture goes on to note,[45] to that which is found on the earth.
Some say that *all things under his feet* refers to metals and plants.

8. SHEEP AND OXEN, ALL OF THEM, YEA, AND THE BEASTS OF THE FIELD.

SHEEP AND OXEN. Scripture mentions sheep and oxen because man needs these for food and clothes. Man needs these animals much more then he needs horses or donkeys to ride on. The psalmist mentions the animals of the field after sheep and oxen.
The word *sadai* means, field.[46] *Sadai* is used in the same way that Scripture employs *yadai* (hands)[47] in *upon all elbows of hands* (Ezek. 13:18).[48]
The word *bahamot* (beasts) takes in all sorts of animals. This is contrary to what Yefet[49] says, for Yefet argues that the term *behemah* only refers to grass eating animals.[50] However, what will Yefet do with *The lion, which is mightiest among beasts* (behemah) (Job 30:30)?[51]

---

43. See Gen. 2:7.

44. Lit. "Because of the power of the breathe of life which You breathed into him."

45. In verses 8 and 9. Lit., as Scripture later mentions.

46. The usual word for field is *sadeh*. Hence I.E.'s comments.

47. The usual word for hands is *yadayim*.

48. Translated lit. *Sadai* like *yadai* is a poetic form.

49. **Yefet ben Ali.** A 10th century, prominent Karaite Bible commentator.

50. Lit., "a grass-eating animal."

51. Job 30:30 classifies the lion as a *behemah*. Hence the latter clearly also refers to carnivorous animals.

9. THE FOWL OF THE AIR, AND THE FISH OF THE SEA; WHATSOEVER PASSETH THROUGH THE PATHS OF THE SEAS.

THE FOWL OF THE AIR. Scripture next[52] mentions the fowl that fly above man and the fish that swim below man.

Over orchot yammim (whatsoever passeth through the paths of the sea)[53] means, man in his wisdom makes ships and knows the paths of the sea. Scripture mentions this, because man catches fish in the midst of the sea.

Others say that *over orchot yammim* (whatsoever passeth through the paths of the sea) refers to the fish, for they pass through[54] the paths of the sea.

10. OH LORD, OUR LORD, HOW GLORIOUS IS THY NAME IN ALL THE EARTH!

OH LORD, OUR LORD. Scripture states this a second time.[55] The repetition indicates that it is so in every generation, for the earth remains forever.

---

52. After mentioning sheep, oxen and beasts of the field.

53. According to I.E. *over orchot yammim* (whatsoever passeth through the paths of the sea) means, he (man) passes through the paths of the sea. See Radak.

54. Lit., "for they end up passing."

55. Verse 10 repeats verse 2.

CHAPTER 9

1. FOR THE LEADER; UPON MUTH-LABBEN.
A PSALM OF DAVID.

FOR THE LEADER; UPON MUTH-LABBEN. *Al mut* (upon muth) are two words. The one who says that *al mut* is like *alamot* (alamoth) in *upon Alamoth. A song.*[1] (Ps. 46: 1)[2] is therefore in error.[3] Furthermore, if *al mut* is a variant of *alamot* why does a *lamed*[4] follow *al mut*?[5]

The one who says that *la-ben* means of Ben[6] and that Ben was a poet like *Ben*[7] in *Ben, and Jaaziel* (1 Chron. 15:18) is also wrong. It is not[8] in keeping with the rules of grammar to place a *pattach* beneath a *lamed* prefixed to a proper name and say *la-yitzchak* (to the Isaac) or *la-ya'akov* (to the Jacob);[9] for the one to whom a proper name refers to is known.[10] I have noted the aforementioned in the *Sefer Ha-Shem*[11]

---

1. In Ps. 46:1, I.E. explains that *alamot shir* means, a song called *alamot*.

2. In other words *al mut* has the same meaning as *alamot*.

3. *Al mut* consists of two words. However, *alamot* is one word.

4. I.E. is referring to the word *la-ben*, which begins with a *lamed*.

5. If *al mut* is a variant of *alamot*, how do we explain the word *la-ben* that follows *al mut/alamot*? The word *shir* (song) should follow.

6. A poem composed by Ben. This interpretation renders *al mut* as, upon the death of. It renders our clause as follows: For the Leader; upon the death of Goliath. [A poem composed] by Ben. A Psalm concerning David. Radak.

7. In other words *Ben* is a proper noun.

8. Lit., "for it is not."

9. The *pattach* beneath a prefixed *lamed* indicates the definite article.

10. Hence there is no need for the definite article.

11. See Chapter 2 of the *Sefer Ha-Shem*. The *Sefer Ha-Shem* is a short work by I.E. explaining the esoteric meaning of the letters making up God's name. *The Sefer Ha-Shem* is included in Israel Levin's *Yalkut Avraham Ibn Ezra*.

Some say that *la-ben* is the name *naval*[12] spelled backwards.[13] Others interpret *al mut la-ben* to mean, upon the death of the champion.[14] Some understand *al mut la-ben* as meaning, upon the death of his son.[15]

Rabbi Dunash[16] explains that *la-ben* was a gentile prince,[17] who as David goes on to explain in this psalm,[18] oppressed Israel. Rabbi Dunash Ha-Levi's interpretation is correct.

2. I WILL GIVE THANKS UNTO THE LORD WITH MY WHOLE HEART; I WILL TELL OF ALL THY MARVELLOUS WORKS.

I WILL GIVE THANKS UNTO THE LORD WITH MY WHOLE HEART. *With my whole heart* means, in secret.

I WILL TELL. In public.

3. I WILL BE GLAD AND EXULT IN THEE; I WILL SING PRAISE TO THY NAME, O MOST HIGH.

I WILL BE GLAD. *I will sing praise to Thy name* because of my great happiness. I will do so even though Your name is beyond praise.[19]

4. WHEN MY ENEMIES ARE TURNED BACK, THEY STUMBLE AND PERISH AT THY PRESENCE.

WHEN MY ENEMIES ARE TURNED BACK. The enemies' men shall not arise again after their king[20] dies.

---

12. A churlish man of Carmel, whose widow David married. See 1 Sam. 25.

13. *La-ben* is spelled *lamed, bet, nun. Naval* is spelled *nun, bet, lamed.* According to this interpretation, *al mut la-ben* should be translated, concerning the death of *la-ben/naval.*

14. Goliath. The latter is referred to as, *ish ha-benayim* (a champion) in 1 Sam. 17:4.

15. David's son Absalom. See 11 Sam. Chap. 18.

16. Dunash ben Labrat (c. 920- c. 990). A grammarian and poet. He was born in Baghdad, studied at Fez and settled in Cordoba.

17. Or king, for that is how I.E. later refers to him.

18. Verses 11, 13, and 14.

19. Lit., "above any psalm."

20. The reference is to *la-ben.*

5. FOR THOU HAST MAINTAINED MY RIGHT AND MY CAUSE, THOU SATTEST UPON THE THRONE AS THE RIGHTEOUS JUDGE.

FOR THOU HAST MAINTAINED MY RIGHT AND MY CAUSE. This shows that
la-ben[21] broke his covenant with David and acted violently towards him. It was on account of this that David prayed. His prayer was accepted.
Thou sattest upon the throne means, You sat on the Throne to execute justice.[22]

6. THOU HAST REBUKED THE NATIONS, THOU HAST DESTROYED THE WICKED, THOU HAST BLOTTED OUT THEIR NAME FOREVER AND EVER.

THOU HAST REBUKED THE NATIONS. When the word *ga'ar* (rebuked) is not fol-
lowed by a *bet*[23] it has the meaning of destroyed.[24] Compare, Behold, *I will destroy* (go'er)
the seed for your hurt (Mal. 2:3).[25]

THOU HAST DESTROYED THE WICKED. The reference is to *la-ben.*
FOR EVER. *Le-olam va-ed* (for ever)[26] is short for *le-olam ve-ad olam* (forever and ever).[27]
The *ayin*[28] is vocalized with a *segol*[29] because it comes at the end of the verse. The *vav*[30]
is vocalized with a *kametz* rather than a *pattach* because the *ayin,* [31]the first letter [of the
word *ed*], is accented.[32] Compare the word *va-yayin* (and wine),[33] in *brought forth bread
and wine* (Gen. 14:18).

---

21. Lit., "he."

22. Our clause should be rendered as follows: *Thou sattest upon the throne to execute justice, O righteous
judge.*

23. It is not followed by a *bet* in our verse.

24. Lit., "cut off." Otherwise, it has the meaning of rebuked. According to I.E. our clause should be
rendered as follows: *Thou hast destroyed* (ga'arta) *the nations.*

25. Translated according to I.E.

26. *Le-olam va-ed* literary means, forever until. Hence I.E.'s comment.

27. Lit. "Forever until ever."

28. Of *va'ed.*

29. The word *ad* (until) is vocalized with a *pattach*. Hence I.E.'s comment. Lit. "The *ayin* changes to a
chataf kametz."

30. Of *va-ed.*

31. Of *va-ed.*

32. A connective *vav* is usually vocalized with a *sheva.* Hence I.E.'s comment.

33. Where the connective *vav* is vocalized with a *kametz* because the letter that follows is accented.

7. O THOU ENEMY, THE WASTE PLACES ARE COME TO AN END FOREVER; AND THE CITIES WHICH THOU DIDST UPROOT, THEIR VERY MEMORIAL IS PERISHED.

O THOU ENEMY. Ben Labrat says that he found an old manuscript wherein the word *choravot* (waste places) is vocalized with a *pattach*.[34] He therefore interpreted the word as meaning swords.[35] Compare, *charvot tzurim* (swords of flint) (Josh. 5: 2).[36] However, in my opinion the *chet* in *choravot* should be vocalized with a *chataf kametz*.[37] Rabbi Moses says that our verse should have read, your very memorial[38] is perished.[39] *Because thou art exalted in stature, and he hath set his top among the thick boughs* (Ezek. 31:10), which should have read, and you have set your top[40] is similar.[41] However, Rabbi Moses[42] is incorrect, for verbs imply nouns.[43] Compare, *Out of the mouth of the Most High comes not evil and good* (Lam. 3:38). The meaning of the latter is, out of the mouth of the Most High comes[44] not the coming, that is the decrees[45] of evil and good.[46] The verse in Ezekiel[47] similarly should be rendered as follows: Because thou art exalted in stature, and your exaltedness[48] hath set its top among the thick boughs.

---

34. *Charavot.*

35. The consonants can spell either word. Its meaning varies with its vocalization. This interpretation renders our verse as follows: *O Thou enemy; Thy swords are come to an end.* See Rashi: "The sword that the enemy placed upon us is come to an end forever."

36. Translated lit.

37. The word should be read, *choravot* (waste places) not *charavot* (swords).

38. Reading *zikhrekha* rather than *zikhram.* Filwarg; Ha-Keter.

39. The Hebrew reads, *avad zikhram hemmah* (their very memorial is perished). This literally means their memory is perished. Rabbi Moses suggests that this be interpreted as if written, *avad zikhrekha attah* (your very memory is perished), for Scripture sometimes employs a third person with the meaning of a first person.

40. Reading *va-titten tzammartekha*, rather than *va-titten tzammarto.*

41. For the verse appears to be in the second person.

42. Lit., "he."

43. See I.E. on Ps. 3:8 and the notes thereto. I.E.'s point is that Scripture at times omits a noun. In such cases the reader supplies the noun that the verb implies.

44. In other words, the term *tetze* (comes) implies the word *yetzi'at* (coming of).

45. Thus the verb *tetze* (comes) implies the noun *gezerot* (decrees).

46. Lam. 3:38 literally reads: *Out of the mouth of the Most High comes not evil and good.*

47. Ezek. 31:10.

48. *Gavhata* (exalted) implies *gavhakha* (your exaltedness).

In my opinion the word *ha-oyev* is similar to the word *ha-kahal* (as for the congregation)[49] in *As for the congregation, there shall be one statute for you* (Num: 15:15). The meaning of our verse is, you the enemy think that you can escape because the places that you wasted are destroyed forever and the memory of the cities that you uprooted is perished.[50] You forgot that the Lord is enthroned forever and that He will exact punishment from you. Scripture therefore next[51] reads, *but the Lord is enthroned forever.* The term *cities* is thus connected to *Their memorial is perished.* [52]

Observe, God, as mentioned above (v. 6), eradicated *La-ben's* name[53].

The meaning of our verse is as follows: God did unto you [54] in accordance with your deeds.[55]

10. THE LORD ALSO WILL BE A HIGH TOWER FOR THE OPPRESSED, A HIGH TOWER IN TIMES OF TROUBLE.

THE LORD ALSO WILL BE A HIGH TOWER FOR THE OPPRESSED.[56] The one who has no strength and is brought low. Therefore *A high tower in times of trouble* is to be taken literally. It refers to a fortress for the oppressed, when they are in trouble.

Rabbi Dunash claims that the word *ba-tzarah* (in ...trouble) is the singular form of the word *batzoret* (drought). It is like *batzoret* in *concerning the droughts* (batzoret) (Jer. 14:1).[57] However, this is not in keeping with the theme of the psalm.[58]

11. AND THEY THAT KNOW THY NAME WILL PUT THEIR TRUST IN THEE, FOR THOU, HAST NOT FORSAKEN THEM THAT SEEK THEE.

WILL PUT THEIR TRUST IN THEE. They will be secure when they see that the Lord will be a tower of hope for the oppressed.

---

49. According to I.E., the meaning of *ha-kahal* is, you the congregation. The literal meaning of *ha-kahal* is, the congregation. Hence I.E.'s comment.

50. Thus, contra Rabbi Moses, *zikhram* means their memorial not your memorial.

51. In verse 8.

52. *Their memorial is perished* means; the memorial of the cities is perished.

53. Lit., "him." See I.E.'s comment on verse 6.

54. *La-ben.*

55. *La-ben* eradicated cities. God eradicated *La-ben's* name.

56. Hebrew *dakh.*

57. Rabbi Dunash interprets *li-ittot ba-tzarah* as, in times of drought.

58. The psalm does not speak of drought.

12. SING PRAISES TO THE LORD, YOU WHO DWELL IN ZION;[59] DECLARE AMONG THE PEOPLES HIS DOINGS.

SING PRAISES. Scripture reads: *Sing praises to the Lord you who dwell in Zion*. It says this, because it earlier mentioned[60] that God had rebuked the nations and destroyed the wicked one[61] who exterminated those who know God.[62] Our verse reads: *Sing praises to the Lord you who dwell in Zion*.[63] Scripture says the latter because those who dwell in Zion know God and seek Him.

14. BE GRACIOUS UNTO ME, O LORD, BEHOLD MINE AFFLICTION AT THE HANDS OF THEM THAT HATE ME; THOU THAT LIFTS ME UP FROM THE GATES OF DEATH.

BE GRACIOUS UNTO ME. The entire root is present in the word *chaneneni* (be gracious unto me).[64] *Chaneneni* is irregular.[65]

BEHOLD MINE AFFLICTION. You always did so.[66]
Thou that liftest me up is in contrast to *the gates of death* which are down below.

15. THAT I MAY TELL OF ALL THY PRAISE IN THE GATES OF THE DAUGHTER OF ZION, THAT I MAY REJOICE IN THY SALVATION.

THE GATES OF THE DAUGHTER OF ZION. *In the gates of the daughter of Zion* is in contrast to *the gates of death*.

16. THE NATIONS ARE SUNK DOWN IN THE PIT THAT THEY MADE; IN THE NET WHICH THEY HID IS THEIR OWN FOOT TAKEN.

---

59. Translated according to I.E.

60. In verse 6.

61. *La-ben*. See I.E. on verse 6.

62. Lit. "Because it earlier mentioned that God had rebuked the nations and destroyed the wicked one who destroyed those who know God."

63. See note 6.

64. Its root is *chet, nun, nun*.

65. *Chaneneni* should have dropped one of the root nuns.

66. Lit. "He always did so to me."

ARE SUNK DOWN. This is the praise spoken of in the previous verse.

IN THE PIT (BE-SHACHAT) THAT THEY MADE. Compare, He *was taken in their pit* (be-shachtam) (Ezek. 19:4).[67]

IN THE NET. In my opinion the word *zu* (the) is to be rendered, these. The same applies to the word *zu* (the) in *The people* (am zu) *which I formed for My-self* (Is. 43:21)[68] and to *zu chatanu lo* (He against whom we have sinned) (Is. 42:24). *Zu chatanu* means, these (zu) say we have sinned.
Be-reshet zu tamanu (in the net which they hid) means, in the net that these nations hid. Others say that the word *zu* means, this.[69]

17. THE LORD HATH MADE HIMSELF KNOWN, HE HATH EXECUTED JUDGEMENT, THE WICKED IS SNARED IN THE WORK OF HIS OWN HANDS. HIGGAION. SELAH.

IS SNARED. The word *nokesh* (is snared) is a *po'el*.[70] Its first root letter is a *nun*.[71] However, in reality the *tzere* [72] (beneath the kof) is most probably in place of a *pattach*, for all the vowels interchange.[73] The interpretation that suggests that *nokesh* is related to the Aramaic word *nekash* (knock) does not make sense.[74]

---

67. In other words *shachat* means, a pit

68. According to I.E., *The people* (am zu) *which I formed for My-self* means, *these people which I formed for My-self* (Is. 43:21).

69. According to this interpretation the meaning of *be-reshet zu* is, in this net. I.E. accepts this interpretation in Is. 42:24. He does not there mention the first interpretation.

70. *Nokesh* is a *kal* participle meaning snares. Compare, *kotev, yoshev, omed*. According to this interpretation, *be-fo'al kappav nokesh rasha* (the wicked is snared in the work of his own hands) means, *with the work of His hands, He* (God) *snares the wicked.*

71. In other words the root of *nokesh* is nun, kof, shin.

72. Lit., "the short *kametz*."

73. According to I.E., *nokesh* is a variant of *nokash*. In other words, *nokesh* comes from the root *yod, kof, shin* and is a third person *nifal* perfect like *noda*, or *nolad*. In this case *nokesh* means, was snared. Our clause is to be rendered as follows: *the wicked was snared in the work of his own hands.*

74. Lit. "There is no sense to the interpretation that suggests that *nokesh* (knock) comes from an Aramaic form." Compare, *da le-da nakeshin* (of knees knocking) (Dan. 5:6). According to this interpretation our clause apparently means, *with the work of His hands, He* (God) *knocks the wicked.*

Should one ask: Do we not find the word *va-yenakkeshu* (they lay snares) in *They also that seek after my life lay snares for me?*[75] The answer is: *We have two roots for snare.*[76]

HIGGAION. I will truly relate this.[77]

18. THE WICKED SHALL RETURN TO THE GRAVE,[78] EVEN ALL THE NATIONS THAT FORGET GOD.

THE WICKED SHALL RETURN TO THE GRAVE. For man is created out of the dust of the ground.[79]

THAT FORGET. *Shekheche* (that forget) is an adjective. It comes in various forms.[80] Compare, *chafetze ra'ati* (that delight in my hurt) (Ps. 40:15).[81]

19. FOR THE NEEDY SHALL NOT ALWAYS BE FORGOTTEN, NOR THE EXPECTATION OF THE POOR PERISH FOREVER.

FOR THE NEEDY SHALL NOT. The word *lo* (not) applies to this clause and to the one that follows.[82] Compare, *Let Reuban live, and not die and let his men not be few* (Deut. 33:6)[83] and *And I have not learned wisdom* (Prov. 30:3).[84]

---

75. Ps. 38:13. We thus see that the root of *nokesh* (snares) is not *yod, kof, shin*, but *nun, kof, shin*, for *nokesh* and *va yeknakkeshu* come from one root.

76. *Yod, kof, shin*, and *nun, kof, shin*.

77. *Higgaion* means, to speak. *Selah* means, truly. See I.E. on Ps. 1:2

78. Translated according to I.E. Hebrew, *she'olah*.

79. I.E. renders *she'ol* as the grave. The grave is in the ground. Hence his comment.

80. If the word were a participle then it would read *shokheche*. In most cases the adjectival form is identical to the participle form. Hence I.E.'s comment.

81. *Shekheche* follows the paradigm of *chafetze*.

82. *Tikvat anavim tovad la-ad* (nor the expectation of the poor perish forever) literally means, the expectation of the poor will perish forever. However, it should be interpreted as if written, *tikvat anavim lo tovad la-ad*, the expectation of the poor will not perish forever.

83. Deut. 33:6 literally reads: *Let Reuben live, and not* (ve-lo) *die/ And let his men be few.* I.E. believes that the word *ve-lo* (and not) also carries over to the second clause. The latter should be read as if written, *And let his men not be few.*

84. Prov. 30:3 literally reads: *I have not* (ve-lo) *learned wisdom, And I have knowledge of the Holy One.* According to I.E. the word *ve-lo* (and I have not) also applies to the second clause. The latter should be read as if written, *And I have no knowledge of the Holy One.*

Tikvat anavim tovad la-ad (nor the expectation of the poor perish forever) means, the expectation of the poor will not perish forever.[85]

20. ARISE, O LORD, LET NOT MAN PREVAIL; LET THE NATIONS BE JUDGED IN THY SIGHT.

ARISE, O LORD. The meaning of *arise* is, show Your might and strength.[86]

MAN. *Enosh* (man) is collective noun.[87] Compare the words *shor* (oxen)[88] and *chamor* (asses)[89] in, *And I have oxen* (shor) *and asses* (chamor) (Gen. 32:6). However, it probably refers to the king.[90] Scripture therefore reads: *the nations,* who are the servants of the king.[91]

21. SET TERROR OVER THEM, O LORD; LET THE NATIONS KNOW THEY ARE BUT MEN. SELAH.

TERROR. The word *morah* (terror) is spelled with a *heh*. However, it has the same meaning as if it was spelled with an *alef*.[92] Our case is the reverse of the word *mara* (bitter)[93] in *call me mara* (Ruth 1:20).[94]

MEN. The word *enosh* (men) is related to the word *ve-anush* (exceedingly weak)[95] in *And it is exceedingly weak* (Jer. 17:9).[96]

SELAH. Truly.[97]

---

85. *Tikvat anavim tovad la-ad* should be read as if written, *Tikvat anavim lo tovad la-ad*.

86. Lit. "The meaning of arise is, to show his might and strength."

87. Its meaning in our verse is, men.

88. Lit., "an ox."

89. Lit., "and an ass."

90. Or prince. See I.E. on verse 1. The reference is to *La-ben*. If the reference is to a king, then *enosh* is not to be taken as a collective noun.

91. Alluded to by the word *enosh* in the first part of the sentence.

92. *Mora* (spelled with an alef) means terror. *Marah* (spelled with a heh) means bitter

93. Spelled *mem, resh, alef.*

94. *Marah* in our verse is spelled with a *heh*, but has the meaning of *mara* spelled with an *aleph*. However, *mara* in Ruth is spelled with an *aleph* but has the meaning of *mara* spelled with a *heh*.

95. The root *alef nun, shin* means, sick or weak.

96. According to this interpretation, *enosh hemmah* (they are but men) means, they are sick.

97. See I.E. on Ps. 3:3.

CHAPTER 10

1. WHY STANDEST THOU AFAR OFF, O LORD? WHY HIDEST THOU THYSELF IN TIMES OF TROUBLE?

WHY STANDEST THOU AFAR OFF, O LORD? There is no doubt that God's glory is all over. However, when God's power is not manifest, then it appears to man that the Almighty is standing far off and therefore does not see,[1] or that He is close, but hides His eyes[2] when we are in trouble.[3]

2. THROUGH THE PRIDE OF THE WICKED THE POOR IS HOTLY PURSUED, THEY ARE TAKEN IN THE DEVICES THAT THEY HAVE IMAGINED.

THROUGH THE PRIDE OF THE WICKED. *Be-ga'avat rasha* (through the pride of the wicked) means, the wicked, in his pride.[4]

THE POOR IS HOTLY PURSUED. *Yidlak* means pursues.[5]
They are taken refers to the wicked person who is the leader, and to his companions who follow him. The wicked person and his followers are taken in the devices *that they have imagined.*

---

1. Our afflictions.

2. God appears to hide His eyes. *Ta'alim* (hidest Thou Thyself) means, you hide. I.E. interprets this as being short for, You hide Your eyes. He interprets our clause as follows: *Why hidest Thou Thy eyes in times of trouble.*

3. I.E.'s interpretation of *Why hidest thou Thyself in times of trouble?*

4. I.E. renders *be-ga'avat rasha yidlak oni* (through the pride of the wicked the poor is hotly pursued) as, The wicked person, in his pride, pursues the poor. See Radak.

5. The word *yidlak* literally means, he sets on fire. Hence I.E.'s comment.

3. FOR THE WICKED BOASTETH OF HIS HEARTS DESIRE, AND THE COVETOUS[6] VAUNTETH HIMSELF THOUGH HE CONTEMN THE LORD.

FOR. Rabbi Moses says that Scripture employs *ki* (for) in place of *asher* (who). *Ki hillel rasha al ta'avat nafso, u- votze'a berekh ni'etz Adonai*[7] (for the wicked boasteth of his heart's desire, And the covetous vaunteth himself, though he contemn the Lord) means, the Lord contemns the person[8] who praises the wicked because he has attained his hearts desire,[9] and the thief[10] who curses God.[11] According to this explanation the word *berakh* (vaunteth) is to be interpreted, curses. It is like *berakh* (curse)[12] in, *Naboth did curse God and the king* (1 King 21:13) and *barekh* (curse) in, *curse God, and die* (Job. 2:9).[13]
It is also possible that the word *berekh* (vaunteth) means, a gift or[14] a present.[15] *Berekh* is a noun.[16] It is like *dibber* (word)[17] in *And the word is not in them* (Jer. 5:13). The same is the case with *u-verekh ve-lo ashivennah* (and when He hath blessed, I cannot call it back) (Num. 23:20).[18]
However the above interpretation is incorrect, for *berekh*[19] is clearly a verb in the perfect.[20] *U-verekh ve-lo ashivennah* (and when He hath blessed, I cannot call it back) is to be read as if written, *u-verekh berakhah ve-lo ashivennah* (and when he hath blessed a blessing, I cannot call it back).

---

6. Hebrew *botze'a*. The word can also mean, a thief.

7. This interpretation reads *ki hillel rasha al ta'avat nafso, u- votze'a berekh ni'etz Adonai* as if written, *asher hillel rasha al ta'avat nafso, u- votze'a berekh ni'etz Adonai*.

8. According to this interpretation, *Adonai* in *nie'etz Adonai* is active and is not the object of *ni'etz*.

9. The meaning of *asher hillel rasha al ta'avat nafso*.

10. See note 6.

11. The meaning of *u- votze'a berekh ni'etz Adonai*.

12. Lit., "bless." Bless in this case is a euphemism for curse.

13. Translated lit.

14. Lit., "and."

15. According to this interpretation *u-votze'a berekh* means, and the one who steals a gift. This interpretation renders our verse as follows: The Lord contemns the person who praises the wicked because he has attained his hearts desire and the one who has stolen a gift i.e. the one who has taken some else's possession.

16. Although it has the form of a verb.

17. Which is a noun even though it has the form of a verb.

18. This interpretation explains the phrase to mean, [God has given] a gift, I cannot take back.

19. Here and in Num. 23:20.

20. Hence it cannot mean a gift.

According to my opinion, *ki hillel rasha al ta'avat nafso, u- votze'a berekh ni'etz Adonai* means, for the wicked, mentioned in the previous verse, praised the evil person[21] who lusted[22] and the thief who contemned God.[23] *Berekh* thus has the meaning of praised.[24]

4. THE WICKED IN THE PRIDE[25] OF HIS COUNTENANCE,[26] [SAITH]: HE WILL NOT REQUIRE; ALL HIS THOUGHTS ARE: THERE IS NO GOD.

THE WICKED. Scripture connects pride to the nose[27] because nothing on the face is higher than it. There is no doubt that pride is in the heart. However, Scripture speaks about that which is out in the open.[28]

HE WILL NOT REQUIRE. In his heart.[29]
The word *kol* (all) in *kol mezimmotav* (all his thoughts) should be read as if written, *be-khol* (with all).[30]

5. HIS WAYS PROSPER AT ALL TIMES; THY JUDGMENTS ARE FAR ABOVE OUT OF HIS SIGHT; AS FOR HIS ADVERSARIES, HE PUFFETH AT THEM.

HIS WAYS PROSPER. Rabbi Moses Ha-Kohen says that *derakhav* (his ways) means, his desires.[31] Compare *darko* (his desire)[32] in, *A man's heart deviseth his desire* (Prov. 16:9).[33]

---

21. Lit., "a fellow wicked one."

22. I.E.'s interpretation of *ki hillel rasha al ta'avat nafso.*

23. I.E.'s interpretation of *u- votze'a berekh ni'etz Adonai.*

24. And *ki* has the meaning of *for* or *because* and not *who* (asher).

25. Heb. *Govah* (height).

26. Heb. *Appo.* Lit., "his nose." Hence I.E.'s comment.

27. *Govah* means both height and pride. Our verse literally reads, *The wicked in the height* (pride) *of his nose*

28. The nose.

29. I.E. interprets *yidrosh* (require), seek. Hence he interprets *bal yidrosh* (He will not require) as, he will not seek the Lord. According to I.E., our clause should be rendered as follows: The wicked in the pride of his nose does not seek the Lord. Radak explains similarly.

30. Lit. "The *bet* is missing from the word *kol mezimmotav.*" According to I.E., the second clause of our verse means, God is not present in any of his thoughts.

31. The literal meaning of *derakhav* is, his ways.

32. Lit., "his way."

33. Translated according to I.E.

Yachilu (prosper) means, they come.[34] Compare *yacholu* (let it come) in *let it come upon the head of Joab* (3:29).[35] *Yachilu derakhav* (his ways prosper) means, all of his needs are fulfilled[36] and established in accordance with his wishes.

It is also possible that *derakhav* (his ways)[37] refers to the ways of God and that *yachilu* (prosper) is related to the word *chil* (fear). In this case *yachilu derakhav* means, the fear of God should have frightened him.[38]

In my opinion *yachilu* is a transitive verb. It is related to the word *chil* (fear)[39] in *And fear* (chil), *as of a women in travail* (Jer. 50:43).[40] The object is missing.[41] Compare, *Thou shalt not murder* (Ex. 20:13).[42] *His ways* refers to the ways of the wicked. His ways[43] frighten the intelligent,[44] for his behavior prospers.

Marom (far above) is similar to *But Thou, O Lord, art on high* (marom) *for evermore* (Ps. 92:9). *Marom* refers to God.[45] *Marom mishpatekha mi-negdo* (Thy judgments are far above out of his sight) means, Thou [who] art on high: Thy judgments are removed from his sight.

Yafi'ach ba-hem (he puffeth at them) is similar to *yafichu kiryah* (set a city at blaze) in *Scornful men set a city at blaze* (Prov. 29:8)[46].

6. HE SAITH IN HIS HEART: I SHALL NOT BE MOVED, I TO ALL GENERATIONS SHALL NOT BE IN ADVERSITY.

SHALL NOT BE IN ADVERSITY. *Asher lo ve-ra* (shall not be in adversity) should be interpreted as if written, *asher lo ereh ve-ra* (I shall not see adversity).[47] Our verse is similar to *let me not look upon my wretchedness* (be-ra'ati) (Num. 11:15).

---

34. The meaning of *yachilu derakhav* (his ways prosper) thus is, his desires come.

35. Translated according to I.E.

36. Lit., "come."

37. In other words we should translate *derakhav* literally.

38. *Yachilu derakhav* means, His (God's) ways [should have] frightened him.

39. As in the second interpretation.

40. Translated according to I.E.

41. In our verse.

42. Scripture does not say whom one is not to murder. The reader must supply the object.

43. The ways of the wicked.

44. The word *ha-maskil* (the intelligent) is the missing object. It has to be supplied by the reader.

45. Not to God's judgments.

46. They "blow" on the fire and cause it to burn with intensity. See Rashi on Prov. 29:8.

47. *Asher lo ve-ra* literally means; that is not in adversity. Hence I.E.'s comment.

7. HIS MOUTH IS FULL OF CURSING AND DECEIT AND OPPRESSION; UNDER HIS TONGUE IS MISCHIEF AND INIQUITY.

AND DECEIT. *Tokh* (deceit) refers[48] to the secret evil thoughts in the midst of the heart of the wicked.[49] Our verse is similar to *Their inward part is a yawning gulf* (Ps. 5:10). The wicked person acts like he is at peace and favorably disposed toward his victim. Scripture therefore afterwards reads, *In secret places doth he slay the innocent.*

8. HE SITTETH IN THE LURKING-PLACES OF THE VILLAGES;[50] IN SECRET PLACES DOTH HE SLAY THE INNOCENT; HIS EYES ARE ON THE WATCH FOR THE HELPLESS.

HE SITTETH. Those who sit in ambush, do so in uninhabited places. However, this one ambushes in inhabited places.

FOR THE HELPLESS. Some say that the *kaf* in *chelekhah* (helpless) refers to God.[51] We ask them: If this is the case, why is there no *yod* in *chelekhah*?[52] The *yod*[53] is not dropped from *bayit,* (house) *zayit* (olive), and *laylah* (night) when they are connected to a pronoun.[54] There is a difference of opinion between the *ketiv*[55] and the *kere*[56] as to whether the word *chelka'im* (helpless) (v. 10) is one or two words.[57]

Ka'im has the same meaning as *nekha'im* (stricken) (Is. 16:7)[58] and is vocalized according to the paradigm of *davvim* (pained) and *rabbim* (many).[59]

---

48. Lit., "this is a sign."

49. The word *tokh* (deceit) means, in the midst of.

50. Lit. *"He sits in ambush in the open places."* Hence I.E.'s comment.

51. In other words the *kaf* is a second person pronominal suffix meaning *your*. This explanation interprets the word *chelekhah* as meaning, Your *chel* (Your army) i.e. Your pious ones.

52. The word *chel* meaning an army has a *yod* in it. There is no *yod* in *chelekhah*. Thus *chelekhah* cannot mean Your army.

53. Lit., "for the *yod.*"

54. Hence the word *chelekhah* cannot mean, your army.

55. The way the word is written in the biblical text.

56. The way the word is read.

57. *Chelka'im* is written as one word but is read as two i.e. *chel ka'im. Chel* in *chelka'im* is spelled without a *yod.*

58. According to Radak the meaning of *chelka'im* is, the congregation (chel) of the stricken (ka'im).

59. It should be noted that these words are vocalized *pattach chirik. Ka'im* is vocalized *kametz chirik*. One cannot place a *dagesh* in an *alef.* To compensate for this the *pattach* (a short vowel) moves up one step and

A great grammarian said that *chelka'im* (helpless) is one word.[60] It comes from a four-letter root.[61] The same is the case with the word *chelekhah*. However, the *heh*[62] takes the place of an *alef* in *chelekhah*.

The Gaon[63] says that the *nun* of *yitzponu* (are on the watch) is superfluous.[64] It should be interpreted as *yitzpu* (are on the watch).[65] The word *enav* (his eyes) proves this. Compare, *His eyes keep watch* (*titzpenah*) *upon the nations* (Ps. 66: 7).

However, in my opinion the wicked seek a secret place for themselves.[66] The meaning of *enav...yitzponu* (his eyes.... on the watch) is: The wicked person's eyes seek a hidden and secret place.[67]

9. HE LIETH IN WAIT IN A SECRET PLACE AS A LION IN HIS LAIR, HE LIETH IN WAIT TO CATCH THE POOR; HE DOTH CATCH THE POOR, WHEN HE DRAWETH HIM UP IN HIS NET.

HE LIETH IN WAIT. Rabbi Moses says that *ve-sukko* (in his lair) has the same meaning[68] as *ve-sukkoto*.[69] We find the same with the word *pinna* (her corner) (Prov. 7:8). It has the same meaning as *pinnatah* (her corner) [70](Job. 38:6).[71]

TO CATCH. *La-chatof* (to catch) is similar to the word *va-chataftem* (and catch you) in *and catch you every man* (Jud. 21:21).[72]

---

becomes a *kametz* (a long vowel).

60. Meaning helpless or oppressed. See Rashi. According to this opinion the *ketiv* is the correct form of the word.

61. Its root is *chet, lamed ,kaf, alef*.

62. Of *chelekhah*.

63. Rabbi Saadiah Gaon.

64. Lit., "added."

65. From the root, *tzadi, peh, heh*.

66. The wicked person searches for a hidden place from which to attack the helpless. See Radak.

67. According to I.E. *yitzponu* (are on the watch) comes from the root, *tzadi, peh, nun* meaning to hide. Thus *enav yitzponu* means *his eyes hide*, that is, his eyes search for a hidden place.

68. That is *sukko* is a variant of *sukkato*.

69. Which is the word *sukkah* (lair) plus the third person pronominal suffix. Rabbi Moses comments thus because the normal word for his lair is *sukkato*.

70. Lit., "its corner." The reference is to a corner stone.

71. Rabbi Moses comments thus because the Hebrew word for "her corner" is *pinnatah*.

72. In other words, *la-chatof* means, to catch.

10. HE CROUCHETH, HE BOWETH DOWN, AND THE HELPLESS FALL INTO HIS MIGHTY CLAWS.

HE CROUCHETH. A lion that desires prey crouches[73] in order to avoid detection. He then jumps on his prey.

INTO HIS MIGHTY CLAWS. *Atzumav* (his mighty claws)[74] refers to the very powerful hands and feet of the lion. This is the correct meaning of *atzumav*. [However, note the following:] We find[75] the word *yegarem* (break)[76] in Scripture (Num. 24:8). *Yegarem* means, to break the bones. *Yegarem* is in the *piel*. We find the same root in the *kal*. Compare, *They leave not a bone* (garemu) *for the morrow* (Zeph. 3:3). We also find the word *itzem* (broken bones) in *hath broken his bones* (itzemo) (Jer. 50:17). The latter is a piel. It, like [garemu] should also come in the *kal*.[77] The meaning of *ba-atzumav*[78] is thus, into his bone breakers.[79] I have already explained the meaning of *chalka'im* (the helpless).[80]

11. HE HATH SAID IN HIS HEART: GOD HATH FORGOTTEN; HE HIDETH HIS FACE; HE WILL NEVER SEE.

HE HATH SAID. The wicked person knows that God exists. However, he maintains that God is unaware of what occurs. Compare,[81] *How doth God know?* (Ps. 73:11).

HE HIDDETH HIS FACE. Our verse, as is the custom,[82] repeats itself.[83]

12. ARISE, O LORD; O GOD, LIFT UP THY HAND; FORGET NOT THE HUMBLE.

---

73. Lit., "acts in this manner."

74. The literal meaning of *atzumav* (his mighty claws) is, his mighty ones. Hence I.E.'s interpretation.

75. Literally, as we find.

76. The word *gerem* means a bone. So does *etzem*. *Yegarem* and *gerem* came from the same root.

77. As in *garemu.*

78. Which comes from the root *ayin, tzadi, mem* (bone).

79. Thus *atzumav* means his bone breakers, that is, his claws.

80. See I.E. on verse 8.

81. Lit., "after the manner."

82. In biblical poetry.

83. This is referred to as synonymous parallelism.

LIFT UP THY HAND. Lift up Your hand and show Your might.[84]

FORGET NOT THE HUMBLE. This is in contrast to *God hath forgotten* (v. 11).

13. WHEREFORE DOTH THE WICKED CONTEMN GOD, AND SAY IN HIS HEART: THOU WILT NOT REQUIRE?

WHEREFORE? *Al meh* (wherefore) introduces a question.[85] Compare, *Why* (lammah) *dost Thou show me iniquity?* (Hab. 1:3).[86]

14. THOU HAST SEEN; FOR THOU BEHOLDEST TROUBLE AND VEXATION, TO REQUITE THEM WITH THY HAND; UNTO THEE THE HELPLESS COMMITTETH HIMSELF; THOU HAST BEEN THE HELPER OF THE FATHERLESS.

THOU HAST SEEN. In Your wisdom.[87] Since it is in Your hand to mete out punishment to the wicked whenever You desire, [88]You[89] undoubtedly behold the trouble and the vexation caused by the wicked[90]

UNTO THEE THE HELPLESS COMMITTETH HIMSELF. *Chelekhah* (helpless) is similar in meaning to *le-chelekah* (for the helpless) (v. 8). The helpless are vexed [91] because they often[92] saw[93] God helping the defenseless orphan.[94]
Rabbi Balaam explains our verse as follows:
The poor cease to rely upon You, for You behold the trouble and the vexation brought about by the wicked and you give him all that he desires.

---

84. Literally, "the lifting of the hand to show strength." One can lift up one's hand for any number of reasons. Hence I.E.'s comment.

85. Lit. "*Al meh* is an expression of wonder." It means, wherefore or why. The literal meaning of *al meh* is, on what. Hence I.E.'s comment.

86. In other words *al meh* and *lammah* mean the same.

87. Seen usually refers to what the eye beheld. Hence I.E.'s comment.

88. I.E.'s explanation of *la-tet be-yadekha* (to requite with Thy hand). The latter literally means, *to give in Thy hand*. I.E. interprets this to mean: It is in Thy hand (be-yadekha) to punish them (la-tet).

89. Lit., "for You."

90. I.E.'s explanation of *For thou beholdest trouble and vexation.*

91. Lit., "this vexation or anger."

92. Lit., "many times."

93. Lit., "see."

94. However, He does not seem to do so now.

The end of the verse shows that Rabbi Balaam is wrong.[95]

15. BREAK THOU THE ARM OF THE WICKED; AND AS FOR THE EVIL MAN, SEARCH OUT HIS WICKEDNES, TILL NON BE FOUND.

BREAK. The *tav*[96] of *tidrosh* (search out) is directed to God. Its meaning is, if You were a man[97] and You sought the wicked person, You would not find him,[98] for he would[99] be destroyed.[100]

Others say that the *tav* of *tidrosh* is a third person prefix[101] referring to the arm of the wicked person. *Tidrosh risho* (search out his wickedness) means, the arm of the wicked will seek to do evil but will not find it possible (bal timtza) to do so. Our verse is similar to *Thy hand shall find* (timtza) *all thine enemies* (Ps. 21:9).[102]

[16. THE LORD IS KING FOR EVER AND EVER; THE NATIONS ARE PERISHED OUT OF HIS LAND]

It will then [103] become clear that God alone is king (v. 16). *The nations are perished out of His land* is proof of this (v. 16).[104]

17. LORD, THOU HAST HEARD THE DESIRE OF THE HUMBLE: THOU WILT DIRECT THEIR HEART, THOU WILT CAUSE THINE EAR TO ATTEND.

THEIR HEART. *Thou hast heard the desire of the humble* means, You have heard the wish of the humble before they expressed it. Our clause is similar to *For there is not a word in my tongue,*

---

95. For the end of the verse states, *Thou hast been the help of the fatherless.*

96. The *tav* is a second person prefix.

97. Lit., "if You were like a man."

98. The word *timtza* (be found) can also be rendered, You will find. The latter is the way I.E. interprets the word.

99. *Timtza* (non be found) can mean, he will find, it will find, or you will find. I.E. interprets it as, you will find.

100. I.E.'s interpretation of why the wicked person will not be found.

101. The *tav* serves both as a second and a third person prefix.

102. Translated according to I.E.

103. When the arm of the wicked is broken.

104. According to I.E. v. 16 should be rendered as follows: Then the Lord alone shall be king for ever and ever; for the nations are perished out of his land.

But, Lo, O Lord, Thou knowest it altogether (Ps. 139:4). The humble only desire that You direct their heart, that is, that You help them to direct their hearts to You.
The *tav* of *takshiv* (to attend) is a feminine prefix.[105]
The second part of this verse repeats the idea expressed in the first part of the verse.[106]

18. TO RIGHT THE FATHERLESS AND THE OPPRESSED, THAT MAN WHO IS OF THE EARTH MAY BE TERRIBLE NO MORE.

TO RIGHT[107] THE FATHERLESS AND THE OPPRESSED. To exact justice[108] on behalf of the orphan and the oppressed.

BE TERRIBLE. The word *la-arotz* (be terrible) is similar to *ta'artzu* (affrighted) in *al ta'artzu* (Num. 20:3; 31:6). The latter means, do not be afraid.
The word *aritz*[109] means, frightening.
The meaning of *la'arotz enosh* (man.... be terrible) thus is, "to fear man;"[110] for we find the Hebrew word for afraid with and with out a *mem*.[111] Compare, *yiru me-Adonai* (fear the Lord) (Ps. 33:8) and *yirau'kha im shemesh* (They shall fear Thee while the sun endureth) (Ps. 72:5).
It is also possible that the word *min* (of) in *min ha'aretz* (of the earth) also applies to the word *enosh* (man).[112] Compare, *odem pitdah u-vareket* (carnelian, topaz, and smaragd) (Ex. 28:17).[113]

---

105. It is a third person feminine prefix rather than a second person masculine prefix. According to this interpretation *takshiv oznekha* (Thou wilt cause Thine ear to attend) is to be rendered, Your ear shall hear.

106. *Thou wilt cause Thine ear to attend* means the same as *Thou hast heard the desire of the humble*.

107. Hebrew, *li-shepot.* Literally, "to judge."

108. In other words *li-shepot* means, to exact justice.

109. In Is. 29:20; 49:25; Jer. 20:11 Ps. 37:35.

110. In other words, the orphans and fatherless will no longer be afraid of man who is of the earth.

111. In other words Scripture employs the forms "fear man" (without a *mem* following the word fear) and "be afraid of man" (with a *mem* following the word *afraid*).

112. Thus *la'arotz enosh* is to be read as if written, *la'arotz min enosh*. In this case the word *of* "appears" in the text.

113. Wherein the *vav* placed before *u-vareket* also applies to *pitdah*. The phrase is thus to be read as if written, *odem u-pitdah u-vareket*.

CHAPTER 11

1. FOR THE LEADER. [A PSALM] OF DAVID. IN THE LORD HAVE I TAKEN REFUGE; HOW SAY YE TO MY SOUL FLEE THOU! TO YOUR MOUNTAIN, YE BIRDS?

FOR THE LEADER… HOW SAY YE TO MY SOUL. *How say ye* is directed to David's enemies, the wicked. It is to them that David speaks.

TO YOUR MOUNTAIN. *Harkhem* means, *your mountain.*
Tzippor (birds)[1] should be interpreted as if written, *ke-tzippor* (like a bird).[2] It is similar to the word *aryeh* (lion) in *And he called a lion: Upon the watch tower O Lord*[3] (Is. 21:8). *Aryeh* (lion) in the latter is to be interpreted as if written *ke-aryeh* (as a lion), for God is the subject of *and he called.*[4] The fact that *mitzpeh* (watchtower) is vocalized with a *segol*[5] and is not[6] in the construct is proof of this.[7]
Tzippor is to be read as if written *ke-tzippor,* for the meaning of our clause is, you say to me, flee by yourself to our mountain[8] for you are like a bird.[9]

---

1. Lit. "Bird." I.E. interprets this word as a singular.

2. Lit. "*Tzippor* is lacking a *Kaf.*"

3. Translated lit.

4. Is. 21:8 should be interpreted, *and God called like a lion.*

5. Rather than a *tzere.*

6. Lit., "for it is not."

7. That *aryeh* is to be read as if written *ke-aryeh.* Is. 21:8 reads: *va-yikra arye al mitzpeh Adonai.* If *mitzpeh* were vocalized with a *tzere* it would be in the construct with what follows. *Va-yikra arye al mitzpeh Adonai* could conceivably be translated as, And a lion called upon the watchtower of the Lord. However, since *mitzpeh* is vocalized with a *segol* the clause ends there and the verse should be read, *vayikra arye al mitzpeh, Adonai.* It should be rendered: God called like a lion on the watchtower. See Filwarg.

8. Scripture employs *your mountain* because David was addressing his enemies. However, when his enemies addressed him they employed the phrase "our mountain."

9. According to I.E. our verse should be understood as follows: How say ye to my soul: Flee thou to our mountain, for you are like a bird.

[2. FOR, LO, THE WICKED BEND THE BOW, THEY HAVE MADE READY THEIR ARROW UPON THE STRING, THAT THEY MAY SHOOT IN DARKNESS AT THE UPRIGHT IN HEART]

The bow is made ready in darkness.

3. WHEN THE FOUNDATIONS ARE DESTROYED, WHAT HATH THE RIGHTEOUS WROUGHT?

WHEN THE FOUNDATIONS ARE DESTROYED. The word *shattot* (foundations) means, traps. Compare, *And her traps* (shatoteha) shall *be crushed* (Is. 19: 10).[10] Others say that the word *shatot* means foundations. Compare, *and with foundations* (shet)[11] *uncovered* (Is. 20:5). The fact that Scripture goes on to say *are destroyed* proves that *shatot* means foundations.
The foundations refer to council. The latter is the foundation of all endeavors.[12]
What hath the righteous wrought means, do not be angry at the righteous, for this is God's work. *The Lord in his holy temple* therefore follows. *His holy temple* refers to heaven.

4. THE LORD IS IN HIS HOLY TEMPLE, THE LORD, HIS THRONE IS IN HEAVEN; HIS EYES BEHOLD, HIS EYELIDS TRY, THE CHILDREN OF MEN.

HIS EYES BEHOLD. This is in contrast to *That they may shoot in darkness* (v. 3).[13]

5. THE LORD TRIETH THE RIGHTEOUS; BUT THE WICKED AND HIM THAT LOVETH VIOLENCE HIS SOUL HATETH.

THE LORD TRIETH. If evil falls upon the righteous it is to afflict him,[14] to test him and to chastise him.[15] Compare, *For whom the Lord loveth He correcteth* (Prov. 3:12). However, God eternally hates the wicked.[16]

---

10. Translated according to I.E. See I. E. on Is. 19:10: "The buildings which they erect to take the fish in." Friedlander, M. *The Commentary of Ibn Ezra on Isaiah*. London: 1873. Radak renders *shatoteha* as, her nets.

11. Translated according to I.E.

12. Lit. "*The foundations* refer to council which is the basis."

13. In other words God sees what is done in the dark.

14. To cleanse him from his sins.

15. See Deut. 8:17.

16. The evil that befalls the wicked does not serve as a corrective.

6. UPON THE WICKED HE WILL CAUSE TO RAIN COALS; FIRE AND BRIMSTONE AND BURNING WIND SHALL BE THE PORTION OF THEIR CUP.

HE WILL CAUSE TO RAIN COALS. David compares the evil which suddenly befalls the wicked to *pachim* (coals). *Pachim* are burning stone like objects which come down with the rain. The word *pachim* is related to *pachim* (plates) in *beaten plates* (Num.17: 3).

AND BURNING WIND. *Zilafot* (burning wind) means shaking. Compare, *zalafah achazatni* (shaking hath taken hold of me) (Ps. 119:53).[17]

PORTION. The meaning of *kosam* (their cup) is, their portion.[18] The word *kosi* (my portion) in *O Lord, the portion of my inheritance and my portion* (kosi) (Ps. 16:5) is similar.[19] *Kosam* and *kosi* come from a double root.[20] The word *takhossu* (make your count) in *ye shall make your count for the lamb* (Ex. 12:4) is proof of this.[21]

7. FOR THE LORD IS RIGHTEOUS, HE LOVETH RIGHTEOUSNESS; THE UPRIGHT SHALL BEHOLD HIS FACE.[22]

FOR …Rabbi Moses says that Scripture employs the word *panemo* (his face)[23] in place of *panav* (his face).[24] The word *alemo* (unto him) in *Or can he that is wise be profitable unto him* (Job 22:2) is similar.[25]

However, Yefet says that our verse employs *panemo* in the same way that it employs *hitu* (caused me to wander)[26] in *when God* (Elohim) *caused me to wander* (hitu) (Gen. 20:13).[27]

---

17. Translated according to I.E.

18. I.E. interprets the latter part of our verse as follows: *Fire and brimstone and burning wind shall be their portion.*

19. Translated according to I.E.

20. *Kaf, samekh, samekh.*

21. *Takhossu* comes from the root *kaf, samekh, samkeh.* Compare, *tasobbu*, from the root *samekh, bet, bet.*

22. Heb. *Fanemo.* Lit., "their faces."

23. Lit., "their face."

24. Our clause reads: *Yashar yechezu fanemo* (The upright shall behold his face). Now *fanemo* literally means, their faces. See Radak. Rabbi Moses argues that Scripture employs a plural with the meaning of a singular. He interprets *yashar yehezu fanemo* as; His face shall behold the upright.

25. *Alemo* literally means unto them. Thus Scripture employs *alemo* with the meaning of *alav* (to him).

26. *Hitu* is a plural. It literally means they caused me to wander.

27. We thus see that Scripture sometimes uses the plural when referring to God. Thus there is no reason to

However, he is mistaken. The plural is never used with God's glorious name.[28] It is only employed with the name *Elohim*. The reason for the latter is a deep secret.[29]

The face does not see. It is only the eyes that are in the face that see.[30]

The face of the Lord hath divided them (Lam. 4: 16) is no argument to the contrary.[31] The latter[32] is similar to *The face of the Lord is against them that do evil* (Ps. 34:17).[33]

In reality *they shall behold* (yechezu) is connected to *the children of men* (v. 4).[34] This is so even though there is some distance between the two.

It is also possible that *shall behold* should be interpreted as if written, those who behold shall behold."[35] It is similar to *Whom she bore to Levi in Egypt* (Num: 25:59).[36]

The word *yashar* (the upright) is an adjective. Its meaning is, *upright judgments.* Compare, *And upright* (yashar) *are Thy judgments* (Ps. 119:137).

---

say that Scripture employs the word *panemo* (his face) in place of *panav* (his face).

28. The reference is to Gods personal name *YHVH*.

29. I.E. might be alluding to his belief that *Elohim* means angels and that the Divine name *Elohim* means, God who works through the angels. Now since *Elohim* is in the plural the verbs pertaining to it are at times in the plural. See I.E. on Gen. 1:1.

30. Thus *yashar yechezu fanemo* (The upright shall behold their face) cannot be rendered; *the face of the Lord shall behold the upright.* Lit. "We do not find that the face sees. It is only with the eyes which are in the face."

31. The face does not divide (Filwarg). We thus see that Scripture is not always exact when it describes the activity of the face. Thus *yashar yechezu fanemo* (The upright shall behold his face) can conceivably be rendered; *the face of the Lord shall behold the upright.*

32. Lit., "for the."

33. *The face of the Lord hath divided them* is to be interpreted, the anger of the Lord hath divided them.

34. In other words, the last part of verse 7 does not continue the thought expressed in the first part of verse 7 but continues the ideas expressed in v. 4. This interpretation renders our clause, *the children of men shall behold* [God's] *upright* [judgment] *before their face.* Filwarg.

35. This interpretation renders *yasher yechezu fanemo* (literally, the upright shall behold their face) as, *those who behold, shall behold* [God's] *upright* [judgment] *before their face.* Filwarg.

36. Num. 25:5 literally reads, *who bore to Levi* (asher yaledah le-levi). Scripture does not identify the bearer. According to I.E. the verse is be explained, *whom the bearer bore* (asher yoledah ha-yoledet). In other words, the verb *yaledah* implies the subject (ha-yoledet). The same is the case here. *Yechezu* (shall see) implies the subject, the one who sees.

CHAPTER 12

1. FOR THE LEADER; ON THE SHEMINITH. A PSALM OF DAVID.

FOR THE LEADER; ON THE SHEMINITH. *On the Sheminith* refers to a tune, or to a poem[1] or to a musical instrument of eight strings.[2]

2. HELP, LORD; FOR THE GODLY MAN CEASETH; FOR THE FAITHFUL FAIL FROM AMONG THE CHILDREN OF MEN.

FOR THE GODLY MAN CEASETH. *Gamar* (ceaseth) is an intransitive verb. On the other hand *gamar* might be transitive. In the latter case *ki gamar chasid* (for the godly man ceaseth) means, for the godly man ceaseth to practice loving-kindness.[3]
The word *passu* (fail) similarly[4] means, are cut off.[5] Compare, *pas yeda* (the palm of the hand) (Ps.8: 5).[6]
Emunim (faithful) is an adjective. This is not the case with *emunim* (faithfulness) in *shomer emunim* (keepeth faithfulness) (Is. 26:2), for *emunim* in the latter is a noun.

3. THEY SPEAK FALSEHOOD EVERY ONE WITH HIS NEIGHBOR; WITH FLATTERING LIP AND WITH A DOUBLE HEART, DO THEY SPEAK.

FLATTERING. *Chalakot* (flattering) is an adjective. The word being described is *imrot*

---

1. See I.E. on Ps. 4:1.

2. Lit., "string." Targum and Rashi interpret similarly.

3. *For the godly man ceaseth* is short for, the godly man ceaseth to practice lovingkindess.

4. Lit. "Also."

5. *Passu* is parallel to *gamer*.

6. Lit., "a piece of the hand, a section of the hand."

(words). However, it is not in the text. Compare, *and spoke rough (kashot) with them*[7] (Gen. 42:7).[8]

AND WITH A DOUBLE HEART, DO THEY SPEAK. They act as if they had two hearts with one tongue speaking on behalf of one of the hearts.[9]

4. MAY THE LORD CUT OFF ALL FLATTERING LIPS,[10] THE TONGUE THAT SPEAKETH PROUD THINGS!

CUT OFF. This is a prophetic statement. It is like *Heal me, O Lord, and I shall be healed* (Jer. 17:14). On the other hand it might be a prayer.[11]

THAT SPEAKETH PROUD THINGS.[12] Compare, *And their food a fat*[13] ... (Hab. 1:16).[14]

5. WHO HAVE SAID: OUR TONGUE WILL WE MAKE MIGHTY; OUR LIPS ARE WITH US: WHO IS LORD OVER US?

OUR TONGUE. *Li-leshonenu* (our tongue) means, because of our tongue.[15] Compare *pen yomeru li* (that men say not of me) (Jud. 9:54).[16]

6. FOR THE OPPRESSION OF THE POOR, FOR THE SIGHING OF THE NEEDY, NOW WILL I ARISE, SAITH THE LORD; I WILL SET HIM IN SAFETY AT WHOM THEY PUFF.

FOR THE OPPRESSION. The *mem* of *mi-shod* (for the oppression) is similar to the *mem* of *me-chamas* (for the violence) in *For the violence done to thy brother* (Obad. 1:10).[17]

---

7. Translated lit.

8. *And spoke rough (kashot) with them* is short for *and spoke rough words with them*. See I.E. on Gen. 42:7.

9. While the other heart has other plans.

10. Lit., "*The Lord will cut off* (yakhrit) *all flattering lips.*" Hence I.E.'s comments.

11. Thus *yakhrit Adonai* (the Lord will cut off) should be rendered: *May the Lord cut off*.

12. Lit. "That speaks proud." Hence I.E.'s comment.

13. Translated according to I.E.

14. *And their food a fat* is short for, and their food a fat lamb. Similarly, *proud* (gedolot) is short for, proud words (dibberot gedolot). (See Radak).

15. Thus *li-leshonenu nagbir* (our tongue will we make mighty) means, we will become mighty because of our tongue.

16. Lit., "that man say to me." In other words the *lamed* means, "because" or "of."

17. The *mem* prefixed to a letter usually means from. Hence I.E. points out that here the *mem* has the meaning of *because* or *for*. Thus *mi-shod* does not mean from the oppression, but because of the oppression. Similarly, *me-chamas* does not mean, from the violence but because of the violence.

NOW WILL I ARISE, SAITH THE LORD. This is a prophetic statement.[18]

I WILL SET HIM IN SAFETY. The *bet* in *be-yesha* (in safety) is similar to the *bet* in *be-lachmi* (of my bread) and the *bet* in *be-yayin* (of the wine) in, *Come eat of my bread, and drink of the wine which I have mingled* (Prov. 9:5).[19]
The word *yafi'ach* (they puff) in *yafi'ach lo* (at whom they puff) means, he will speak. Compare *yafi'ach kezavim* (speaks lies) (Prov. 6:19).[20]
Ashit be-yesha yafi'ach lo (I will set him in safety at whom they puff) means, I will set salvation[21] to the one who speaks to himself the words of the Lord. This verse is connected to the sentence that follows.[22]

7. THE WORDS OF THE LORD ARE PURE WORDS, AS SILVER TRIED IN A CRUCIBLE ON THE EARTH, REFINED SEVEN TIMES.

THE WORDS OF THE LORD. "I will save the one who speaks the words of the Lord"[23] (v. 6) means, God immediately saves those who make mighty their tongue, that is, those who study the Lord's Torah.[24] Hence Scripture goes on to say, *Thou wilt keep them… from this generation for ever…* (v. 8).
The *lamed* of *ba-alil*[25] (in a crucible) is doubled like the *resh* of *sagrir* (stormy).[26] *Ba-alil* comes from the same root that *ba'al* (owner) does. *Ba-alil la-aretz* (in the crucible of the earth) is thus like *ba'al ha-retz*. Its meaning is, the owner of the earth. *Kesef tzaruf ba-alil la-aretz* (as silver tried in the crucible of the earth) should be rendered as, the tried silver of the Lord of the earth.

---

18. For David is quoting God.

19. A *bet* prefixed to a word usually has the meaning of, before. Thus *be-yesha* should be rendered, in salvation. However, I.E. maintains that in our verse the *bet* should be omitted, for *ashit be-yesha* (I will set him in safety) should be rendered: I will set salvation i.e. I will save.
The same applies to the *bet* in *be-lachmi* (of my bread) and the *bet* in *be-yayin* (of the wine) in, *Come eat of my bread, and drink of the wine which I have mingled* (Prov. 9:5). The aforementioned *bets* are to be omitted when translating the verse.

20. Translated according to I.E.

21. That is, I will save.

22. Its meaning is as follows: I will save the one who speaks the words of the Lord, for the words of the Lord are pure words…

23. I.E.'s paraphrase of *ashit be-yesha yafi'ach lo* (I will set him in safety at whom they puff).

24. In contrast to the wicked spoken of in v. 5.

25. In other words *ba-alil* comes from the root *bet, ayin, lamed*. According to this interpretation the *bet* of *ba-alil* is a root letter and not a preposition. *Ba-alil* should be transliterated *ba'alil*.

26. From the root *samekh, gimel, resh*..

SEVEN TIMES. Many times.[27]

8. THOU WILT KEEP THEM, O LORD; THOU WILT PRESERVE US FROM THIS GENERATION FOREVER.

THOU WILT KEEP THEM. The *mem* of *tishmerem* (Thou wilt keep them) most probably refers to *The words of the Lord* (v. 7).
Titzrennu (Thou wilt preserve us) refers to the one[28] who carries God's laws on his tongue.
The word *zu* (this) means, these.[29]
The people of David's generation were wicked.[30] Hence the next verse reads: *The wicked walk on every side.* The meaning of the latter is, they go all over to do evil.

[9. THE WICKED WALK ON EVERY SIDE, WHEN VILENESS IS EXALTED AMONG THE SONS OF MEN]

The meaning of *zullot* (vileness) is, vile. Compare, *the precious out of the vile* (mi-zolel) (Jer. 15:19); *How vile* (zolelah) *I am* (Lam. 1:11);[31] *All that honored her despise her* (hizziluha) (ibid. v. 8).
A word is missing in our clause. Our text should read as if written, when vile men are exalted.[32] Our verse is similar to, *And thy mighty in the war* (Is. 3:25);[33] *be not thou rebellious* (Ezek. 2:8);[34] *But I am prayer* (Ps. 109:4).[35]
Some say that the word *zullot* is related to the word *zollel* (glutton) in *a glutton and a drunkard* (Deut. 21:20).[36] However, the first interpretation is correct.[37]

---

27. Seven is not to be taken literally.

28. *Titzrennu* (Thou wilt preserve us) is a singular. *Titzrennu* literally means, You will preserve him. Hence I.E.'s comment.

29. The reference being to the evil people of David's generation. For the meaning of *zu* see I.E. on Ps. 35:5.

30. I.E. interprets our verse as follows: You will preserve Your commandments; You will preserve the person, who keeps these commandments, from the evil men of this generation.

31. Translated according to I.E.

32. In other words *zullot* (vileness) is short for *anshe zulllot* (vile men). According to I.E. the second part of our verse should be rendered: *When vile men, among the sons of men are exalted.*

33. *And thy mighty in the war* should be read as if written, *And thy mighty men in the war.*

34. *Be not thou rebellious* is short for, *be not thou a rebellious person.*

35. Translated literally. *But I am prayer* is short for, *but I am a man of prayer.*

36. According to this interpretation our clause should be rendered as follows: *When gluttons are exalted among the children of men.*

CHAPTER 13

1. FOR THE LEADER. A PSALM OF DAVID.

2. HOW LONG, O LORD, WILT THOU FORGET ME FOREVER? HOW LONG WILT THOU HIDE THY FACE FROM ME.

HOW LONG. If David is not saved from his enemies then people will think that God[1] has forgotten him and is not aware of what happened to him.[2]

3. HOW LONG SHALL I TAKE COUNSEL IN MY SOUL, HAVING SORROW IN MY HEART BY DAY? HOW LONG SHALL MY ENEMY BE EXALTED OVER ME?

HOW LONG. How long shall I plan and continually take counsel in my soul, due to the sorrow that is in my heart[3] by day, because my enemy is exalted over me.

4. BEHOLD THOU, AND ANSWER ME, O LORD MY GOD; LIGHTEN MINE EYES, LEST I SLEEP THE SLEEP OF MY DEATH.

BEHOLD THOU, AND ANSWER ME. This is in contrast to *How long wilt Thou hide Thy face from me?* (V.1).

LEST I SLEEP. The sleep of death, for verbs imply nouns.[4]

---

1. Lit., "his God."

2. Lit. "Its meaning is, If he is not saved from his enemies then people will think that his God has forgotten him and is not aware of what happened to him."

3. Our verse literally reads: *How long shall I take counsel in my soul, sorrow in my heart.* I.E. explains that *sorrow in my heart* is to be interpreted, due to the sorrow that is in my heart.

4. Our text reads, *pen ishan ha-mavet.* This literally means, *lest I sleep of death.* According to I.E., the verb

5. LEST MINE ENEMY SAY: I HAVE PREVAILED AGAINST HIM; LEST MINE ADVERSARIES REJOICE WHEN I AM MOVED.

LEST MINE ENEMY SAY: I HAVE PREVAILED AGAINST HIM. *Yakhol* (I have prevailed) is intransitive.[5] Hence the meaning of *yekholtiv* is, I have prevailed against him.[6] Compare, *va-yizakukha*[7] (Neh. 9: 28). The latter means, *They cried unto Thee* (elekaha) or *thy cried to Thee*[8] (lekha).[9]

6. BUT AS FOR ME, IN THY MERCY DO I TRUST; MY HEART SHALL REJOICE IN THY SALVATION. I WILL SING UNTO THE LORD, BECAUSE HE HATH DEALT BOUNTIFULLY WITH ME.

BUT AS FOR ME. There is no mercy for me to trust in but Yours. It is because of this trust that my heart rejoices.

---

ishan implies the noun *shenat* (sleep of). Thus *pen ishan ha-mavet* should be rendered, *lest I sleep the sleep of death*.

5. Even though it has the form of a transitive verb. Intransitive verbs are not combined with personal pronouns. However, *yekholtiv* which is a combination of *yakholti* (I have prevailed) and *oto* (him) is. Hence I.E.'s comment.

6. Rather than I have prevailed him. See previous note.

7. This rather than *va-yizaku* (and they cried) appears to be the correct reading. Filwarg; *Ha-Keter*.

8. Rather than *they cried you*. The point is *va-yizakukha* is intransitive even though it has the form of a transitive verb.

9. In Hebrew there is a difference in nuance between *elekha* and *lekha*. The difference does not come through in English translation.

CHAPTER 14

1. FOR THE LEADER. [A PSALM] OF DAVID. THE FOOL HATH SAID IN HIS HEART THERE IS NO GOD; THEY HAVE DEALT CORRUPTLY, THEY HAVE DONE ABOMINABLY; THERE IS NONE THAT DOETH GOOD.

THE FOOL HATH SAID. *Naval* (fool) is the reverse of *Chakham* (wise man)[1]. The fools have corrupted their ways[2] and have committed abominable acts, for they think there is no God. There is none that does good.

The word *alilah* (done) means, deeds. Compare, *u-va-alilotekha asichah* (and muse on Thy doings) (Ps. 77:13).[3]

2. THE LORD LOOKED FORTH FROM HEAVEN UPON THE CHILDREN OF MEN, TO SEE IF THERE WERE ANY MAN OF UNDERSTANDING, THAT DID SEEK AFTER GOD.

THE LORD LOOKED FORTH FROM HEAVEN. Scripture says *The Lord looked forth from heaven,* because God's glory is in a highly exalted place, that is, it is in heaven.[4] Scripture speaks metaphorically, for God knows all. God knows all via all.[5]

3. THEY ARE ALL CORRUPT, THEY ARE TOGETHER BECOME IMPURE; THERE IS NONE THAT DOETH GOOD, NO, NOT ONE.

---

1. In other words *naval* means a fool.

2. *Hishchitu* (dealt corruptly) is short for *hishchitu darkam* (they have corrupted their ways).

3. In other words the term *alilah* (done) means deeds.

4. Heaven is high above the earth.

5. Hence it is not necessary for God to look down from heaven to know what is occurring on earth. See I.E. on Ps. 2:6.

THEY ARE ALL CORRUPT. *Ha-kol sar* (they are all corrupt) means, all of them have turned away from the right path.[6]

THEY ARE TOGETHER BECOME CORRUPT. *Ne'elahu* means, they are become corrupt.

NO, NOT ONE. The meaning of *gam echad* (not one) is, even one.[7] Compare the word *gam* in the following verses: *Even (gam)*[8] *in laughter the heart acheth* (Prov. 14:13); *The poor is hated even (gam)*[9] *of his own neighbor* (ibid. v. 20).
The wicked spoken of in our verse refers to those who hate Israel. *Who eat up My people* which follows[10] is proof of the latter.

4. SHALL NOT ALL THE WORKER OF INIQUITY KNOW IT, WHO EAT UP MY PEOPLE AS THEY EAT BREAD, AND CALL NOT UPON THE LORD.

SHALL NOT ALL THE WORKER OF INIQUITY KNOW IT. The psalmist wonders and as it were says, "Did not these workers of iniquity know and consider, when they ate My people like one eats bread, that God gave them the power to do so." Compare, *Our hand is exalted And not the Lord hath wrought all this* (Deut. 32:28). This is what our verse means by *And call not upon the Lord.*

5. THERE ARE THEY IN GREAT FEAR; FOR GOD IS WITH THE RIGHTEOUS GENERATION.

THERE ARE THEY IN GREAT FEAR. They are in great fear in the place where they ate My people, for in that very place they trembled because of the great trouble, which befell them. As a result of the aforementioned they learned that God comes to the aid of the righteous generation.[11] *For God is with the righteous generation* is similar to *To the Lord's help of the mighty*[12] (Jud. 5:23).

---

6. *Ha-kol sar* (they are all corrupt) literally means, they all turned. I.E.'s believes that *they all turned* is short for, they all turned away from the right path.

7. *Gam echad* literally means, also one. Hence I.E.'s comment.

8. Lit., "also."

9. Lit., "also."

10. In verse 4.

11. I.E.'s interpretation of *For God is with the righteous generation.*

12. Translated according to I.E.

6. YE WOULD PUT TO SHAME THE COUNSEL OF THE POOR, BUT THE LORD IS HIS REFUGE.

THE COUNSEL OF THE POOR The *poor* refer to Israel. Israel's entire counsel[13] is, *the Lord is his refuge.*[14]

7. OH THAT THE SALVATION OF ISRAEL WERE COME OUT OF ZION! WHEN THE LORD TURNETH THE CAPTIVITY OF HIS PEOPLE, LET JACOB REJOICE, LET ISRAEL BE GLAD.

OH THAT THE SALVATION OF ISRAEL WERE COME OUT OF ZION! The meaning of our verse is similar to that of, *The rod of thy strength the Lord will send out of Zion* (Ps. 110:2); and *And support thee out of Zion* (Ps. 20:3). Scripture speaks of God's salvation and support coming out of Zion[15] because God's glory was with the ark in the days of David.

[WHEN THE LORD TURNETH THE CAPTIVITY OF HIS PEOPLE.] It is possible that our verse speaks of some Israelites who were taken captive.[16] On the other hand it is possible that our verse speaks of the future.[17] In this case *Oh that the salvation of Israel were come out of Zion! When the Lord turneth the captivity of his people* means, when God's Glory that dwells in Zion will return the captivity of His people.[18]
Mi yitten (Oh that)[19] is similar to *mi yitten* (would that) in *Would that all the Lord's people were prophets* (Num. 11:29).[20]

---

13. Reading *atzato*. See Radak.

14. I.E.'s interprets our verse as follows: You would put to shame Israel's belief that God will save them. In other words, you want to destroy Israel and thus show that God does not protect them.

15. Even though the temple did not yet exist. See I.E. on Ps. 15:1.

16. I.E. comments thus, because there was no Diaspora in David's time.

17. It is a prophetic statement.

18. Lit., "when the glory out of Zion."

19. Lit., "who will give."

20. In other words *mi yitten* means, oh that, I hope, or something similar.

CHAPTER 15

1. A PSALM OF DAVID. LORD, WHO SHALL SOJOURN IN THY TABARNACLE? WHO SHALL DWELL UPON THY HOLY MOUNTAIN?

A PSALM OF DAVID. LORD, WHO SHALL SOJOURN IN THY TABARNACLE? *Oholekha* (thy tabernacle)[1] means, Thy house. *Every man to your tents* (ohalekah) *O Israel* (11 Chon. 10:16) is similar.

WHO SHALL DWELL UPON THY HOLY MOUNTAIN? Mount Moriah. Or, Mount Zion, before it was known that it[2] was to be identified with Mt. Moriah. The Ark at that time rested in a house that David prepared for it on Mt. Zion, as the Book of Chronicles records.[3]

2. HE THAT WALKETH UPRIGHTLY, AND WORKETH RIGHTEOUSNESS, AND SPEAKETH TRUTH IN HIS HEART.

HE THAT WALKETH UPRIGHTLY. This is the answer to *Who shall sojourn in Thy tabernacle?*
UPRIGHTLY. The word *tamim* (uprightly)[4] is an adjective. However, the word that it describes[5] is missing. *Holekh tamim* (he that walketh uprightly)[6] means, he that walks in an upright way[7] with regards to his affairs and speech.

---

1. Lit. "Thy tent."

2. God's holy mountain.

3. See 1 Chron. 16:1. Actually Chron. tells us that David placed the ark in a tent. I.E. refers to the tent as a house.

4. Lit., "upright."

5. *Be-derekh* (in a way).

6. Lit., "he that walks upright."

7. In other words *holekh tamim* (he that walketh uprightly) is short for *holekh be-derekh tamim* (he that

AND WORKETH RIGHTEOUSNESS. In his dealing with his friends.

AND SPEAKETH TRUTH IN HIS HEART. This is the essence of man.[8]

3. THAT HATH NO SLANDER UPON HIS TONGUE, NOR DOETH EVIL TO HIS FELLOW, NOR TAKETH UP A REPROACH AGAINST HIS NEIGHBOR.

THAT HATH NO SLANDER UPON HIS TONGUE. The word *ragal* (slander) is similar to the word *va-yeraggel* (and hath slandered) in *And he hath slandered* (va-yer-aggel) *thy servant* (11 Sam. 19:28). It refers to one who acts like a spy and reveals that which is hidden.[9]

NOR TAKETH UP A REPROACH AGAINST HIS NEIGHBOR. The word *nasa* (taketh up) is similar to the word *tissa* (utter) in *Thou shalt not utter a false report* (Ex. 23:1). Some say that *ve-cherpah lo nasa al kerovo* (nor taketh up a reproach against his neighbor) means, he did not do anything that would bring shame upon his relatives.[10]

4. IN WHOSE EYES A VILE PERSON IS DESPISED, BUT HE HONORETH THEM THAT FEAR THE LORD; HE THAT SWEARETH TO HIS OWN HURT, AND CHANGETH NOT.

A VILE PERSON. The words *nivzeh* (a vile person)[11] and *nimas* (despised) are both tied to *be-enav* (in whose eyes). Our clause teaches that the one who serves God considers every commandment that he observes, and any good that he does of no account, when weighed against that which he is obligated to do in honor of His creator. This is the way of the righteous. They aspire to ascend to a more holy and exalted level. *Honoreth* is in contrast to *vile*.[12]

---

walks in an upright path).

8. Lit. "This is the whole man." See Ecc. 12:13.

9. Thus *lo ragal al leshono* (that hath no slander upon his tongue) means, he who does not reveal the secrets of his fellows.

10. The word *kerovo* (his neighbor) literally means, his relative.

11. The word *nivzeh* literally means, vile. I.E. interprets our verse accordingly.

12. The first half of the clause is in contrast to the second half.

HE THAT SWEARETH TO HIS OWN HURT. He swears to harm his body, that is,[13] he swears to fast. Fasting[14] weakens the flesh.

5. HE THAT PUTTETH NOT OUT HIS MONEY ON INTEREST, NOR TAKETH A BRIBE AGAINST THE INNOCENT. HE THAT DOETH THESE THINGS SHALL NEVER BE MOVED.

HIS MONEY. *Nor taketh* is parallel to *putteth not. Nor taketh a bribe against the innocent* means, he does not take a bribe to pervert justice.

HE THAT DOETH THESE THINGS. The reference is to all the positive and negative commandments.[15] The word *oseh* (doeth) here is similar to the word *la'asot* (to observe) in *to observe the sabbath* (Ex. 31:16).[16] The meaning of *la'asot*[17] is, to fix. Compare, *va-yemaher la'asot oto* (and he hastened to dress it) (Gen. 18:6).[18]

13. Lit. "For example."
14. Lit., "for fasting."
15. All the positive and negative commandments mentioned in this chapter. Filwarg.
16. The word *la'asot* refers to both the positive and negative commandments related to the Sabbath. Similarly, the word *oseh*. It refers both to positive and negative commandments.
17. Lit. For the meaning of *la'asot*.
18. In other words, *la'asot* implies wholeness. Thus *la'asot et ha-shabbat* means to make the Sabbath whole, that is, to completely observe it by keeping the positive and negative commandments pertaining to the Sabbath. Similarly, *oseh elleh* means, he that completely observes these things, that is keeps the positive and negative commandments mentioned above.

CHAPTER 16

1. MIKHTAM OF DAVID. KEEP ME, O GOD; FOR I HAVE TAKEN REFUGE IN THEE.

MIKHTAM. The reference is to a very precious Psalm. Compare, *ketem paz* (the most fine gold) (Song of Songs 5:11).[1] The reference might also be to a tune beginning with the word *mikhtam*.[2]

KEEP ME, O GOD.[3] The following is the meaning of our verse: *Keep me,* for I have taken refuge in Thee; keep me, for Thou art the Lord. The meaning of the latter[4] is, You are mighty and have the power to save me.

2. I HAVE SAID UNTO THE LORD:[5] THOU ART MY LORD; I HAVE NO GOOD BUT IN THEE.

I HAVE SAID UNTO THE LORD. David spoke to his soul.[6] He said to it, you have confessed in times past that the Lord is your master and that you are obligated to serve Him even if He does not deal well with you.[7] The concept conveyed in our verse is similar to that of the rabbinic statement: *Do not be like servants who serve their masters in order to*

---

1. *Mikhtam* and *ketem* come from the same root.

2. See I.E. on Ps. 4:1 and the notes thereto.

3. Heb. *El.*

4. The word used for God in our verse is *El*. I.E. interprets *El* as meaning powerful. See I.E.'s long commentary on Ex. 34:6.

5. Lit. "**You** have said (amart) unto the Lord." Hence I.E.'s comment.

6. The word *amart* (you have said) is in the feminine. So is *nefesh* (soul). Hence I.E.'s comment.

7. *Tovati bal alekha* (I have no good but in Thee) literally means, my good is not upon You. I. E. reads our verse as follows: *You [my soul] have said unto the Lord: Thou art My Lord; You are not obligated to do good to me.*

receive a reward.[8] Rabbi Solomon the Spaniard[9] similarly writes in one of the prayers that he composed:

> *I stand before You for Your sake, not for my sake.*
> *I stand before You for the sake of Your glory.*
> *I do not stand before You to receive a reward for my deeds.*

Rabbi Moses explains that *tovati bal alekha* (I have no good but in Thee)[10] means, You are not obligated to deal kindly with me, for unlike *the holy that are in the earth* (v. 3),[11] I am unworthy of your kindness.

According to my opinion David is beseeching God to deal kindly with the holy that are in the earth.[12] David had to add the words *that are in the earth* because the holy usually refers to angels.[13] Compare, *And all the holy ones with Thee* (Zech. 14:5).

David then said, Cause the sorrows of them that do not serve You but serve others to be multiplied. Hence Scripture reads: *Yirbu atzvotam acher maharu*[14] (let the pain of them be multiplied that make suit unto another) (v. 4).[15]

[3. AS FOR THE HOLY THAT ARE IN THE EARTH, THEY ARE THE EXCELLENT IN WHOM IS ALL MY DELIGHT.]

TO THE HOLY.[16] David said, You do not have to deal kindly with me. However, be good to the holy and the excellent of the earth in whom is all my delight.[17] The latter means, my entire desire is to be like them.

The interpretation that *the holy* refers to the patriarchs, is not is not in keeping with the meaning of this verse.

---

8. *Abot* 1:3.

9. The reference is apparently to Solomon ibn Gabirol.

10. The literal meaning of *tovati bal alekha* is, my good is not upon You. Hence Rabbi Moses' comment.

11. According to this interpretation verse 3 is connected to verse 2.

12. In other words verse 3 is not connected to verse 2. It rather expresses a new idea, namely God be kind to the righteous.

13. Whereas the holy that are on the earth refers to the righteous on earth.

14. The printed texts of I.E. have, *al ken yirbu atzvotam li-kedoshim*. This is an obvious error. The correct reading is, *al ken yirbu atzvotam. Li-kedoshim* is the heading for the next comment. See *Ha-Keter*.

15. Translated according to I.E.

16. See note 15.

17. Heb. *Cheftzi*. Lit., "my desire." Hence I.E.'s comment.

4. LET THE IDOLS OF THEM BE MULTIPLIED THAT MAKE SUIT UNTO ANOTHER;[18] THEIR DRINK OFFERINGS OF BLOOD WILL I NOT OFFER, NOR TAKE THEIR NAMES UPON MY LIPS.

LET THE IDOLS OF THEM BE MULTIPLIED THAT MAKE SUIT UNTO ANOTHER. *Acher mahar* (make suit unto another) should be read as if written, *asher acher maharu* (that make suit unto another).[19]
Maharu (that make suit) comes from the same root as *mahor yimharennah* (he shall surely pay a dowry for her)[20] (Ex. 22:15). *Acher maharau* means that have tied themselves to another nation.[21]

[THEIR DRINK- OFFERINGS OF BLOOD WILL I NOT OFFER, NOR TAKE THEIR NAMES UPON MY LIPS] I, in contrast to them,[22] will not offer their drink-offerings that are mixed with the blood of their sacrifices. I will not even mention their names.[23]

5. O LORD, THE PORTION OF MINE INHERITANCE AND OF MY CUP, THOU MAINTAINEST MY LOT.

AND OF MY CUP. The word *kosi* (my cup) means my portion.[24] It is related to the word *takhossu* (ye shall apportion) *in ye shall apportion the lamb*[25] (Ex. 12:4). The word *kosam* (their portion) that we encountered earlier in *menat kosam* (their portion) (Ps. 11:6)[26] is similar. It is incorrect to interpret *kosi* as referring to drink,[27] as in *kosi revayah* (my cup runneth over) (Ps. 23:5).

---

18. According to I.E., this should be rendered as follows: *Let the sorrows of them be multiplied that make suit unto another.*

19. The literal reading of our verse is as follows: *Let the pains* (or idols) *be multiplied make suit unto another.* Hence I.E.'s comment. The printed texts of I.E. have *ashre.* The latter is an obvious error for *asher.* See *Ha-Keter.*

20. According to I.E. *mahor yimharennah* means, he shall surely tie her [to himself], that is, he should marry her.

21. To a nation that serves another god.

22. Heb. *Rak ani.* I, in contrast to those who make suit unto another god.

23. Lit., "I will not mention them with my mouth."

24. I.E. renders our clause as follows: *O Lord, the portion of mine inheritance and of my lot.*

25. Translated according to I.E.

26. Translated according to I.E. See I.E. on Ps. 11:6.

27. That is, to render *kosi* as my cup.

The word *tomikh* (maintainest) is similar to the word *tomekh* (holdeth)[28] in *And him that holdeth the scepter* (Amos 1:5; 1:8), for the word *motze* (bringeth forth) in *He bringeth forth the wind* (Ps. 135:6) is similar to the word *motzi* (bringeth forth).[29] It is very farfetched to maintain that *tomikh*[30] is similar to the word *moshiv* (causes to sit).[31]

6. THE LINES ARE FALLEN UNTO ME IN PLEASANT PLACES; YEA, I HAVE A GOODLY HERITAGE.

THE LINES. [The word *chavalim* (lines)] means, portions. Compare, *yosef chavalim* (Joseph receiving two portions) (Ezek. 47:13).
The word *ne'imim* [32] (in pleasant places) is an adjective. Compare, *ha-ne'ehavim ve-hane'imim* (the lovely and the pleasant) (11 Sam. 1:23).
The word "places" has been omitted from our verse.[33]
Our verse is metaphoric.[34]

[YEA, I HAVE A GOODLY HERITAGE.] Rabbi Moses Ha-Kohen says that *af nacha-lat* (yea...a...heritage) is to be read as if written, *af nachalati* (yea my heritage).[35] I will yet explain my opinion on the word *nachalat* when commenting on the verse; *The Lord is my strength and song (Ex. 15:2).*[36]

---

28. *Tomikh* looks like a *hifil*. If *tomikh* is a *hifil* then *tomikh gorali* is to be rendered, *You cause my lot to be maintained*, rather than *You maintain my lot*. I.E. rejects the former because we do not find the root *tav, mem, kaf* in the *hifil* (Filwarg). Hence he argues that *tomikh* is a variant of *tomekh*, which is a *kal*, and means, maintains.

29. *Motze* is a *kal* form. *Motzi* is a *hifil* form. I.E. believes that *motze* (bringeth forth) in Ps. 135:6 is in reality a *hifil*. We thus see that the *hifil* and *kal* participle forms occasionally interchange.

30. Lit., "that it is."

31. In other words *tomikh* is a *kal* and not a *hifil*.

32. Lit. "*Ba-ne'imim* (in pleasant places) is an adjective."

33. Our verse literally reads: *The lines are fallen unto me in pleasant*. I.E. maintains that this be interpreted as if written, *The lines have fallen unto me in pleasant places*. In other words, *ba-ne'imim* is to be interpreted as if written, *bi--mekomot ne'imim*.

34. The reference to God as a portion of David's inheritance is not to be taken literally.

35. In other words, *nachalat* is short for *nachalati*. The usual form for the word heritage is *nachalah*. Hence Rabbi Moses' interpretation. According to this interpretation, our verse reads, "yea, my inheritance was pleasant to me."

36. In Ex. 15:2 I.E. explains the word *nachalat* as being in the construct. He believes this to be the case even though *nachalat* is vocalized with a *kametz* rather than with a *pattach*.

In my opinion, the word *nachalat* is connected to the Lord.[37] It like the word *mizreke* (bowls of) in *That drink wine in bowls of...* (Amos 6:6).[38]

7. I WILL BLESS THE LORD, WHO HATH GIVEN ME COUNSEL; YEA, IN THE NIGHT SEASONS MY REINS INSTRUCT ME.

I WILL BLESS THE LORD. This counsel[39] originally came to me from God,[40] for the Lord endows[41] man with wisdom.

Scripture reads: *in the night seasons*. It so reads, for David was then separated from worldly affairs.[42]

The *reins* allude to the natural powers, which like the kidneys are hidden.

Scripture reads *yisseruni* (instruct me), because David thought about what happened to all those who departed from this world. David was therefore instructed.[43]

8. I HAVE SET THE LORD ALWAYS BEFORE ME; SURELY HE IS AT MY RIGHT HAND, I SHALL NOT BE MOVED.

I HAVE SET THE LORD. The counsel and instruction[44] caused David to set the Lord before him day and night. Thus David's soul cleaved to its creator before it separated from its body.[45]

I shall not be moved from the straight path,[46] because *I have set the Lord always before me at my right hand.*

---

37. In other words our text should be interpreted as if written, *af nachalat Adonai shaferah alai* (Yea, the Lords heritage was pleasant to me). It should be noted that the word Lord does not appear in our text. Hence I.E. goes on to explain why *nachalat* is be read as if written, *nachalat Adonai*.

38. Translated Lit. *Mizreke* (bowls of) is short for bowls of gold or bowls of silver (Filwarg). Similarly, *nachalat* is short for *nachlat Adonai*.

39. That the Lord is his portion v. 5. See Radak.

40. Lit., "came to me from God at the first."

41. Lit., "gives."

42. Lit. "When he was alone from worldly affairs".

43. See Chap. 11 of I.E.'s *Yesod Mora*: "The intelligent will understand that life is short, that the soul is in the hand of its creator, and that one does not know when God will reclaim it. He will therefore seek after things that lead a person to the love of God." (*Secret of the Torah*, p. 107).

44. Spoken of in verse 7.

45. "[The intelligent] person...will isolate himself for the purpose of studying and meditating upon God's law and observing the Lord's precepts. God will then open the eyes of his heart and create a new and different spirit in him. He will be beloved of his creator while he is yet alive. His soul will cleave to God and enjoy the fullness of the joy of God's presence." Ibid.

46. In other words *I shall not be moved* means, I shall not be moved from the straight path.

9. THEREFORE MY HEART IS GLAD, AND MY GLORY REJOICETH; MY FLESH ALSO DWELLETH IN SAFETY.

MY HEART. The reference is to the intellect, by which one acquires knowledge.[47]

AND MY GLORY. *My glory* refers to the soul.

MY FLESH ALSO. *My flesh* refers to the body.
The meaning of our verse is as follows: David's soul will rejoice because it clings to a power that is most high.[48] The power to which David clings will protect him from illness when things turn in the future.[49] David's body will therefore dwell in safety in this world.

10. FOR THOU WILT NOT ABANDON MY SOUL TO THE NETHER WORLD; NEITHER WILT THOU SUFFER THY GODLY ONE TO SEE THE PIT.

FOR THOU WILT NOT ABANDON MY SOUL. David states why[50] his soul rejoices. His soul rejoices because it will not die nor perish.

11. THOU MAKEST ME TO KNOW THE PATH OF LIFE; IN THY PRESENCE IS THE FULNESS OF JOY, IN THY RIGHT HAND IS BLISS FOR EVERMORE.

THOU MAKEST ME TO KNOW THE PATH OF LIFE. When my body dies, You will teach me the path of life. You will show me the way to take to ascend to heaven, to be with the angels who are on high.
In Thy presence is fullness of joy means that David will enjoy the splendor of God's *shekhinah*.[51]

---

47. The rational soul. Literally, "To the intelligence of knowledge."

48. Heb. *Ko'ach elyon*. The reference is to God.

49. Lit. "When the future changes." See Chap. 12 of the *Yesod Morah*: "It is because of the...heavenly motions ...that change comes to all things born of the earth, be they metal, plants, or living bodies." (*Secret of the Torah*, p. 173).

50. Lit. "David mentions the reason."

51. According to medieval Jewish thinking, the *shekhinah* refers to something created by God to manifest His presence. See Chap. 2: of Saadiah Gaon's *Book of Beliefs And Opinions* and Book 2 of Rabbi Judah Ha-Levi's *Kuzari*.

Thou makest me to know means that the soul will then[52] overcome the concerns of this world[53] and it will directly see the truth.

In Thy right hand bliss means, the soul will delight itself in the Lord.[54]

In Thy right hand means, God will act like a person who gives pleasant gifts to his beloved with his right hand.

For evermore means, God's gifts will not cease.

Observe, this chapter describes the reward of the righteous.

---

52. At the time of death.

53. Lit., "be powerful from the concerns of this world."

54. See Ps. 37:4.

CHAPTER 17

1. A PRAYER OF DAVID. HEAR THE RIGHT, O LORD, ATTEND UNTO MY CRY; GIVE EAR UNTO MY PRAYER FROM LIPS WITHOUT DECEIT.

A PRAYER OF DAVID. HEAR THE RIGHT, O LORD. Hear O Lord because I will rightfully speak, for God does not listen to lies.[1]

ATTEND UNTO MY CRY. *Rinnati* (my cry) refers to supplications uttered loudly. Compare, *And there went a cry* (rinnah) *throughout the host* (1 Kings 22:36). *Tefilati* (my payer) refers to prayers offered in a whisper.

2. LET MY JUDGEMENT COME FORTH FROM THY PRESENCE;[2] LET THINE EYES BEHOLD EQUITY.

LET MY JUDGEMENT COME FORTH FROM THY PRESENCE. You will punish me, if Your eyes do not behold equity.

3. THOU HAST TRIED MY HEART, THOU HAST VISITED IT IN THE NIGHT; THOU HAST TESTED ME, AND THOU FOUNDEST NOT THAT I HAD A THOUGHT WHICH SHOULD NOT PASS MY MOUTH.

THOU HAST TRIED MY HEART. You are cognizant of all of my thoughts. [THOU HAST VISITED IT IN THE NIGHT.] When people are away and I am alone.[3]

---

1. Hence Scripture reads: *From lips without deceit.*

2. I.E. takes *my judgment* to mean, my punishment. Hence his interpretation.

3. Lit. "*In the night* means, when he is alone from people."

THOU FOUNDEST NOT. Something unseemly or a blemish.

THAT I HAD A THOUGHT WHICH SHOULD NOT PASS (YA'AVOR) MY MOUTH. *Ya'avor* (pass) is similar to *ya'avru* (should...transgress) in *That the waters should not transgress* (ya'avru) *His commandment* (Prov. 8:22).[4] Observe, David's thoughts were expressed by his mouth. His words were not the reverse of his thoughts.[5]

4. AS FOR THE DOINGS OF MEN, BY THE WORDS OF THY LIPS I HAVE KEPT ME FROM THE WAYS OF THE VIOLENT.

AS FOR THE DOINGS OF MEN. I see to it that people do what You commanded them.[6] I do this because I greatly desire that everyone serve you.

I HAVE KEPT ME FROM THE WAYS OF THE VIOLENT.[7] I ordered that the steps of the violent be guarded to ensure that he does not violate the words of Thy lips. I acted in this way because he is a violent man.[8]

5. MY STEPS HAVE HELD FAST TO THY PATHS, MY FEET HAVE NOT SLIPPED.

MY STEPS HAVE HELD FAST TO THY PATHS. Howbeit, as for me, my steps have always held fast to Thy paths.

6. AS FOR ME, I CALL UPON THEE, FOR THOU WILT ANSWER ME, O GOD; INCLINE THINE EAR UNTO ME, HEAR MY SPEACH.

AS FOR ME... O GOD. The meaning of *El (God)* is, the Almighty.[9]

---

4. In other words *ya'avor* (pass) is to be rendered, transgress. According to I.E., *zammoti bal ya'avor pi* (that I had a thought which should not pass my mouth) means, my mouth did not trespass my thoughts. In other words, David did not misrepresent himself. He did not lie.

5. David did not say one thing and think another.

6. I.E. interprets *As for the doings of men, by the words of Thy lips* as follows: I see to it that the doings of men are by the words of Thy lips.

7. Our clause literally reads: *I guarded* (shamarti) *the ways of the violent.* Hence I.E.'s interpretation.

8. I.E. interprets our verse as follows: I see to it that the acts of men are in accordance with the words of Your lips. I place guards on the steps of the violent.

9. See I.E. on Psalm 16:1 and the notes thereto.

---

7. MAKE PASSING GREAT THY MERCIES, O THOU THAT SAVEST BY THY RIGHT HAND FROM ASSAILENTS THEM THAT TAKE REFUGE IN THEE.

MAKE PASSING GREAT THY MERCIES. *Hafleh* (make passing great) means make clear and separate. The word *hafleh* is similar to *yafleh* (declare) in *that the Lord doth put a difference* (Ex. 11:7).
The word *bi-yeminekha* (in Thy right hand) is connected to the word *chosim* (that take refuge), for we do not find words from this root[10] unconnected to a *bet*.[11] Others say that the word *chosim* is connected to *moshi'a* (that savest).[12]

9. FROM THE WICKED THAT OPPRESS, MY DEADLY ENEMIES, THAT COMPASS ME ABOUT.

FROM THE WICKED. The word *zu* (the) means, *these*.[13]
The word *shadduni* (oppress) is similar to word *sevavuni* (they... encompassed us) (vs. 11).[14]
MY DEADLY ENEMIES. They surround me with the desire to take my soul.[15]

10. THEIR GROSS HEART THEY HAVE SHUT TIGHT, WITH THEIR MOUTH THEY SPEAK PROUDLY.

THEIR GROSS HEART. The word *chelbamo* (their gross heart) is missing a *bet*. It should be interpreted as if written, *be-chelbamo*.[16] *Chelbamo sageru pimo dibberu ve-ge'ut* (Their

---

10. *Chet, vav, samekh.*

11. It is always followed by a word that begins with a *bet*. According to I.E. our verse should be read as if written, *Moshi'a chosim bi-yeminekha*. Our verse literally reads: *Declare Thy mercies, O Thou that savest them (moshi'a) that take refuge (chosim) from assailants in Thy right hand* (bi-yeminekha). According to I.E., this should be interpreted as follows: *Declare Thy mercies, O Thou that savest from assailants them that take refuge in Thy right hand.*

12. According to this interpretation our verse literally reads: *Declare Thy mercies, O Thou that savest them that take refuge in Thee* [moshi'a chosim], *by Thy right hand, from assailants*

13. According to I.E., *mi-pene resha'im zu shadduni* (from the wicked that oppress me) means, from these wicked [men] that oppress me.

14. Both words come from double roots. The word *shadduni* comes from the root *shin, dalet, dalet*, while *sevavuni* (they compass me about) comes from the root *samekh, bet, bet*. Filwarg suggests reading: *shadduni* is similar to *sabbuni* (they compass me about)(Ps. 118:11). In this case I.E. is noting that both words come from a double root and are similarly vocalized.

15. See Rashi and Radak. The verse literally reads: *my enemies with soul* (oyevai be-nefesh). Hence I.E.'s comment.

16. *Chelbamo* (their gross heart) literally means, their fat. Hence I.E.'s interpretation.

gross heart they have shut tight, With their mouth they speak proudly) means, they have closed with their fat (be-chelbamo)[17] their proudly speaking mouths.

It is also possible that chelbamo sageru pimo dibberu ve-ge'ut (Their gross heart they have shut tight, With their mouth they speak proudly) means,[18] their fat (chelbamo) is closed in their innards,[19] and their mouths speak proudly.

I prefer the first interpretation because our verse is similar to *Because he hath covered his face with his fatness* (Job. 15:27).

11. AT EVERY STEP THEY HAVE NOW ENCOMPASSED US; THEY SET THEIR EYES TO CAST US DOWN TO THE EARTH.

AT EVERY STEP. The word *im* (with)[20] or *li-fe'at* (the side of) is missing from our verse. Our text should be interpreted as follows: They surrounded us at the side of our steps. They set their eyes to see whether our steps have turned (li-netot) on the earth.[21] Compare, *If my step hath turned* (yitteh)[22] *out of the way* (Job. 31:7).[23]

12. HE IS LIKE A LION THAT IS EAGER TO TEAR IN PIECES, AND LIKE A YOUNG LION LURKING IN SECRET PLACES.

HE IS LIKE A LION. The form of each one of those who has encompassed us is like a lion that is eager to tear in pieces.[24]

13. ARISE, O LORD, CONFRONT HIM, CAST HIM DOWN; DELIVER MY SOUL FROM THE WICKED BY THY SWORD.

ARISE, O LORD. To show Your might.[25]

---

17. Fat indicates self-indulgence and smugness.

18. Lit. Or its meaning is.

19. In other words *chelbamo sagaru* is short for *chelbamo sageru be-kirbam* (their insides [their hearts] is covered with fat).

20. Our verse literally reads: *Our steps they have now surrounded us. Ashurenu* (step) means, our steps. I.E. suggests that *ashurenu* should be interpreted *im ashurenu*, with our steps or at the side of our steps i.e. at every step.

21. According to I.E. *li-netot ba-aretz* (to cast us down to the earth) means, *to turn aside on the earth*. He interprets the latter to mean, they spy on us and follows us.

22. *Li-netot* and *yitteh* come from the same root.

23. *If my step hath turned out of the way* means, if I have turned away from the righteous path.

24. Hence, the switch from the plural in the previous verse, to the singular in this verse.

25. Lit., "to show Your might."

CONFRONT HIM. When he comes to tear me.

DELIVER MY SOUL. From the wicked who serve as Your sword.

14. FROM MEN, BY THY HAND, O LORD, FROM MEN OF THE WORLD, WHOSE PORTION IS IN THIS LIFE, AND WHOSE BELLY THOU FILLEST WITH THY TREASURE; WHO HAVE CHILDREN IN PLENTY, AND LEAVE THEIR ABUNDANCE TO THEIR BABES.

FROM MEN. This clause is connected to the previous verse. Its meaning is, save me from men who serve as Your hand[26] and are the instruments of Your blow. Scripture speaks of God's blow as God's hand.[27] Compare, *behold, the hand of the Lord is upon thy cattle which are in the field* (Ex. 9:3).[28]

FROM MEN OF THIS WORLD. From men whose entire desire is to be a creature of this world.
Cheled (world) refers to that which is not everlasting.[29] *And mine age* (cheldi) *is as nothing before Thee* (Ps. 39:6) and *all ye inhabitants of the world* (chaled) (ibid. 49:2) is proof of this.
Men of this world refers to people whose entire desire is to live a long life and to have their bellies in this world filled with all of God's[30] hidden treasure so that they and their children can enjoy themselves and then leave what is left over to their small grandchildren.[31]

15. AS FOR ME, I SHALL BEHOLD THY FACE IN RIGHTEOUSNESS; I SHALL BE SATISFIED, WHEN I AWAKE, WITH THY LIKENESS.

AS FOR ME I SHALL BEHOLD THY FACE IN RIGHTEOUSNESS. My sole desire is to behold Your face. The righteousness that I kept was the cause of the pleasure that I experienced in beholding Your face.

26. Our verse literally reads, *From men, Thy hand.* I.E. explains this as, from men who serve as Thy hand.

27. Lit. "Because it is by hand."

28. The murrain, which was God's instrument in killing Egypt's cattle, is described by Scripture as a blow struck by God's hand.

29. I.E. takes the word *cheled* to mean time. See Radak's *Sefer Ha-Shoroshim*, N.Y. 1948.

30. Lit. "Your."

31. Lit. The babes of their children. See Radak.

Beholding God's face refers to knowing[32] God's work, which consists of the categories into which all creation falls. They are wisely made and are eternal.[33]

I, unlike those who rejoice when You fill their bellies, delight from the pleasure that I experience when I behold Your image.[34]

The above[35] does not occur in a dream. It is experienced while awake. This sight is not seen by the eye but is a vision brought about by rational thinking. The latter are the true visions of God. Only those who have studied the psychology of the soul can understand these things.

---

32. Lit., "recognizing."

33. The categories are eternal. The individual who is part of the categories perishes. God created the categories. The particulars naturally follow.

34. According to I.E. seeing God's face means knowing how God works in the world. See Chapter 12 of *The Yesod Mora* (*The Secret of the Torah*, p. 178) and I.E. on Ex. 33:19.

35. Beholding God's face.+

CHAPTER 18

1. FOR THE LEADER. [A PSALM] OF DAVID THE SERVANT OF THE LORD. WHO SPOKE UNTO THE LORD THE WORDS OF THIS SONG IN THE DAY THAT THE LORD DELIVERED HIM FROM THE HAND OF ALL HIS ENEMIES, AND FROM THE HAND OF SAUL.

FOR THE LEADER. [A PSALM] OF DAVID THE SERVANT OF THE LORD. David refers to himself as *the servant of the Lord* because he kept the ways of the Lord. Compare, *For I have kept the ways of the Lord* (11 Sam. 2:22) and *The Lord rewarded me according to my righteousness* (ibid. v. 21).

David composed this poem when his men swore that he would no longer join them when they went out to war.[1] David mentioned Saul along with his enemies.[2]

2. AND HE SAID: I LOVE THEE, O LORD, MY STRENGTH.

AND HE SAID: I LOVE THEE. The transitive verbal form of the word *rachamim* (pity)[3] always appears in Scripture in the piel.[4] *Erchamekha* (I love thee) is a *kal*.[5] *Erchamekha* is intransitive.[6] It is similar to *banai yetzau'ni* (Jer. 10:20) and to *chazaktani* (Thou hast

---

1. See 11 Sam. 21:17: *Then the men of David swore unto him saying: Thou shalt go no more out with us to battle that thou quench not the lamp of Israel.* Since David would no longer go out to war he could now thank God for saving him from the hand of all of his enemies.

2. Even though Saul was long dead at this point in time.

3. From the root *resh, chet, mem*.

4. Lit., "in the heavy conjugation." I.E.'s point is that whenever Scripture wants to employ the root *resh, chet, mem* in the sense of pitying it employs the *piel* form.

5. Transitive and intransitive verbs come in the *Kal* form.

6. *Erchamekha* appears to be transitive for it has an adjective pronounal suffix affixed to it. Thus prima facie, *erchamekha* means, I will be compassionate to You. However, David would not address God in this manner. Hence I.E. goes on to suggest that the meaning of *erchamekha* is, I will seek compassion from You.

overcome me) (Jer. 20:7). *Banai yetzau'ni* means, my children are gone from of me.[7] *Chaz-aktani* means, it is stronger than I.[8] *Erchamekha* means, I will seek compassion from You. Others[9] in keeping with the Aramaic say that *erchamekha* means; I will love You.[10]

3. THE LORD IS MY ROCK, AND MY FORTRESS, AND MY DELIVERER; MY GOD, MY ROCK, IN HIM I TAKE REFUGE; MY SHIELD, AND MY HORN OF SALVATION, MY HIGH TOWER.

THE LORD IS MY ROCK. *The Lord is my rock* is a metaphor. I am like a person who is on a high place[11] and is unafraid of those who are below him.

4. PRAISED, I CRY[12] IS THE LORD AND I AM SAVED FROM MINE ENEMIES.

PRAISED, I CRY IS THE LORD. When I call upon Him with words of praise, I am instantly saved.

5. THE CORDS (CHAVLE) OF DEATH COMPASSED ME, AND THE FLOODS OF BELIAL ASSAILED ME.

THE CORDS (CHAVLE) OF DEATH COMPASSED ME. *Chevle* means *throes of.* Compare, *Pangs and throes* (chavalim) (Is. 13:8).[13] *Chevle* (cords of) is vocalized with a *segol*[14] to distinguish it from the word *chavle* (parts) in *ten parts to Manasseh* (Josh. 17:5).

AND THE FLOODS OF BELIAL ASSAILED ME. David compares his enemies[15] to a flood. The king of Assyria is similarly compared to *The waters of the River* (Is. 8:7). Scripture likewise reads: *Then waters*[16] *had overwhelmed us* (Ps. 124:4).

---

7. *Yetza'uni* is a transitive form. Its literal meaning is, gone out me. Thus *banai yetza'uni* means; My children have gone out me. However, this makes no sense. We thus must render *yetza'uni* as, " have gone out from me." We thus see that Scripture sometimes uses a transitive form with the meaning of an intransitive.

8. Here too Scripture employs a transitive form with the meaning of an intransitive.

9. See Rashi and Radak.

10. The Targum renders *erchamekha, ahabbvinakh.* The root *resh, chet mem* in Aramaic means, to love.

11. A high rock or a fortress built of rocks.

12. Heb., *ekra.* Lit., "I call."

13. Our clause should thus be rendered, *The throes of Death compassed me.*

14. Rather than with a *pattach.* Compare, *malkhe.*

15. Lit., "the enemy."

16. The reference is to Israel's enemies.

Rabbi Judah Ha-Levi, who rests in glory, says that the word *beliya'al* (Belial) means, he should not go up.[17] It refers to the enemy[18] and was uttered in prayer.[19] The word *chevle* (cords) is used metaphorically. It refers to the pangs of death.[20]

[6. THE CORDS OF SHEOL SURROUNDED ME; THE SNARES OF DEATH CONFRONTED ME.]

7. IN MY DISTRESS I CALLED UPON THE LORD, AND CRIED UNTO MY GOD; OUT OF HIS TEMPLE HE HEARD MY VOICE, AND MY CRY CAME BEFORE HIM INTO HIS EARS.

IN MY DISTRESS. *His temple* refers to heaven,[21] for all of God's decrees are written and sealed there.

8. THEN THE EARTH DID SHAKE AND QUAKE, THE FOUNDATIONS ALSO OF THE MOUNTAINS DID TREMBLE; THEY WERE SHAKEN BECAUSE HE WAS WROTH.

THEN THE EARTH DID SHAKE. David mentions the earth and the mountains because they stand and do not move. Our verse is metaphoric. It means; God's anger caused David's enemies to quake, even though they were as strong as the mountains.

9. SMOKE AROSE UP IN HIS NOSTRILS AND FIRE OUT OF HIS MOUTH DID DEVOUR; COALS FLAMED FORTH FROM HIM.

SMOKE AROSE UP IN HIS NOSTRILS. Compare, *Thou sendest forth Thy wrath, [it consumeth them as stubble]* (Ex.15: 7) and similarly, *Shall even be for burning, for fuel of fire* (Is. 9:4). The reference is to death.[22]

---

17. According to Rabbi Judah Ha-Levi the word *beliya'al* is a composite of the words *beli* (without) and *ya'al* (he will go up).

18. Symbolized by the floods.

19. According to Rabbi Judah Ha-Levi our clause should be translated as follows: And the floods, may my enemy not arise, assailed me.

20. See note 13.

21. Lit., "the heaven."

22. Our verse metaphorically speaks of the destruction of the wicked.

10. HE BOWED THE HEAVENS ALSO, AND CAME DOWN; AND THICK DARKNESS WAS UNDER HIS FEET.

HE BOWED THE HEAVENS ALSO, AND CAME DOWN. *He bowed the heavens also, and came down* means, God the glorious sent down a decree from heaven upon David's enemies.[23]

11. AND HE RODE UPON A CHERUB, AND DID FLY; YEA, HE DID SWOOP DOWN UPON THE WINGS OF THE WIND.

AND HE RODE UPON A CHERUB... A metaphor describing the quick, uninterrupted and continuous descent of God's decree.

12. HE MADE DARKNESS HIS HIDING-PLACE, HIS PAVILION ROUND ABOUT HIM; DARKNESS OF WATERS, THICK CLOUDS OF THE SKIES.

HE MADE DARKNESS HIS HIDING-PLACE. When the waves of the sea roar and its water storm, the mist that arises from the water and ascends to the sky increases. This gives birth to darkness in the sky.[24] This is what the *darkness of the waters* refers to. It adverts to the thickness of the mist. It speaks of the denseness of the mist. The aforementioned gives birth to the cloud.[25]

Our verse metaphorically describes the coming down of the decrees.[26] No one sees them descending.

13. AT THE BRIGHTNESS BEFORE HIM, THERE PASS THROUGH HIS THICK CLOUDS HAILSTONES AND COALS OF FIRE.

AT THE BRIGHTNESS BEFORE HIM, THERE PASS THROUGH HIS THICK CLOUDS *Avav averu* (there pass through His thick clouds) means, the clouds violated their widely known laws.[27]

---

23. Lit., "upon the enemies."

24. Lit. "Darkness is therefore born there."

25. Lit. "It adverts to the thickness of the mist, when it is thick, which is the cloud."

26. From heaven.

27. The literal meaning of *avav averu* (there pass through His thick clouds) is, *His clouds passed.* I.E. interprets this to mean, *His clouds* (aviv) *surpassed* (averu) natural law, for they produced hailstones and coals of fire rather than rain.

HAILSTONES AND COALS OF FIRE. *Gachale esh* (coals of fire) refers to iron like objects, which set fire to that which they strike, and whose fumes cause death.[28] The allusion is to the fear and terror which David's enemies[29] experienced, when they heard the sound of the thunder.

14. THE LORD ALSO THUNDERED IN THE HEAVENS, AND THE MOST HIGH GAVE FORTH HIS VOICE; HAILSTONES AND COALS OF FIRE.

THE LORD ALSO THUNDERED. The *mem* of *va-yarem* (thundered) is a root letter.[30] Scripture mentions *hailstones and coals of fire* a second time because they[31] all came together at one moment.[32]

15. AND HE SENT OUT HIS ARROWS, AND SCATTERED THEM, AND HE SHOT FORTH LIGHTNINGS, AND DISCOMFITED THEM.

AND HE SENT OUT HIS ARROWS… AND HE SHOT. The word *rav* (he shot) is a verb in the perfect.[33] It comes from a double stem.[34] *Rav* follows the paradigm of *tam* (spent)[35] in *how that our money is all spent* (Gen. 47:18). It is related to *va-robbu* (and shot)[36] (Gen. 49:23). Observe, *And He shot* is parallel to *And He sent.*

---

28. So Filwarg. Lit. "It also kills by wind."

29. Lit., "the enemies."

30. It is not a third person plural pronoun, for the root of *va-yarem* is *resh, ayin, mem.*

31. The hailstones, the coals of fire, and the thunder.

32. Had Scripture omitted the hailstones and stones of fire from our verse, we might have supposed that the former came together and that God thundered at another time. Hence our verse indicates that the hailstones, stones of fire and the thunder came at one and the same time.

33. *Rav* might be taken to be an adjective. In the latter instance *u-varakim rav* (and He shot forth lightnings) would mean, and much lightning. Hence I.E.'s comment.

34. Its root is *resh, bet, bet.*

35. From the root *tav, mem, mem.*

36. Its root is *resh, bet, bet.*

16. AND THE CHANNELS OF WATERS APPEARED, AND THE FOUNDATIONS OF THE WORLD WERE LAID BARE, AT THY REBUKE, O LORD, AT THE BLAST OF THE BREATH OF THY NOSTRILS.

AND THE CHANNELS OF WATERS APPEARED. The mighty places.[37] Our verse speaks of the uncovering of the secret place of those who arose against David.

I will now offer a general statement. [38] Our verse probably has a different meaning.[39] God[40] causes the world to quake, when He so desires. The meaning of our verse is as follows: God removes the earth from its foundations and he causes water to descend from the heavens. David, as it were, says, the One who has the power to do the aforementioned will save me.

17. HE SENT FROM ON HIGH, HE TOOK ME, HE DREW ME OUT OF MANY WATERS.

HE SENT. *He sent* means, He sent His word or He sent His angel. *He took me* from those who surrounded me.

HE DREW ME OUT OF MANY WATERS. This is in contrast to *and the floods of belial assailed me* (v. 5).

18. HE DELIVERED ME FROM MINE ENEMY MOST STRONG, AND FROM THEM THAT HATED ME, FOR THEY WERE TOO MIGHTY FOR ME.

HE DELIVERED ME. The waters [mentioned in the previous verse] appear to symbolize David's enemies. The word *she-hu* (who is) has been omitted from our verse.[41] Our text should be interpreted as if written, *she-hu az* (who is most strong).

---

37. *The channels of water and the foundations of the world* are metaphors for the strongholds of David's enemies.

38. So *Ha-Keter.* The standard printed texts read, Hillel says.

39. *The channels of water and the foundations of the world* are not metaphors for strongholds. Our verse does not speak of the uncovering of the secret place of those who arose against David.

40. Lit., for God.

41. Our verse reads: *yatzileni me-oyevi az* (from mine enemy most strong). This literally means; He delivered me from mine enemy strong. I.E. suggests that our verse be read as if written, *yatzileni me-oyevi she-hu az,* He delivered me from mine enemy who is strong.

19. THEY CONFRONTED ME IN THE DAY OF MY CALAMITY; BUT THE LORD WAS A STAY UNTO ME.

THEY CONFRONTED ME IN THE DAY OF MY CALAMITY. *They confronted me in the day of my calamity* corresponds to *The snares of death confronted me* (v. 6).[42]

20. HE BROUGHT ME FORTH ALSO INTO A LARGE PLACE; HE DELIVERED ME, BECAUSE HE DELIGHTED IN ME.

HE BROUGHT ME FORTH ALSO INTO A LARGE PLACE. *Into a large place* is the reverse of *In my distress* in, *In my distress I called upon the Lord* (v. 7).

21. THE LORD REWARDED ME ACCORDING TO MY RIGHTEOUSNESS; ACCORDING TO THE CLEANNESS OF MY HANDS HATH HE RECOMPENSED ME.

THE LORD REWARDED ME. This is connected to the preceding verses. It means that God[43] did all of this[44] to reward me *according to my righteousness.*

ACCORDING TO THE CLEANLINESS OF MY HANDS HATH HE RECOMPENSED ME. Compare, *In the simplicity of my heart* (Gen. 20:5).[45] David describes his hands as being clean because most deeds are done by the hands. Compare, *and the innocency of my hands* (ibid.).[46]

22. FOR I HAVE KEPT THE WAYS OF THE LORD, AND HAVE NOT DEPARTED WICKEDLY FROM MY GOD.

FOR I HAVE KEPT THE WAYS OF THE LORD. The positive commandments. The word *darkhe* (the ways) also applies to the word *rashati* (wickedly).[47]

---

42. In other words our clause refers to *The snares of death.*

43. Literally, "He."

44. The things mentioned in the preceding verses.

45. In other words *cleanliness of hands* is similar in meaning to *simplicity of…heart.*

46. Lit. "Because, most deeds are done by the hands our verse mentions purity with them as in, *and the innocency of my hands* (ibid.)."

47. The second part of our verse is to be read as if written, *And have not wickedly departed from the ways of my God.* The second part of our verse literally reads: *I have not wickedly from my God.* Hence I.E.'s comment.

AND HAVE NOT WICKEDLY DEPARTED FROM MY GOD. From the ways of my God. The reference is to the negative commandments.

23. FOR ALL HIS ORDINANCES WERE BEFORE ME; AND I PUT NOT AWAY HIS STATUTES FROM BEFORE ME.

FOR ALL HIS ORDINANCES WERE BEFORE ME. I will not forget His ordinances. This is the meaning of, *before me.*

24. AND I WAS SINGLE-HEARTED WITH HIM; AND I KEPT MYSELF FROM MINE INIQUITY.

AND I WAS SINGLE-HEARTED[48] WITH HIM. Compare, *Thou shalt be whole-hearted* (tamim) *with the Lord thy God* (Deut. 18:13].

AND I HAVE KEPT MY SELF FROM MINE INIQUITY. From having *a distorted heart* (Prov. 12:8).[49]

25. THEREFORE HATH THE LORD RECOMPENSED ME ACCORDING TO MY RIGHTEOUSNESS, ACCORDING TO THE CLEANNESS OF MY HANDS IN HIS EYES.

THE LORD RECOMPENSED ME. *The cleanness of my hands* corresponds to *For all his ordinances were before me* (v. 23).

26. WITH THE MERCIFUL THOU DOST SHOW THYSELF MERCIFUL, WITH THE UPRIGHT MAN THOU DOST SHOW THYSELF UPRIGHT.

WITH THE MERCIFUL. *Titchassad* means, *Thou dost show thy self merciful.*[50]

---

48. Hebrew, *tamim.*

49. Translated according to I.E. The printed edition of I.E. reads: Compare, *ma'aneh lev.* There is no such verse in Scripture. Filwarg emends to *ma'avveh lev* (a distorted heart). According to I.E. verse 22, speaks of sins committed by action, while our verse speaks of sins of the heart such as disbelief. For the commandments relating to the heart see pages 91-105 of *The Secret of the Torah.*

50. Lit. "He shows himself merciful."

WITH THE UPRIGHT MAN. *Gevar* (man) is an adjective.[51] It is not in the construct with *tamim* (upright).[52]

THOU DOST SHOW THYSELF UPRIGHT. The third *tav* that should have appeared in the word *tittamam* (Thou dost show Thyself upright) is swallowed by the *dagesh*.[53] Compare, *titchazzek* (you will strengthen yourself).[54]
Tittamam means, Your deeds that are upright are revealed. *Tittamam* might also mean, You show Yourself to be upright in thought.[55]

27. WITH THE PURE THOU DOST SHOW THYSELF PURE; AND WITH THE CROOKED THOU DOST SHOW THYSELF SUBTLE.

WITH THE PURE. The word *navar* (pure) comes from a double root.[56] Compare, *nakel* (of no account)[57] (11 Kings 3:18) and *names*[58] (feeble) (1 Sam. 1:9).

AND WITH THE CROOKED THOU DOST SHOW THYSELF SUBTLE. The word *titpattal* (Thou dost show thyself subtle) is similar to the word *naftule* (wrestlings)[59] in *With mighty wrestlings* (Gen. 30:8).[60] *Ve-im ikkesh titpattlal (And with the crooked thou dost show thyself subtle)* means, You will fight with the crooked until you overcome him.

51. According to I.E., *gevar tammim* is to be rendered a man who is upright.

52. Even though its vocalization is that of a noun, in the construct, I.E. refers to modified nouns as adjectives.

53. The root of *tittamam* is *tav, mem, mem*. *Tittamam* is spelled with two *tavs*. However, *tittamam* is in the *hitpa'el*. It should thus have been spelled with three *tavs*, namely with the *tav* that serves as a second person prefix, the *tav* of the *hitpa'el*, and the root *tav*.

54. *Titchazzek* is in the *hitpa'el* and has two *tavs* added to its root. Similarly the root, *tav, mem, mem* should have two *tavs* prefixed to its root.

55. Or perfect in knowledge. Heb. *Temim de'im*. See Job 36:4; 37:16.

56. Its root is *bet, resh, resh*.

57. From the root *kof, lamed, lamed*.

58. From the root *mem, samekh, samekh*.

59. In other words *titpattal* means, You will wrestle.

60. Both words come from the root *peh, tav, lamed*.

28. FOR THOU DOST SAVE THE AFFLICTED PEOPLE; BUT THE HAUGHTY EYES THOU DOST HUMBLE.

FOR THOU DOST SAVE THE AFFLICTED PEOPLE. *Ani* (afflicted) is the reverse of *ikkesh* (the crooked) and *toshi'a* (Thou dost save) is the opposite of *titpattal* (Thou dost show Thyself subtle).[61]

Scripture reads *people*,[62] because it is a greater wonder to save a large nation than to save one person.[63]

Scripture reads: *But the haughty eyes Thou dost humble.* The latter means, the haughty do not see at night.[64]

29. FOR THOU DOST LIGHT MY LAMP; THE LORD MY GOD DOTH LIGHTEN MY DARKNESS.

FOR THOU DOST LIGHT MY LAMP. David goes on to say,[65] *For Thou dost light my lamp.* The latter is a metaphor for David's good luck.[66]

30. FOR BY THEE I RUN UPON A TROOP; AND BY MY GOD DO I SCALE A WALL.

FOR BY THEE I RUN UPON A TROOP. *Arutz* (I run)] is similar to *aratzetz* (I break).[67] The word *merutzatam* (their breaking)[68] (Jer 23:10) is similar.[69]

Others say that *arutz gedud* (I run upon a troop) means, I run after a troop. *Arutz* (I run) is similar to *erdof* (I will pursue),[70] which is sometimes connected to that which follows and at other times stands alone. *Be-kha arutz gedud* (for by Thee I run upon a troop)

---

61. Which I.E. renders, Thou dost wrestle.

62. The entire psalm is in the singular. Hence our psalm should have read, "For Thou dost save the afflicted **person**" rather than *For Thou dost save the afflicted **people**.*

63. The plural is used in order to more fully praise God.

64. God lightens David's Darkness (v. 29). However, the haughty will be enveloped by darkness.

65. Lit. "He mentions."

66. In other words David goes on to say *For Thou dost light my lamp,* because the latter is a metaphor for David's good luck.

67. In other words *arutz* (I run) comes from the root *resh, tzadi, tzadi.* It is to be rendered, I break or I shatter. Comp. *Ratzutz* (bruised or broken) in Is. 36:6.

68. Translated according to I.E.

69. According to this interpretation the meaning of *arutz gedud* (I run upon a troop) is, I shatter a troop.

70. According to this interpretation *arutz* comes from the root *resh, vav, tzdadi,* and means, I run.

means, for by You alone do I defeat my many enemies. *Be-kha* (by Thee) means, with You or by Your name, which I call.[71]

31. AS FOR GOD (EL), HIS WAY IS PERFECT; THE WORD OF THE LORD IS TRIED; HE IS A SHIELD UNTO ALL THEM THAT TAKE REFUGE IN HIM.

AS FOR GOD (EL), HIS WAY IS PERFECT. This is to be understood as follows: As for God, He is mighty[72] and does no wrong. On the contrary His way is perfect. God has promised,[73] that He will be a shield unto those who take refuge in Him.[74] God's word is unblemished and unsoiled, for it is tried

32. FOR WHO IS GOD SAVE THE LORD? AND WHO IS A ROCK, EXCEPT OUR GOD?

FOR. No one can oppose and refuse to fulfill His word,[75] for there is no God aside from the Lord.

33. THE GOD THAT GIRDETH ME WITH STRENGTH, AND MAKETH MY WAY STRAIGHT.

THE GOD. As He is a mighty God,[76] He girded me with some of His strength. As His way is straight, He made my way straight.
Scripture says *And maketh my way straight*, because God is the cause of the good.[77]

34. WHO MAKETH MY FEET LIKE HINDS', AND SETTETH ME UPON MY HIGH PLACES.

WHO MAKETH MY FEET LIKE HINDS'. David mentions *my feet*, because he previously spoke of *His way* (v. 31).

---

71. Thus our verse means, for with You (or when I call upon Your name) I defeat my enemies.

72. The term used for God in our clause is *El*. *El* means mighty. Hence I.E.'s comment.

73. Lit. "He has already said." God had promised David that He would be a shield to those who take refuge in Him.

74. I.E.'s interpretation of the second part of our verse.

75. Lit. "No one can stand up to Him in that he does not fulfill his word."

76. The name used for God in our verse is El. El means majesty.

77. Lit. "The meaning of *And maketh*, because from Him the good is caused."

The word *meshavveh* (who maketh) is similar to the word *shaveh* (equivalent) or to the word *shivviti* (I have set). Compare, I *have set* (shivviti) *the Lord always before me* (Ps.16:8).[78]

AND SETTETH ME UPON MY HIGH PLACES. So that I do not stumble.

35. WHO TRAINETH MY HANDS FOR WAR, SO THAT MINE ARMS DO BEND A BOW OF BRASS.

WHO TRAINETH MY HANDS. The word *melammed* means, who trains.[79] Scripture thus speak of *limmude ha-ra* (trained in evil)[80] and *limmud midbar* (trained in the way of the wilderness)(Jer. 2:24).

SO THAT MINE ARMS DO BEND A BOW OF BRASS. So that each one of my arms do bend a bow of Brass.[81] This clause is similar to *Its branches run over the wall* (Gen. 49:22).[82]

The *nun* of *ve-nichatah* (do bend)[83] is a root letter.[84] Compare, *Va-tinchat* (is come down) in *And Thy hand is come down upon me* (Ps. 38:3).[85]

It is also possible that *ve-nichatah* is similar to the word *nichat* (broken)[86] in *And was broken before My name* (Mal. 2: 5).[87] In this case the *nun* of *ve-nichatah* is the *nun* of the *nifal* conjugation and a *bet* should have been prefixed to the word *zero'otai* (mine arms).[88]

---

78. According to the first interpretation our verse reads as follows: *Who maketh my feet like hinds.* According to the second interpretation our verse reads as follows: *Who sets my feet like hinds.* The difference between the two interpretations is semantic.

79. Its usual meaning is, who teaches. Hence I.E.'s comment.

80. Cf. Jer. 2:33

81. *Nichatah* (bend) is in the singular. However, *zero'otai* (mine arms) is in the plural. According to I.E., when a noun in the plural is governed by a verb in the singular, then the verb refers to each one of the singular. Hence his interpretation.

82. *Banot* (its branches) is in the plural. *Tza'adah* (run) is in the singular. According to I.E. the meaning of *banot tza'adah* is, *each one of its branches run over the wall.* See I.E. on Gen. 49:22.

83. Its root is *nun, chet, tav.*

84. It is not the *nun* of the *nifal.* *Ve-nichatah* is in the *nifal.* Hence I.E.'s comment.

85. According to this interpretation our clause reads: *So that my arms do bring down a bow of brass.*

86. From the root *chet, tav, tav.* In this case the *nun* of *nichatah* is the *nun* of the *nifal.*

87. Translated literally.

88. According to I.E., *ve-nichatah keshet nechushah zero'otai* (so that mine arms do bend a bow of brass) is to be rendered: *So that a bow of brass is broken in my arms,* or *So that a bow of brass is broken with by my arms.* Hence our verse is to be read as if written, *ve-nichatah keshet nechushah be- zero'otai.*

It is like the phrase *bet Adonai* (house of the Lord) in *that was found in the house of the Lord* (11 Kings 12:11).[89]

36. THOU HAST ALSO GIVEN ME THY SHIELD OF SALVATION; AND THY RIGHT HAND HATH HOLDEN ME UP; AND THY CONDESCENSION HATH MADE ME GREAT.

THOU HAST ALSO GIVEN ME. Scripture mentions *and Thy right hand*, because it had earlier said,[90] *Who traineth my hands for war* (v. 35).
And Thy condescension hath made me great means, the humility that You placed in me, will exalt and strengthen me. Observe, *Tarbeni* (made me great) is similar to *rav* (great) in *all the great* (officers) of *his house* (Esther 1:8).[91]

37. THOU HAST ENLARGED MY STEPS UNDER ME, AND MY FEET HAVE NOT SLIPPED.

THOU HAST ENLARGED MY STEPS. [*Karsulai* (feet) is to be rendered knees.] Compare, the Aramaic rendition of the word *kera'ayim* (jointed legs) in *which have jointed legs* (Lev. 11:21).[92]
The meaning of our verse is; my knees have not slipped because *Thou hast enlarged my steps under me*.[93]

38. I HAVE PURSUED MINE ENEMIES, AND HAVE OVERTAKEN THEM; NEITHER DID I TURN BACK TILL THEY WERE CONSUMED.

I HAVE PURSUED MINE ENEMIES. And did not turn back from pursuing them till they were consumed.[94]

---

89. 2 Kings 12:11 literally reads: *that was found house of the Lord*. However, this makes no sense. Hence a *bet* must be placed before the Hebrew word for house and the word read as *be-vet*, in the house of. We thus see that Scripture occasionally omits a preposition.

90. Lit., " in correspondence to."

91. Translated lit. I.E.'s point is that *tarbeni* means made me great and not made me numerous.

92. The Targum to Lev. 11:21 renders *kera'ayim*, *karsule*.

93. Lit. "The meaning of *Thou hast enlarged* is because…"

94. In other words, *Neither did I turn back till they were consumed* should be interpreted as: *Neither did I turn back from pursuing them till they were consumed*.

39. I HAVE SMITTEN THEM THROUGH, SO THAT THEY ARE NOT ABLE TO RISE; THEY ARE FALLEN UNDER MY FEET.

I HAVE SMITTEN THEM THROUGH, SO THAT THEY ARE NOT ABLE TO RISE. The word *kum* (rise) is an infinitive.[95] *They are unable to rise* means; they are unable to rise when they fall.

40. FOR THOU HAST GIRDED ME WITH STRENGTH UNTO THE BATTLE, THOU HAST SUBDUED UNDER ME THOSE THAT ROSE AGAINST ME.

FOR THOU HAST GIRDED ME WITH STRENGTH. You gave the organs of my body the strength to bear the difficulties of war.

41. THOU HAST ALSO MADE MINE ENEMIES TURN THEIR BACKS UNTO ME, AND I DID CUT OFF THEM THAT HATE ME.

THOU HAST ALSO MADE MINE ENEMIES TURN THEIR BACKS UNTO ME. David as it were said, You gave the backs of my fleeing enemies to me.[96]
Compare, *Thy hand shall be on the neck of thine enemies* (Gen. 49:8).

42. THEY CRIED, BUT THERE WAS NONE TO SAVE; EVEN UNTO THE LORD, BUT HE ANSWERED THEM NOT.

THEY CRIED… EVEN UNTO THE LORD. *Al Adonai* means *unto the Lord*.[97] It is similar to *and Hannah prayed unto the Lord* (al Adonai)[98] (1 Sam. 1:10).

---

95. Meaning to rise. In other words *kum* is short for *la-kum. Kum* is usually an imperative. Hence I.E.'s comment.

96. The first part of our verse literally reads: *And my enemies You gave me the back.* Hence I.E.'s comment.

97. *Al* means on. Thus *al Adonai* would ordinarily be rendered on the Lord. However, this makes no sense. Hence I.E. points out that *al* sometimes has the meaning of *to.* Thus *al Adonai* should be rendered, *el Adonai.*

98. Here too the word *al* has the meaning of *el.*

43. THEN DID I BEAT THEM, SMALL AS THE DUST BEFORE THE WIND; I DID CAST THEM OUT AS THE MIRE OF THE STREETS.

THEN DID I BEAT THEM… I DID CAST THEM OUT. The word *arikem* (I did cast them out) is similar to *ve-rakkot* (and lean) in *and lean-fleshed* (Gen. 41:19).[99] The aforementioned is so even though the *kof* of *ve-arikem* should have a *dagesh*.[100]

44. THOU HAST DELIVERED ME FROM THE CONTENTIONS OF THE PEOPLE, THOU HAST MADE ME THE HEAD OF THE NATIONS; A PEOPLE WHOM I HAVE NOT KNOWN SERVE ME.

THOU HAST DELIVERED ME FROM THE CONTENTIONS OF THE PEOPLE. The word *people* refers to Israel.[101] It alludes to Saul.
A people whom I have not known therefore follows.[102]

45. AS SOON AS THEY HEAR OF ME, THEY OBEY ME; THE SONS OF THE STRANGER DWINDLE AWAY BEFORE ME.

AS SOON AS THEY HEAR OF ME, THEY OBEY ME. *Yishame'u* (they obey) means, they gather.[103] Compare, *And Saul gathered* (va-yeshamma) *the people* (1 Sam. 15:4).

THE SONS OF THE STRANGER DWINDLE AWAY BEFORE ME.[104] The latter means that the sons of the stranger will deny (lie) to my face that they boasted that they were mightier than I. Compare, *Through the greatness of Thy power shall Thine enemies dwindle away* (yekhachashu) *before Thee* (Ps. 66:3).[105]

---

99. According to I.E. our clause should be rendered, I will make them as thin as the mire of the streets.

100. To compensate for the missing *kof*, for the root of the Hebrew word for thin is *resh, kof, kof*.

101. The parallel verse in 2 Sam. 22:44 reads: *Thou also hast delivered me from the contentions of my people.*

102. David first speaks of God's saving him from his Jewish enemies, then of being made king, and finally of ruling over foreign nations.

103. If Scripture intended to say they obey me, it would have read *yishme'u li*. I.E. renders our clause: As soon as they hear of me, they gather to me.

104. The Hebrew reads, *yikhachashu li*. The latter literally means, will lie to me. Hence I.E.'s comment.

105. I.E. renders this verse as follows: *Through the greatness of Thy power shall Thine enemies lie to Thee* (Ps. 66:3).

46. THE SONS OF THE STRANGER FADE AWAY, AND COME TREMBLING OUT OF THEIR CLOSE PLACES.

FADE AWAY. The word *yibbolu* (fade away) is similar to *navol tibbol* (thou wilt surely wear away) (Ex. 18:17).

AND COME TREMBLING (VE-YACHROGU) OUT OF THEIR CLOSE PLACES. [*Ve-yachrogu* means, and come trembling]. Compare the Aramaic phrase *chargat mota* (the fear of death).[106] This is the only place that this word[107] appears in Scripture.

OUT OF THEIR CLOSE PLACES.[108] Out of their mighty palaces wherein they shut themselves in because of their fright.

47. THE LORD LIVETH, AND BLESSED BE MY ROCK; AND EXALTED BE THE GOD OF MY SALVATION.

THE LORD LIVETH ... Our clause means, my Rock lives forever and the God of my salvation is eternally exalted. I therefore do not fear.

48. EVEN THE GOD THAT EXECUTETH VENGEANCE FOR ME, AND SUBDUETH PEOPLES UNDER ME.

The word *va-yadber* (and subdued) is similar to the word *ha-davero* (their pasture) in *As a flock in the midst of their pasture* (Micah 2:12).[109]

49. HE DELIVERETH ME FROM MINE ENEMIES; YEA, THOU LIFTEST ME UP ABOVE THEM THAT RISE UP AGAINST ME; THOU DELIVEREST ME FROM THE VIOLENT MAN.

HE DELIVERETH ME FROM MINE ENEMIES. Some say that *mine enemies* refers to Saul and his men.

---

106. *Targum Onkelos* on Deut. 32:25.

107. *Yachrogu.*

108. Hebrew. *Misgerotehem.* Its root *is samekh, gimel, resh* (close).

109. *Va-yadber ammim tachtai* literally means, You caused peoples to pasture under me, i.e. You subdued peoples under me.

YEA, THOU LIFTEST ME UP ABOVE THEM THAT RISE UP AGAINST ME. The reference is to the inhabitants of foreign countries.

THOU DELIVEREST ME FROM THE VIOLENT MAN. The king of the Philistines, for it is very unlikely that David would refer to Saul as *the violent man*. However, it is possible that the reference is to Saul, for David said regarding Saul, *Out of the wicked cometh forth wickedness* (1 Sam. 24:14).

50. THEREFORE I WILL GIVE THANKS UNTO THEE, O LORD, AMONG THE NATIONS, AND WILL SING PRAISES UNTO THY NAME.

THEREFORE I WILL GIVE THANKS UNTO THEE. With my mouth, for might is Yours.[110]

51. GREAT SALVATION GIVETH HE TO HIS KING; AND SHOWETH MERCY TO HIS ANNOINTED, TO DAVID AND TO HIS SEED FOR EVERMORE.

GREAT SALVATION. I will sing praises to Your name and declare that *Great Salvation Giveth He to His king*.[111]

---

110. Lit., "for the might is yours. I will declare that might is Yours."

111. *And showeth mercy* etc.

CHAPTER 19

1. FOR THE LEADER. A PSALM OF DAVID.

2. THE HEAVENS DECLARE THE GLORY OF GOD, AND THE FIRMAMENT SHOWETH HIS HANDIWORK.

THE HEAVENS DECLARE THE GLORY OF GOD This is a very important Psalm. It deals[1] with the heavenly apparatus.[2] I will now briefly explain it. However, only one who has studied the science of the stars[3] will understand my explanation.[4]

THE HEAVENS. The reference is to the movement of the spheres that are equal in one way[5] but differ in another way.[6] They[7] travel in an in of itself straight path.[8] However, from the standpoint of the people of the earth their path does not appear to be straight.[9]

1. Lit. "It is tied."

2. Heb., *melekhet ha-shamayim*. The *melekhet ha-shamayim* consists of the sun, moon, the five visible planets (Mercury, Venus, Mars, Jupiter and Saturn) and the constellations. Each of these celestial bodies was believed to be embedded in its own sphere. These spheres were propelled by the diurnal sphere, which enclosed all of the spheres. The earth was believed to be in the center of the aforementioned heavenly apparatus. For a description of the *melekhet ha-shamayim* see W.M. Feldman, *Rabbinical Mathematics and Astronomy*, New York, 1978.

3. Or the science of the constellations. Heb., *chokhmat ha-mazalot*. In either case the reference is to astrology.

4. Lit., "understand it."

5. The reference is apparently to the movement of the eight spheres containing the sun, the moon, the five visible planets and the sphere of the constellation. These spheres move from west to east.

6. The reference is apparently the daily motion of spheres due to the effect upon them of the diurnal sphere, which moves east to west. See *Yalkut Ibn Ezra* p. 270.

7. The reference is apparently to the movement of the heavenly bodies that are embedded in the spheres. See *Yalkut Ibn Ezra* p. 270.

8. The planets move from west to east.

9. To the people on earth planets appear at times to go from east to west. This movement was explained by positing epicycles, small spheres within the larger spheres. A planet could travel west to east in its large sphere while moving east to west in its epicycle. I.E. makes a similar point in Chap. 12 of his *Yesod Mora*.

There is positive proof that the pace of their[10] movement does not speed up or slow down. However, to the eye their movement[11] appears to increase or slow down.

Note the following: One who knows the ways of the spheres knows the mind of the Most High.

Observe, the heavens are teachers. They are righteous teachers. The heavens are said to instruct in the same sense that the earth is said to teach. Compare, *Or speak to the earth, and it tell thee* (Job 12:8).

Note, the heavens are the dwelling place of the stars.

Scripture reads *declare* because the heavens are unchangeable. This is God's glory.[12]

God is referred to by the term *El*,[13] because the heavens declare God's might.[14]

AND THE FIRMAMENT SHOWETH HIS HANDIWORK. *The firmament*[15] refers to the air. I have noted the aforementioned in my comments on the Torah portion *Be-reshit*.[16] New things come into being every day. Hence Scripture states: *And the firmament showeth his handiwork. The heavens declare the glory of God*[17] is in contrast to *And the firmament showeth his handiwork.* This is truly so, for the air[18] is under the influence of the planets and the constellations.[19]

3. DAY UNTO DAY UTTERETH SPEECH, AND NIGHT UNTO NIGHT REVEALETH KNOWLEDGE.

DAY UNTO DAY. There is positive proof from the science of mathematics that all parts of the arrangement of the seven heavenly bodies[20] are in flux.[21] If the world were to exist

---

See page 172 of *The Secret of the Torah*.

10. Lit., "its movement."

11. Lit., "its movement."

12. Which the heavens declare. In other words the heavens declare that God created that which is unchangeable. See Chap. 12 of The Secret of the Torah, p. 170.

13. Our Psalm reads, *kevod El* (the glory of God).

14. The term *El* means, God the Mighty. See I.E. on Ex. 34:5.

15. Hebrew, *raki'a*.

16. See I.E. on Gen. 1:1. The firmament is part of the sub lunar world.

17. The heavens, which are unchangeable, bear witness to the unchangeability of their creator. See 170-171 of *The Secret of the Torah*.

18. The firmament. The firmament and what is below it is under the influence of the planets and the constellations.

19. Lit. "This is truly so, for the air receives the power of the ministers and the great host."

20. Lit., "of the seven." The reference is to the sun, moon, and the five visible planets.

21. With regard to the constellations.

for thousands of thousands of ten thousands of years no two arrangements would dupli-
cate each other. The aforementioned[22] is also explained in the *Sefer Yetzirah*.[23]
It is because of the changes in the arrangement of the seven planets[24] that what comes
into being today is made known by one day to the next day; this day to the next day,
and one generation to the next generation. This goes on forever, for there is something
new each day.
The statement by Solomon *there is nothing new under the sun* (Ecc. 1:9) does not disprove
the above, because Solomon speaks of the whole.[25]

UTTERETH. The word *yabbia* (uttereth) means flows.[26] It does not stop. On the other
hand the meaning of the word *yabbia* might mean, uttereth.[27] Compare, *Behold they bark
out* (yabbi'un) *with their mouths* (Ps. 59:8).

[AND NIGHT UNTO NIGHT REVEALETH KNOWLEDGE.] [The word *yechav-
veh*[28] (revealeth) means, tells]. Compare, *Achavkha* (I will tell thee) in *I will tell thee, hear
thou me* (Job. 15:17).
Day unto day and night unto night means, constantly.[29]

4. THERE IS NO SPEECH (OMER), THERE ARE NO WORDS (DEVARIM), NEITHER IS THEIR VOICE (KOLAM) HEARD.

THERE IS NO SPEECH. Scripture notes that unlike people the heavens have no mouth.[30]

---

22. Lit., "this too."

23. *The Book of Creation.* A mystical work written in the Land of Israel or Babylonia between the 3rd-6th centuries. The *Sefer Yetzirah* derives the structure of the cosmos from the Hebrew alphabet and the ten primary numbers.

24. Lit. "It is because of this."

25. The whole is eternal. It is only the individual parts that are transient. See I.E.'s introduction to *Koheleth.*

26. Lit. "It is like a fountain." The root of *yabbia* is *nun, bet, ayin,* meaning to flow, spring, or bubble up. Thus *yabbia omer* (uttereth speech) means, speech flows. Our clause should thus be rendered: *Day unto day speech flows.*

27. Lit., "tells or relates." In this case the root *nun, bet, ayin,* means both to flow and to speak, for figuratively speaking speech flows from the lips.

28. From the root, *chet, vav, heh.*

29. Lit. "The time stands."

30. In other words verse 3 is not to be taken literally.

Omer (speech)[31] refers to statements that convey a complete thought. *Reuben lives* is an example of an *omer*.[32]

Speech is composed of words (devarim). The term Reuben is an example of a word (dibbur). The voice (kol) sounds out the letter *resh* of Reuben.[33]

Scripture notes that a human being's rational faculty can comprehend the truth that the heavens declare and the firmament shows. It can accomplish the aforementioned by employing the vision of the corporeal eye and the perception of the eye of the inner soul.[34]

5. THEIR LINE IS GONE OUT THROUGH ALL THE EARTH, AND THEIR WORDS TO THE END OF THE WORLD. IN THEM HATH HE SET A TENT FOR THE SUN,

6. [WHICH IS AS A BRIDEGROOM COMING OUT OF HIS CHAMBER, AND REJOICETH AS A STRONG MAN TO RUN HIS COURSE.]

THEIR LINE IS GONE OUT THROUGH ALL THE EARTH. *Kavvam* (their line) is similar to *kav la-kav* (line by line). The reference[35] is to their writing.[36] The *mem*[37] of the word *kavvam* refers to the heavens.[38]

The meaning of our verse is that the writing of the heavens is read in all places.[39] Intelligent people all over the world understand it.[40]

AND THEIR WORDS TO THE END OF THE WORLD. *Tevel* (world) refers the inhabited world. The heavens[41] make their words heard throughout the inhabited world.

---

31. Lit. The word *omer*.

32. The word *omer* looks like a participle. Hence I.E. points out that it can also be noun. He explains its meaning and goes on to do the same for the terms *davar* and *kol* that are employed in our verse.

33. I.E. is being brief. What he means is that one's voice sounds out each one of the letters that make up a word. The *resh* in *re'uven* is an example of the aforementioned.

34. Lit. "Scripture notes that wisdom will show the truth which heaven declares, and likewise what the firmament shows, by the vision of the corporeal eye and the perception of the eye of the inner soul."

35. Reading *ta'amo* rather then *ta'ame*.

36. Lit. "The writing." The line refers to the line that makes up the letter. According to I.E., our clause should be rendered, *Their writing is gone out through the earth.*

37. A suffix meaning *their.*

38. It does not refer back to day or night.

39. It is read all over the world.

40. Intelligent people the world over understand the heavenly writing.

41. Lit., "they."

Observe, Scripture mentions *words*.[42] The lines refer to writing.[43] The aforementioned are spoken of in the *Sefer Yetzirah*, for the latter states that God created the world through numbers, letters, and words.[44] These three[45] are the bases of all the sciences.

Scripture mentions the sun because it is larger than any other body[46] and all of the movements of the celestial bodies[47] are tied to it. The sun gives birth to equal[48] and changing time.[49] Day,[50] night,[51] metals, plants, and all life are dependent on the sun. Solomon similarly says, *under the sun* (Ecc.1: 3).[52]

The word *ohel* (tent) means a dwelling place. Compare, *ish le-ohalav* (every man unto his tent)(11 Sam. 20:1). The sun[53] is fixed in the sphere.[54] The science dealing with the heavenly apparatus offers definitive proof to the aforementioned.

Others say that the word *ohel* (tent) means light as in *lo yahil* (hath no brightness) (Job 25:5).[55] However in my opinion the *alef* of *yahil* is superfluous.[56] It is like the *alef* in *ve-he'eznihu*[57] (shall become foul) in *And the rivers shall become foul* (Is. 19:6). *Yahil* comes from the same root as the *yahellu* (give their light)[58] in *Shall not give their light* (Is. 13:10).

In them means, in the heavens. The sun itself[59] is hidden from the eyes of the inhabitants of the world in accordance to their distance from the eastern edge of the earth.[60]

---

42. I.E. will soon explain why.

43. Our verse speaks of words and writing.

44. *Sefer Yetzirah* 1:1.

45. Lit., "for these three."

46. The reference is to the moon and the five visible planets. Levin.

47. The reference here too is to the moon and the five visible planets.

48. The reference is apparently to the sun's 24-hour cycle around the earth that makes for a full day. This cycle is always equal. It should be recalled that I.E. believed the sun to circle the earth.

49. The reference is to the yearly cycle. This cycle various a bit. Levin.

50. Daylight.

51. Darkness.

52. Lit., "Solomon similarly said."

53. Lit., "for the sun."

54. In other words, the sun's tent refers to the place in the solar sphere where the sun is embedded.

55. This opinion renders our verse as follows: *In them hath He put the sun for a light* (ohel).

56. In other words the root of *yahil* is not *alef, heh, lamed*. Thus *ohel*, which comes from the stem *alef, heh, lamed*, is not connected to *yahil* and does not mean to give light.

57. Whose *alef* is superfluous and is not a root letter.

58. From the root *heh, lamed, lamed*.

59. Lit. "And it, it, (ve-hu hu)." Scripture tells us: *And there is nothing hid from the heat* [of the sun]. Hence I.E. points out that the sun is not seen all over the earth at the same time.

60. The sun rises later in the west.

Scripture describes the sun as a bridegroom because all who see the sun rejoice in it.[61] Scripture reads: *as a strong man*. It so reads, because the solar sphere is propelled by the power of the sun and it[62] does not tire nor grow weary.

7. HIS GOING FORTH IS FROM THE END OF THE HEAVEN, AND HIS CIRCUIT UNTO THE ENDS OF IT; AND THERE IS NOTHING HID FROM THE HEAT THEREOF.

FROM THE END OF THE HEAVEN. Our verse deals with the sun's movement[63] according to its true nature.[64] This movement is the reverse of the large movement.[65] The word *tekufah* (circuit) is similar to the word *hikkifu* (were gone about) in *when the days of their feasting were gone about* (Job 1:5) and *hikkifuni* (have encircled me)[66] (Ps. 22:17).[67]

[AND THERE IS NOTHING HID FROM THE HEAT THEREOF.] Its meaning is that the heat of the sun in the world is similar to the heat of the heart in the human body. There is proof to the aforementioned from the natural sciences. The sun is thus the life of all bodies.

8. THE LAW OF THE LORD IS PERFECT RESTORING THE SOUL; THE TESTIMONY OF THE LORD IS SURE, MAKING WISE THE SIMPLE.

THE LAW OF THE LORD. Rabbi Saadiah Gaon says that the word *yomar* (it says) has been eliminated from our text; for the meaning of our verse is, the sun says, " the law of the Lord is perfect."[68]
However, I disagree.[69]

---

61. Lit., "rejoice in the sun."

62. The sun.

63. Lit. "Scripture mentions its movements."

64. The sun's natural annual movement in its sphere is west to east. See note 5.

65. The diurnal sphere moves from east to west. See note 2. The diurnal sphere propels the sun east to west in its daily motion around the earth.

66. Translated according to I.E.

67. In other words *tekufah* means a circuit.

68. And what follows. In other words the sun says, *The law of the Lord is perfect...making wise the simple.*

69. Lit. "In my opinion."

Up till now[70] Scripture explained how an intelligent person can find proof of God's existence and recognize God's deeds.[71] Now David goes on to say that there is a better, more precious and more believable witness[72] then the above. That witness is provided by God's law, His testimonies, precepts, positive commandments, negative commandments[73] and His ordinances.[74] The word *Torah* (law) means direction, for the *Torah* directs (torah) us on the straight path. It does this by the signs that are in it.[75] Compare, *The law* (torat) *of leprosy* (Lev. 14: 57) and *the law of the Nazirite* (Num. 6:13).[76]

Scripture reads[77] *restoring the soul*: It says this, because the Torah removes doubt from the soul.

Scripture says that the law of the Lord is perfect. Its perfection corresponds to the sun's perfection, for the sun unlike the moon is a perfect source of light.[78]

The meaning of *restoring the soul* is *restoring the soul* like the sun, for when the sun is in the ascending half of its sphere it restores the soul of many who are ill.[79] The action of the sun in its ascending half of its sphere is in contrast to its effect when it is in the descending half of its sphere.

The effect of the sun on the ill[80] is known to physicians.

The *testimonies* refer to ancient things[81] known to us from the mouth of witnesses who saw these things with their eyes.[82] Scripture says *making wise the simple*, because a person cannot

---

70. Verses 1-7 deal with God as he is revealed in the world of nature. Scripture now speaks of God as he is revealed in the Torah.

71. By studying the heavens.

72. For God's existence.

73. Lit. "His fear." See I.E. on verse 10.

74. Revelation is the ultimate proof of God's existence.

75. In other words, the *Torah* teaches us how to act in certain circumstances. For example, the *Torah* tells us that a person with certain skin ailments is unclean. It then lists the signs by which we can identify the skin diseases that render a person unclean.

76. Num. 6:13 reads: *And this is the law* (torat) *of the Nazirite.*

77. Lit., "mentions."

78. Lit. "Scripture says that the law of the Lord is perfect in correspondence to the sun's perfection, for the sun unlike the moon is perfect with regards to its light."

79. The sun travels in an eccentric sphere. When the sun is in that part of the sphere that moves away from the earth it is said to be ascending, when it travels in that part of the sphere that moves toward the earth it is said to be descending.

80. Lit., "this."

81. Such as the parting of the Sea of Reeds, the revelation at Sinai and other miracles which prove God's existence and concern for Israel.

82. In other words, the testimonies refer to the historical narratives in Scripture. These are only known by tradition.

know these things by employing proofs. Scripture says *The testimony of the Lord is sure* because they are true and not false even though intelligent people do not know these things.[83] David says that the Torah is perfect, because one has no need for another witness along with it.[84]

9. THE PRECEPTS OF THE LORD ARE RIGHT, REJOICING THE HEART; THE COMMANDMANT OF THE LORD IS PURE, ENLIGHTENING THE EYES.

THE PRECEPTS OF THE LORD. The word *pikkude* (the precepts) comes from the same root as *pikkadon* (deposit). The reference is to those precepts that are found in every human being's soul when he reaches the age of the observance of the commandments.[85] These precepts were deposited in the heart by God.[86] They are potential.[87]
Scripture tells us that *The precepts of the Lord are right*,[88] because all intelligent people can discover them by taking the straight road,[89] which has no stumbling block.
Scripture tells us that God's precepts rejoice the heart, because a wise man attains eternal happiness through them.
Scripture employs the term *yashar* (right)[90] because the sun travels on the axle of the sphere of the constellations.[91] The latter is a straight path. However,[92] the precepts have an advantage over the sun, for the sun at times inclines from the straight sphere.[93]
God's precepts *rejoice the heart*. The sun only gladdens the heart during the day but not at night. However, God's precepts always gladden the heart.
Mitzvah (Commandment) refers to the positive commandments. They are called commandments because in most cases Scripture does not tell us why they were commanded.[94]

---

83. Unless they have studied the Torah. Scientists and philosophers cannot know the events recorded in the Bible by the use of their rational powers. I.E. makes this point because he soon goes on to note that the human mind can arrive at knowledge of the rational laws of Judaism on its own.

84. One does not need any outside proof to verify, that which is recorded in the *Torah*. Two witnesses are ordinarily required to establish a fact. Hence I.E.'s comments.

85. The age of thirteen.

86. See chapter 5, of the *Yesod Morah* and page 75 of *The Secret of the Torah*.

87. If a person does not develop his mind he will not discover these precepts.

88. Lit. "Scripture mentions *are right* with them."

89. Following one's intelligence.

90. Lit., "straight."

91. The sun and constellations share one central point.

92. Furthermore.

93. The sun's sphere inclines above and below that of the sphere of the constellations.

94. One has to observe these commandments, because God ordered us to do so.

Scripture tells us that God's commandment *is pure,* because they are so for those of a pure heart. The psalm therefore goes on to say, *enlightening the eyes* of the man who is, at it were, in the dark.

Scripture uses the term *barah* (pure) in order to contrast the purity of the commandments with the purity of the sun. Now[95] the sun unlike the moon has no darkness in it.[96] However, the commandments have an advantage over the sun, because the clouds cover the sun during the day and nothing covers the commandments.

The Psalm reads *enlightening the eyes* because God's commandments are the light of the world both during the day and during the night, for the light of the moon instructs with definite proofs.[97]

10. THE FEAR OF THE LORD IS CLEAN, ENDURING FOREVER; THE ORDINANCES OF THE LORD ARE TRUE, THEY ARE RIGHTEOUS ALTOGETHER.

THE FEAR OF THE LORD. *The fear of the Lord* refers to the negative commandments. Scripture describes the negative commandments as *clean*[98] because a clean person is a person who does not defile himself by violating any of the negative commandments.

ENDURING FOREVER. It is inconceivable for God to permit what is prohibited.[99]

Scripture says *The fear of the Lord is clean* in order to contrast the fear of the Lord with the sun that at times darkens.[100] Scripture makes this comparison even though the sun itself is pure. It only appears to darken.[101] The sun endures forever,[102] for unlike all things that are created out of the four elements the sun is not made up of parts. The aforementioned is true even though the position of the sun changes in accordance with the compass points.

---

95. Lit., "for."

96. Hence the sun is pure.

97. It has astrological or calendar significance. I.E.'s point is that the commandments of God, unlike the sun and moon, give light both during the day and during the night.

98. Lit. "Scripture says clean."

99. The commandments are eternally valid. God would not later permit that which he earlier prohibited. Saadiah Gaon makes the same point in Chapter 3 of his *Emunot Ve-De'ot.* According to Maimonides this point is one of the principles of Judaism. See Maimonides' introduction to Chapter 11 of tractate *Sanhedrin.*

100. During an eclipse.

101. Lit. "It only [is so] with regards to others."

102. I.E. believed the heavens to be eternal. See I.E. on Gen. 1:1.

It is known that laws of the science of astrology are based on the alignment of the planets to the sun.[103] Some of these laws contradict each other. This is the reason the astrologers err.[104] Hence David says, *the ordinances of God they are righteous altogether.*

After David concludes speaking of the advantage of the Torah,[105] which is efficacious to the intelligent in the world to come, he contrasts its pleasures with the pleasures of this world.

11. MORE TO BE DESIRED ARE THEY THAN GOLD, YEA, THAN MUCH FINE GOLD; SWEETER ALSO THAN HONEY AND THE HONEYCOMB.

MORE TO BE DESIRED ARE THEY THAN GOLD. *Paz* (fine gold) means precious stones. People desire to possess a large amount of gold and precious stones because they last and are at hand when one needs them. They are always available because they endure[106] and do not decompose. However, wisdom has an advantage over them, for wisdom is at one's disposal during ones life and after one's death.[107]

Scripture states *Sweeter also than honey,* because all living things both good and evil need to eat. David is telling us that the pleasure of wisdom is greater than the pleasure of sweet food. There is nothing-sweeter then honey.

The Psalm states that wisdom is sweeter than honey because the pleasure of eating lasts for a moment. However, that of wisdom is eternal.

Sweeter also than honey and the honey comb also means that the *Torah* is sweeter[108] *than honey and the honeycomb* only for the intelligent. It is not so for all men. Hence Scripture goes on to say, *Moreover by them is Thy servant*[109] *warned.*[110] The word *ba-hem* (by them) refers to *ha-nechemadim* (more desired are they).[111]

---

103. Lit. "It is known that the science of astrology is in accordance with the arrangement of the planets in their alignment to the sun. There are ordinances in the arrangements that contradict one another."

104. Heb. *Ba'ale ha-din.*

105. Over the sun.

106. Lit., "they stand by themselves." They do not need any preservatives.

107. According to I.E., the wisdom that a person attains develops his soul and gains him eternal life. See Chapter One of *The Secret of the Torah.*

108. Lit., "they are sweeter."

109. Who is one of the intelligent.

110. In other words our verse is to be rendered: Moreover by that which is desired more than gold is your servant warned.

111. In other words, *by them* refers to that which is more desired than gold, viz. God's precepts.

[12 MOREOVER BY THEM IS THY SERVANT WARNED; IN KEEPING OF THEM THERE IS GREAT REWARD.]

In keeping them is much reward (ekev rav) means; I know that only the one who keeps Your Laws[112] will receive great reward.[113] God's commandments[114] are thus beneficial in this world and in the world to come.

13. WHO CAN DISCERN ERRORS? CLEAR THOU ME FROM HIDDEN FAULTS.

ERRORS. It is possible that the *alef* in *shegi'ot* (errors) is in place of a doubled root letter.[115] On the other hand it might be in place of a *yod*.[116] Compare, *sekhiyot* (imagery)[117] in *delightful imagery* (Is. 2:16).
Who can discern errors means, I try with all of my might to keep Your commandments. However, I am afraid that I might err. Hence Scripture goes on to say *Clear Thou me from hidden faults.*

14. KEEP BACK THY SERVANT ALSO FROM PRESUMPTUOUS SINS, THAT THEY MAY NOT HAVE DOMINION OVER ME; THEN SHALL I BE FAULTLESS, AND I SHALL BE CLEAR FROM GREAT TRANSGRESSION.

ALSO FROM PRESUMPTUOUS SINS. David prays to God, for *by Him all actions are weighed* (1. Sam. 4:3), to arrange things so that he will avoid the company and the evil of the presumptuous.[118]
Az etam means, then I shall be faultless. *Etam* is irregular.[119]
The following is the meaning of our verse: I cannot keep the commandments if the presumptuous rule over me, for they will force me to violate God's laws.

---

112. Lit., "them."

113. The word *ekev* refers to the reward, which is ultimately given. See I.E. on Deut. 7:12.

114. Unlike the pleasures of this world.

115. A *gimel,* for the root of *she'gi'ot* is *shin, gimel, gimel.*

116. In this case the root of *shegi'ot* is *shin, gimel, heh,* and *shegi'ot* is a variation of *shegiyot.*

117. From the root *sin, kaf, heh.*

118. According to I.E., *zedim* (presumptuous sins) refers to sinners and not to sin. He renders our clause: *Keep back Thy servant also from presumptuous people.*

119. The word should have read *ettam,* for its root is *tav, mem, mem,* and the word is in the *nifal* (Filwarg).

15. LET THE WORDS OF MY MOUTH AND THE MEDITATION OF MY HEART BE ACCEPTABLE BEFORE THEE, O LORD, MY ROCK, AND MY REDEEMER.

LET THE WORDS OF MY MOUTH...BE ACCEPTABLE. *The words of my mouth* refers to David's supplication that the presumptuous should not rule over him. *My rock* implies that David prayed that he not fear that the presumptuous rule over him.[120] If they were to rule over him then no one except for the Lord can save him from their hand. Hence David goes on to say, *O Lord, My rock and my redeemer.*

---

120. Lit. "The meaning of *My rock* is that he should not fear that the presumptuous rule over him."

CHAPTER 20

1. FOR THE LEADER. A PSALM OF DAVID.

2. THE LORD ANSWER THEE IN THE DAY OF TROUBLE; THE NAME OF THE GOD OF JACOB SET THEE UP ON HIGH.

THE LORD ANSWER THEE IN THE DAY OF TROUBLE. It is possible that this psalm was composed by one of the poets concerning David[1] and that *le-david* (of David) has the same meaning as *al david* (concerning David).[2] The word *le-david* is similar to *li-shelomo* (of Solomon) in *(A psalm) Of Solomon. Give the king Thy judgments, O God* (Ps. 72:1).[3] Do not be surprised by the *lamed* prefixed to the word David.[4] Observe, the *lamed* is used in an unusual manner[5] in *A Psalm, a Song For the sabbath day* (le-yom ha-shabbat)[6] (Ps. 92:1). On the other hand it is possible[7] that David composed this psalm.[8] David said to his prince:[9] *The Lord answer thee in the day of trouble.*[10] It is also possible that David was addressing himself.[11]

Other say that David was speaking of the messiah.

---

1. Heb. *Al david.*

2. Our verse reads, *mizmor le-david* (a Psalm of David). This is usually rendered a psalm written by King David. However, this cannot be the case here, for the psalm appears to be directed to David. Hence I.E.'s interpretation.

3. I.E. renders *li-shelomo* (of Solomon) as *al shelomo* (concerning Solomon), for the psalm appears directed to Solomon. He renders Ps. 72:1: *(A psalm) concerning Solomon. Give the king Thy judgments, O God.*

4. Which seems to indicate that the meaning of *mizmor le-david* (a psalm of David) is, a psalm written by David.

5. Lit. In another manner, i.e. with the meaning of "concerning" rather than "by."

6. For *le-yom ha-shabbat* means, *for the sabbath day* not *to the sabbath day.*

7. Lit., "or."

8. In this case *mizmor le-david* means, a psalm written by David.

9. Heb. *Nesikho.* I.E. does not identify the prince. He probably had Solomon in mind.

10. The point is, the word *thee* does not refer to David. Hence it is possible that David composed this psalm.

11. In this psalm. Thus David is the author of this psalm.

The Lord answer thee in the day of trouble means, the Lord answer thee in battle.[12]
Our verse reads *the God of Jacob,* because many troubles came upon Jacob on the way[13]
and God set him on high.[14]

3. SEND FORTH THY HELP FROM THE SANCTUARY, AND SUPPORT THEE OUT OF ZION.

FROM THE SANCTUARY. From the place of the Ark.

4. RECEIVE THE MEMORIAL OF ALL THY MEAL-OFFERINGS, AND ACCEPT THE FAT OF THY BURNT-SACRIFICE. SELAH.

RECEIVE THE MEMORIAL OF ALL THY MEAL-OFFERINGS. The meaning of
our verse is; why will God help you? (v. 2). He shall help you, because He will remember all of your meal offerings. [15] The Torah means the same when it states: *then you shall sound an alarm with the trumpets, and you shall be remembered before the Lord your God, and you shall be saved from your enemies* (Num. 10:9).[16]
Others say that they used to offer sacrifices when waging war. Compare, *I forced myself therefore, and offered the burnt-offering* (1 Sam. 13:12).[17]

AND ACCEPT THE FAT (YEDASHENEH) OF THY BURNT-SACRIFICE. The fire
of the altar will consume the burnt offering and turn it into ashes.[18]
The word *yedashena* (accept the fat)[19] is similar to the word *va-ekra'eh* (I have called) in *I have called thee* (1 Sam. 28:15); wherein the *alef* which is followed by the *heh* is not vo-

---

12. Lit. "He said: The *Lord answer thee in the day of trouble,* that is, in war."

13. From the time that Jacob left his father's house, until he returned to Canaan. See Gen 28-33.

14. God saved him.

15. In other words, God shall help you (v. 3) *because* He will remember all of your meal offerings. I.E.
renders *yizkor kol minchotekha* (receive the memorial of all thy meal-offerings) as: He will remember all of
your meal offerings. Hence his interpretation.

16. When you sound the trumpets, God shall recall your sacrifices

17. God will accept the sacrifices offered during the battle.

18. I.E. renders *yedasheneh* (accept the fat) as: *it* (the fire*) will turn it into ashes.* According to I.E., our
verse should be understood as follows: *He will accept* (or remember) *all of thy meal-offerings and whole-offerings* (olatekha) *that the fire of the altar will turn into ashes.* According to I.E., the word *yedasheneh* is
connected to *deshen,* ashes. Hence his interpretation.

19. According to the rules of Hebrew grammar *yedasheneh* should be vocalized *yedashenah,* for *yedasehneh*
is a combination of the verb *yedashen* (will burn) and the pronoun *otah* (it). Hence I.E.'s comment.

calized with a *kametz*, as is the rule.[20] Many therefore say that these words[21] are similar to verbs from a four-letter stem.[22]

5. GRANT THEE ACCORDING TO THINE OWN HEART, AND FULFIL ALL THY COUNSEL.

GRANT. Its meaning is that David will overcome his enemy.[23]

6. WE WILL SHOUT FOR JOY IN THY VICTORY AND IN THE NAME OF OUR GOD WE WILL SET UP OUR STANDARDS; THE LORD FULFIL ALL THY PETITIONS.

WE WILL SHOUT FOR JOY IN THY VICTORY. Each one of David's men will say this to David,[24] for the *kaf* of *bi-shu'atekha* (in thy victory) refers to David.[25]

AND IN THE NAME OF OUR GOD WE WILL SET UP OUR STANDARDS; THE LORD FULFIL ALL THY PETITIONS. Our standards will be raised when the Lord fulfils all your petitions.[26]

7. NOW KNOW I THAT THE LORD SAVETH HIS ANNOINTED; HE WILL ANSWER HIM FROM HIS HOLY HEAVEN, WITH MIGHTY ACTS OF HIS SAVING RIGHT HAND.

NOW KNOW I. Each one of David's men shall say, *Now I know that the Lord Saveth His annointed*.[27]

On the other hand *Now I know that the Lord Saveth His annointed*[28] might be the words of the poet[29] under the influence of the Holy Spirit. The latter interpretation is in my

---

20. We thus see that at times Scripture employs a *segol* when the rules of grammar require a *kametz*.

21. Lit. , "they."

22. In other words, the *heh* of *yedasheneh* and of *ekra'eh* are root letters and are vocalized as such. According to this interpretation the root of *yedashenah* is *dalet, shin, nun, heh*, and that of *ekra'eh kof, resh, alef, heh* (Filwarg).

23. For this is what David desires.

24. Lit., "to him."

25. Lit., "to him."

26. David's men will say this to David.

27. Lit., "shall say this."

28. Lit., "it."

29. See I.E. on verse 1.

opinion correct.

His anointed refers to David or to the messiah his son.[30]

How shall God answer him?[31] The Lord shall answer him with the mighty acts that His right hand shall do.[32] That which follows indicates that *His... right hand* does not refer to David's right hand.[33]

8. SOME TRUST IN CHARIOTS, AND SOME IN HORSES; BUT WE WILL MAKE MENTION OF THE NAME OF THE LORD OUR GOD.

SOME TRUST IN CHARIOTS. *Elleh va-rekhev* should be rendered: *Some trust in chariots.*[34]

The *bet* of *be-shem* (of the name) is there for poetic purposes.[35] Compare, *lachamu ve-lachami* (eat of my bread) (Prov. 9:5).[36]

9. THEY ARE BOWED DOWN AND FALLEN; BUT WE ARE RISEN AND STAND UPRIGHT.

THEY ARE BOWED DOWN AND FALLEN. The reference is to the charioteers.[37]

AND FALLEN. The reference is to the horsemen. Compare, *So that his rider falleth backward* (Gen. 49:18).

BUT WE ARE RISEN. The word *kamnu* (risen) is related to the word *kam* (shall be made sure) in *the house...shall be made sure* (Lev. 25:30).[38]

---

30. That is, the messiah who is descended from David.

31. In other words, our verse corresponds to verse 2.

32. In other words, our verse is to be understood as follows: *He will answer him from his holy heaven.* How? *With mighty acts of His saving hand.*

33. The verses which follow show that the hand spoken of in our verse refers to God's and not David's hand, for these verses speak of God's might.

34. *Elleh va-rekhev* literally means, these in chariots. Hence I.E.'s comment.

35. Our clause reads: *va-anachnu be-shem Adonai Elohenu nazkir* (But we will make mention of the name of the Lord our God). The latter literally reads: *But we will make mention in the name of the Lord our God.* "In the name" does not make sense. It was placed there for poetic purposes, possibly to rhyme with the *bets* of *va-rekhev* and *va-susim* in the first part of the verse.

36. The *bet* placed before *lachami* has no meaning, for the meaning of *lachamu ve-lachami* is the same as *lachamu lachami.*

37. Mentioned in verse 8.

38. According to I.E., the meaning of *va-anachnu kamnu* (But we are risen) is, but we are made sure.

AND STAND UPRIGHT. *Nitodad* (stand upright) means, we will be proud and exalt our-selves; for *me'oded*[39] (upholdeth) (Ps.147: 6) is the reverse of *mashpil* (lowers).[40]

10. SAVE, LORD; LET THE KING ANSWER US IN THE DAY THAT WE CALL.

LORD. Some say that the word *ha-melekh* (the king) is connected to the word *hoshi'ah* (save).[41] However, this is incorrect because of the *etnach* beneath the *shin* of *hoshi'ah*.[42] Others say that the words in our verse are out of order. Our verse should be read as if written, *In the day that we call: Save, Lord* - as is the custom of warriors when they come to do battle- *let the king answer us.*[43]

LET THE KING ANSWER US. David who is the king will respond: Amen, so be it.[44] Our verse is similar to my upcoming interpretation of *Blessed be he that cometh in the name of the Lord* (Ps. 118:26).[45]

However the correct interpretation of *Adonai hoshi'ah* (Save, Lord) is: "Lord save us", for God knows the mind of the poet.[46] The same is the case with *We beseech Thee, O Lord, save now* (Ps. 118:25).[47]

Our verse[48] omits the object.[49]

The king refers to God[50] who is the true king. David is His anointed.

---

39. Same root as *nitodad*.

40. In Psalm 147:6. The latter reads: *The Lord upholdeth* (me'oded) *the humble; He bringteth the wicked down* (mashpil) *to the ground* (Psalm 147:6).

41. Our verse reads: *Adonai hoshi'ah ha-melekh...* If we connect *hoshi'ah* to *ha-melekh* then our verse reads: *Lord, save the king.*

42. The *etnach* (a musical note) divides the verse in half. Hence our verse reads: *Adonai hoshi'ah; ha-melekh* (Save, Lord; Let the king...).

43. These commentators read our verse as if written, *be-yom korenu Adonai hoshi'ah, ha-melekh ya'anenu.*

44. David who is the king will respond: Amen, so be it, to the cry of *Save O Lord.*

45. Psalm 118:26 reads: *Blessed be he that cometh in the name of the Lord; We bless you out of the house of the Lord.* According to I.E., *Blessed be he that cometh in the name of the Lord* was said by the celebrant. *We bless you out of the house of the Lord* was the response of the *kohen.* Similarly in our verse. The warriors said, *Save, Lord. So be it,* was said by the king.

46. Hence the poet leaves out the word *otanu* (us). In other words, even though the poet said *Adonai hoshi'ah,* he knew that God understood that his intention was *Adonai hoshi'ah otanu.*

47. For the meaning of *We beseech Thee, O Lord, save now* is, *We beseech Thee, O Lord, save us now.*

48. Like Ps. 118:25.

49. Us.

50. Not to David. In other words, *His anointed* (v.7) refers to David. King refers to God.

CHAPTER 21

1. FOR THE LEADER. A PSALM OF DAVID.

2. O LORD, IN THY STRENGTH THE KING REJOICETH; AND IN THY SALVATION HOW GREATLY DOTH HE EXULT.

O LORD, IN THY STRENGTH THE KING REJOICETH. Its meaning is as follows: O Lord, the king rejoices in the strength which You have given him.[1] The same applies to *And in Thy salvation*[2] *how greatly doth he exult.*

3. THOU HAST GIVEN HIM HIS HEART'S DESIRE, AND THE REQUEST OF HIS LIPS THOU HAST NOT WITHHOLDEN. SELAH.

HIS HEART'S DESIRE. *Ta'avat libbo* (his heart's desire) means, what is in his heart.

AND THE REQUEST OF HIS LIPS THOU HAST NOT WITHHOLDEN. *Areshet sefatav* (the request of his lips) means, what he utters with his lips. The *alef* of *areshet* is superfluous. It is like the *alef* of *ve-ezro'ekha* (and your arm).[3] *Areshet* is similar to the word *rishayon* (utterance) in *according to the utterance of Cyrus king of Persia upon them* (Ezra 3:7).[4]

---

1. In other words, *Thy strength* means, the strength that You have given him.

2. It means, *and in the salvation which you brought on his behalf.*

3. The reference is probably to Jer. 32:21. However, the reading there is *u-ve-ezro'a.* I.E.'s point is that the *alef* of *ezro'a* is superfluous, for the word for arm is *zero'a.* I.E. probably added the suffix *kha* because Ezekiel is addressing the Lord.

4. Translated according to I.E.

4. FOR THOU MEETEST HIM WITH CHOICEST BLESSINGS; THOU SETTEST A CROWN OF FINE GOLD ON HIS HEAD.

FOR THOU MEETEST HIM. The *tav* of *tekaddemennu* (Thou meetest him) refers to God. *Tekaddemennu* is thus a verb with two objects.[5] Our verse should be rendered as follows: For Thou meetest with choicest blessings the king who is met by the blessings.

THOU SETTEST A CROWN OF FINE GOLD ON HIS HEAD. *Paz* (fine gold) means, precious stones. *Ateret paz* (a crown of fine gold) means, a crown of gold[6] with precious stones round about it.

[The Psalmist says *Thou settest a crown of fine gold on his head,*] because it is the practice of kings to wear such a crown.

It is possible that the *tav* of *tekaddemennu* (Thou meetest him) is a third person feminine prefix[7] and refers to the word *birkhot* (blessings). In this case our verse is similar to *Its branches* (banot) *run* (tza'adah) *over the wall* (Gen. 49:22).[8]

5. HE ASKED LIFE OF THEE, THOU GAVEST IT HIM; EVEN LENGTH OF DAYS FOR EVER AND EVER.

LIFE. The word *chayyim* (life) is a noun that always comes in the plural. It never comes in the singular. It is similar to the words: *ne'urim* (youth), *betulim* (virginity), *zekunim* (old age), and *me'lu'im* (investure).[9]

EVEN LENGTH OF DAYS FOREVER AND EVER. The word *olam* (for ever) refers to at least two generations.

---

5. The king and the blessings.

6. *Atarah* means a crown. I.E. explains that the reference here is to a gold crown.

7. In this case the meaning of *tekaddemennu* is, they meet him. According to this interpretation, the meaning of *tekaddemennu birkhot tov* (Thou meetest him with choicest blessings) is, choicest blessings meet him.

8. *Its branches* (banot) *run* (tza'adah) *over the wall* (Gen. 49:22). *Banot* is in the plural, *tza'adah* is in the singular. According to I.E., a verb in the singular with a noun in the plural refers to each one of the singular. Thus the meaning of Gen. 49:22 is, each one of the branches run over the wall. (See I.E. on Gen. 49:22). The same applies to our verse, wherein *tekaddemennu* is in the singular and *birkhot* is in the plural. Its meaning is, each one of the blessings shall meet him.

9. These words never come in the singular.

6. HIS GLORY IS GREAT THROUGH THY SALVATION, HONOR AND MAJESTY DOST THOU LAY UPON HIM.

HIS GLORY IS GREAT. Whomever God saves always increases in glory.

HONOR AND MAJESTY DOST THOU LAY UPON HIM. The word *teshavveh* (dost Thou lay) means, You place.

7. FOR THOU MAKEST HIM MOST BLESSED FOREVER; THOU MAKEST HIM GLAD WITH JOY IN THY PRESENCE.

FOR THOU MAKEST HIM MOST BLESSED FOREVER. God told Abraham *and be thou a blessing* (berakhah)[10] (Gen. 12:19). The poet said, *blessed* (berakhot) *for ever,*[11] that is, for eternity, for him and his seed.[12]

THOU MAKEST HIM GLAD WITH JOY. The word *techaddehu* (Thou makest him glad) comes from the same root as the word *chedvah* (gladness).[13]

8. FOR THE KING TRUSTETH IN THE LORD, YEA, IN THE MERCY OF THE MOST HIGH; HE SHALL NOT BE MOVED.

Its meaning is, the king does not trust in his own might. He puts his faith only in God and His mercy.
Scripture reads *Most High* because it goes on to say, *he shall not be moved.*[14]

9. THY HAND SHALL BE EQUAL TO ALL THINE ENEMIES; THY RIGHT HAND SHALL OVERTAKE THOSE THAT HATE THEE.

THY HAND SHALL BE EQUAL TO ALL THINE ENEMIES. God's statement to David promising him, *Thy hand shall be equal to all thine enemies,* is the mercy of the Most High.[15]

---

10. *Berakhah* is in the singular.

11. *Berakhot* is in the plural. Thus our verse literally reads: *blessings forever.* Hence I.E.'s comments.

12. The point is: Gen 12:19 employs the singular because the blessing refers to Abraham. Our verse employs the plural because it refers to the king and his descendants.

13. In other words *techaddehu* means, *Thou makest him glad.*

14. *The Most High* implies that God is master over all. Hence David can be certain that *he shall not be moved.*

15. Our verse defines the mercy of the *Most High* spoken of in the previous verse.

Thy hand refers to the left hand.[16] Similarly, *Her hand she put to the tent-pin, and her right to the workman's hammer* (Judges 5:26).[17]

The word *timtza* (shall be equal)[18] is similar to *yimtze'u* (will find) in, *and will distress them, so that* the slingers[19] *will find them* (Jer. 10:18).[20] Its meaning is that God' enemies will not be able to flee, escape, and save themselves.[21]

10. THOU SHALT MAKE THEM AS A FIERY FURNACE IN THE TIME OF THINE ANGER; THE LORD SHALL SWALLOW THEM UP IN HIS WRATH, AND THE FIRE SHALL DEVOUR THEM.

THOU SHALT MAKE THEM AS A FIERY FURNACE IN THE TIME OF THINE ANGER. The word *panekha* means, *thine anger.*[22] Compare, *pene Adonai chillekam* (the anger of the Lord hath divided them) (Lam. 4:16) and *u-fanhah lo hayu lah od* (and her countenance was no more sad) (1 Sam. 1:18).[23]

Some say that the *kaf* placed in front of the word *tannur* (furnace) in *ke-tannur esh* (as a fiery furnace) has the meaning of a *bet*.[24] It is similar to *ba-chatzi ha-layelah* (at midnight) (Ex.12: 29) and *ka-chatzot ha-laylah* (about midnight) (Ex. 11:4).[25]

---

16. For the second part of the clause reads: *Thy right hand shall overtake those that hate thee.*

17. *And her right to the workman's hammer* indicates that *her hand* refers to the left hand.

18. *Timtza* literally means, will find. Hence I.E.'s interpretation.

19. The words "the slingers" are I.E.'s. They are not found in the Biblical text.

20. Translated according to I.E. See Radak on Jer. 10:18.

21. According to I.E. our verse should be rendered: *Thy right hand shall find all thine enemies.*

22. The word *panim* means a face. Thus *panekha* would ordinarily be rendered your face. Hence I.E. points out that the word *panim* occasionally has the meaning of anger.

23. I.E. renders this verse, and she no longer had her anger.

24. The *kaf* usually has the meaning of like or as. The *bet* prefixed to a word means in. According to this interpretation *teshitemo ke-tannur esh le-et panekha* (Thou shalt make them as a fiery furnace in the time of thine anger) should be translated: *You will place them in a fiery furnace, in the time of your anger.*

25. *Ka-chatzot ha-laylah* (about midnight) (Ex. 11:4) has the same meaning as *ba-chatzi ha-layelah* (at midnight) (Ex.12: 29). We thus see that the *kaf* at times has the same meaning as a *bet*.

11. THEIR FRUIT SHALT THOU DESTROY FROM THE EARTH, AND THEIR SEED FROM AMONG THE CHILDREN OF MEN.

THEIR FRUIT SHALT THOU DESTROY. The *tav*[26] prefixed to the word *te'abbed* (shalt thou destroy) refers to David or to the messiah.[27] The aforementioned is indicated by what follows.[28]

12. FOR THEY INTENDED EVIL AGAINST THEE, THEY IMAGINED A DEVICE, WHEREWITH THEY SHALL NOT PREVAIL.

FOR THEY INTENDED EVIL. The word *natu* (they intended) is transitive.[29] Its object is *ra'ah* (evil).

THEY IMAGINED A DEVICE, WHEREWITH THEY SHALL NOT PREVAIL. They imagined a prospective act, but were not able to bring it to fruition.[30]

13. FOR THOU SHALT MAKE THEM TURN THEIR BACK, THOU SHALT MAKE READY WITH THY BOWSTRINGS AGAINST THE FACE OF THEM.

FOR THOU SHALT MAKE THEM TURN THEIR BACK. The word *shekhem* (back)[31] is short for *shekhem echad* (one group),[32] for the word *shekhem* has an *etnachta* below it.[33] *Ki teshitemo shekhem echad* (for thou shalt make them turn their back) means, they form

---

26. The *tav* prefixed to a word means you.

27. In other words our verse is directed to David or to the messiah. It is not directed to God mentioned in the previous verse.

28. The next verse reads: *For they intended evil against thee.* I.E. believes that the psalmist would not address God in this way, for one cannot harm God.

29. The word *natu* usually means they turned aside and is intransitive. Hence I.E.'s comment.

30. Our verse literally reads: *They imagined a device, they were not able.* Hence I.E. points out that "they were not able" is short for, they were not able to being it to fruition.

31. The word *shekhem* can mean shoulder or back. The former is its usual meaning.

32. Our verb reads: *ki teshitemo shekhem* (for thou shalt make them turn their back). This literally means, *for you shall make them* (ki teshitemo) *back* (shekhem). I.E. believes that *shekhem* is short for *shekhem echad,* one portion. (See Gen. 48:22) He thus renders our clause: *For Thou shalt make them one portion* (one group), that is they will all form one group and suffer God's wrath together.

33. A note that indicates a pause. Hence our clause must be read *ki teshitemo shekhem.* In other words, *shekehm* ends our clause. It is not to be connected to that which follows.

one group. It is similar to, and will squeeze them into one place *so that* [the slingers] *will find them* (Jer. 10:18).[34]

The word *tekhonen* (Thou shalt make ready) is short for *tekhonen ha-keshet be-chitzim* (You will make ready the bowstring with arrows).[35]

14. BE THOU EXALTED, O LORD, IN THY STRENGTH; SO WILL WE SING AND PRAISE THY POWER.

BE THOU EXALTED, O LORD. David once again praises God at the conclusion of this psalm. He does so because all that he describes in this psalm will ultimately come upon the enemy by the might of God. David concludes this psalm in the same manner that He began it. He opened the psalm with, *O Lord, in Thy strength the king rejoiceth.*

---

34. Translated according to I.E. See Radak on Jer. 10:18.

35. Our verse reads: *be-metarekha tekhonen al penehem* (Thou shalt make ready with thy bowstrings against the face of them). I.E. believes that our verse should be interpreted as if written, *tekhonen be-metarekha ha-keshet be-chitzim al penehem*, with Your bowstring, You will make ready the arrows against their face.

CHAPTER 22

1. FOR THE LEADER; UPON AYYELET HA-SHACHAR. A PSALM OF DAVID.

FOR THE LEADER; UPON AYYELET HA-SHACHAR. *Upon Ayyelet ha-shachar* means, when the power of the rising of the dawn is manifested.[1]

Others say that *ayyelet ha-shachar* is the name of a musical instrument.

We know that the *yod* in *eyaluti* (my strength) (v. 20) and the *yod* in *eyal* (help) in *I am become as a man that hath no help* (Ps. 88:5) have no *dagesh*.[2] It is therefore improbable for the word *ayyelet* to be related to *eyaluti* or *eyal*.[3]

It appears to me that *ayyelet ha-shachar* is the beginning of a love poem.[4] Compare, *ayyelet ahavim* (a lovely hind) (Prov. 5:19).[5] This psalm was to be performed according to its melody.[6]

2. MY GOD, MY GOD, WHY HAST THOU FORSAKEN ME, AND ART FAR FROM MY HELP AT THE WORDS OF MY CRY?

MY GOD, MY GOD. The word *Eli* (My God) is repeated because David was in trouble. David employs the term *Eli* (my God) because he goes on to ask:[7] *Why hast Thou forsaken me?*[8]

---

1. This poem was composed at the rising of the dawn. This opinion apparently connects *ayyelet* with the word *eyal* (power). See Radak.

2. Whereas *ayyelet* does.

3. Thus *ayyelet* is not connected to the word *eyal*, and *ayyelet ha-shachar* does not mean the strength of dawn.

4. Lit. *A poem dealing with desire.*

5. Prov. 5:19 reads: *A lovely hind and a graceful doe, Let her breasts satisfy thee at all times.*

6. To the tune of a well known song beginning with the words *ayyelet ha-shachar.*

7. Lit., "to ask."

8. According to I.E., the meaning of our verse is as follows: Why have You O Mighty God, who was the source of my strength in the past, now forsaken me and are no longer my strength? *El* means God the mighty. Hence I.E.'s interpretation. See I.E. on Ps. 16:1. Also see Radak.

The word *Eli* (my God) should be inserted in the second part of our verse.[9] It should be interpreted as follows: *my God Thou art far from my help; These are the words of my cry.*[10] *Sha'agati* (my cry) is similar to *sha'agti* (I groan) in I *groan by reason of the moaning of my heart* (Ps. 38:9).[11]

David adds *words of*[12] to *my cry* because he was human.[13]

3. O MY GOD, I CALL BY DAY, BUT THOU ANSWEREST NOT; AND AT NIGHT, AND THERE IS NO SURCEASE FOR ME.

O MY GOD. I am amazed.[14] Why don't You answer me, for You are my God? The following is the meaning of our verse: I have no God but You. I don't call for a moment and remain silent. On the contrary, I do not cease to call.[15]

4. YET THOU ART HOLY, O THOU ART ENTHRONED UPON THE PRAISES OF ISRAEL.

YET THOU ART... ENTHRONED UPON THE PRAISES OF ISRAEL. The house that contains the Ark.[16] Our verse is similar to *Our holy and our beautiful house, Where our fathers praised Thee* (Is. 64:10).[17] One is forced to interpret our verse in this manner because the verb *yoshev* (enthroned) is connected to *tehillot yisra'el* (praises of Israel).[18] Others say[19] that *yoshev* (enthroned) means, You who exist *and are enthroned of old. Selah.* (Ps. 55:20). It is similar to *Thou, O Lord, art enthroned for ever* (Lam. 5:19). These commentators interpret *tehillot yisrael* (the praises of Israel) to mean, and You are the praises of Israel. It is like, *He is thy praise, and He is thy God* (Deut. 10:21).[20]

---

9. Lit. "The word *Eli* is missing."

10. The second part of our verse literally reads: *Far from my help, the words of my cry.* Hence I.E.'s interpretation.

11. In other words, *sha'agati* means, my cry or my groaning.

12. *Words of my cry* appear to be verbose. The text could have conveyed the same idea by reading, *my cry.*

13. Animals cry out. Human beings verbalize their pain. Hence our verse reads: *The words of my cry.*

14. Lit. "It is amazing."

15. I.E.'s interprets *ve-lo dumiyyah li* (and there is no surcease for me) as meaning, and there is no silence for me i.e. I constantly call unto You.

16. You are enthroned in the house that contains the ark. See I.E. on Ps. 15:1. The Temple had not yet been built. Hence I.E. speaks of a house.

17. In other words *praises of Israel* refers to the house where Israel praised God.

18. Our verse reads: *yoshev tehillot yisra'el* (upon the praises of Israel).

19. Literally, for others say.

20. These commentators explain *O Thou that art enthroned upon the praises of Israel* (ve-attah yoshev

Others say that the meaning of our verse is as follows: You are found amidst the praise of Israel and You are the Holy one who is praised.[21] It is similar to *For great is the Holy One of Israel in the midst of thee* (Is. 12:6).

5. IN THEE DID OUR FATHERS TRUST; THEY TRUSTED AND THOU DIDST DELIVER THEM.

IN THEE DID OUR FATHERS TRUST. When our ancestors were at ease, they trusted in You and were secure. When they were in trouble, they trusted in You and You delivered them.

6. UNTO THEE THEY CRIED, AND ESCAPED; IN THEE DID THEY TRUST, AND WERE NOT ASHAMED.

UNTO THEE THEY CRIED. Our fathers cried only to You. They did not rely on others. They therefore were not ashamed.

7. BUT I AM A WORM, AND NO MAN; A REPROACH OF MEN, AND DESPISED OF THE PEOPLE.

BUT I AM A WORM, AND NO MAN. It is very unlikely that an intelligent person would say, "I am no man" about himself. On the contrary David speaks on behalf of his enemies.[22] His enemies insult him. They do not think that he is of any worth.

8. ALL THEY THAT SEE ME LAUGH ME TO SCORN; THEY SHOOT OUT THE LIP, THEY SHAKE THE HEAD.

ALL THEY THAT SEE ME LAUGH ME TO SCORN. The word *la'ag* (scorn) in all of its forms is always connected to a *lamed*.[23]

---

tehillot yisra'el) to mean as follows: You are enthroned forever and are the praises of Israel. I.E. disagrees, for *yoshev* is connected to *tehillot yisra'el.*

21. Our verse literally reads: *And You are holy* (ve-attah kadosh), *enthroned prayers of Israel* (yoshev tehillot yisra'el). This commentator interprets this as, *You are the Holy One who is found amidst the praise of Israel.*

22. David's enemies consider him a worm and subhuman.

23. Our verse reads, *yilag li* (laugh me to scorn). Hence I.E. points out that the word *la'ag* is always followed by *li* (to me), *lo* (to him), *lehkha* (to you), or the like.

THEY SHOOT OUT THE LIP, THEY SHAKE THE HEAD. The word *yaftiru* (they shoot out) means, they open. Compare, *peter*[24] *rechem* (openeth the womb) (Ex. 13:12).[25]

The *bet* placed in front of the word *safah* (lip) is there for poetic purposes.[26] It is like the *bet* of *ve-lachmi* (of my bread) in *eat of my bread* (Prov. 9:5). It is also possible that a word has been omitted from our verse.[27]

9. LET HIM COMMIT HIMSELF UNTO THE LORD! LET HIM RESCUE HIM; LET HIM DELVER HIM, SEEING HE DELIGHTETH IN HIM.

LET HIM COMMIT HIMSELF. The word *gol* (let him commit himself) is an adjective[28] in the form of a *po'el*. It is vocalized like *lechom* (warmth) (Hagai 1:6) and *chom* (heat) (1 Sam. 11:11).[29]

Gol is an adjective, for *gol el Adonai* means, one who commits his needs upon the Lord.[30] Compare, *Commit* (gol) *thy way unto the Lord* (Ps. 37:5).[31]

LET HIM DELIVER HIM, SEEING HE DELIGHTETH IN HIM. *He delighteh in him* refers to God.[32] The one who says that the reference is to the one who commits himself unto the Lord[33] errs. Scripture reads: *If the Lord delight in us* (Num. 14:8). There are many other similar verses.[34]

---

24. *Peter* and *yaftiru* come from the same root (*peh, tet, resh*).

25. I.E. renders *yaftiru ve-safah* (they shoot out the lip), they open the lip.

26. The *bet* usually has the meaning of *in* or *with*. Thus *yaftiru ve-safah* would ordinary mean, they open in the lip, or they open with the lip. Each one of these translations makes no sense. Hence I.E. points out that the *bet* placed before *safah* is there for poetic purposes.

27. See Radak who interprets our verse as if written, *yaftiru alai ve-safah,* they send words against me with their lips. In this case the *bet* has its usual meaning.

28. Not a verb. *Gol* looks like a verb. Hence I.E.'s comment.

29. These words are adjectives vocalized with a *cholam.* According to I.E., *gol el Adonai* (let him commit himself unto the Lord) means, *a God committed person,* that is, a person who places his trust in God.

30. Thus *gol* refers to commitment. So too Radak.

31. According to I.E., *gol el Adonai yefaltehu* (Let him commit himself unto the Lord! let Him rescue him) should be interpreted, God will save the person who places his trust in the Lord.

32. Its meaning is, God delights in him.

33. According to this interpretation, *He delighteth in him* means, the God trusting person delights in the Lord.

34. Wherein God is said to take delight in his creatures.

10. FOR THOU ART HE THAT TOOK ME OUT OF THE WOMB; THOU MADEST ME TRUST WHEN I WAS UPON MY MOTHER'S BREAST.

THAT TOOK ME OUT. The word *gochi* (took me out) is either a verb[35] or an adjective.[36] *Gochi* is like[37] *gozi* (make bald) (Micah 1:16). *Gochi* comes from the same root as the word *va-tagach* (and thou didst gush forward) in *And thou didst gush forth with thy rivers* (Ezek. 32:2). *Gochi* is similar[38] to the word *motzi'iy* (that bringeth me forth)(1 Sam. 22:49). The psalmist says: God will deliver the person who commits himself unto the Lord (v. 9); for behold, God took me out of the womb and cared for me when I had no wisdom and no strength.[39]

11. UPON THEE I HAVE BEEN CAST FROM MY BIRTH; THOU ART MY GOD FROM MY MOTHER'S WOMB.

UPON THEE... Its meaning is as follows: I have been cast upon You and not upon my mother's breast, for You feed her and you feed me. You are the one who gave[40] me the strength to receive sustenance until I grew up.[41] Scripture therefore reads: *Thou art my God from my mother's womb.*

12. BE NOT FAR FROM ME; FOR TROUBLE IS NEAR; FOR THERE IS NONE TO HELP.

BE NOT FAR FROM ME; FOR TROUBLE IS NEAR. It is stylish to combine far and near in poetry.[42]

---

35. Meaning, *He that took me out.*

36. According to the latter our verse should be rendered, *Thou art my taker out* (gochi) *of the womb.*

37. Is similar in form.

38. Is similar in meaning.

39. Lit. "When we had no wisdom and no strength."

40. Lit., "gives."

41. And am able to feed myself.

42. Our verse reads: *Be not far.* However, God is never far off. Hence I.E.'s comment.

13. MANY BULLS HAVE ENCOMPASSED ME; STRONG BULLS OF BASHAN HAVE BESET ME ROUND.

Rabbim (many) means, from all sides.[43]

STRONG BULLS OF BASHAN HAVE BESET ME ROUND. The word *abbire* (strong bulls) means, calves. Our verse is similar to *ye kine of Bashan* (Amos 4:1).[44]

HAVE BESET ME ROUND. The word *kitteruni* (have beset me round) comes from the word *keter* (crown) in *the royal crown* (Esther 2:17). The royal crown (keter) is round.[45]

14. THEY OPEN WIDE THEIR MOUTH AGAINST ME, AS A RAVENING AND A ROARING LION.

THEY OPEN WIDE THEIR MOUTH. The word *patzu* (they open wide) means, they open. It is like *patzetah* (open) in *and the ground open her mouth* (Num. 22:30).
The word *aryeh* (lion) should be read as if written, *ke-aryeh* (as a lion).[46] It is similar to *esh okhelah* (a devouring fire) (Deut. 9:3).[47]
Our verse says that the above-mentioned bulls[48] tear apart and roar like lions.

15. I AM POURED OUT LIKE WATER, AND ALL MY BONES ARE OUT OF JOINT; MY HEART IS BECOME LIKE WAX; IT IS MELTED IN MINE INNERMOST PARTS.

I AM POURED OUT LIKE WATER. This is metaphoric. The psalmist[49] is so frightened that he is like spilled water that cannot be gathered. His organs are scattered and his bones, which are the body's foundation, have come apart. His heart has melted within him as if he lost his mind.

---

43. According to I.E., our clause means, many bulls have encompassed me on all sides.

44. *The kine of Bashen* refers to the evil women of Bashen. Similarly here the phrase *strong bulls of Bashen* is not to be taken literally. It is a metaphor for evil people.

45. Similarly *kitteruni* means have surrounded me.

46. Lit. "A *kaf* has been omitted from *aryeh*." Our verse literally reads: *They open their mouth against me, a ravening, a roaring lion.* Hence I.E.'s comment.

47. *Esh okhelah* should be read as if written, *ke-esh okhelah,* as a devouring fire.

48. Lit. "These bulls." The bulls mentioned in verse 13.

49. Lit., "he."

16. MY STRENGTH IS DRIED UP LIKE A POTSHERD; AND MY TONGUE CLEAVETH TO MY THROAT; AND THOU LAYEST ME IN THE DUST OF DEATH.

The psalmist cannot speak.[50] One of the Geonim therefore[51] said that *kochi* (my strength) is a scrambled form of the word *chikki* (my palate).[52] However in my opinion the natural moisture that is in the body unites it and sustains it. Hence the body's moisture is referred to as strength. Look, the psalmist complains that he is dry like an old man who is advanced in age.[53] The word *malkochai* (my throat) is related to the word *u-malkacheha* (and the tongs thereof) (Ex. 25:38) even though it does not follow its paradigm.[54]

AND THOU LAYEST ME IN THE DUST OF DEATH. In the dust of those who are dead.[55] Compare, *And thy mighty in the war* (Is. 3:25).[56] The word *tishpeteni* (and thou layest me) is similar to the word *sefot* (set) in *Set on the Pot* (Ezek. 24:3).[57]

17. FOR DOGS HAVE ENCOMPASSED ME; A COMPANY OF EVILDOERS HAVE INCLOSED ME; LIKE A LION, THEY ARE AT MY HANDS AND MY FEET.

FOR DOGS HAVE ENCOMPASSED ME. David says that a company of evil-doers, have surrounded him. The aforementioned are adversaries and enemies more infuriating[58] and of a lower class then the bulls.[59]

---

50. I.E.'s interpretation of *And my tongue cleaveth to my throat.*

51. So that the first and second part of the verse will be in harmony.

52. *Kochi* and *chikki* are made up of the same consonants, *chet, kaf, yod.* According to the Gaon, the first part of our verse should be rendered: *My palate* (kochi/chikki) *is dried up like a potsherd.*

53. Lit. "However, in my opinion because the natural moisture which unites all and which sustains the body is referred to as strength. Look, he is dry like that which occurs to an old man who is advanced in age."

54. According to I.E., *malkochai* (my throat) refers to the inside of the mouth, which like a tong holds on to the food. He renders our clause: *And my tongue cleaveth to the inside of my mouth* (malkochai).

55. In other words *ve-la'afar mavet* (in the dust of death) is short for *ve-la'afar bene mavet* (in the dust of those who are dead).

56. *And thy mighty in the war* (Is. 3:25) is short for "and thy mighty *by men* of war."

57. So too Rashi.

58. The dogs symbolize brazenness.

59. Mentioned in verse 17.

Like a lion is connected to *encompassed me.* It means; they have enclosed my hands and feet like a lion.[60]

David mentions his hands because he uses them to wage war. He mentions his feet because he can use them to escape.

18. I MAY COUNT ALL MY BONES; THEY LOOK AND GLOAT OVER ME.

I MAY COUNT ALL MY BONES. Some say that the word *asapper* (I may count) is similar to the word *esperem* (I would count them) in *If I would count them, they are more in number than the sand* (Ps. 139:18). The word *yisapper* (number) in *Who can number the clouds by wisdom* (Job 38:37) is similar. *Asapper kol atzmotai* (I may count all my bones) means, I am thin and have no flesh.[61]

However in my opinion David says the following: When I recount (asapper) the number of bones that have separated themselves from me, my enemies laugh.[62] He says this because he had earlier said, *And all my bones are scattered* (v. 15). [63]

The meaning of *yiru vi*[64] is *they gloat over me.*[65] Compare, *le-ra'avah bakh* (that they may gaze upon thee) (Ezek. 28:17).[66]

It is possible that the bones are a metaphor for David's men, who separated themselves from David, when he experienced adversity in war.

19. THEY PART MY GARMENTS AMONG THEM, AND FOR MY VESTURE DO THEY CAST LOTS.

THEY PART. The verse speaks of what is in the mind of David's enemies and what they speak of.[67] They intend to divide David's garments because they are royal garments.

---

60. According to I.E., we should interpret our verse as follows: *For dogs have encompassed me, a company of evildoers; They have enclosed my hands and feet like a lion.*

61. Lit., "that he is thin and has no flesh."

62. I.E. renders our verse: *I tell of my bones; they look and gloat over me.*

63. Translated according to I.E.

64. Lit. "*They gaze upon me.*"

65. Lit., "my enemies laugh."

66. *Yiru* and *ra'avah* come from the same root, *resh, alef, heh*

67. In other words, *They part my garments* means, they intend to part my garments and speak of parting my garments. David's enemies never divided up David's garments. Hence I.E.'s interpretation.

If David was not king, their words would not make sense.[68] The verse is a hint.[69]

20. BUT THOU, O LORD, BE NOT FAR OFF; O THOU MY STRENGTH, HASTEN TO HELP ME.

BUT THOU… MY STRENGTH. My strength refers to God.[70] Do not ask: How could David call out that God is his strength, his light, his salvation and his help, when all of these are accidents?[71] The answer is: David wants to declare the might of the power from above[72] that he accepted.[73]

21. DELIVER MY SOUL FROM THE SWORD; MINE ONLY ONE FROM THE POWER OF THE DOG.

DELIVER MY SOUL FROM THE SWORD. For *A company of evildoers have inclosed me* (v. 17).

MINE ONLY ONE FROM THE POWER OF THE DOG. For *dogs have encompassed me* (ibid).

22. SAVE ME FROM THE LION'S MOUTH; YEA, FROM THE HORNS OF THE WILD-OXEN DO THOU ANSWER ME.

SAVE ME FROM THE LION'S MOUTH. David said that his enemy acted *As a raven-ing and a roaring lion* (v. 14). He therefore now says, *Save me from the lion's mouth.* The meaning of *mine only one* (v. 21) is, my soul. The soul is referred to in this manner because the soul of every person is unique and apart in its body from the soul of all.[74] When it separates itself from its body it joins the all.[75]

---

68. Otherwise, why would David's enemies want David's garments?

69. That David's enemies wanted to depose and replace David.

70. The second part of our verse literally reads, *My strength, hasten to help me.* Hence I.E.'s interpretation.

71. Our text of I.E. reads *makdim.* This is an obvious error for *mikrim* (accidents). See Filwarg and *Ha-Keter.* Accidents refer to the properties of substance such as an object's color, shape and viscosity. God is beyond the accidents.

72. *The power from above* refers to God.

73. David declares that God's acts are mighty. Thus strength is an attribute of action. It does not apply to God's essence. See Chapter 54 of Maimonides' *Guide for the Perplexed.*

74. The reference is probably to the universal soul.

75. The universal soul.

The horns of the *remim* (wild-oxen) are stronger than all other horns. Hence Scripture reads: *from the horns of the wild -oxen.*[76]

I have heard people saying that the *re'em* (wild-ox) throws itself from a high mountain. It falls on its horns and they do not break.

The word *remim* is missing an *alef.*[77] It is similar to the word *chemah* (butter)[78] in *When my steps were washed with butter* (Job 29:6).

Anitani[79] (do Thou answer me) means, do Thou answer me as you did in times past, for you acted kindly towards me in the past, when I was in similar adversity.

From the horns of the wild-ox means, I am, as it were, on the horns of a wild-ox.

Some say that the horns of the *re'am* (wild-ox) are higher than all other horns. *But my horn hast Thou exalted like the horn of the wild-ox* (re'em) (Ps. 92:11) is proof of this.

You answered me[80] is in contrast to *I call by day, but Thou answerest not* (v. 3).

23. I WILL DECLARE THY NAME UNTO MY BRETHERIN; IN THE MIDST OF THE CONGREGATION WILL I PRAISE THEE.

I WILL DECLARE THY NAME UNTO MY BRETHERIN. *Asapperah* (I will declare) is in contrast to *asapper* (I relate) in *I relate the number of my bones that have separated from me.* (v. 18).[81]

My bretherin means my confidants.

IN THE MIDST OF THE CONGREGATION WILL I PRAISE THEE. I will praise you with the following: [Ye *that fear the lord, praise him...*(v. 6).]

---

76. Lit. "This is the meaning."

77. The singular of *remim* is *re'em,* thus its plural should be *re'emim.*

78. Which is also missing an *alef.*

79. Lit. "You answered me." Our clause literally reads: *From the horns of the wild oxen you answered me.* Hence I.E.'s interpretation.

80. See note 77.

81. Translated according to I.E. See I.E. on verse 18.

24. YE THAT FEAR THE LORD, PRAISE HIM; ALL YE THE SEED OF JACOB, GLORIFY HIM; AND STAND IN AWE OF HIM, ALL YE THE SEED OF ISRAEL.

YE THAT FEAR THE LORD, PRAISE HIM. The *vav* of *haleluhu*[82] (praise him) refers to *shimkha* (Thy name) that is mentioned in the previous verse.[83]

Ye that fear the Lord refers to non-Jews. Hence the word "all" is not prefaced to it, as it is in the case of *All ye the seed of Jacob.*[84]

David addresses Israel and tells them to stand in awe of God. He says that all of Israel should fear God. Israel should attribute all strength to God. They should do so, even when they over power their enemies.

25. FOR HE HATH NOT DESPISED NOR ABHORRED THE LOWLINESS OF THE POOR; NEITHER HATH HE HID HIS FACE FROM HIM; BUT WHEN HE CRIED UNTO HIM, HE HEARD.

FOR HE HATH NOT DESPISED NOR ABHORRED THE LOWLINESS OF THE POOR. *Ve-lo shikketz* (nor abhorred) means, nor distanced or despised.

The word *enut* (the lowliness of) comes from the word *oni* (affliction).[85] Others say that *enut* is connected to the word *ma'aneh*[86] (answer) in *the answer of the tongue* (Prov. 16:1).[87] *Enut* follows the form of *shevut* (captivity) (Ezek. 29:14).[88]

26. FROM THEE COMETH MY PRAISE IN THE GREAT CONGREGATION; I WILL PAY MY VOWS BEFORE THEM THAT FEAR HIM.

FROM THEE COMETH MY PRAISE. You are the cause and the object of my praise. *My praise* is in keeping with *In the midst of the congregation will I praise Thee* (v. 23).

---

82. Which is a pronominal suffix meaning *him* or *it*. I.E. interprets it here as meaning, *it*.

83. In the previous verse. I.E. interprets our verse as follows: *Ye that fear the Lord, praise his name.*

84. For not all gentiles fear the Lord.

85. According to this interpretation, our verse should be rendered: *For he hath not despised nor abhorred the affliction of the poor.*

86. From the root *ayin, nun, heh.*

87. According to this interpretation, our verse should be rendered: *For He hath not despised nor abhorred the prayer of the poor.*

88. *Enut* is vocalized *sheva (chataf segol), shuruk.* So is *shevut.*

27. LET THE HUMBLE EAT AND BE SATISFIED; LET THEM PRAISE THE LORD THAT SEEK AFTER HIM; MAY YOUR HEART BE QUICKENED FOREVER.

LET THE HUMBLE EAT AND BE SATISFIED. Its meaning is, the humble will eat, rejoice, and be full of great joy when they see that God saved the meek person who has no one to help him.

May your heart be quickened forever means, each man will say to his neighbor, *May your heart be quickened forever.*

The word *yechi* (be quickened) is used in the same sense that the word *va-techi* (revived) is in *the spirit of Jacob their father revived* (Gen. 45: 27), for his heart was, as at it were, dead.[89]

28. ALL THE ENDS OF THE EARTH SHALL REMEMBER AND TURN UNTO THE LORD; AND ALL THE KINDREDS OF THE NATIONS SHALL WORSHIP BEFORE THEE.

ALL THE ENDS OF THE EARTH SHALL REMEMBER. *All the ends of the earth* means, all who hear even though they are at the ends of the earth will remember the wonder[90] that God performed and will turn to serve the Lord. Our verse does not speak of the humble. It therefore reads: *all the kindreds of the nations.*

29. FOR THE KINGDOM IS THE LORD'S; AND HE IS THE RULER OVER ALL THE NATIONS.

FOR THE KINGDOM IS THE LORD'S. They will then admit that the kingdom is the Lord's alone. This verse is also to be interpreted like the verse *and even the prophecy of Oded the prophet* (11 Chron. 15:8). The meaning of the latter is, even *the prophecy, the prophecy of Oded the prophet.*[91] There are many such verses. Our verse is to be interpreted as if written, *For the kingdom is the Lord's and the Lord is ruler over all the nations.*[92]

---

89. *Yechi levavekhem la-ad* (may your heart be quickened forever) literally means; may your heart live forever. Hence I.E.'s interpretation.

90. Lit., "this wonder."

91. 11 Chron. 15:8 literally reads: *And even the prophecy Oded the prophet.* Hence I.E.'s comment.

92. Our verse literally reads: *For the kingdom is the Lord's; and ruler over the earth.* Hence I.E.'s comment.

30. ALL THE FAT ONES OF THE EARTH SHALL EAT AND WORSHIP; ALL THEY THAT GO DOWN TO THE DUST SHALL KNEEL BEFORE HIM, EVEN HE THAT CANNOT KEEP HIS SOUL ALIVE.

ALL THE FAT ONES OF THE EARTH SHALL EAT. This verse is in contrast to *Let the humble eat and be satisfied* (v. 27), for *the fat ones of the earth* refer to those who enjoy themselves in this world. They eat all kinds of fat food. *The fat ones* are the opposite of *the humble*.

The meaning of *All the fat ones shall eat and worship.... [they] shall kneel before him* is: If the fat ones enjoy themselves in this world, they will ultimately bow to God who gathers their spirit at the end of their lives. They will then not have the strength to rebel. Similarly, *All they that go down to the dust* shall bow down before God.

Even he that cannot keep his soul alive is similar to *its branches run over a wall* (Gen. 49:22).[93] Its meaning is, each one of the fat ones[94] will not be able to keep his soul alive.[95] The verse hints that their souls will perish in this world.[96] The latter is in contrast to the humble concerning whom it is said: *May your heart be quickened forever* (v. 27).

31. A SEED SHALL SERVE HIM; IT SHALL BE TOLD OF THE LORD UNTO THE NEXT GENERATION.

A SEED. The *vav* in the word *le-fanav* (before Him)(v. 30) and also the *vav* of *ya'avdennu* (shall serve him) refer back to the Lord in *For the kingdom is the Lord's* (v. 29).

Our verse has the same meaning as *But the mercy of the Lord is from everlasting to everlasting upon them that fear Him* (Ps. 103:17). It is also similar to *The children of Thy servants shall dwell securely, [and their seed shall be established before Thee]* (ibid. 102:29).

The word *asher* (that) is missing from our text, as it is in *levavkhem shalem* (your heart whole) (1 Kings 8:61).[97] Our verse[98] should be read as if written, *zera asher ya'avdennu*

---

93. The meaning of *its branches run over a wall* is, each one of its branches run over the wall. *Banot* (its branches) is a plural. *Tza'adah* (run) is a singular. I.E. explains that the combination of the plural *banot* and the singular *tza'ada*, means, each one of the branches run over the wall.

94. Lit., "not one of them."

95. The first part of the verse is in the plural. The last clause is in the singular. Hence I.E.'s interpretation.

96. Their souls will cease to exist after they die.

97. *Levavekhem shalem* should be read as if written, *levavekhem asher shalem*.

98. Which reads, *zera ya'avdennu* (a seed shall serve him).

(a seed that shall serve Him).[99] The reference is to the children of the humble mentioned above.

The meaning of *la-dor* is, the next generation.[100] Hence They *shall come* (v. 32) follows. It is similar to *One generation passeth away, and another generation commeth* (Ecc.1: 4).[101]

32. THEY SHALL COME AND SHALL DECLARE HIS RIGHTEOUSNESS UNTO A PEOPLE THAT SHALL BE BORN, THAT HE HATH DONE IT.

UNTO A PEOPLE THAT SHALL BE BORN. *Unto a people that shall be born* refers to the third generation.

His righteousness is similar to *his[102] righteousness endureth forever* (Ps. 112:9). The latter also refers to this world.[103]

---

99. God. I.E. reads our verse as follows: *It will told of the Lord unto the next generation, what he did to the seed that serves Him.* So Filwarg.

100. *La-dor* literally means, to the generation. Our clause thus literally reads: *It shall be told of the Lord unto the generation.* Hence I.E.'s comment.

101. In other words *la-dor* (to the generation) is short for *le-dor ha-ba* (to the coming generation).

102. The God fearing man.

103. Not only in the word to come. See Radak on Ps. 112:2. Our verse which reads, *They shall come and declare His righteousness unto a people that shall be born* is similar to *his righteousness endureth for ever,* for both verses speak of God's lasting acts of righteousness to the descendents of the pious.

CHAPTER 23

1. A PSALM OF DAVID. THE LORD IS MY SHEPHERD; I SHALL NOT WANT.

This is a very precious psalm. David compared himself to a lamb that relies on the shepherd. David says: Behold, God is my shepherd. I therefore do not lack anything. *Lo echsar* (I do not want) means; I do not lack anything that I need. *Echsar* (want) is similar to *male* (full).[1]

2. HE MAKETH ME TO LIE DOWN IN GREEN PASTURES; HE LEADETH ME BESIDE THE STILL WATERS.

IN GREEN PASTURES. The meaning of *He maketh me to lie down in green pastures* is that the lamb finds grass when it lies down. The grass is found in a place that is close by, so that the lamb does not tire itself out in the mountains looking for pasture

HE LEADETH ME BESIDE THE STILL WATERS. David makes mention of the still waters. The still waters are the reverse of *an overflowing stream* (Is. 30:28).[2]

3. HE RESTORETH MY SOUL; HE GUIDETH ME IN STRAIGHT PATHS FOR HIS NAMES SAKE.

HE RESTORETH MY SOUL. David notes that the shepherd does not urgently drive the lamb from pasture to pasture. On the contrary the shepherd calms (yeshovev) its soul

---

1. "I am full (male)" is not a complete statement. It does not tell us what the individual is satiated with. Hence one has to complete the sentence and say, I am full of food or the like. The same applies to the word *chaser* (lacking). If a person says *lo echsar* I do not want, one does not know what that person does not lack. Hence *lo echsar* should be interpreted *lo echsar kelum*, I do not lack anything. See Filwarg.

2. God leads David by still waters rather than by torrential streams.

in tranquility (be-shuvah)[3] *and rest* (Is. 30:15).[4]

[HE GUIDETH ME IN STRAIGHT PATHS FOR HIS NAMES SAKE.]

He guideth me in straight[5] paths means, He does not lead me upon the high mountains and in valleys.

God does not act in this manner for my sake. He acts in this manner for His name's sake. He guides me *in straight paths* so that His name will be declared all over the world.[6] It will be related to all, that God is a good and merciful shepherd and there is none like Him.

4. YEA, THOUGH I WALK THROUGH THE VALLEY OF THE SHADOW OF DEATH, I WILL FEAR NO EVIL, FOR THOU ART WITH ME; THY ROD AND THY STAFF, THEY COMFORT ME.

YEA, THOUGH I WALK THROUGH THE VALLEY OF THE SHADOW OF DEATH. David compares the evil that comes upon the world to *the valley of the shadow of death.* The following is the meaning of our verse: *I will not fear* when the decrees from heaven that God decreed from the days of old for evil to come upon the world come to pass. I am not afraid that harm shall come upon me, for Your rod directs me towards the way that I should take in order to escape. This is the rod and the staff that David comforts his heart in. The meaning of the aforementioned is, when an evil year comes upon the world, God will arrange things, so that those who take refuge in Him shall survive. He will keep them alive in time of hunger and will save them from death, that is, from an unnatural death such as death in war or death from plague.

5. THOU PREPAREST A TABLE BEFORE ME IN THE PRESENCE OF MINE ENEMIES; THOU HAST ANNOINTED MY HEAD WITH OIL; MY CUP RUNNETH OVER.

THOU PREPAREST A TABLE BEFORE ME IN THE PRESENCE OF MINE EN-EMIES. In contrast to *the valley of the shadow of death. The valley of the shadow of death* is similar to the *gloom of anguish* (Is. 8:22).[7]

---

3. Translated according to I.E.

4. I.E. connects the word *yeshovev* (he restoreth) to the word *shuvah* (tranquility). He thus interprets *nafshi yeshovev* (He restoreth my soul) as, He calms my soul.

5. Hebrew, *be-magle tzedek.* Literally, in righteous steps. Hence I.E.'s explanation.

6. See Ex. 9:16.

7. In other words *ge tzalmavet* (the valley of the shadow of death) means, a dark valley (Filwarg).

Note, the *table* is parallel to the *green pastures. My cup runneth* over is parallel to *the still waters* (v. 2).[8]

Revayah (runneth over) is an adjective.[9] *Revayah* (runneth over) is similar to *chakhamah* (wise)[10] in *a wise women* (11 Sam. 14:2).

My head is, at it were, anointed with fresh oil, because it is fattened from the fat of the dainties that are on the table.

This psalm speaks of the servants of the Lord who forsake all the pleasures of this world and are satisfied with their lot. They consider bread and water the equivalent of the delights provided by any and all dainties, for their thoughts and hearts are directed to the pleasures of the world to come. Hence they forsake the pleasures of the moment for the eternal pleasures. David therefore said: *Surely* my only thought is that *goodness and mercy shall follow me all the days of my life; And I shall dwell in the house of the Lord for ever* (v 6).

Goodness and mercy shall follow me means, I shall train my self to do goodness and kindness,[11] that is, goodness to myself and kindness to others. I will teach and instruct people to serve God. I will be so habituated to act in this manner, that even if I wanted to stop doing good for even one moment, then the good would pursue me.

Ve-shavti (and I shall dwell) means, I shall return time and time again.[12] *Ve-shavti* is similar to the word *shav* (return)[13] in *Every one returns in his course* (Jer. 8:6).[14]

Some say[15] that *ve-shavti* means; I shall be tranquil. *Ve-shavti* is similar to *shuvah* (tranquility)[16] in; *in tranquility and rest shall ye be saved* (Is. 30:15).[17]

The meaning of our verse thus is as follows: I shall always do good and kindness. I will spend my entire life in God's house so that I will recognize the Lord's deeds. This is a true prayer,[18] for the individual is then isolated from people.

---

8. The idea is the same, though the metaphor changes.

9. The meaning of *revayah* is, saturated.

10. *Chakhamah* is an adjective. Both words are similarly vocalized.

11. The Hebrew term *chesed* (mercy) means, kindness or mercy.

12. According to I.E. our verse should be rendered: *And I shall keep on returning to the house of God forever.*

13. For the root of *ve-shavti* is *shin, vav, bet.*

14. Translated according to I.E.

15. Lit. "Others say."

16. The root of *shuvah* is *shin, vav, bet.*

17. Translated according to I.E. According to this interpretation our clause should be rendered: *And I will be tranquil in the house of the Lord.*

18. This is what a person should truly pray for.

CHAPTER 24

1. A PSALM OF DAVID. THE EARTH IS THE LORD'S, AND THE FULLNESS THEREOF; THE WORLD, AND THEY THAT DWELL THERIN.

2. FOR HE HATH FOUNDED IT UPON THE SEAS; AND ESTABLISHED IT UPON THE FLOODS.

FOR HE HATH FOUNDED IT UPON THE SEAS. There are places[1] upon the earth that receive power from above as in, *and this is the gate of heaven* (Gen. 28:17). David therefore opens his psalm with *The earth is the Lord's.* He does so, because our psalm speaks *of the mountain of the Lord* (v. 3).[2]

The earth is the Lord's means, according to the laws of nature the earth was created to be below the waters.[3] However God willed that some of the land dry up.[4] This is the half of the earth that is revealed.[5] Hence Scripture states: *For He hath founded it upon the seas.* Rabbi Moses says that the meaning of *al* (upon) is *with*, as in *And they came, the men with* (al) *the women* (Ex.35: 22).[6] The meaning of our verse is that the earth was not created

---

1. Lit. "Because there are places."

2. I.E.'s point is, even though all the earth belongs to God, there are places where His presence is more manifest than others. Radak.

3. When God first created the earth, it was covered with water. See Gen. 1:1,2. According to medieval science there are four elements, fire, air, water, and earth. Earth is the heaviest element. Hence its place is below the water. See I.E. on Genesis 1:1.

4. It took a special act of Divine providence for the dry land to appear. Hence *The earth is the Lord's,* that is, God is its master.

5. The other half is below the waters as required by the laws of nature.

6. According to Rabbi Moses, our verse should be rendered: *For He has founded it with the seas, and established it with the rivers/floods.*

in a way that would allow for people to dwell upon its entire surface.[7] It was created with seas and rivers surrounding it.[8]

Ben Balaam[9] says that the meaning of our verse is that the land is not far from a river or a sea.[10]

3. WHO SHALL ASCEND INTO THE MOUNTAIN OF THE LORD? AND WHO SHALL STAND IN HIS HOLY PLACE?

WHO SHALL ASCEND INTO THE MOUNTAIN OF THE LORD. *The mountain of the Lord* refers to Mount Moriah.[11]

David composed this psalm after he bought[12] the threshing floor of Aruanah the Jebusite.[13]

AND WHO SHALL STAND IN HIS HOLY PLACE. This means, who shall dwell in it?[14]

4. HE THAT HATH CLEAN HANDS, AND A PURE HEART; WHO HATH NOT TAKEN MY NAME IN VAIN, AND HATH NOT SWORN DECEITFULLY.

CLEAN HANDS. Scripture speaks of *clean hands,* because the hands perform all actions. *He that hath clean hands* means, he who has done no evil. In addition to not doing evil the person who shall ascend the mountain of God must have a pure heart. The latter is what is most important.

---

7. Lit. "The meaning of our verse is that the earth was not originally created in a united form allowing for people to dwell upon all of it."

8. It was originally covered with water. See Gen. 1:2.

9. The reference is probably to Judah ben Balaam. See I.E. on Ps. 10:14.

10. Ben Balaam apparently renders *al* near. He translates our verse as follows: *For he has founded it near the seas, and established it alongside the rivers.*

11. Where the temple stood.

12. Lit., "after the incident."

13. See 11 Sam. 2:24. The threshing floor of Arunah was on Mt. Moriah. The Temple was there erected. Before David bought this threshing floor, the mount of God was not in Jewish hands. Hence I.E.'s comment. See I.E. on Ps. 15:1

14. In other words *yakum* (stand) is to be interpreted as, dwell. See Ps. 15:1.

Nafshi (My name)[15] refers to God's very glory. Compare, *The Lord… hath sworn by Himself* (be-nafsho)[16] (Amos 6:8). Our text euphemistically reads *nafshi* (my soul).[17] It so reads out of respect for God.[18] It is like *that I and my son Solomon shall be counted offenders* (1 Kings 1:21).[19] I have already explained this.[20]

Observe, our verse mentions deeds,[21] heart,[22] and speech.[23]

5. HE SHALL RECEIVE A BLESSING FROM THE LORD; AND RIGHTEOUSNESS FROM THE GOD OF HIS SALVATION.

HE SHALL RECEIVE A BLESSING. *Yissa berakha* (He shall receive a blessing) was said in contrast to *lo nasa la-shav nafshi* (who hath not taken My name in vain).[24]

6. SUCH IS THE GENERATION[25] OF THEM THAT SEEK AFTER HIM; THAT SEEK THY FACE, EVEN JACOB. SELAH.

SUCH IS THE GENERATION. The allusion is to the generation in whose days the temple was built. This occurred after David's death.

David then[26] turns to God and says, this generation is a generation that seeks Your face.[27]

SELAH. In truth.[28] *Ya'akov selah* (even Jacob. Selah) means, *they are* truly *the seed of Jacob*. There is a commentator who says that our clause should be read as if written, *even the God of Jacob. Selah*. However, his interpretation is unnecessary.

---

15. The literal meaning of *nafshi* is my life or my soul. According to I.E., God's life or God's soul means God's glory.

16. Lit. "By His soul."

17. It should read *nafsho*, His (God's) life, for David is the speaker.

18. It would be disrespectful for David to say, who has not taken (sworn by) God's life in vain.

19. What Bath Sheba meant was, you David will be guilty. However, she used the first person out of respect for the king.

20. In I.E.'s now lost commentary on Kings.

21. Hands.

22. Heart is a synonym for thought.

23. *Hath not sworn falsely*. Man functions on these three levels. According to I.E. the commandments are observed in three ways, by deeds, by speech and thought. See Chap. 7 of the *Yesod Mora*.

24. *Yissa* and *nasa* come from the same root. Hence I.E.'s comment.

25. Lit. "This is the generation." Hence I.E.'s comment.

26. After addressing Israel.

27. Hence the change from third to first person.

28. See I.E. on Ps. 4:3.

7. LIFT UP YOUR HEADS, O YE GATES, AND BE LIFTED UP, YE EVERLASTING DOORS; THAT THE KING OF GLORY MAY COME IN.

LIFT UP YOUR HEADS. The sages of the Talmud of blessed memory say[29] that this alludes to the entrance of the ark into the holy of holies.[30] Hence Scripture above states, *in His holy place* (v. 3).

That which David says to the gates is to be taken metaphorically.[31] Its meaning is that the place where the ark is positioned is established and exalted above all high mountains,[32] for God's glory rests there.

Scripture speaks of *gates* and *everlasting doors,* because there were many doors and gates in the temple.[33]

Pitche olam (everlasting doors) means, the doors that are everlasting because of the glory of God's presence.[34]

Scripture speaks of *the King of glory,* for the glory of the Temple was great because of God.

8. WHO IS THE KING OF GLORY? THE LORD STRONG AND MIGHTY, THE LORD MIGHTY IN BATTLE.

WHO IS THE KING OF GLORY? Should some one ask: *Who is the King of glory?* The answer will be: *The Lord strong and mighty.* The latter means, the Lord shows his might in His deeds and He fights on behalf of His holy ones.

The meaning of our verse is, when God's glory rests amidst Israel, Israel dwells in security, for they do not fear their enemies.

---

29. Lit. "The ancient ones."

30. See Sabbath 30a.

31. One does not talk to gates.

32. See Is. 2:2.

33. Fillwarg believes that the words "and everlasting doors" are the result of a scribal error. Our text of I.E. should read: Scripture reads *gates* because there were many gates in the temple.

34. Lit. "The glory of God's glory."

9. LIFT UP YOUR HEADS, O YE GATES, YEA LIFT THEM UP, YE EVERLASTING DOORS; THAT THE KING OF GLORY MAY COME IN.

LIFT UP YOUR HEADS, O YE GATES. Scripture repeats itself.[35] This alludes to the return of God's glory when the redeemer[36] comes, for God's glory was not manifest in the second temple.[37]

The first *your heads*[38] also applies to the next clause. The latter should be read as if written, *Yea lift up your heads, O ye everlasting doors.*[39]

10. WHO THEN IS THE KING OF GLORY? THE LORD OF HOSTS; HE IS THE KING OF GLORY. SELAH.

WHO THEN IS THE KING OF GLORY? This is added[40] because the third temple will last forever. Scripture does not here state, *The Lord mighty in battle*[41] because *they shall beat their swords into plowshares* (Is. 2: 4) and all war will disappear from the earth.[42] Our verse refers to God as *The Lord of hosts,* because the people of that generation[43] will be like angels of God.[44]

The phrase *The Lord of hosts* should be understood as follows: God is referred to as the Lord of hosts because of the hosts of heaven. He is not so referred to because of the hosts of Israel, as the Gaon[45] maintains. I have already explained the meaning of *The Lord of hosts.*[46]

---

35. Verse 9 repeats verse 7.

36. The messiah.

37. In other words, verse 7 deals with the first temple and verse 9 with the messianic era.

38. In our verse.

39. Our verse literally reads: *Lift up your heads, O ye gates, And lift up ye everlasting doors.* It should be interpreted as if written, *Lift up your heads, O ye gates, And lift up your heads, ye everlasting doors.*

40. In other words our verse repeats verse 8.

41. As it does in verse 8.

42. In the messianic era.

43. The generation of the messiah.

44. According to I.E., *Lord of hosts* means, Lord over the angels. Hence his interpretations. See I.E. on Gen. 1:1.

45. Rabbi Saadiah Gaon.

46. See I.E. on Gen. 1:1; 26.

CHAPTER 25

1. [A PSALM] OF DAVID. UNTO THEE, O LORD, DO I LIFT UP MY SOUL.

Rabbi Moses says that *nafshi essa* (I lift up my soul) means, I offer my soul as a gift.[1] *Essa* (I lift up) in our verse is similar to *va-yissa*[2] *masot* (and portions[3] were taken) (Gen. 43:34). However, in my opinion our verse is similar to *and setteth* (nose) *his heart upon it* (Deut. 24:15).[4] The following is the meaning of our verse: *Unto You O Lord do I set my soul* and not to any one else.

2. O MY GOD, IN THEE HAVE I TRUSTED, LET ME NOT BE ASHAMED; LET NOT MINE ENEMIES TRIUMPH OVER ME.

O MY GOD, IN THEE HAVE I TRUSTED. It is possible that the *bet* of *be-kha ba-tachti* (In Thee have I trusted) is in place of the *bet* with which our verse should have opened.[5] It is similar to the *vav* of *vi-lammedeni* (and teach me) (v. 5), which is in place of the *vav* [with which verse six should have opened]. On the other hand it is possible that such is the case.[6]

[David said:] Behold. I have trusted in You. It is unfitting for me to be ashamed.[7]

---

1. I.E. renders our clause as follows: *Unto Thee, O Lord, do I offer up my soul as a gift.* See *Metzudat David*.

2. *Va-yissa* and *essa* come from the same root.

3. Gifts.

4. In other words, *nafshi essa* (I lift up my soul) means, I set my soul.

5. The verses in our psalm follow the order of the alphabet. However, there is no verse opening with a *bet* or a *vav*. Hence I.E.'s comment.

6. That a *bet* and a *vav* do not open any verse in our psalm.

7. In other words, *al evoshah (let me not be ashamed)* means, it is unfitting for me to be ashamed.

3. YEA, NONE THAT WAIT FOR THEE SHALL BE ASHAMED; THEY SHALL BE ASHAMED THAT DEAL TREACHEROUSLY WITHOUT CAUSE.

YEA… The truth is, it is fitting that those who deal treacherously without cause be ashamed.

The word *rekam* means, without cause. The *mem* is superfluous.[8]

4. SHOW ME THY WAYS, O LORD; TEACH ME THY PATHS.

THY WAYS. *Thy ways* refers to the ways of God and of nature that He brought into being by employing the ways of wisdom.

Teach me Thy paths means, teach me Thy paths that You revealed by the hand of the prophet.[9] The reference is to the ways that God commanded us to walk in.

5.GUIDE ME IN THY TRUTH, AND TEACH ME; FOR THOU ART THE GOD OF MY SALVATION; FOR THEE DO I WAIT ALL THE DAY.

GUIDE ME IN THY TRUTH. This is an important verse. In it[10] David Asks God to help him walk in the way of truth until he is habituated to walk in this way.[11]

Ve-lammedeni (and teach me) is similar in meaning to *limmud* (used to) in *A wild ass used* (limmud) *to the wilderness* (Jer. 2:24) and to *limmud* (trained) in as *a calf untrained* (lo lummad) (Jer. 31:18).[12]

For Thou art the God of my salvation; For Thee do I wait all day means, You save me from all things that hinder me from walking in the path of truth, for I have no one to wait for but you.

---

8. The *mem* has no meaning.

9. Moses.

10. Lit., "its meaning is."

11. Without Divine aid.

12. Thus the meaning of *ve-lammedeni* (and teach me) is, and train me. I.E. renders our clause as follows: Guide me in Thy truth and train me [in Thy truth].

6. REMEMBER O LORD, THY COMPASSIONS AND THY MERCIES; FOR THEY HAVE BEEN FROM OF OLD.

REMEMBER O LORD. David seeks God's compassions and mercies so that the Lord will not punish him for his earlier deeds that till now prevented him to truly understand the ways of God. Hence that which follows in the next verse.

7. REMEMBER NOT THE SINS OF MY YOUTH, NOR MY TRANSGRESSIONS; ACCORDING TO THY MERCY REMEMBER THOU ME, FOR THY GOODNESS SAKE, O LORD.

THE SINS… NOR MY TRANSGRESSIONS. *Pesha* (transgressions) refers to acts that signify that the trespasser has removed himself from God's authority.[13] *For every matter of trespass* (pesha) (Ex. 22:8) is proof of this.[14]

According to Thy mercy Remember Thou me, For Thy goodness sake O, Lord means, I ask the aforementioned of You because You are the source of mercy[15] and the fountain of the good.[16] Hence that which follows [in the next verse].

9. GOOD AND UPRIGHT IS THE LORD; THEREFORE DOTH HE INSTRUCT SINNERS IN THE WAY.

GOOD. The *bet* in the word *ba-derekh* (in the way) is vocalized with a *pattach*[17] because it refers to the ways of God.[18]

David asks God to show him where the way of God way begins.[19]

Note the following: God shows the sinners the right path. He guides the humble in His paths and trains them therein[20] until it becomes their law and statute.[21]

---

13. It refers to sins committed with the intention of rebelling against God.

14. Ex. 22:28 deals with theft, the removal of property from its owners.

15. Lit., "the mercy."

16. I.E.'s paraphrase of *for Thy goodness sake.*

17. The *pattach* beneath the *bet* indicates the definite article.

18. In other words *the way* (ba-derekh) refers to the way of God.

19. Lit. "When (ka'asher) Your way Lord begins, make it known to me." Perhaps we should read *ba'asher* in place of *ka'asher.*

20. I.E.'s interpretation of verse 9.

21. It becomes their second nature.

10. ALL THE PATHS OF THE LORD ARE MERCY AND TRUTH UNTO SUCH AS KEEP HIS COVENANT AND HIS TESTIMONIES.

ALL THE PATHS OF THE LORD ARE MERCY AND TRUTH. First *mercy* then *truth*.[22] UNTO SUCH AS KEEP HIS COVENANT. The word *notzere* (keep) is used in the same way that *notzer* (keeping) is in *Keeping* (notzer) *mercy unto the thousandth generation* (Ex. 34:7).[23]

11. FOR THY NAME'S SAKE, O LORD, PARDON MINE INIQUITY, FOR IT IS GREAT.

FOR THY NAME'S SAKE... FOR IT IS GREAT. *Ki rav hu* (for it is great) means *even though it is great*.[24] It is similar to *ki am keshe oref* (for it is a stiff-necked people) (Ex. 34:9)[25] and to *ki chatati lakh* (for I have sinned against Thee) (Ps. 41:5).[26] Some say that *For Thy name's sake* means, so that I will make Your name known. However its correct meaning is, so that it will come to be known that Your name is "Forgiver."

12. WHAT MAN IS HE THAT FEARETH THE LORD? HIM WILL HE INSTRUCT IN THE WAY THAT HE SHOULD CHOOSE.

WHAT MAN IS HE. *Ish* (man) refers to an important man. Compare, *and show thyself a man* (ish)[27] (1 Kings 2:2). The meaning of our verse is, the fear of God will bring man[28] to the way that he should choose.[29]

---

22. Our text mentions mercy before truth because it recalls *keeping mercy unto the thousandth generation.* See next note.

23. In other words our verse is similar to Ex. 34:7. God will keep (notzer) mercy to those who keep (notzere) his covenant (Filwarg).

24. *Ki* usually means *for, if* or *when.* Hence I.E. points out that its meaning here is *even though.* I.E. comments thus because he does not believe that David would say, pardon my iniquity for it is great.

25. I. E. renders Ex: 34:9, *even though it is a stiff-necked people.*

26. I.E. renders Ps. 41:5, even *though* (ki) *I have sinned against Thee.*

27. The meaning of which is, and show thyself to be a worthy man.

28. Lit., him.

29. I.E. renders our verse as follows: *Who is an important Man? The fear of God will instruct him in the way that he should choose.* He interprets it as meaning, who is an important man? He whom the fear of God instructs to chose the proper path.

13. HIS SOUL SHALL ABIDE IN PROSPERITY; AND HIS SEED SHALL INHERIT THE LAND.

HIS SOUL. The word *nafsho* (his soul) is similar in meaning to the words *nefesh* and *nafsho* in *For as to the soul (nefesh) of all flesh, the blood thereof is all one with the soul thereof* (nafsho) (Lev. 17:11).[30] The *nefesh* refers to the soul that dies when the rational soul (neshamah) separates from the body.[31]

The meaning of *talin* (abide) is, lie down.[32]

The meaning of *His soul shall lie down in prosperity*[33] is, he will enjoy this world until the day of his death.

Others say that *His soul shall lie down in prosperity* alludes to the life of the [rational] soul. It will enjoy the good.[34]

14. THE COUNSEL OF THE LORD IS WITH THEM THAT FEAR HIM; AND HIS COVENANT, TO MAKE THEM KNOW IT.

The secrets of God are revealed[35] only to those who fear the Lord. This will certainly be the case after their[36] *soul shall abide in prosperity*.[37] Scripture reads: *with them that fear Him*. The latter means, when they begin to fear the Lord.

15. MINE EYES ARE EVER TOWARD THE LORD; FOR HE WILL BRING FORTH MY FEET OUT OF THE NET.

It appears to me that the net in *my feet out of the net* refers to the lust of the evil inclination. The soul (neshamah) is caught in the net of lust. The term *net* is used metaphorically. The psalmist does not have the power to escape from the evil one[38] with out God's help. Hence our verse reads; *He will bring forth [my feet out of the net]*.

---

30. Translated according to I.E.

31. According to I.E. there are three souls in the human body, *neshamah* (rational soul), *ru'ach* (spirit) *and nefesh* (life). Only one, the rational soul (neshamah) survives death. See *The Secret of the Torah*, p. 96.

32. I.E. renders our clause as follows: *His soul shall lie down in prosperity.*

33. Lit., "our verse."

34. For eternity.

35. In this world.

36. Lit. "His."

37. After their deaths. See I.E. on verse 13.

38. The evil inclination.

16. TURN THEE UNTO ME, AND BE GRACIOUS UNTO ME; FOR I AM SOLITARY AND AFFLICTED.[39]

TURN THEE. The soul is solitary.[40] So too the heart. Scripture reads *and poor* because the psalmist[41] lacks the strength to stand up to his lust.

17. THE TROUBLES OF MY HEART ARE ENLARGED; O BRING THOU ME OUT OF MY DISTRESS.

THE TROUBLES OF MY HEART ARE ENLARGED. My heart refers to the intelligence that is implanted in the heart. Hence intelligence is referred to as the heart.[42] *Hirchivu* (are enlarged) is an intransitive verb.[43] Its meaning is, they are many.[44] Others say that *my heart* is the object of *hirchivu*.[45] However, this interpretation is far-fetched, for the text goes on to say, *O bring Thou me out of distress.*[46]

18. SEE MINE AFFLICTION AND MY TRAVAIL; AND FORGIVE ALL MY SINS.

SEE MINE AFFLICTION. *Onyi* (affliction) is derived from *oni* (affliction) (Ps. 107:10).[47] Our clause means; see mine affliction and the much travail that I suffer in keeping myself from giving in to my lusts.

AND FORGIVE ALL MY SINS. Which I committed.[48]

---

39. Translated according to I.E.

40. Man has only one rational soul. Lit. "For the soul is solitary."

41. Lit. "He."

42. See I.E. on Gen. 1:1.

43. *Hirchivu* (are enlarged) is generally transitive. Its usual meaning is, *enlarged.* Thus our clause should be literally rendered: Troubles of my heart enlarged. Hence I.E.'s comment.

44. I.E. renders our clause: *The troubles of my heart are many.*

45. In other words *hirchivu* is transitive. The meaning of our clause is as follows: *The troubles have enlarged my heart,* i.e. the troubles made my heart large so that it could contain a lot of pain (Filwarg).

46. Our clause literally reads: *O bring Thou me out of my straits* (metzukotai). Hence the psalmist does not speak of his heart being "enlarged."

47. It, unlike the word *oni* in verse 16, does not mean poor.

48. Lit., "which he committed"

19. CONSIDER HOW MANY ARE MINE ENEMIES; AND THE CRUEL HATRED WHEREWITH THEY HATE ME.

CONSIDER HOW MANY ARE MINE ENEMIES. Furthermore,[49] I fear my enemies who hate me without reason. I am afraid that they might keep me from learning Your ways.

20. O KEEP MY SOUL, AND DELIVER ME; LET ME NOT BE ASHAMED, FOR I HAVE TAKEN REFUGE IN THEE.

O KEEP MY SOUL... LET ME NOT BE ASHAMED. From my hope of being a servant of the Lord.

21. LET INTEGRITY AND UPRIGHTNESS PRESERVE ME; BECAUSE I WAIT FOR THEE.

INTEGRITY. The integrity of my heart and the uprightness of my deeds will guard me[50] so that I do not walk in a crooked way. It is also possible that the meaning of our clause is, the integrity of David's heart and the uprightness of his deeds will protect David from his enemies. Hence what follows.

22. REDEEM ISRAEL, O GOD. OUT OF ALL HIS TROUBLES.

REDEEM ISRAEL. Just as David prayed that God protect him and that his enemies not rule over him so did he pray that God redeem all of Israel.

---

49. In addition to my affliction, my travail and my sins.

50. Lit., "will guard him."

CHAPTER 26

1. A PSALM OF DAVID. JUDGE ME O LORD, FOR I HAVE WALKED IN MINE INTEGRITY; AND I HAVE TRUSTED IN THE LORD WITHOUT WAVERING.

A PSALM OF DAVID. JUDGE ME O LORD. Rabbi Moses says that *shofteni* (judge me) means, take up my cause and punish my enemies for what they did to me.[1] However, I believe that *shofteni* (judge me) means, punish me[2] if my heart has turned aside from You. *For I have walked in mine integrity* (tummi) is therefore similar to *tamim* (whole-hearted) in *Thou shalt be whole-hearted* (tamim) (Deut. 18:13).[3]

AND I HAVE TRUSTED IN THE LORD WITHOUT WAVERING.[4] I have trusted in the Lord to help me be whole-hearted. Hence I do not waver.

2. EXAMINE ME, O LORD, AND TRY ME; TEST MY REINS AND MY HEART.

EXAMINE ME, O LORD. It is well known that God knows all hidden things. *Tzorfah* [5]... *libbi* (test... my heart) means, for You know my heart[6] like the one who refines silver.[7]

---

1. Rabbi Moses interprets *shofteni* (judge me) as, execute judgment on my behalf.

2. According to I.E., the meaning of *shofteni* (judge me) is, punish me.

3. The word *tummi* can also be translated as, my simplicity. Hence I.E.'s comment.

4. Our verse literally reads: *I have trusted in the Lord. I do not waver.* Hence I.E.'s interpretation.

5. Hebrew, *tzorfah*. Literally, refine or smelt.

6. And reins.

7. I.E. renders our verse: Examine me O Lord, and try me, for you know my heart and reins like a refiner of silver knows his silver.

3. FOR THY MERCY IS BEFORE MINE EYES; AND I HAVE WALKED IN THY TRUTH.

FOR THY MERCY IS BEFORE MINE EYES. I, as it were, always see Your mercies before me.

AND I HAVE WALKED IN THY TRUTH. *Ve-hithallakhti* (and I have walked) means, *I trained myself.*[8] Compare, *Va-yithallekh*[9] *chanoch et ha-elohim* (and Enoch walked with God) (Gen. 5:22).[10]

IN THY TRUTH. In the way of truth.

4. I HAVE NOT SAT WITH MEN OF FALSEHOOD; NEITHER WILL I GO IN WITH DISSEMBLERS.

I HAVE NOT SAT WITH MEN OF FALSEHOOD. Sitting with men of falsehood is the reverse of the way of truth.
NEITHER WILL I GO IN WITH DISSEMBLERS. The word *na'alamim* (dissemblers) is related to the word *ve-ne'elam* (hid) in *the thing being hid* (Deut. 4: 13). *Na'alamim* are people who do unseemly things in secret. Others say that *na'almim* (dissemblers) is connected to the word *elem* (youth), which refers to one who loves levity and sport.

5. I HATE THE GATHERING OF EVIL DOERS, AND WILL NOT SIT WITH THE WICKED.

I HATE THE GATHERING OF EVIL DOERS. The psalm mentions *walking, namely And I have walked* (v. 3). It then mentions *sitting*, namely *I have not sat* (v. 4). It next mentions *going in*, namely *Neither will I go in* (v. 4).[11] I believe that the correct meaning of *Neither will I go in* is, I will not go into their council.[12]

---

8. *Ve-hithallakhti* (and I have walked) is in the *hitpa'el*. It literally means; I will make myself walk. Hence I.E.'s interpretation.

9. *Va-yithallekh* too is in the *hitpa'el*,

10. I.E. explain this as, *and Enoch trained himself to walk with God.* See I.E. on Gen. 5:22.

11. Hebrew, *avo*. Literally, "I will come." Hence I.E.'s comment.

12. See Gen. 49:6:

David once again mentions *And will not sit with the wicked*,[13] for the men of falsehood[14] sin with their lips and the wicked sin by deed.

6. I WILL WASH MY HANDS IN INNOCENCY; SO WILL I COMPASS THINE ALTAR, O LORD.

I WILL WASH MY HANDS IN INNOCENCY. *I will wash my hands in innocency* means; I will not violate any of the negative commandments.[15] I will then *compass Thine altar with burnt offerings.*

7. THAT I MAY MAKE THE VOICE OF THANKSGIVING TO BE HEARD, AND TELL OF ALL THY WONDROUS WORKS.

MAKE… TO BE HEARD. The word *la-shemi'a* (make… to be heard) is to be interpreted as if written, *le-hashmi'a*.[16] The same is the case with the word *la-shemid* (to destroy)[17] in *To destroy the strongholds thereof* (Is. 23:11).
Nifle'otekha (Thy wondrous works) is the object of *lashmi'a* (make to be heard) and *u-le-sapper* (and tell).[18]

8. LORD, I LOVE THE HABITATION OF THY HOUSE, AND THE PLACE WHERE THY GLORY DWELLETH.

I LOVE THE HABITATION OF THY HOUSE. This verse is parallel to *I have not sat with men of falsehood* (v. 4).
Thy house refers to the place of the righteous who serve God's[19] name in truth.
[I love the habitation of Your house,] because the righteous are always there.

---

13. After stating in v. 4, *I have not sat with men of falsehood.*

14. Mentioned in v. 4.

15. Lit. "He did not violate any of the negative commandments."

16. *La-shemi'a* is in the *hifhil*. The usual form of the *hifil* infinitive of this word is *le-hashmi'a.* Hence I.E.'s comment.

17. *La-shemid* is to be interpreted as if written *le-hashmid.*

18. I.E. interprets our verse as follows: *That I may make to be heard Thy wondrous works with the voice of thanksgiving and tell of all Thy wondrous works.*

19. Literally, Your.

[9. GATHER NOT MY SOUL WITH SINNERS, NOR MY LIFE WITH MEN OF BLOOD]

Rabbi Moses says that *Gather not my soul with sinners* means, I pray that my end not be like their end. However, I believe that its meaning is, do not permit things to be so arranged that I spend all of my days with sinners and certainly not with men of blood who are more evil than sinners.

10. IN WHOSE HANDS IS CRAFTINESS; AND THEIR RIGHT HAND IS FULL OF BRIBES.

IN WHOSE HANDS IS CRAFTINESS. They have the ability to plan and arrange things[20] so that they receive bribes of gifts and money. Others say that it means; all of their thoughts are to take with their hands. *And their right hand is full of bribes* means the same. The second part of the verse repeats the first part.

11. BUT AS FOR ME, I WILL WALK IN MINE INTEGRITY; REDEEM ME, AND BE GRACIOUS UNTO ME.

BUT AS FOR ME, I WILL WALK IN MINE INTEGRITY. I will not walk craftily. Scripture states this now because the psalm opened with *I have walked in mine integrity* up till now.[21] David now says: I will continue to walk in my integrity and You will redeem me from their crafty plans.

12. MY FOOT STANDETH IN AN EVEN PLACE; IN THE CONGREGATION WILL I BLESS THE LORD.

MY FOOT. *Be-tummi* (in mine integrity) (v. 11) means, in the wholeness of my heart.
My foot standeth in an even place means, I walk[22] in a straight path.
In my opinion the interpretation of our verses is as follows: For You will redeem me.[23] I shall praise You in the congregation. My feet will stand before them.[24]

---

20. I.E.'s interpretation of *In whose hands is craftiness.*

21. In other words *I have walked in mine integrity* means, I have walked in my integrity until now.

22. Lit., "to walk."

23. Verse 11.

24. I.E.'s interpretation of, *my foot standeth in an even place.*

CHAPTER 27

1. A PSALM OF DAVID. THE LORD IS MY LIGHT AND MY SALVATION; WHOM SHALL I FEAR? THE LORD IS THE STRONGHOLD OF MY LIFE; OF WHOM SHALL I BE AFRAID.

A PSALM OF DAVID. THE LORD IS MY LIGHT AND MY SALVATION; WHOM SHALL I FEAR? Some say *The Lord is my light and my salvation whom shall I fear?* means, the Lord is my light at night when there is no illumination and the soul is frightened.[1] Furthermore, God is my salvation during the day.[2]

Others say that *My light* is connected to things pertaining to the soul; *and my salvation* to things pertaining to the body. *The Lord is the stronghold of my life* pertains to the union[3] of the soul with the body. David therefore does not fear that any man will separate them.

2. WHEN EVILDOERS CAME UPON ME TO EAT UP MY FLESH, EVEN MINE ADVERSARIES AND MY FOES, THEY STUMBLED AND FELL.

WHEN EVILDOERS CAME UPON ME. Some say that the word *be-kerov* (when...came upon me) is connected to the word *kerav* (battle) in *And my fingers for battle* (Ps. 144:1).[4] Others say that *bi-kerov alai* (when...come upon me) means, when they draw close to me.[5]

---

1. Lit., "for the soul is then frightened."

2. These commentators read this verse as follows: *The Lord is my light at night and my salvation during the day; whom shall I fear.*

3. Lit., "the binding."

4. According to this interpretation *bi-kerov alai me-re'im* (when evil-doers came upon me) means, when evildoers wage war against me.

5. According to this interpretation *bi-kerov alai mere'im means,* when evildoers came upon me. The root *kof, resh, bet* can mean to draw close or to wage war. Hence these two interpretations.

Rabbi Moses says *mine adversaries and my foes* means, people who are known as my adversaries and foes.

3. THOUGH A HOST SHOULD ENCAMP AGAINST ME, MY HEART SHALL NOT FEAR; THOUGH WAR SHOULD RISE AGAINST ME, IN THIS DO I TRUST.[6]

THOUGH A HOST SHOULD ENCAMP AGAINST ME. Even if a large camp of gentiles should encamp against me, *My heart shall not fear.* If I have to wage war against them *in this* (be-zot*) do I trust:*[7] I trust that *the Lord is my light and my salvation (v. 1).* Others say that *be-zot* (in this) refers to the request that follows.[8]

4. ONE THING HAVE I ASKED OF THE LORD, THAT WILL I SEEK AFTER: THAT I MAY DWELL IN THE HOUSE OF THE LORD ALL THE DAYS OF MY LIFE, TO BEHOLD THE GRACIOUSNESS OF THE LORD, AND TO VISIT EARLY IN HIS TEMPLE.

ONE THING HAVE I ASKED OF THE LORD. It appears to me that David composed this psalm in his latter days, when his men swore that David would no longer accompany them to war.[9] I will explain this[10] in my comments on *The Lord saith unto my Lord* (Ps. 110:10).

TO BEHOLD THE GRACIOUSNESS OF THE LORD. That the secrets of God's actions that I do not as of yet know [11] will now be revealed to me.[12] Hence David goes on to say the following:

AND TO VISIT EARLY IN HIS TEMPLE. *Le-vakker* (to visit early) is related to the word *yevakker* (inquire) in *He shall not inquire whether it be good or bad* (Lev. 27:33).[13]

6. Translated lit. The Hebrew reads: *be-zot ani bote'ach.*

7. See note 5.

8. In the next verse.

9. See II Sam. 21: 17. Also see Ps. 18 note 1.

10. Lit., "as I will explain."

11. Reading, *ye'da'am.*

12. Literally, "him."

13. I.E. renders our clause: *and to inquire in His temple.*

The meaning of *le-vakker be-hekhalo* (to visit early in his temple) is that the *Kohanim* who are always in the house of God will instruct and teach him.

Others say that the meaning of *le-vakker be-hekhalo* is to go each morning to God's temple.[14] It is similar to *morning and evening* (1 Sam. 17:16).

5. FOR HE CONCEALETH ME IN HIS PAVILION IN THE DAY OF EVIL; HE HIDDETH ME IN THE COVERT OF HIS TENT; HE LIFTETH ME UP UPON A ROCK.

FOR HE CONCEALETH ME. For He conceals me, and my enemies cannot touch me. HIS PAVILION. *Be-sukkoh* (his pavilion) refers to Jerusalem. Compare, *In Salem also is set His tabernacle* (sukkoh) (Ps. 76:3).

IN THE DAY OF EVIL. When the stars[15] are evilly arranged against my[16] star.[17]

[HE LIFTETH ME UP UPON A ROCK.] I will be hidden in the covert of His tent and be as safe as if I were on a high rock.

6. AND NOW SHALL MY HEAD BE LIFTED UP ABOVE MINE ENEMIES ROUND ABOUT ME; AND I WILL OFFER IN HIS TABARNACLE SACRIFICES WITH TRUMPET SOUND; I WILL SING, YEA, I WILL SING PRAISES UNTO THE LORD.

AND NOW SHALL MY HEAD BE LIFTED UP ABOVE MINE ENEMIES. Even though I will from this day on no longer go to war, my head shall be lifted up because I am[18] in the covert of the Most High.[19]

AND I WILL OFFER IN HIS TABERNACLE SACRIFICES WITH TRUMPET-SOUND. As in, *Also in the day of your gladness, ...ye shall blow with trumpets over your burnt-offerings* (Num. 10:10). Such an event occurred in the days of Hezekiah's gladness.[20]

---

14. In other words *le-vakker* is related to the word *boker*.

15. Or planets.

16. Lit. "His."

17. Or planet.

18. Lit. "He is."

19. See Ps. 91:1.

20. See 11 Chron. 29: 20-36.

7. HEAR, O LORD, I CALL WITH MY VOICE; AND BE GRACIOUS UNTO ME AND ANSWER ME.[21]

HEAR, O LORD. The word *asher* (when) is missing in our text.[22] Or the meaning of our text is, this glorious God that I call and mention.[23]

AND BE GRACIOUS UNTO ME AND ANSWER ME. This is a sign that David prayed on behalf of Israel[24] who fought against the enemy. David employed the first person because he prayed on behalf of his men.[25]

8. IN THY BEHALF MY HEART HATH SAID; SEEK YE MY FACE; THY FACE, LORD, WILL I SEEK.

IN THY BEHALF MY HEART HATH SAID. Rabbi Moses says that the meaning of *lekha* (in Thy behalf) is, because of you.[26] *Lekha* is like *li* (because of me)[27] in, *say because of me: He is my brother*[28] (Gen. 20:13). The following is the meaning of our verse: I declare what You commanded us[29] through the hand of Your messengers. You said to us, seek My face. I therefore seek Your face O Lord.

---

21. Translated lit.

22. Our clause reads: *shema YHVH koli ekra.* The latter literally reads: *Hear, O Lord, my voice, I call.* According to I.E. *shema YHVH koli ekra* should be read as if written , *shema YHVH koli asher ekra,* Hear, O Lord, my voice when I call.

23. In other words *shema YHVH koli ekra* should be rendered: Hear O Lord, whom I call with my voice.

24. For David himself no longer went out to war when he offered this prayer.

25. Literally, "because they were his men."

26. The literal meaning of *lekha* is, to you. Hence our clause literally reads: *To You (lekhah) my heart hath said, seek ye my face.* However, this makes no sense. Hence I.E.'s interpretation.

27. The word *li* literally means to me. However, it makes no sense to translate Gen 20:13, say to me he is my brother. Hence *li* in Gen. 20:3 must be rendered *because of me.* See I.E. on Gen. 20:13.

28. I.E.'s translation.

29. I.E.'s paraphrase of *In Thy behalf my heart hath said.*

9. HID NOT THY FACE FROM ME; PUT NOT THY SERVANT AWAY IN ANGER; THOU HAST BEEN MY HELP; CAST ME NOT OFF, NEITHER FORSAKE ME, O GOD OF MY SALVATION.

PUT NOT THY SERVANT AWAY IN ANGER. The word *tat* (put away) is a transitive verb. Its object is *avdekha* (thy servant).[30] The word *tat* is similar to the word *natuy* (leaning)[31] in *As a leaning wall* (Ps. 62:4). *Thou hast been my help* therefore[32] follows. The latter means, help me now as You helped me from my youth until now.

10. FOR THOUGH MY FATHER AND MY MOTHER HAVE FORSAKEN ME, THE LORD WILL TAKE ME UP.

FOR THOUGH MY FATHER AND MY MOTHER HAVE FORSAKEN ME. My father and mother who were the cause of my coming into this world have forsaken me by dying,[33] but You have always taken me up. This is its meaning even though *ya'asfeni* (will take me up) is an imperfect.[34] Compare, *I will give* (natati)[35] *the price of the field: take it of me* (Gen. 23:13) and *They made* (ya'asu)[36] *a calf in Horeb* (Ps. 106:19).

11. TEACH ME THY WAY, O LORD; AND LEAD ME IN AN EVEN PATH, BECAUSE OF THEM THAT LIE IN WAIT FOR ME.

TEACH ME THY WAY, O LORD. One of the wise men said: He who wants to defeat his enemies should increase his efforts[37] in the service of the Lord.

---

30. The text reads: *al tat be-af avdekha*. This literally means, put not away in anger Thy servant. I.E. insists that this be interpreted as if written, *al tat avdekah be-af*, put not away Thy servant in anger.

31. A wall about to fall. According to I.E. our clause should be rendered as follows: *Cast not down (tat) Thy servant in anger.*

32. Because of what is written in the first part of the clause.

33. Lit., when they died.

34. In other words *ya'asfeni* is to be rendered, *has taken me up* rather than *will take me up*.

35. *Natati* is a perfect. Nevertheless it has the meaning of an imperfect.

36. *Ya'asu* is an imperfect. However, it has the meaning of a perfect. We thus see that the tenses are not always to be taken literally.

37. Lit., "works."

12. DELIVER ME NOT OVER UNTO THE WILL OF MY ADVESARIES; FOR FALSE WITNESSES ARE RISEN UP AGAINST ME, AND SUCH AS BREATHE OUT VIOLENCE.

DELIVER ME NOT OVER UNTO THE WILL OF MY ADVESARIES. The word *be-nefesh*[38] means, unto the will of.[39] Compare, *bi-she'at be-nefesh* (with disdain of soul) (Ezek. 25:15).[40]

FOR FALSE WITNESSES ARE RISEN UP AGAINST ME, AND SUCH AS BREATHE OUT VIOLENCE. Who speak violently. The word *vi-fe'ach* (and such as breathe out) means, and such as speak.[41]

13. IF I HAD NOT BELIEVED TO LOOK UPON THE GOODNESS OF THE LORD IN THE LAND OF THE LIVING.

IF I HAD NOT BELIEVED… This is connected to the previous verse. Its means, my enemies would have ruled over me[42] if I had not believed to look to the Lord and said to myself, *Wait for the Lord.* Now then, let the truth of my words with which I used to direct myself and say, *Yea, wait for the Lord*, be shown to be true.

14. WAIT FOR THE LORD; BE STRONG, AND LET THY HEART TAKE COURAGE, YEA WAIT THOU FOR THE LORD.

BE STRONG, AND LET THY HEART TAKE COURAGE. *Ya'ametz* (take courage) is a transitive verb.[43] *Ve-ya'metz libbekha* (and let thy heart take courage) means, God will strengthen your heart.[44] *Yea, wait for the Lord* means, always wait for the Lord. Wait for the Lord at the first and at the last.[45]

---

38. The word *nefesh* usually means, soul. Hence I.E.'s note.

39. Lit., "the lust of."

40. I.E. renders Ezek. 25:15, with disdain of desire, or disdain of will.

41. Heb. *Yafi'ach.* See I.E. on Ps. 12:6.

42. Lit., "almost ruled over me."

43. Meaning, he will strengthen.

44. I.E. renders our verse: *Wait thou for the Lord, be strong, God will strengthen your heart, and wait for the Lord.*

45. If God does not fulfill your request at first wait for Him to eventually do so.

CHAPTER 28

1. A PSALM OF DAVID. UNTO THEE O LORD, DO I CALL; MY ROCK, BE NOT THOU DEAF UNTO ME; LEST, IF THOU BE SILENT UNTO ME, I BECOME LIKE THEM THAT GO DOWN INTO THE PIT.

A PSALM OF DAVID. UNTO THEE O LORD, DO I CALL. This psalm was composed by David. On the other hand it is possible that one of the poets composed this psalm about David.

The psalmist says, *My rock.*[1] *My rock* is in contrast to, *them that go down in the pit.* The word *techerash* (be not Thou deaf) means, be not Thou silent. Scripture employs the word *tacharosh* (devise) in *Devise* (tacharosh) *not evil against thy neighbor* (Prov. 3:29) because it wants to distinguish between to be silent (techerash) and to devise (tacharosh),[2] for both words share a common root.[3]

2. HEAR THE VOICE OF MY SUPPLICATIONS, WHEN I CRY UNTO THEE, WHEN I LIFT UP MY HANDS TOWARD THY HOLY SANCTUARY.[4]

HEAR THE VOICE OF MY SUPPLICATIONS… WHEN I LIFT UP MY HANDS. Toward the place of the ark. The place of the ark is called the *devir* (sanctuary).

---

1. The Rock is situated on high ground. My rock is thus in contrast to the pit that is down below.

2. Lit., "because it wants to distinguish between the meanings."

3. *Chet, resh, shin.* Hence it was necessary to differentiate their vocalizations.

4. Heb. *Devir.*

3. DRAW ME NOT AWAY WITH THE WICKED; AND WITH THE WORKERS OF INIQUITY; WHO SPEAK PEACE WITH THEIR NEIGHBORS, BUT EVIL IS IN THEIR HEARTS.

DRAW ME NOT AWAY WITH THE WICKED. Do not arrange things in such a way that I mix with the wicked and I am drawn along with them.

3. GIVE THEM ACCORDING TO THEIR DEEDS, AND ACCORDING TO THE EVIL OF THEIR ENDEVORS; GIVE THEM AFTER THE WORK OF THEIR HANDS; RENDER TO THEM THEIR DESERT.

GIVE THEM ACCORDING TO THEIR DEEDS. This was said in reference to *the workers of iniquity* (v. 3).

5. BECAUSE THEY GIVE NO HEED TO THE WORKS OF THE LORD, NOR TO THE OPERATION OF HIS HANDS; HE WILL BREAK THEM DOWN AND NOT BUILD THEM UP.

BECAUSE THEY GIVE NO HEED TO THE WORKS OF THE LORD. *The works of the Lord* (pe'ullot Adonai) is in contrast to *their deeds* (po'olam) (v. 4).

NOR TO THE OPERATION OF HIS HANDS. This is in contrast to *after the work of their hands* (v. 4). Our verse means, if *the workers of iniquity* would understand *the works of the Lord* they would not do evil, for they would know that God would break them down. Others say that *He will break them down and not build them up* is a prayer or a prophecy. *He will break them down and not build them up* means; they will fall and not arise again.

6. BLESSED BE THE LORD, BECAUSE HE HATH HEARD THE VOICE OF MY SUPPLICATIONS.

BLESSED BE THE LORD… A prophetic statement to the effect that David's prayer was heard and that God heard the voice of David's supplications. *Because He hath heard the voice of my supplications* is similar to *And my prayer came unto Thee* (Jonah 2:8).[5]

---

5. Jonah 2:8 was uttered prophetically when Jonah was in the fish's belly.

7. THE LORD IS MY STRENGTH AND MY SHIELD, IN HIM HATH MY HEART TRUSTED, AND I AM HELPED; THEREFORE MY HEART GREATLY REJOICETH, AND WITH MY SONG WILL I PRAISE HIM.

THE LORD IS MY STRENGTH. According to my opinion *In Him hath my heart trusted, and I am helped* means, I have trusted in Him alone and many others helped me, for the Lord commanded them to do so.

THEREFORE MY HEART GREATLY REJOICETH, AND WITH MY SONG WILL I PRAISE HIM. *Mi-shiri* (with my song)[6] has the same meaning as *be-shiri* (with my song).[7] The reverse is the case with the word *ba-basar* (of the flesh) in *And that which remaineth of the flesh* (ba-basar) *and of the bread* (Lev. 8:32).[8] However, Rabbi Moses Ha-Kohen says that *mi-shiri ahodennu* (with my song will I praise him) means, I will praise Him above and beyond this song.[9]

8. THE LORD IS STRENGTH UNTO THEM; AND HE IS A STRONGHOLD OF SALVATION TO HIS ANOINTED.

THE LORD IS STRENGTH UNTO THEM. *Unto them* (lamo) refers to those who help David,[10] for the meaning of our verse is that the Lord is a strength to those who help me and a stronghold to the one who is helped, that is, to David His anointed.
Rabbi Moses says that *oz lamo* (unto them) means, strength unto him.[11] *Lamo* (to him) in *to him the stroke was due* (Is. 53:8)[12] is similar. However, this is incorrect, for *lamo*[13] refers to the servant of God and his people.[14]

---

6. The *mem* is a preposition meaning, from. Thus *mi-shiri* literally means, from my song.

7. In other words the *mem* sometimes has the meaning of the *bet.*

8. In Lev. 8:32 the *bet* has the meaning of a *mem,* for *ba-basar* (lit. with the flesh) is to be rendered *of the flesh* (mi-besar).

9. Rabbi Moses renders our verse as follows: *Therefore my heart greatly rejoiceth, and more than with my song will I praise Him.* One of the meanings of the preposition *mem* is *more than.* Hence Rabbi Moses' interpretation.

10. Lit., "me."

11. In other words Scripture employs a plural (lamo) with the meaning of a singular.

12. Translated according to Rabbi Moses.

13. In Is. 53:8.

14. It is thus a plural. I.E. renders Is. 53:8, *to them the stroke was due.*

9. SAVE THY PEOPLE, AND BLESS THINE INHERITANCE; AND TEND THEM, AND CARRY THEM FOR EVER.

SAVE THY PEOPLE. David earlier mentioned that God is his strength and that his heart greatly rejoices.[15] He now prayed that God tend Israel. Scripture therefore reads: *Save Thy people, and bless Thine inheritance.*
And bless Thine inheritance means, may God increase his people.[16]
David prayed that God protect Israel[17] as a shepherd his flock. Hence Scripture reads: *And tend them, and carry them.*
And carry them (ve-nasse'em) means, may God place them in a high place [18] so that the wild beasts will not be able to harm them.
Rabbi Moses says that *ve-nasse'em* (and carry them) means, and provide for all of their needs. Compare, *yenasse'uhu* (help him) in *let the men of his place help him* (Ezra 1:4).[19]

15. Verse 7.

16. According to I.E. to bless means, to increase. See I.E. on Gen. 2:3.

17. Lit. "Them."

18. *Ve-nasse'em* literally means, and lift them up. Hence I.E.'s interpretation.

19. *Ve-nasse'em* and *yenasse'uhu* come from the same root, *nun, sin, alef.*

CHAPTER 29

1. A PSALM OF DAVID. ASCRIBE UNTO THE LORD, O YE SONS OF MIGHT, ASCRIBE UNTO THE LORD GLORY AND STRENGTH.

A PSALM OF DAVID. ASCRIBE UNTO THE LORD, O YE SONS OF MIGHT. It is possible that the *heh* in the word *havu* (ascribe ye) is irregularly vocalized because it is a guttural.[1] *Havu* is like *efu* (bake)[2] in *Bake that ye will bake* (Ex. 16:23).

The *bene Elim* (sons of might) are the stars. *When the morning stars sang together* (Job 38:7) which is followed by *And all the sons of God* (bene Elohim) *shouted for joy* (ibid.) is proof of this, for the second half of the verse means the same as the first part of the verse.[3]

Scripture mentions the stars because, with the help of the God of gods[4] the rains come down in accordance with the arrangements of the stars.[5]

Scripture repeats the phrase *Ascribe unto the Lord* for this is always the case.[6] It is similar to *The floods have lifted up, O Lord, The floods have lifted up their voice* (Ps. 93:3).[7]

Ascribe (havu) *unto the Lord* means, offer blessings unto the Lord. It is similar to *Ascribe* (tenu) *ye strength unto the Lord* (Ps. 68:35).[8]

---

1. Lit. "Perhaps the vowel of the *heh* was changed because of the guttural." A plural imperative in the *kal* is usually vocalized with a *sheva* beneath the first stem letter when its last root letter is a *heh*. Compare, *benu*, *penu* etc. Thus the *heh* of *havu* should have been vocalized with a *chataf pattach* rather than with a *kametz*. Hence I.E.'s comment.

2. *Efu* too is irregularly vocalized. It should have been vocalized with a *chataf pattach* (afu) rather then with a *tzere* (efu). Here too the anomaly is due to the guttural, the *alef*.

3. In biblical poetry, the second half of the verse often repeats the first half in different words.

4. According to I.E., the phrase *God of gods* refers to God who works through the angels. See I.E. on in Gen. 1:1.

5. The coming down of the rain is a manifestation of God's might.

6. God is consistently glorious and mighty.

7. There too, Scripture repeats itself to indicate that this is always the case.

8. The word used for *ascribe* in our verse is *havu*, which literally means, give. We find a similar instance in Ps. 68:35, wherein the word used for ascribe is *tenu*, which literally means, give.

Declare[9] that might and glory are the Lords alone.[10]

Bow before the Lord[11] (v. 2) means, bow before the Lord like a servant bows before his master, when he wants to do all that his master will command him. Its import is that the stars cannot change their movements or the way that they are arranged.

3. THE VOICE OF THE LORD IS UPON THE WATERS; THE GOD OF GLORY THUNDERETH, EVEN THE LORD UPON MANY WATERS.

THE VOICE OF THE LORD. God's name[12] is mentioned[13] because His power, strength and might are revealed when the rains come down. The Book of Job similarly states: *Who doeth great things and unsearchable* (Job 5:9).[14] The latter is followed by *Who giveth rain upon the earth* (Job 5:10).

Scripture refers to the Lord as *God of glory* in *The God of glory thunderteth* because it earlier stated *Ascribe unto the Lord the glory due unto His name.*[15]

The God of glory thunderteth explains[16] *The voice of the Lord is upon the waters.*[17]

The meaning of *Even the Lord upon many waters* is that the Lord brings thunder. Thus the word *thundereth* is to be read as if written twice.[18]

4. THE VOICE OF THE LORD IS IN POWER; THE VOICE OF THE LORD IS IN MAJESTY.[19]

THE VOICE OF THE LORD. Some say that *in power* refers to the power that God placed in nature. The same applies to *in majesty.*

Others say that *in power* means in the bodies which are powerful and that *in majesty* (behadar) refers to the mountains. Compare, *And make the mountains* (hadurim) *straight* (Is.

---

9. Literally; admit, confess.

10. I.E.'s interpretation of *Ascribe unto the Lord glory and strength.*

11. Translated lit. Heb. *Hishtachavu la-Adonai.*

12. The Tetragrammaton, *YHVH.*

13. Our verse reads, *The voice of YHVH (the Lord) is upon the waters.*

14. In reality I.E. quotes Job 9:10, which is very close in reading to Job 5:9. If our text is not based on a scribal error, then I.E. quoted from memory and erred.

15. Lit. "Scripture calls Him *The God of glory,* because it earlier stated *the glory due unto His name.*"

16. Lit. "This explains."

17. The latter means that God thunders over the waters.

18. Our verse should be read as if written, *The God of glory thundereth, the Lord thundereth upon many waters.*

19. Translated literally.

45:2).[20] According to this interpretation the word *ko'ach* (power) is an adjective rather than a noun. Our text should be read as if written, in those who are powerful.[21] It is similar to *But I am prayer* (Ps. 109:4).[22]

It is also possible that *in power* refers to the power that is mentioned in the following verse, namely *The voice of the Lord breaketh the cedars.* Scripture speaks of cedars because they are very strong. The cedars of Lebanon are mentioned because they are the most famous of the cedars.

6. HE MAKETH THEM ALSO TO SKIP LIKE A CALF; LEBANON AND SIRION LIKE A YOUNG WILD-OX.

HE MAKETH THEM ALSO TO SKIP. This is a well-known effect of thunder.[23]

LEBANON AND SIRION LIKE A YOUNG WILD-OX. *Ben re'emim* (a young wild ox) is similar to *ben torim* (a young turtle dove)[24] and *ben atonot* (a young ass) (Zech. 9:9).[25]

7. THE VOICE OF THE LORD HEWETH OUT FLAMES OF FIRE.

Rabbi Moses says that this alludes to steel like stone that destroys.[26] *Heweth* means, He hewed them from the rock. *Heweth* is used metaphorically. It means, it is as if He hewed.

However, in my opinion our verse speaks of lightening. Compare, *And the Most High gave forth His voice* (Ps. 18: 14). The latter is followed by *He sends out*[27] *His arrows* (ibid. v. 15).

---

20. Translated according to I.E.

21. In other words, *ko'ach* is short for *be-va'ale ha-ko'ach.* Thus *ko'ach* modifies *ba'ale.*

22. Translated literally. According to I.E. *va-ani tefillah* (but I am prayer) is short for *va-ani ish tefillah* (but I am a man of prayer).

23. To make the mountains quake.

24. This phrase does not appear in the Bible. However, see Lev. 1:4.

25. *Ben* (a young wild ox) is a singular. *Re'emim* is a plural. To be consistent our text should read *bene re'emim.* According to I.E., the combination of a plural and singular indicates one of the group. Thus *ben re'amim,* literally a son of wild oxen means, a wild ox. The same applies to *ben torim* (a young turtle dove) and *ben atonot* (a young ass).

26. Heb., *torefet* (weakens). Rabbi Moses is probably thinking of a stone made out of basalt or a similar material. According to Rabbi Moses, we may paraphrase our verse as follows: *The voice of the Lord heweth a flaming sword out of the rock.*

27. Ps. 18:15 reads, *and he sent out.* If not a scribal error then I.E. quoted from memory and erred.

8. THE VOICE OF THE LORD PAINS[28] THE WILDERNESS; THE LORD PAINS[29] THE WILDERNESS OF KADESH.

THE VOICE OF THE LORD PAINS THE WILDERNESS. This is said metaphorically. It is like *you shall hurt the land[30] with stones* (11 Kings 3:19)[31]. On the other hand the wilderness might allude to the animals of the wilderness that Scripture goes on to mention.[32]

9. THE VOICE OF THE LORD MAKETH THE HINDS TO CALVE, AND STRIPPETH THE FORESTS BARE; AND IN HIS TEMPLE ALL SAY : 'GLORY.'

THE VOICE OF THE LORD MAKETH THE HINDS TO CALVE. The psalmists mentions *the wilderness* (v. 8), because he had earlier said *in majesty* (v. 4).[33]
Scripture mentions *the wilderness of Kadesh*(v. 8) because it is great and awe inspiring.
Scripture mentions *hinds,* because they give birth in difficulty.
Note, the thunder causes the hinds to calve, that is, the thunder causes their birth pains to come quickly.[34] The womb of the hinds then open and they give birth. They also give birth because they are frightened.[35]
And strippeth the forests bare means, the area taken up by the forest is revealed when the trees fall.
Some say that *and in His temple* refers to the heavens. Compare, *But the Lord in His holy temple* (Hab. 2:20).[36] The meaning of *and in His temple all say glory* is:[37] those who dwell there[38] ascribe glory to God and say, "how great is Your glory."
Others say the reference is to the *Kohanim* and the Levites who stand in prayer.[39]

---

28. Translated lit. The Hebrew reads *yachil.*

29. Translated lit.

30. Lit. "It."

31. Translated lit.

32. The hinds mentioned in the next verse.

33. Literally, He mentions *the wilderness* (v. 8) is parallel to *in majesty.*

34. I.E. interprets *The voice of the Lord* as referring to the thunder.

35. By the thunder.

36. The meaning of which is, *but the Lord in heaven.*

37. Lit., "its meaning is."

38. In heaven. The reference is to the angels.

39. Lit., "who stand to pray."

Rabbi Moses says that in *His temple* refers to those who dwell in God's palace, that is, in the Holy Temple.[40] They are not afraid, for God will honor them and ensure that no harm will come to them because of the thunder. Scripture therefore next reads: *The Lord sat enthroned at the flood Yea, the Lord sitteth as King forever* (v.10). The meaning of the latter is that the waters destroyed the wicked. This resulted in the revelation of God's Kingship, for God executed judgment against the wicked. God thus saves the pious,[41] such as Noah and his sons, and destroys[42] His enemies.

Others say that the flood is mentioned because Scripture earlier mentioned part of God's glory[43] namely the coming down of rain.[44] Scripture therefore goes on to mention the great wonder, namely the great amount of rain that came down in the days of Noah. This is a sign that the Lord is enthroned from eternity, and his mercy is eternally upon His people. Scripture therefore next reads: *The Lord will give strength to His people.*

Others say that Scripture mentions the flood because of the oath taken by God that the waters will not destroy the entire earth and that the kingdom of God[45] who is the king of life will not be destroyed.[46] Scripture therefore immediately reads: *Yea, the Lord sitteth as King forever.*

Others say that the meaning of *The Lord sat enthroned at the flood Yea, the Lord sitteth as King for ever* is that God's kingdom[47] was revealed[48] from the time that God sat in judgment in the days of the flood. Therefore the people who live after the flood should fear God. Scripture reads: *The Lord sat enthroned at the flood.* It says this, because there was no flood before Noah.[49]

11. THE LORD WILL GIVE STRENGTH UNTO HIS PEOPLE; THE LORD WILL BLESS HIS PEOPLE WITH PEACE.

THE LORD... This is a prayer. On the other hand it might be a prophecy that God will give strength to His people in the time of thunder and that they will have peace.

---

40. Lit. "The holy house."

41. Lit. "His pious."

42. Lit., "kills."

43. In verse 3.

44. See I.E.'s comment on verse 3.

45. The earth.

46. Gen. 9:15.

47. That God acts as a king and punishes transgressors.

48. Was clearly revealed to the entire world.

49. In reality God is king from eternity. However, His acting as judge was revealed at the flood. Hence the reading of our verse.

CHAPTER 30

1. A PSALM; A SONG AT THE DEDICATION OF THE HOUSE; OF DAVID.

A PSALM; A SONG AT THE DEDICATION OF THE HOUSE. Some say that David commanded that the singers play this psalm at the dedication of the first temple.[1] Others say at the dedication of the second or the third temple,[2] for David, as I will explain, compares the days of exile to days of illness.[3]

It appears that David composed this psalm when he dedicated his house, the house of cedars,[4] for our psalm does not mention God's house.[5] The same, as I have explained in its place, is the case with *There are the blind and the lame; he cannot come into the house* (11 Sam. 5:8).[6] David fell ill at that time,[7] and recovered from his illness.

Rabbi Moses says that David mourned when Nathan told him that he would not build a house for God.[8] However, when the Lord told him that his son Solomon would build the house[9] he girded himself with joy in place of mourning, for his son is like himself[10] and the enemy[11] would not taunt David.[12] Rabbi Moses says that affliction of the spirit

---

1. Which was built after the death of David.

2. In other words this is a prophetic psalm.

3. This psalm speaks of David's recovery from illness. These commentators believe that David's illness is a metaphor for redemption from exile.

4. See 11 Sam. 5:11.

5. Our verse speaks of *the dedication of the house*. It does not speak of the dedication of God's house.

6. There too *house* refers to David's cedar house.

7. When he dedicated his house.

8. 11 Sam. 7:5.

9. Ibid. v. 13.

10. A person lives on in his children.

11. David's enemies. See 11 Sam. 16:5-8.

12. By saying that he was unworthy to build God's house.

is like the affliction of the body.[13] It is even worse. Compare, *The spirit of a man will sustain his infirmity* (Prov. 18:14).

2. I WILL EXTOL THEE, O LORD, FOR THOU HAST RAISED ME UP, AND HAST NOT SUFFERED MINE ENEMIES TO REJOICE OVER ME.

I WILL EXTOL THEE. *I will extol Thee because Thou hast raised me up.* David says, *for Thou hast raised me up* because he thought[14] that he was going to die.
And hast not suffered mine enemies to rejoice over me is similar to what is written in the psalm opening with *Happy is he that considereth the poor* (Ps. 41:2),[15] for they both have one theme.

3. O LORD MY GOD, I CRIED UNTO THEE, AND THOU DIDST HEAL ME.

O LORD. Its meaning is, I cried only unto You and not to a physician,[16] and You healed me.

4. O LORD, THOU BROUGHTEST UP MY SOUL FROM THE GRAVE;[17] THOU DIDST KEEP ME ALIVE, THAT I SHOULD NOT GO DOWN TO THE PIT.

O LORD. *Thou broughtest up my soul from the grave* means, I almost went down to the grave.
We find the word *yaredi* (that I should go down)[18] in *that I should not go down to the pit* to be fully spelled out.[19] It is similar to the word *radefi* (I follow) in *because I follow the thing that is good* (Ps. 38:21).[20]

---

13. In other words, the illness spoken of in this verse refers to David's spiritual anguish.

14. Reading *machashavto*, rather than *machashavti*. Ha-Keter.

15. Psalm 41 deals with David's illness. It is there stated that David's enemies were waiting for David to die (Ps. 41:6). However, God healed David and disappointed his enemies. This is the meaning of *And hast not suffered mine enemies to rejoice over me.*

16. According to I.E., the truly pious man has no need of physicians. See *The Secret of the Torah*, page 98.

17. Translated according to I.E. Heb. *She'ol.*

18. *Yaredi* is the *kere.*

19. The *ketib* reads *yoredi. Yoredi* is spelled with a *vav.*

20. In the *ketib*, the *ketib* reads *redofi. Redofi* is spelled with a *vav.*

5. SING PRAISE UNTO THE LORD, O YE HIS GODLY ONES; AND GIVE THANKS TO HIS HOLY NAME.

SING PRAISE UNTO THE LORD. David says this because he was a godly person as it is written, *Neither wilt Thou suffer Thy godly ones to see the pit*[21] (Ps. 16:10) and *the faithful godly deeds of David* (Is. 55:3). [22] David informs the godly that if what happened to him[23] happens to them, then God will save them.

6. FOR HIS ANGER IS BUT FOR A MOMENT, HIS FAVOR IS FOR LIFE; WEEPING TARRIES FOR THE NIGHT BUT JOY IN THE MORNING.[24]

FOR HIS ANGER... *For life* means for a long life.[25] It is similar to *men of stature*[26] (Num.14: 33).[27] The latter means, men of great stature.

[WEEPING TARRIES FOR THE NIGHT BUT JOY IN THE MORNING.] *Weeping tarries for the night* is a metaphor.[28] On the other hand the subject might have been omitted as in, *whom she bore to Levi* (Exodus 26:59).[29] The meaning of our clause is, the One who makes a person tarry in weeping, does so for the night, but in the morning He brings joy.[30] We may so interpret our verse because the prepositional *bet* is omitted in many places in Scripture.[31] Compare the word *bet* (house of) in, *found in the house of the Lord* (11 Kings 12:11).[32]

---

21. Translated literally.

22. Ps. 17:10 speaks of David.

23. What happened to David is described in verse 4.

24. Translated according to I.E.

25. In other words *life* is short for a long life.

26. Translated literally.

27. For *stature* is short for great stature.

28. For weeping is personified.

29. Here too Scripture omits the subject, for Scripture does not identify the one who bore.

30. Literally, "in the morning in joy."

31. Our verse reads: *ba-erev yalin bekhi, ve-la-boker rinnah.* I.E. suggests that this be read as if written: *ba-erev yalin ha-melin be-vekhi, ve-laboker be-rinnah.*

32. 11 Kings 12:11 literally reads, *found in house* (bet) *of the Lord.* I.E. says this should be read as if written, *found in the house* (be-vet) *of the Lord.* In other words a prepositional *bet* should be placed before the Hebrew word for house.

7. NOW I HAD SAID IN MY SECURITY: I SHALL NEVER BE MOVED.

NOW I... Rabbi Moses explained this verse as referring to the time concerning which Scripture states, *It came to pass, when the king*[33] *dwelt in his house* (11 Sam. 7:1)[34] and Nathan[35] told him: *Go, do all that is in your heart* (ibid. v. 3).[36] However, this is far fetched. In my opinion our verse reflects the thinking of a strong healthy person who thinks that things shall always be the same. He believes that he will not fall ill and that his strength will never fail.

8. THOU HADST ESTABLISHED, O LORD, IN THY FAVOR MY MOUNTAIN AS A STRONGHOLD- THOU DIDST HIDE THY FACE; I WAS AFFRIGHTED.

O LORD. I now know that my strength came from You when I was healthy, for when You hid Your face; *I was affrighted.*
Rabbi Moses says that *he'emadtah* (Thou hast established) means, You have established me[37].
Le-hareri (for a mountain)[38] in *le-hareri oz* (for a mountain which is a stronghold) is similar to the word *kavod* (glory) in *So that my glory* (kavod) *may sing praise to Thee* (v. 13).[39] *Kavod* in the latter is to be interpreted as if written *kevodi* (my glory).
Others say that the *yod* of *le-hareri* (my mountain) is a first person suffix.[40] Its meaning is that God made David like a mountain.[41]

---

33. King David.

34. And wanted to build a temple to God on Mt. Moriah.

35. The prophet.

36. However, God soon told David that he would not build the temple.

37. In other words *he'emadtah* (Thou hast established) is short for *he'emadtani* (Thou hast established me).

38. This interpretation explains *le-harri* (my mountain) as meaning, for a mountain (le-har). The word *harri* presents a problem. The word appears to mean, my mountain. However, the Hebrew word for my mountain in Jer. 17:3 is *harari*. Hence the various interpretations which follow.

39. *Harri* is to be read as if written *har* (mountain) in the same way that *kavod* is to be interpreted as if written *kevodi*. According to this interpretation our clause reads as follows: You have established me for a mountain stronghold.

40. In other words, *harri* means my mountain. According to this interpretation *he'emadtah le-harri oz* means, *Thou hast established my mountain as a stronghold*.

41. In other words *mountain* is a metaphor for David. This comment also applies to Rabbi Moses' interpretation.

Rabbi Judah Ha-Levi says that *le-harri* is similar to the word *harari* (My mountain)[42] in *My mountain*[43] *in the field* (Jer. 17:3), for the forms of nouns change.[44]

9. UNTO THEE, O LORD, DID I CALL, AND UNTO THE LORD I MADE SUPPLICATION:

UNTO THEE. David relates that he could not do any thing but call unto the Lord and make supplication unto Him and say: *What profit is there in my death* (v. 10).
What profit is there in my blood (v. 10) means, what profit is there in my death? *for the blood is life* (nefesh) (Deut. 12:23).[45] Compare, *Ye shall not make any cuttings in your flesh for a life*[46] *(nefesh)*[47] (Lev. 19:28).

10. WHAT PROFIT IS THERE IN MY BLOOD, WHEN I GO DOWN TO THE PIT? SHALL THE DUST PRAISE THEE? SHALL IT DECLARE THY TRUTH?

SHALL THE DUST PRAISE THEE? As Scripture states: *And the dust returneth to the earth as it was* (Ecc. 12:7).[48]

12. THOU DIDST TURN FOR ME MY MOURNING INTO DANCING; THOU DIDST LOOSE MY SACKCLOTH, AND GIRD ME WITH GLADNESS.

THOU DIDST TURN FOR ME MY MOURNING INTO DANCING. David was happy because he would now live until his soul was satiated with serving God and recognizing His works, for this is the purpose that man was created for.
Thou didst loose my sackcloth is to be understood as a metaphor for one who mourns for his life.[49]
And gird me means, and strengthen me.

---

42. Thus *hareri* means, my mountain.

43. Translated lit.

44. Thus *hareri* and *harari* mean the same.

45. Translated literally.

46. Translated literally.

47. The meaning of Lev 19:28 is, Ye shall not make any cuttings in your flesh for a life (nefesh) that has passed away. We thus see that the meaning of *nefesh* is life.

48. In other words *dust* refers to the human body. *Shall the dust praise Thee* therefore means, shall man who is ultimately buried in the dust praise You?

49. Our verse speaks of one who wears sackcloth because he expects to soon die.

13. SO THAT[50] GLORY[51] MAY SING PRAISE TO THEE, AND NOT BE SILENT; O LORD MY GOD, I WILL GIVE THANKS UNTO THEE FOR EVER.

SO THAT... *Glory* (kavod) refers to the rational soul. The following is the meaning of our verse: I will praise You as long as I live, so that all people who posses a rational soul will sing praises and give thanks to You. Scripture reads *glory* and not all glory because the intelligent are few in number.

50. Translated according to I.E.

51. Translated lit.

CHAPTER 31

1 FOR THE LEADER. A PSALM OF DAVID.

David handed this psalm over to one of the musicians so that he would play it.[1]

2. IN THEE, O LORD, HAVE I TAKEN REFUGE; LET ME NEVER BE ASHAMED; DELIVER ME IN THY RIGHTEOUSNESS.

IN THEE, O LORD, HAVE I TAKEN REFUGE; LET ME NEVER BE ASHAMED. For my enemies are people, who without cause, act violently towards me.

3. INCLINE THINE EAR UNTO ME, DELIVER ME SPEEDILY; BE THOU TO ME A ROCK OF REFUGE, EVEN A FORTRESS OF DEFENCE, TO SAVE ME.

INCLINE THINE EAR UNTO ME. The Torah employed human language for *He*[2] *that planted the ear* (Ps. 94:9) hears without an ear.[3]
EVEN A FORTRESS OF DEFENCE. A high place, so that in it, I[4] will not fear the enemy.

4. FOR THOU ART MY ROCK AND MY FORTRESS; THEREFORE FOR THY NAME'S SAKE LEAD ME AND GUIDE ME.

FOR THOU ART MY ROCK. *My rock* corresponds to *a rock of refuge* (v. 3) and *my fortress* corresponds to *a fortress of defense* (ibid.).

---

1. This musician was designated to "eternally" play this psalm. According to this interpretation, the word *la-mena'tze'ach* (for the leader) is related to the word *netzach* (forever). See I.E. on Ps. 4:1.

2. God.

3. See I.E. on Ps. 2:4 and the notes thereto.

4. Lit., "he."

Scripture reads: *and lead me.* It so reads, because it is difficult to walk on a mountain[5] due to its height.[6] *Lead me* means; lead me according to my pace.

5. BRING ME OUT FORTH OUT OF THE NET THAT THEY HAVE HIDDEN FOR ME; FOR THOU ART MY STRONGHOLD.

BRING ME OUT FORTH OUT OF THE NET. *Me-reshet zu tamenu li* (out of the net that they have hidden for me) means, out of the net that these[7] have hidden for me.[8] Others say that *zu* (they) means, this.[9]

6. INTO THY HAND I COMMIT MY SPIRIT; THOU HAST REDEEMED ME, O LORD, THOU GOD OF TRUTH.

INTO THY HAND I COMMIT MY SPIRIT. So that the enemy cannot take it away. [10] David says *O Lord, Thou God of truth,* because he deposited his soul with God. He refers to God as a *God of truth* (El emet) because of this[11] deposit.[12] Scripture refers to the Lord by the term *El*[13] because no one, no matter how strong, can overcome God.[14]

7. I HATE THEM THAT REGARD LYING VANITIES; BUT I TRUST IN THE LORD.

I HATE THEM THAT REGARD LYING VANITIES. Those who employ magic and soothsaying in choosing the day on which to go out to war. I rely only on the Lord.[15]

---

5. That is, to climb a mountain.

6. The fortress spoken of in our verse was located on a mountain. Hence I.E.'s comment.

7. These wicked men.

8. According to this interpretation *zu* means, these. See I.E. on Ps. 12:8.

9. According to this interpretation the word *zu* is connected to *me-reshet.* Our verse should be read as if written, *me-reshet zu, tamnu li,* out of this net that they have hidden for me.

10. Lit. "This means, so that the enemy cannot take it away."

11. Lit., "the."

12. One places a deposit only with a trust worthy individual.

13. Reading *El* rather than *Adonai.* The latter is an obvious error. The word *El* means mighty.

14. Lit., "because a powerful man cannot force Him."

15. Not upon magic (lying vanities).

8. I WILL BE GLAD AND REJOICE IN THY LOVINGKINDNESS; FOR THOU HAST SEEN MINE AFFLICTION, THOU HAST TAKEN COGNIZANCE OF THE TROUBLES OF MY SOUL.

I WILL BE GLAD AND REJOICE IN THY LOVINGKINDNESS. If my hand grows mighty, I will only rejoice in your loving kindness.

9. AND THOU HAST NOT GIVEN ME OVER INTO THE HAND OF THE ENEMY; THOU HAST SET MY FEET IN A BROAD PLACE.

AND THOU HAST NOT GIVEN ME OVER. The word *hisgartani* (hast given me over) is related to the word *segirah* (closure).[16] It refers to a person who is closed in, someone who is placed in bonds.[17]

THOU HAST SET MY FEET IN A BROAD PLACE. I[18] can go to any place that I want to. This is the reverse of being enclosed into the hands of the enemy.[19]

10. BE GRACIOUS UNTO ME O LORD, FOR I AM IN DISTRESS; MINE EYE WASTETH AWAY BECAUSE OF ANGER[20], YEA, MY SOUL AND MY BELLY.[21]

BE GRACIOUS UNTO ME O LORD. It is possible that *Thou hast set my feet in a broad place* means; I rejoice in the kindness that You showed me in days past, when You[22] did not enclose me in the hands of my enemies. However, I am now in straits and not in a broad place.[23]
Many say that this psalm refers to an illness that befell David.[24]

---

16. I.E. renders our clause as follows: *And hast not enclosed me* (hisgartani) *in the hands of my enemies.*

17. Lit., "in a bond." So too Menachem ben Seruk. See Rashi.

18. Lit., "he."

19. See note 20. One who is enclosed in the hands of the enemy is not free to go at will.

20. Translated lit.

21. Translated lit.

22. Lit., "and You did not."

23. Therefore *be gracious unto me.*

24. In other words the enemy spoken of in this psalm is a metaphor for David's illness.

Osheshah be-kha'as (wasteth away because of anger) means, I am, as it were, totally eaten by a moth,[25] for the wrath of the enemy is directed at me.[26] David compares the pain in the heart to a fever in the body.[27]

Scripture reads: *mine eye.* It so reads, because a sick person despises all food that he sees. The spirit of a sick person can't stand any food.

My soul[28] refers to the lusting[29] soul, whose power is implanted in the liver.[30] Scripture similarly says, *the soul* (nefesh) *that eateth* (Lev. 7:18).[31]

My belly alludes to the upper innards wherein the food is.

The meaning of our verse is, the power of my[32] body has been weakened like a garment that has been eaten by a moth.

11. FOR MY LIFE IS SPENT IN SORROW, AND MY YEARS IN SIGHING; MY STRENGTH FAILETH BECAUSE OF MINE INIQUITY, AND MY BONES ARE WASTED AWAY.

FOR MY LIFE IS SPENT IN SORROW …AND MY BONES ARE WASTED AWAY. Because of lack of food. This is a metaphor.[33] The psalmist mentions the bones,[34] because they are the foundations of the body.

12. BECAUSE OF ALL MINE ADVERSARIES I AM BECOME A REPROACH, YEA, UNTO MY NEIGHBORS EXCEEDINGLY, AND A DREAD TO MY ACQUAINTENCE; THEY THAT SEE ME WITHOUT FLEE FROM ME.

BECAUSE OF ALL MINE ADVERSARIES I AM BECOME A REPROACH. The psalmist notes that reproach comes to him from his enemies.

---

25. The word *ash* means a moth. Hence *osheshah* means "mothed" that is, eaten by a moth. According to I.E., *osheshah be-kha'as eni* means, mine eye has been eaten by a moth (ash).

26. *Because of anger* is short for *because of the anger of the enemy.*

27. Literally, *to the heat of the body.* The anger of the enemy causes David to worry. This worry is compared to a fever that wastes the body.

28. Heb., *nafshi.*

29. According to I.E. there are three souls or powers in the human body, *neshamah, ru'ach* and *nefesh.* "The *nefesh* is corporeal and it is that part of the psyche that desires food and sex." See *The Secret of the Torah*, p. 96.

30. See, *The Secret of the Torah*, Page 96.

31. I.E. takes this verse literally and refers it to the lusting soul which is in the liver.

32. Literally, *the.*

33. David's bones did not actually waste away.

34. Even though it is the whole body that wastes away.

YEA, UNTO MY NEIGHBORS EXCEEDINGLY. David became a reproach to his neighbors[35] because they were close to him.

THEY THAT SEE ME WITHOUT FLEE FROM ME. As people do [36] when they see a very sick person, or a something that is disgusting to look at.

13. I AM FORGOTTEN AS A DEAD MAN OUT OF MIND; I AM LIKE A USELESS VESSEL.

I AM FORGOTTEN. No one remembers me. I am like a vessel that no one wants. When it is lost no one looks for it.

14. FOR I HAVE HEARD THE WHISPERING OF MANY, TERROR ON EVERY SIDE; WHILE THEY TOOK COUNSEL TOGETHER AGAINST ME, THEY DEVISED TO TAKE AWAY MY LIFE.

FOR I HAVE HEARD THE WHISPERING OF MANY. It is possible that *I am forgotten* (v. 13) means; I am forgotten by God; for since God does not save me it is as if He has forgotten me. We may interpret the verse is this manner, because *for I have heard the whispering of many*[37] follows.
For I have heard the whispering of many, terror on every side means, I have heard the evil report that they spread about me. They invent things about me that frighten all those who hear it.
On the other hand it is possible that *For I have heard the whispering of many, terror on every side* means, *For I have heard the whispering of many,* the purpose of which is that I be surrounded by terror on all sides.
WHILE THEY TOOK COUNSEL TOGETHER AGAINST ME. *Be-hivvasedam* (while they took counsel) comes from the same root as the word *sod* (counsel).[38]

15. BUT AS FOR ME, I HAVE TRUSTED IN THEE, O LORD; I HAVE SAID: THOU ART MY GOD.

BUT AS FOR ME… Even though my enemies think that You have forgotten me, I trust in You and give thanks to You, for You are my God.

---

35. Lit., "them."

36. Lit., "as a person."

37. This verse indicates that he has not been forgotten by man.

38. Its root is *samekh, vav, dalet.*

16. MY TIMES ARE IN THY HAND: DELIVER ME FROM THE HAND OF MINE ENEMIES, AND FROM THEM THAT PERSECUTE ME.

MY TIMES ARE IN THY HAND. In contrast to those who put their faith in lying vanities,[39] I trust only in You, for the time of my salvation is in Your hand alone.[40]

17. MAKE THY FACE TO SHINE UPON THY SERVANT; SAVE ME IN THY LOVINGKINDNESS.

MAKE THY FACE TO SHINE UPON THY SERVANT. The word *al* (upon) is to be rendered *el* (to).[41] Compare, *and prayed unto* (al) *the Lord* (1 Sam. 1:10).[42] Our verse is similar to *The Lord make his face to shine towards*[43] *thee* (Num. 6:25).[44] One[45] who is in distress is like one who sits in the dark. Hence Scripture reads: *Make Thy face to shine.*

19. LET THE LYING LIPS BE DUMB, WHICH SPEAK ARROGANTLY AGAINST THE RIGHTEOUS, WITH PRIDE AND CONTEMPT.

LET THE LYING LIPS BE DUMB. The psalmist now says this because he earlier stated: *For I have heard the whisperings of many* (v. 14).[46] *Atak* (arrogantly) [is to be read as if written, *devar atak* (arrogant words).[47]] Compare, *and spoke rough*[48] *with them*[49] (Gen. 42:7).[50] The word *davar* has been omitted from our verse. *Righteous* means, a righteous person such as I.

---

39. See Jonah 2:9.

40. In other words *My times are in Thy hand* means, the time of my salvation is in Your hand.

41. According to I.E. our verse should be rendered as follows: *Make Thy face shine towards Thy servant.*

42. In 1 Sam. 1:10 the word *al* which usually means *upon* has the meaning of *el* (to). So too in this verse.

43. Translated lit. Hebrew, *elekha.*

44. Hence *al* in our verse has to be rendered *el.*

45. Literally, "for one."

46. The word translated as whispering in verse 14 reads *dibbatam. Dibbatam* means, their defamation. Thus according to I.E. verse 14 reads: *For I have heard the defamation of many.* Hence his comment.

47. Our text literally reads, *which speaks arrogant* (atak) *against the righteous.* Hence I.E.'s comment that our verse is to be read as if written, *which speaks arrogant* words *against the righteous.*

48. Hebrew, *kashot* (hard, rough).

49. Translated lit. According to I.E., this verse should be read as if written, *and spoke rough words with them.*

50. Lit. "Behold, *atak* (arrogantly) is like, *and spoke rough with them* (Gen. 42:7). Behold, the word *davar* is missing."

20. OH HOW ABUNDANT IS THY GOODNESS WHICH THOU HAST LAID UP FOR THEM THAT FEAR THEE; WHICH THOU HAST WROUGHT FOR THEM THAT TAKE THEIR REFUGE IN THEE, IN THE SIGHT OF THE SONS OF MEN.

OH HOW ABUNDANT IS THY GOODNESS … Those who speak arrogantly do not know of the good that You have laid up for those who fear You. In fact You have already openly done a number of good deeds for those who take refuge in You. This is the meaning of *in the sight of the sons of men*.

21. THY HIDEST THEM IN THE COVERT OF THY PRESENCE[51] FROM THE PLOTTINGS OF MAN; THOU CONCEALEST THEM IN A PAVILION FROM THE STRIFE OF TONGUES.

THY DIDST HIDE THEM. You will similarly hide all those who fear You. You will hide them, by hiding Your face from crooked men.[52]
FROM THE PLOTTINGS. The word *rukhse* (plottings) is related to the word *rekhasim* (crooked places) in *And the crooked places a plain* (Is. 40:4).[53]
Some say that *tastiram be-seter panekha*[54](Thy didst hide them in the covert of Thy presence) means; You will hide them[55] from the strife of tongues.[56] You will conceal them in a hidden place, where they shall see Your face.
Others say that *tastiram be-seter panekha* means; You will hide them[57] by hiding Your anger and Your wrath[58] from them.

---

51. Heb. *Tastirem be-seter penekha*. The latter literally means, You will hide them in the covert (*be-seter*) of Your face, or You will hide them by hiding (*be-seter*) Your face.

52. By turning His face away from the wicked, God is in effect hiding the righteous from the wicked. I.E. interprets the opening of our verse as follows: *You hide them* [all God fearing people] *by removing Your face from the crooked people.*

53. Translated according to I.E.

54. *Be-seter panekha* (in the covert of Thy presence) literally means, in a hidden place of Your face. I.E. interprets this as, in a hidden place where they will see Your face.

55. This opinion explains *tastirem* (Thou didst hide them) as *You will hide them*, and *be-seter panekha* (in the covert of Thy face) as *in a hidden place where they shall behold Thy face.*

56. This is possibly an error for *from crooked men*.

57. The righteous.

58. This interpretation renders *panekha* (your face) as: Your wrath. It renders *be-seter* as: when you hide.

FROM THE STRIFE OF TONGUES.[59] Compare, the *whispering of many* (v. 14).[60]

22. BLESSED BE THE LORD; FOR HE HATH SHOWN ME HIS WONDROUS LOVINGKINDNESS IN AN ENTRENCHED CITY.

BLESSED BE THE LORD. Some say that *Blessed be the Lord... in an entrenched city* means, as if I were in an entrenched city.[61]

On the other hand the meaning of our clause might be, I will then say in an entrenched city, *Blessed be the Lord...*

23. AS FOR ME, I SAID IN MY HASTE: I AM CUT OFF FROM BEFORE THINE EYES; NEVERTHELESS THOU HEARDEST THE VOICE OF MY SUPPLICATIONS WHEN I CRIED UNTO THEE.

AS FOR ME, I SAID IN MY HASTE: I AM CUT OFF FROM BEFORE THINE EYES. The word *nigrazti* (I am cut off) is related[62] to the word *garzen* (axe) which is an instrument used in killing. Other say that they[63] are the same word with their letters inverted. The psalmist says, *Thine eyes.* He similarly says, *Thou heardest.*[64]

24. O LOVE THE LORD, ALL YE GODLY ONES; THE LORD PRESERVETH THE FAITHFUL, AND PLENTIFULLY REPAYETH HIM THAT ACTETH HAUGHTILY.

O LOVE THE LORD. *Ehevu* (love) is an imperative.[65] It is like the word *echezu* (take us) in *Take us the foxes* (Songs 2:15). [66]

59. Reading *me-riv* for *be-riv.*

60. Reading *kemo dibbat rabbim* rather than *ki dibbat rabbim.*

61. According to this interpretation our verse should be read as follows: Blessed be the Lord; for He has shown me His loving kindness, as if I was in an entrenched city.

62. Has a similar meaning.

63. *Ngrz* (nigraz) and *grzn* (garzen). The *ti* in *nigrazti* is a perfect suffix.

64. Both terms are metaphoric, for God has neither eyes nor ears. Or, since David uses the image of God's eyes he uses the image of God's ears, for both of these organs are located in the head.

65. An imperative in the *kal* is usually vocalized with a *chirik* under the first letter. Hence I.E.'s comment.

66. *Ehevu* is an imperative.

THE LORD PRESERVETH THE FAITHFUL. The word *emunim* (faithful) is an adjective.[67] It is similar to *emunim* (faithful) in *the faithful fail* (Ps. 12:2).[68]

AND PLENTIFULLY REPAYETH HIM THAT ACTETH HAUGHTILY. Its meaning is that God repays[69] the remnants of the haughty.[70]
The word *la'asot* (acteth)[71] means to arrange the out come. Compare, *and he[72] hastened to prepare* (la'asot) [73] *it*.[74] (Gen. 18:7).[75]
It is possible that the word *ga'avah* (haughtily) is lacking a *bet*.[76] The word *ma'aseh* (deeds) is also missing.[77] Our clause should thus be rendered: And repays the remnant of those who do deeds in haughtiness.[78]

25. BE STRONG, AND LET YOUR HEART TAKE COURAGE, ALL YE THAT WAIT FOR THE LORD.

BE STRONG. David told the godly ones, *O love the Lord* (v. 24). He said this to them because of their exalted status.[79] He told those *that wait for the Lord, Be strong.*

---

67. *The Lord preserveth the faithful* (emunim) is short for *The Lord preserveth the faithful people* (anashim emunim). Thus *emunim* describes *anashim*.

68. *The faithful fail* is short for *The faithful people fail*. Thus here too *emunim* is short for *anashim emunim*.

69. That is, punishes.

70. Our clause reads, *u-meshalem al yeter oseh ga'avah*. I.E. renders *al yeter* (plentifully), the remnant. He believes *al yeter oseh ga'avah* is short for, *al yeter me-anshe oseh ga'avah*. Hence his interpretation.

71. *Oseh* and *la'asot* come from the same root, *ayin, sin, heh. Oseh* literally means, makes. *La'asot* literally means, to make. Hence I.E. points out that these verbs are not always used in their literal sense.

72. Abraham's young man.

73. The young man prepared the calf. He did not make it.

74. The calf.

75. According to I.E, *And plentifully repayeth him that acteth haughtily* means, God repays the remnants of those who arrange (commit) haughty acts.

76. In other words *ga'avah* should be read as if written, *be-ga'avah* . The word *ga'avah* means, pride, haughtiness. *Be-ga'avah* means haughtily.

77. This also applies to the previous comment. Our text should be read as if written, *oseh ma'aseh be-ga'avah*.

78. Or who act haughtily.

79. One has to be of a high moral and intellectual stature to truly love the Lord.

CHAPTER 32

1. A PSALM OF DAVID. MASCHIL. HAPPY IS HE WHOSE TRANSGRESSION IS FORGIVEN, WHOSE SIN IS PARDONED.

A PSALM OF DAVID. MASCHIL. HAPPY IS HE WHOSE TRANSGRESSION IS FORGIVEN. It is possible that the word *maskil* indicates that this psalm is to be performed to the tune of a poem beginning with the word *maskil*.[1] It is also possible that the word *maskil* is used because this psalm has the word *askilekha* (I will instruct thee) (v. 8) in it.[2]

The word *nesuy* (forgiven) in *nesuy pesha* (whose transgression is forgiven) comes from a root ending in an *alef*.[3] However, it is treated as if it came from a root ending in a *heh*.[4] On the other hand it is possible that there are two roots for the word pardoned.[5] The word *ve-nasu*[6] (and they shall bear) in *And they shall bear their shame* (Ezek. 39:26) is proof of this.[7]

The word *kesuy* (pardoned) is passive,[8] for the word *koseh* (concealeth) in *But a prudent man concealeth shame* (Prov. 12:16) is a transitive verb.[9]

---

1. See I.E. on Ps. 4:2 and the notes thereto.

2. In other words *[A Psalm] Of David. Maschil* means, a Psalm of Enlightenment written by David. See I.E. on Ps. 42:1.

3. Its root is *nun, sin, alef.* Compare, *nose avon* (forgiving iniquity) (Ex. 33:7).

4. If it followed the normal conjugation of a word ending in an *alef* then the word would have been spelled with an *alef* and without a *yod* and would have read *nesu* rather than *nesuy.*

5. Or carry or bear. One *nun, sin, alef,* and one *nun, sin, heh.* The latter is used in this verse.

6. It should be noted that the *mikra'ot gedolot* edition of I.E. reads *ve-nase'u.* However, this is an error, for the text in Ezekiel reads *ve-nasu.* See Filwarg.

7. The usual word used for bear is *nose. Nose* comes from the root *nun, sin, alef.* However, the word *ve-nasu* in Ezek 39:26 comes from the root *nun, sin, heh,* for if it came from the root *nun, sin, alef* then Ezek. 39:26 would read: *Ve-nase'u.* We thus see that there are two roots for the word to bear (and thus also for forgive).

8. Heb., *pa'ul.*

9. In other words *koseh* is the active (po'el) form of the verb and *kesuy* the passive form (pa'ul).

Scripture uses the phrase *kesuy chata'ah* (whose sin is pardoned),[10] because one is beaten or smitten in public because of sins that he committed. The psalmist therefore states: *I will make confession*[11] *concerning my transgression unto the Lord* (v. 5).[12]

We encounter a great difficulty in the book of Psalms. Note, we find David saying, *for I am godly* (Ps. 86:2) and *Neither wilt Thou suffer Thy godly one to see the pit* (Ps. 16:2). Now if this is so, then why do we find a number of psalms saying that David was guilty of trespasses and sins? [For Example, we find David saying,] *For I know my transgressions* (Ps. 51:5). The answer is:

David's heart was whole with regard to God. He did not sin nor trespass. However, he unintentionally transgressed in the eyes of human beings.[13]

Others say that David spoke on behalf of others, who were in exile.[14] However, if this is the case, what will they[15] do with *for I know my transgressions* (Ps. 51:5)? The latter was said with regard to the incident of Bat Sheba. I will yet explain this.[16]

2. HAPPY IS THE MAN UNTO WHOM THE LORD COUNTETH NOT INIQUITY, AND IN WHOSE SPIRIT THERE IS NO GUILE.

HAPPY IS THE MAN. The phrase *kesuy cha'ta'ah* (whose transgression is pardoned)[17] refers to one who repents and God's fierce anger is turned away from him. Such a person's sin is not seen, for he is not punished for trespassing.[18]

The word *yachashov* (counteth) refers to a thought (machashavah)[19] or to an account (cheshbon).[20]

The word *remiyyah* (guile) means, deceit.

---

10. Lit., "whose sin is covered. Hence I.E.'s comment."

11. Before people.

12. There is thus no reason for public punishment. Fillwarg.

13. What David did appeared to people to be a sin. It thus entailed desecration of God's name. However, David did not intentionally desecrate God's name. Hence he confessed his "sin." See Filwarg.

14. When David speaks of his sins, he refers to the sins of the Jews in exile.

15. Lit., "he."

16. According to I.E. David did not actually commit adultery with Bat Sheba. It only appeared so to people. See I.E. on Psalm 51:2, 5.

17. Lit., "whose sin is covered."

18. Hence it is said to be covered.

19. According to this interpretation, our clause should be rendered as follows: *Happy is the man that the Lord does not think of his sin.*

20. According to this interpretation, our clause reads as follows: *Happy is the man unto whom the Lord counteth not iniquity.*

Some say that *And in whose spirit there is no deceit* (remiyyah) means, and in whose spirit there is no thought of acting like a deceitful bow (remiyyah)." [21] I will yet explain this.[22]

3. WHEN I KEPT SILENCE, MY BONES WORE AWAY; THROUGH MY GROANING ALL THE DAY LONG.

WHEN I KEPT SILENCE, MY BONES WORE AWAY. If[23] I kept silent and did not speak as people speak[24] then my bones wore away.
Bi-sha'agati (through my moaning) means, I acted like a lion that lifts up his voice.[25]

4. FOR DAY AND NIGHT THY HAND WAS HEAVY UPON ME; MY SAP WAS TURNED AS IN THE DROUGHTS OF THE SUMMER. SELAH.

FOR … THY HAND. Thy blow, for blows are delivered by the hand.

MY SAP. The word *leshaddi* (my sap) is related to the word *leshad* (moisture) in *leshad ha-shamen* (moisture of oil) (Num. 11:8). The reference in our verse is to the body's warm liquids upon which human life depends.[26] *The droughts of the summer* is[27] similarly[28] a metaphor. It means that the liquids in David's body[29] were dried up and the days of his death were drawing close.

5. I ACKNOWLEDGED MY SIN UNTO THEE, AND MINE INIQUITY HAVE I NOT HID; I SAID: I WILL MAKE CONFESSION CONCERNING MY TRANSGRESSIONS UNTO THE LORD; - AND THOU FORGAVEST THE INIQUITY OF MY SIN. SELAH.

---

21. Ps. 78:57. A deceitful bow is a bow that does not accomplish its task.

22. See I.E. on Ps. 78:57.

23. I.E. renders *ki hecherashti* (when I kept silent) as, if I kept silent.

24. When they are in pain. David did not fully verbalize his pain. However, he was not totally silent. I.E. comments thus so that part one and part two of the verse will not contradict each other. Filwarg.

25. *Bi-sha'agati* (through my moaning) literally means, through my roaring. People do not roar. Hence I.E.'s comment.

26. In other words *my sap* is a metaphor for the warm liquids in the body.

27. Like *my sap.*

28. Lit., "also."

29. Lit., "his body."

MY SIN. *I acknowledged my sin* corresponds to *whose sin is pardoned* (v. 1); *mine iniquity* corresponds to *unto whom the Lord counteth not iniquity* (v. 2), and *my transgressions* corresponds to *whose transgression is forgiven* (v. 1).

Odeh (I acknowledged) means, I will make confession.

And Thou forgavest the iniquity of my sin was said under the influence of the Holy Spirit.[30] Or, it indicates that God forgave David's sin in the past.[31]

6. FOR THIS LET EVERY ONE THAT IS GODLY PRAY UNTO THEE IN A TIME WHEN THOU MAYEST BE FOUND; SURELY, WHEN THE GREAT WATERS OVERFLOW, THEY WILL NOT REACH UNTO HIM.

FOR THIS. That You forgive sin.

IN A TIME WHEN THOU MAYEST BE FOUND. This is similar to *Seek ye the Lord while He may be found* (Is. 55:6) and to *But from thence ye will seek the Lord thy God; and thou shalt find Him* (Deut. 4:29). Or *in a time when Thou mayest be found* means, the godly person will pray when he finds his mind free from ruminations of business, other needs, and extraneous thoughts.[32] Our verse is similar to *therefore hath Thy servant found his heart to pray this prayer unto Thee* (11 Sam. 76:27).[33]

When the great waters overflow alludes to David's[34] enemies who roar like water.[35] It is similar to *He drew me out of many waters* (Ps. 18:17).[36] Or, *the great waters* (which) *overflow* refers to death and illness. David compared the latter to waters that greatly increase.

---

30. I.E. renders *nasata* (forgavest) as, will forgive. The question thus arises: How does David know that God will forgive his sin? Hence I.E.'s comment that David knew this because he was prophetically inspired. See Radak.

31. Lit., *until that very day.* Hence David was confident that God would forgive his sin.

32. Lit., "his thoughts." According to this interpretation *le-et metzo* (in a time when Thou mayest be found) means, in a time when one finds one's mind free.

33. According to I.E., our verse means, Your servant has found his heart fit to pray to You.

34. Lit., "his."

35. So Filwarg, reading *ka-mayim* for *ba-mayim.*

36. Where *the waters* refer to David's enemies.

The meaning of *Surely, when the great waters overflow, they will now reach unto him* is that the waters will harm others but not him. The word *surely* (rak) is tied to *they will not reach him*.[37] There are many similar such cases in our language.[38]

7. THOU ART MY HIDING-PLACE; THOU WILT PRESERVE ME FROM THE ADVERSARY; WITH SONGS OF DELIVERANCE THOU WILT COMPASS ME ABOUT. SELAH.

THOU ART MY HIDING-PLACE. It is possible that *mi-tzar* (from the adversary) means, from the enemy. It might also refer to the sorrow caused by illness.[39] Compare, the word *tzar* (trouble) in *Trouble and anguish have overtaken me* (Ps. 119:143). *Many are the sorrows of the wicked* (v. 10) is proof of this.

WITH SONGS OF DELIVERANCE THOU WILT COMPASS ME ABOUT. Rabbi Moses says that the word *tesoveveni* (thou wilt compass me about) is a verb with two objects.[40] *Ranne falet* (songs of deliverance) refers to the voices of the angels saying that I will be saved. Note, the word *ranne* (songs of) is similar to the word *rinnah* (cry) in *And there went a cry* (1 Kings 22:36).[41] These angels correct me and say, *I will instruct thee...* (v. 8).

8. I WILL INSTRUCT THEE AND TEACH THEE IN THE WAY WHICH THOU SHALT GO; I WILL GIVE COUNSEL, MINE EYE BEING UPON THEE.

IN THE WAY WHICH THOU SHALT GO. The word *zu* (the) means, this.[42] The word *bet* is missing in the word *eni* (eye).[43] Some say that *I will give counsel... with mine eye* means, I will hint.[44]

---

37. Our text should be read as if written, When the great waters overflow, surely (rak) they will not reach him.

38. Where a word is not connected to what immediately follows.

39. The word *tzar* means adversity, trouble or sorrow. Hence the two interpretations.

40. It refers to David and to the voice of the angels.

41. I.E. reads: *va-ta'avor*. However, the reading in 1 kings 22:36 is: *va-ya'avor*.

42. I.E. reads our verse as follows: *I will instruct you and teach you: This is the way you shall walk in.*

43. In other words *eni* (mine eye) should be read as if written, *be-eni* (with mine eye). According to I.E. our clause is to be interpreted, *I will counsel you with Mine eye.*

44. "I will hint with my eyes as to how you should act." Rashi.

9. BE NOT AS THE HORSE, OR AS THE MULE, WHICH HAVE NO UNDERSTANDING; WHOSE MOUTH MUST BE HELD IN WITH BIT AND BRIDLE, THAT THEY COME NOT NEAR UNTO THEE.

BE NOT. This is the counsel.

BE NOT AS THE HORSE, OR AS THE MULE. There is no *vav*[45] in front of the word *ke-fered* (as the mule).[46] Scripture does this because it wants to employ an elegant style.[47] Compare *ke-re'a ke-ach li*[48] (my friend or my brother) (Ps. 35:14). [49] Sometimes the comparative *kaf* (as)[50] is also omitted.

Rabbi Moses says that *Be not as the horse… whose mouth must be held in with bit and bridle* means, don't be like a horse[51] that requires a bit and a bridle.

Edyo (whose mouth) means, cheeks.[52] Compare, *who satisfieth thine mouth* (edyekh) *with good things* (Ps. 103:5).[53]

MUST BE HELD. The word *li-velom* (be held) is a well-known Talmudic term.[54]

That they come not near unto thee means, that they come not near unto you to harm you.

Others say that *That they come not near you* means, far be it from you to act like a horse.[55] It is similar to, *But the counsel of the wicked is far from me* (Job 22:18).

Others say that the word *oto* (him) is missing from our text.[56] Our clause should be read as if written, *whose glory it is to be held in with bit and bridle*.[57] I will yet explain the word

---

45. Which here would have the meaning of, *or*.

46. Our verse literally reads: *Be not as the horse, as the mule.* Hence I.E.'s comment.

47. In poetry one often omits a word.

48. Rather than *ke-re'a u-khe'ach li.*

49. Ps. 35:14 literally reads: *my friend, my brother.*

50. Which grammar requires to be prefixed to each of two things being compared.

51. Or a mule.

52. Or mouth. See I.E. on Ps. 103:5.

53. Translated according to I.E.

54. In other words, the meaning of *li-velom* can be ascertained from Talmudic use. See Hull. 89a: *He who restrains* (she-bolem) *himself in strife.* The word *balam* thus means to muzzle or to restrain.

55. Or a mule.

56. In other words *li-velom* (be held) should be read as if written, *li-velom oto,* to hold him (or it) in.

57. I.E. renders *edyo* as *his glory.*

Edyekh (thine old age) (PS. 103: 5).[58] Our verse is similar to *Until his iniquity be found, and he be hated* (Ps. 36:3).[59]

10. MANY ARE THE SORROWS OF THE WICKED; BUT HE THAT TRUSTETH IN THE LORD, MERCY COMPASSETH HIM ABOUT.

MANY ARE THE SORROWS OF THE WICKED. Rabbi Moses says that the *wicked* refers to one who did not set his heart to watch his ways and to see if his steps have slipped. It is because of this that he is called wicked.[60] It is therefore likely that our verse speaks of the one *whose sin is pardoned* (v. 1.).[61]

But he that trusteth in the Lord refers to a person who does not rely on physicians as King Asa did.[62]

Note the following: Scripture only permits one to be healed from a human blow, for God alone is the healer of Israel. One's healing consists in strengthening one's spirit and increasing his fear of God.[63]

11. BE GLAD IN THE LORD, AND REJOICE, YE RIGHTEOUS; AND SHOUT FOR JOY, ALL YE THAT ARE UPRIGHT IN HEART.

The righteous who have not sinned are glad because no illness will befall them, for God who is their physician watches over them, and he will remove all disease which is found in their food.[64]

---

58. I.E. connects the word *edyo* with *adah* an ornament. Hence his rendering of *Edyo* as his glory. See Filwarg.

59. Literally, to hate (li-seno). Here too *li-seno* is to be read as if written, *li-seno oto* (that he be hated; literally, to hate him) See I.E. on Ps. 36:3).

60. In other words, our verse speaks of a person who was not scrupulous with regard to his religious behavior.

61. This type of individual sinned only in error and repented when God brought pain upon him. Filwarg.

62. When king Asa fell ill, he sought the help of physicians. I.E. notes that Scripture criticizes the king for doing this. See 2 Chron. 16:12.

63. According to I.E., illness is to be healed only by God. See I.E. on Ex. 21:19. Also See Chapter 7 of *The Secret of The Torah*.

64. People in the middle ages often fell ill from contaminated food. I.E.'s comment reflects the latter.

CHAPTER 33

1. REJOICE IN THE LORD, O YE RIGHTEOUS, PRAISE IS COMELY FOR THE UPRIGHT.

REJOICE IN THE LORD. *Rannenu* (rejoice) means, make your voice heard.[1]
The word *navah* (comely) is related to the word *ta'avah* (desire).[2] Its *nun* is the *nun* of the *nifal* form. *Ta'avah* follows the paradigm of *na'asah* (dressed)[3] in *and all that is dressed (na'asah) in the stewing-pan* (Lev. 7:9). Others say that *navah* is similar to the Talmudic word *na'ah* (comely).[4]

2. GIVE THANKS UNTO THE LORD WITH HARP, SING PRAISES UNTO HIM WITH THE PSALTERY OF TEN STRINGS.

GIVE THANKS UNTO THE LORD WITH HARP. Rabbi Moses says that *nevel asor* (psaltery of ten strings)[5] refers to a jar like musical instrument[6] that has ten holes. However, he is incorrect, for the terms *nevel* (psaltery) and *asor* (ten strings) refer to different musical instruments.[7] Our text should be interpreted as if written *be-nevel, be-asor* (with psaltery, with a ten stringed instrument).[8] It is like *ke-re'a ke'ach li* (like my friend or like

---

1. I.E. renders *rannenu* as, shout. He interprets our clause as follows: *Shout joyfully to the Lord*, or *Shout joyfully invoking God's name*. (See Radak).

2. According to this interpretation our clause should be rendered: *Praise is desirable for the upright*.

3. *Na'aseh* (dressed) is a *nifal*. Its *nun* is the *nun* of the *nifal*.

4. In other words *navah* means, comely. Its root is *nun, alef, heh*.

5. *Nevel asor* (psaltery of ten strings) literally means, a psaltery of ten. Rabbi Moses claims that ten is short for ten holes.

6. A *nevel* is a bottle or jar made out of skin. According to Rabbi Moses, the musical instrument bearing this name is a wind instrument made out of skin.

7. I.E. does not believe that *nevel* is connected to *asor*. He reads our phrase as follows: *be-nevel, [be-] asor*.

8. According to I.E. our clause reads: *Sing praises unto Him, with psaltery, with a ten [stringed instrument]*.

my brother) (Ps. 35:14).[9] The phrase *ke-keves alluf* (like a docile lamb) (Jer. 11:19) is similar. The latter is to be interpreted as if written, *ke-keves ke-alluf* (like a lamb, like cattle), for the *kaf* applies to both words as in the case of the *bet* in *be'el Shaddai* (as God Almighty) (Ex. 6:3)[10] and the *bet* of *be-bavel* (on Babylon) in *shall perform His pleasure on Babylon* (Is. 48:14).[11] The verse, which reads *With an instrument of ten, strings* (ale asor) and *with psaltery* (navel) (Ps. 92:4), proves that *nevel* and *asor* are two different instruments.[12]

3. SING UNTO HIM A NEW SONG; PLAY SKILLFULLY AMID SHOUTS OF JOY.

SING UNTO HIM A NEW SONG. The word *lo* (unto him) is to be read as if written twice. Our verse is to be read as if written, *Play skillfully unto him amid shouts of joy.*[13] Our verse is like, *Rebuke me not in Thine anger, Chasten me not in Thy wrath*[14] (Ps. 6:2).[15]

4. FOR THE WORD OF THE LORD IS UPRIGHT; AND ALL HIS WORK IS DONE IN FAITHFULNESS.

FOR THE WORD OF THE LORD IS UPRIGHT. The reference is to the decrees that the Lord decreed. They are called God's words[16] because all of the Lord's edicts are executed by the angels who do God's will.[17]

All the prophets and similarly all intelligent people give thanks to God in this way.[18] Rejoice with what is here written because the righteous are happy and break forth in song.

---

9. Translated lit. Friend and brother do not refer to the same person.

10. According to I.E., the *bet* of *be'el* also applies to the word *shemi* that follows the word *Shaddai*. Thus I.E. reads Ex. 6:3 as if written, *be'el Shaddai u-ve-shemi YHVH* (with the name El Shaddai and with the name YHVH). See I.E. on Ex. 6:3.

11. According to I.E. the *bet* of *be-bavel (on Babylon)* also applies to the word *kasdim* (Chaldeans) that follows. Thus the word *kasdim* in Is. 48:14 is to be rendered *be-kasdim* (on the Chaldeans). The verse is to be translated as follows: *He whom the Lord loveth shall perform His pleasure on Babylon, and show His arm **on the** Chaldeans;* rather than *He whom the Lord loveth shall perform His pleasure on Babylon, and show His arm Chaldeans.*

12. Lit. "That they are two."

13. In other words *hetivu naggen* (play skillfully) is to be interpreted as if written, *hetivu naggen lo* (play skillfully to Him).

14. Translated lit.

15. Wherein the second part of the verse repeats the first half.

16. Lit. "The words."

17. God's word is a metaphor for God's will.

18. By saying, *For the word of the Lord is upright* etc.

The righteous are never sad regarding what God decreed upon them, for all of God's decrees are upright and faithful.

5. HE LOVETH RIGHTEOUSNESS AND JUSTICE; THE EARTH IS FULL OF THE LOVINGKINDNESS OF THE LORD.

HE LOVETH RIGHTEOUSNESS. Scripture mentions *uprightness* with God' word[19] to indicate that God's word is correct.

It mentions *faithfulness* with God's work[20] because God will bring all hidden things to light.

Tzedakah means, righteousness. God' treats all equally.[21]

Justice means that God demands the cause of the victimized from those who harmed them. God extends his loving kindness to all. Hence Scripture reads: *The earth is full of the loving-kindness of the Lord.*

6. BY THE WORD OF THE LORD WERE THE HEAVENS MADE; AND ALL THE HOST OF THEM BY THE BREATH OF HIS MOUTH.

BY THE WORD OF THE LORD. Scripture backtracks and once again mentions God's word, because the parts by themselves are not connected to God's word. It is only their roots that are connected to God's word.[22]

By the breath of His mouth means the same as *the word of the Lord.*

Our verse mentions the heavens and their hosts, because all things that were created and exist upon the earth are dependent on the arrangement of the heavenly bodies.[23]

7 HE GATHERETH THE WATERS OF THE SEA TOGETHER AS A HEAP; HE LAYETH UP THE DEEPS IN STOREHOUSES.

HE GATHERETH THE WATERS. Scripture mentions the earth first,[24] for[25] it is a solid mass and we are its offspring. It then mentions the heavens and afterwards the sea.

---

19. In verse 4.

20. In verse 4.

21. Literally, "to equalize all."

22. The reference is to the genus or category to which an individual being belongs. The specie is connected to God and thus eternal. The individual is transient and thus not directly connected to God.

23. Literally, "the heavens."

24. In verse 6.

25. Unlike the sky and sea.

It does not mention the sphere of the wind and the fire,[26] for Scripture only speaks about that which is visible to the eye.

Rabbi Moses says that the dry land[27], which forms the surface of the earth,[28] would remain unrevealed if the waters did not stand like a heap, that is, if the waters were not gathered together.[29] Note, the word *kones* (gathereth) is connected to the word *kenos* (gather) [30]in *Go, gather together all the Jews* (Esther 4:16).[31]

He layeth up the deeps in storehouses means the same as *He gathereth the waters of the sea*.[32]

8. LET ALL THE EARTH FEAR THE LORD; LET ALL THE INHABITANTS OF THE WORLD STAND IN AWE OF HIM.

LET ALL THE EARTH FEAR THE LORD. Note, everything was created by God's word. It is thus fitting that all people of the earth fear Him and tremble at His word.[33] Our verse reads all the *earth*. The latter is similar to, *And all the earth came into Egypt*[34] (Gen. 41:57).[35]

9. FOR HE SPOKE, AND IT WAS; HE COMMANDED, AND IT STOOD.

FOR HE SPOKE, AND IT WAS. By His will and His desire and not through any instrument.

HE COMMANDED, AND IT STOOD. Scripture repeats itself.[36] Our verse should be read as if written, For He spoke and His word was,[37] and He commanded a command and it stood. Our verse is to be understood according to my earlier interpretation.[38] It is

---

26. I.E. believed that a sphere of fire and air surrounds the earth.

27. See Gen. 1:9.

28. Lit. "The dry land, that is, the surface of the earth."

29. Ibid.

30. Translated lit.

31. In other words, *kones* means *gathers*.

32. Lit. "The meaning is doubled in *He layeth up the deeps in storehouses.*"

33. See Is. 66:5.

34. Translated literally.

35. In other words, *earth* means the people of the earth.

36. *He commanded, and it stood* is parallel to *For he spoke and it was*.

37. His word was fulfilled.

38. That all verbs imply a noun. See I.E. on Ps. 3:8. Thus *He spoke* implies, He spoke a word. Similarly, *He*

similar to And *when He hath blessed*,[39] *I cannot call it back* (Num. 23:20), for a noun is implied in every perfect and imperfect verb.

10. THE LORD BRINGETH THE COUNSEL OF THE NATIONS TO NOUGHT; HE MAKETH THE THOUGHTS OF THE PEOPLES TO BE OF NO EFFECT.

THE LORD. Since God's counsel *standeth forever* no nation has the power to overturn His counsel. On the contrary God overturns their counsel.

11. THE COUNSEL OF THE LORD STANDETH FOREVER; THE THOUGHTS OF HIS HEART TO ALL GENERATIONS.

THE COUNSEL OF THE LORD STANDETH FOREVER. In contrast to the counsel of the nations.

THE THOUGHTS OF HIS HEART. This is metaphoric.[40]
The thoughts of His heart is in contrast to *the thoughts of the peoples* (v. 10).[41]

13. THE LORD LOOKETH FROM HEAVEN; HE BEHOLDETH ALL THE SONS OF MEN.

FROM HEAVEN. Scripture tells us that God knows the secrets of the hearts.[42] God is thus wise and omnipotent. Scripture says this here, because it earlier[43] mentioned God's might.
He beholdeth means, God, as it were, [44] sees all with His eyes.
Our verse mentions the heavens because they surround the earth.
Scripture reads *all the inhabitants* (v. 8) to indicate that no one is missing.[45]

---

commanded implies, He commanded a command.

39. According to I.E., *And when He hath blessed* means, and when He has blessed a blessing.

40. For God is incorporeal.

41. In other words, God nullifies the counsel of the nations (v. 10), but His counsel endures forever.

42. I.E.'s interpretation of *The Lord... beholdeth all the sons of men.*

43. Verses 6-11.

44. I.E.'s comment eliminates any question of God's corporeality. See I.E. on Ps. 2:4 and the notes thereto.

45. God does not miss anyone.

15. HE THAT FASHIONETH THE HEARTS OF THEM ALL, THAT CONSIDERETH ALL THEIR DOINGS.

HE THAT FASHIONETH THE HEARTS OF THEM ALL. He that fashioneth them is one, even though those who are fashioned[46] differ from each other. Therefore God alone knows all their doings.

16. A KING IS NOT SAVED BY THE MULTITUDE OF A HOST; A MIGHTY MAN IS NOT DELIVERED BY GREAT STRENGTH.

A KING IS NOT SAVED BY THE MULTITUDE OF THE HOST. God's decrees[47] are not like the thoughts of the king, who is the great counselor among men. Thus what purpose is there to the King's Counsel? Behold, the king is not saved by his many troops[48] that are his strength.

17. A HORSE IS A VAIN THING FOR SAFETY; NEITHER DOTH IT AFFORD ESCAPE BY ITS GREAT STRENGTH.

A VAIN THING. Scripture states: *A horse is a vain thing for safety.* Thus[49] God said [to Job:] *Hast thou given the horse its strength* (Job 39:19)?[50] Our verse refers to the horse of the king and to the horses of his army.[51]

NEITHER DOTH IT AFFORD ESCAPE BY ITS GREAT STRENGTH.[52] The object of *lo yimallet* (neither doth it afford escape) is missing. Our text should be read as if written, *lo yimallet nafsho* (neither save himself).[53]

---

46. Reading *ha-yetzurim* for *ha-yotzerim.*

47. Lit. "The decrees."

48. Lit. "Camps."

49. Literally, "because."

50. Our verse says that *A horse is a vain thing for safety,* to indicate that even the mighty horse cannot serve as an instrument of survival.

51. Lit. "Its meaning is, the horse of the king and the army."

52. The Hebrew reads, *u-ve-rov chelo lo yimallet.* This literally reads: Neither will he save by its great strength.

53. I.E. renders our clause as follows: *Neither will he* (the rider) *save himself by its great strength.*

18. BEHOLD, THE EYE OF THE LORD IS TOWARD THEM THAT FEAR HIM, TOWARD THEM THAT WAIT FOR HIS MERCY.

BEHOLD, THE EYE OF THE LORD IS TOWARD THEM THAT FEAR HIM. This[54] is similar to *that I may set my eyes upon him* (Gen. 44:21)[55] and to *place your eyes on him*[56] (Jer. 39:12).[57]

The eye of the Lord is toward those who do not fear a king of flesh and bones, but fear the Lord alone and wait only for His mercy.

19. TO DELIVER THEIR SOULS FROM DEATH; AND TO KEEP THEM ALIVE IN FAMINE.

TO DELIVER THEIR SOULS FROM DEATH. *To deliver their souls from death* refers to deliverance from the sword or the plague.[58]

20. OUR SOUL HATH WAITED FOR THE LORD; HE IS OUR HELP AND OUR SHIELD.

OUR SOUL… Our soul waited for the Lord because we saw that those who fear the Lord and put their trust in Him were saved.

He is our help is in contrast to the large army, which is mentioned with regard to *the king*.[59]

The Lord in contrast to *the king*[60] is *our shield*.[61] Compare, *Behold, O God our shield* (Ps. 84:10).

---

54. *The eye of the Lord is toward them.*

55. The meaning of which is, I will take care of him. However, in Gen. I.E. interprets *that I may set my eyes upon him* as, that I may see him.

56. Translated literally.

57. The meaning of which is, take care of him.

58. Not from natural death, for all people must ultimately die.

59. Verse 16.

60. Mentioned in verse 16.

61. Literally, "our *shield* is in contrast to *the king*."

21. FOR IN HIM DOTH OUR HEARTS REJOICE; BECAUSE WE HAVE TRUSTED IN HIS HOLY NAME.

FOR IN HIM DOTH OUR HEARTS REJOICE. *Our hearts* refers to the hearts of those who fear God.

22. LET THY MERCY, O LORD, BE UPON US, ACCORDING AS WE HAVE WAITED FOR THEE.

LET THY MERCY, O LORD, BE UPON US. Scripture mentions *Thy mercy*, and *we have waited for Thee* because it earlier stated, *Behold, the eye of the Lord is toward them.... that wait for His mercy* (v. 18).

CHAPTER 34

1. [A PSALM] OF DAVID; WHEN HE CHANGED HIS DEMEANOR BEFORE ABIMELECH; WHO DROVE HIM AWAY, AND HE DEPARTED.

[A PSALM] OF DAVID; WHEN HE CHANGED HIS DEMEANOR. *Ta'amo* (demeanor) means, his heart, his intelligence and his reason. Compare, *meshive ta'am* (that give wise answer) (Prov. 26:16).
Achish (1 Sam. 21: 13-16) had two names.[1] There are many other similar cases.[2]

2. I WILL BLESS THE LORD AT ALL TIMES; HIS PRAISE SHALL CONTINUALLY BE IN MY MOUTH.

I WILL BLESS THE LORD AT ALL TIMES. *At all times* means, when at ease and when in dire straits; when of sound mind and when acting insane.[3]

3. MY SOUL SHALL GLORY IN THE LORD; THE HUMBLE SHALL HEAR THEREOF, AND BE GLAD.

MY SOUL... I shall glory in the Lord[4] until the humble hear my praise[5] and be glad.

---

1. According to 1 Sam. 11-16 the king before whom David feigned madness was named Achish. However, here he is referred to as Abimelech. Hence I.E. points out that Achish had two names, Achish and Abimelech.

2. In Scripture of a person having more then one name.

3. Lit. "At all times, when he is at ease or in straits, when he is of sound mind and when changing it."

4. I shall recite God's glory.

5. Of the Lord.

4. O MAGNIFY THE LORD WITH ME; AND LET US EXALT HIS NAME TOGETHER.

O MAGNIFY THE LORD WITH ME. David speaks, as it were, with the humble and request of them to help him magnify the Lord.[6]

5. I SOUGHT THE LORD, AND HE ANSWERED ME, AND DELIVERED ME FROM ALL MY FEARS.

I SOUGHT THE LORD. David tells the humble[7] that he sought the Lord when he was in straits and the Lord answered him

6. THEY LOOKED UNTO HIM, AND WERE RADIANT; AND THEIR FACES SHALL NEVER BE ABASHED.

THEY LOOKED UNTO HIM. *They looked unto Him* refers to *this poor man cried* which follows.[8] *I see him, but not now* (Num. 24:17), which refers to *There shall step forth a star out of Jacob*[9] (ibid) is similar to our verse.

AND WERE RADIANT. Their faces were radiant. *Radiant* is in contrast to *abashed* in *shall never be abashed.* The word *ve-naharu* (and were radiant) is related to the word *ha-minharot* (the dens)[10] (Judges 6:2). There is a verse in Aramaic that reads, *And the light* (nehorah) *dwelleth with Him* (Dan. 2:22).[11]

Some say[12] that *ve-naharu* (and were radiant) is related to the word *ve-naharu* (shall flow) in *shall flow unto it* (Is. 2: 2). *Ve-naharu* is derived from the word *nahar* (river).[13]

6. David calls upon them to join him in praising God.

7. Lit., "them."

8. According to I.E. our clause is to be understood as, the poor looked upon Him, and were radiant.

9. Which follows.

10. A *minharah* is a hole in the ground with an opening for light to come in. I.E.'s point is that **nahar** means light.

11. We thus once again see that the word *nahar* means light.

12. Lit. "Others say."

13. These commentaries render our clause as follows: *They looked unto Him and flowed [unto Him].*

7. THIS POOR MAN CRIED, AND THE LORD HEARD; AND SAVED HIM OUT OF ALL HIS TROUBLES.

THIS POOR MAN CRIED, AND THE LORD HEARD. *Shame'a* (heard) is a perfect.[14] Compare, *ahev* (loveth)[15] *in such as he loveth* (Gen. 27:9). *Shame'a* is so vocalized because it has an *ethnachta*[16] beneath it.[17]

8. THE ANGEL OF THE LORD ENCAMPETH ROUND ABOUT THEM THAT FEAR HIM; AND DELIVERETH THEM.

ENCAMPETH. God sent an angel to save David because the servants of Achish surrounded him. Compare, *He will send His angel before thee* (Gen. 24:7). Scripture reads *round about* because *angel* is used as a collective noun.[18] Compare, *And I have an ox, and an ass*[19] (Gen. 32:6).[20] Thus *angel* means many angels, as we find in the account of Elisha.[21] Note the following: Even though the angels[22] are not seen by the eye, they are truly known by the heart.[23]

9. O CONSIDER AND SEE THAT THE LORD IS GOOD; HAPPY IS THE MAN, THAT TAKETH REFUGE IN HIM.

O CONSIDER. The word *ta'amu* (consider) is related to the word *ta'amo* (demeanor) (v. 1). It refers to what the heart perceives. However, the word *see* refers to what the eye sees.

---

14. The usual vocalization of this word is *shama*. Hence I.E.'s comment.

15. The usual vocalization of which is *ahav*.

16. A musical note that indicates a pause.

17. At a pause the word *shama* is vocalized, *shame'a*, and *ahav*, *ahev*.

18. In other words *angel* means, angels. One angel can't surround a person. Hence I.E.'s comment.

19. Translated lit.

20. The meaning of which is, and I have oxen and assess.

21. The prophet Elisha was surrounded by angels sent by God to protect him. See 11 Kings 6:17.

22. Sent by God to protect the righteous.

23. I.E. interpretation of 11 Kings 6:17.

10. O FEAR THE LORD, YE HIS HOLY ONES; FOR THERE IS NO WANT TO THEM THAT FEAR HIM.

O FEAR THE LORD. Rabbi Moses says that the word *yeru* (fear)[24] should have been vocalized *yiru*.[25] Compare, the word *kiru* (call).[26] However, it is irregularly vocalized so that it will not be confused with the word *yiru*[27] (saw)[28] in *The righteous saw it* (Job 22:19).

His holy ones refer to those who forsake the pleasures[29] and affairs of this world.

O fear the Lord ...for there is no want to them that fear Him means, do not fear that harm shall come upon you.[30] Do not even fret that your strength will diminish.[31]

11. THE YOUNG LIONS DO LACK, AND SUFFER HUNGER; BUT THEY THAT SEEK THE LORD WANT NOT ANY GOOD THING.

THE YOUNG LIONS. Some say that the *kefirim* (young lions) refer to those who deny God's existence.[32] However, it appears to me that the *kefirim* refer to those who are extremely gluttonous. They are like young lions with regard to the large amount of food that they tear apart. These people now lack food and suffer hunger.[33]

BUT THEY THAT SEEK THE LORD WANT NOT ANY GOOD THING. They seek their bread from God alone.[34]

---

24. *Yeru* is vocalized *sheva, shuruk*. Its *alef* is silent.

25. *Chirik, sheva, shuruk*, with the *alef* sounded.

26. For both words come from a root that ends in an *alef*. The root of *yeru* is *yod, resh, alef*. The root of *kiru* is *kof, resh, alef*.

27. From the root *resh, alef, heh*.

28. Lit., "will see."

29. Lit., "lusts."

30. From an outside source.

31. Lit. "The meaning of *O fear* is that they should not fear that harm shall befall them, or even that their strength will diminish."

32. Lit. "Some say, [those] who deny the root." The word *kofer* means a heretic. Hence this interpretation. It should be noted that the word *kofer*, with the meaning of heretic, is Rabbinic and not Biblical.

33. I.E. considers gluttony a major moral defect.

34. That is, for they seek their bread from God alone.

Some say that when the men of Achish seized David,[35] they starved him. David was thus hungry when he stood before Achish. However, God in his mercy helped him as he did Elijah.[36]

12. COME, YE CHILDREN HEARKEN UNTO ME; I WILL TEACH YOU THE FEAR OF THE LORD.

COME, YE CHILDREN HEARKEN UNTO ME. David mentions children because they are in need of instruction.

13. WHO IS THE MAN THAT DESIRETH LIFE, AND LOVETH DAYS, THAT HE MAY SEE GOOD THEREIN?

WHO IS THE MAN THAT DESIRETH LIFE? All people desire to live many years. Therefore *and loveth days* means, and loveth many days.[37] Compare, *men of size*[38] (Num. 14:32);[39] *men of heart*[40] (Job 34:10).[41] *Days* thus refers to well known days. It means, like the days of a certain individual who lived such and such a number of days.[42]

14. KEEP THY TONGUE FROM EVIL; AND THY LIPS FROM SPEAKING GUILE.

KEEP THY TONGUE FROM EVIL. David told the holy ones to fear God in their hearts,[43] for their status is very high.[44] He now tells them to keep themselves from sinning by tongue and deed.[45]

---

35. See 1 Sam. 21: 12-16.

36. See 1 Kings 17:2-6.

37. Lit., long days i.e. a long life.

38. Translated lit.

39. The meaning of which is, men of great size.

40. Translated lit.

41. The meaning of which is, men of a wise heart.

42. *And loveth days* thus means, he loves the days of so and so, who lived a long life. In other words he wants to live as long as the aforementioned did.

43. In verse 10. According to I.E. *O fear the Lord* means, fear the Lord in you hearts.

44. According to I.E. the mitzvot are observed by the heart, mouth and deed. He believes that the commandments given to the heart are the most important commandments. See *The Secret of the Torah*, Chapter 7.

45. Lit. "He told the holy ones to fear God in the heart, for their status is very high, to keep themselves from sinning by tongue and deed."

15. DEPART FROM EVIL, AND DO GOOD; SEEK PEACE AND PURSUE IT.

DEPART FROM EVIL. Do not violate any of the negative commandments.

AND DO GOOD. Observe the positive commandments.

SEEK PEACE. For it is unfit for children to seek lordship[46] and to overpower each other.

16. THE EYES OF THE LORD ARE TOWARD THE RIGHTEOUS; AND HIS EARS ARE OPEN UNTO THEIR CRY.

THE EYES… David mentions the eyes and the ears, that which is hidden and that which is open.[47]

17. THE FACE OF THE LORD IS AGAINST THEM THAT DO EVIL; TO CUT OFF THE REMEMBERENCE OF THEM FROM THE EARTH.

THE FACE OF THE LORD. God's rage, for anger is expressed by the face. Compare, *and her face was no more*[48] (1 Sam. 1: 18).[49]

18. THEY CRIED, AND THE LORD HEARD; AND DELIVERED THEM OUT OF ALL THEIR TROUBLES.

THEY CRIED, AND THE LORD HEARD. When they turned from their evil ways. Some say that this verse applies to the cry of the righteous.[50] However, what I said was correct. *The Lord is nigh unto them that are of a broken heart* (v. 19) proves it.[51]

---

46. To desire to rule over each other.

47. God sees what is done to them in public and hears their private prayers.

48. Translated literally.

49. Its meaning is, she was no longer angry.

50. See verse 16.

51. For *them that are of a broken heart* refers to those who repent their sins.

19. THE LORD IS NIGH UNTO THEM THAT ARE OF A BROKEN HEART; AND SAVETH SUCH AS ARE OF A CONTRITE SPIRIT.

OF A BROKEN HEART. The reference is to those who turned from their evil ways.

20. MANY ARE THE ILLS OF THE RIGHTEOUS, BUT THE LORD DELIVERETH HIM OUT OF THEM ALL.

MANY ARE THE ILLS OF THE RIGHTEOUS … Our clause means, if evil comes upon a righteous person, let him not give up hope, for God will save him from all evils.

21. HE KEEPETH ALL HIS BONES; NOT ONE OF THEM IS BROKEN.

HE KEEPETH ALL HIS BONES. This means that no great harm shall even fall upon his organs.[52] The psalmist mentions the bones because they are the foundations of the body.

22. EVIL SHALL KILL THE WICKED: AND THEY THAT HATE THE RIGHTEOUS SHALL BE HELD GUILTY.

EVIL SHALL KILL THE WICKED. One act of evil shall immediately kill the wicked.[53] Our verse is in contrast to *Many are the ills of the righteous* [*But the Lord will deliver him out of them all*] (v. 20).

23. THE LORD REDEEMETH THE SOUL OF HIS SERVANTS; AND NONE OF THEM THAT TAKE REFUGE IN HIM SHALL BE DESOLATE.

REDEEMETH… SHALL BE DESOLATE. The word *yeshmu* (shall be desolate) is similar to the word *yeshamu* (shall be desolate) in *but they that hate the righteous shall be desolate* (v. 22).[54] *Tesham* (shall be desolate) in *tesham shomron*[55] (Samaria shall be desolate) (Hosea 14:1) is similar to these two words. [56]

---

52. God shall not only protect his life, He will also protect his body.

53. One evil act that befalls the wicked shall kill them. The word for evil (ra'ah) is in the singular. Hence I.E.'s comment.

54. Translated according to I.E. The latter interprets *yeshamu* to mean, *shall be desolate*. See Radak.

55. I.E. renders this as, *Samaria shall be desolate*.

56. To *yeshamu* and to *yeshmu*.

CHAPTER 35

1. [A PSALM] OF DAVID. STRIVE, O LORD, WITH THEM THAT STRIVE WITH ME; FIGHT AGAINST THEM THAT FIGHT AGAINST ME.

[A PSALM] OF DAVID. STRIVE, O LORD, WITH THEM THAT STRIVE WITH ME. Some say that the word *yerivai* (them that strive with me) is based on an inverted root.[1] Compare, the word *shov* (abide)[2] in *If you will abide* (shov teshevu)[3] *in this land* (Jer. 42:10) and the word *yashov* (bring back) in *The Lord shall indeed bring me back* (yashov yeshiveni)[4] (11 Sam. 15:8).[5] However, it appears to me that we are dealing with two different roots.[6]

2. TAKE HOLD OF SHIELD AND BUCKLER; AND RISE UP TO MY HELP.

TAKE HOLD OF SHIELD AND BUCKLER. The following is the meaning of our text: I do not rely on the shield and buckler which I take to war. I rely only on You. I trust that You will strengthen me and that You will strengthen my shield.

---

1. *Yerivai* comes from the root *yod, resh, bet*. The Hebrew word for strife *riv* comes from the root *resh, yod, bet*. Thus *yerivai* can be traced to the root *resh, yod, vav*, which when inverted gives birth to the root *yod, resh, bet*.

2. The word *shov* in Jer. 42:10 comes from the root *shin, vav, bet*. However, the Hebrew word for abide comes from the root *yod, shin, bet*. Thus our text should have read, *yashov teshevu*. Thus *shov* in Jer. 42:10 is based on an inverted root.

3. This is the correct reading. The *Mikra'ot Gedollot* edition of I.E. reads, *shov tashuvu*.

4. This is the correct reading. The *Mikra'ot Gedollot* edition of I.E. reads, *shov yeshiveni*.

5. The Hebrew root for return comes from the root *shin, vav, bet*. Thus our text should have read *shov*, rather than *yashov*. Hence *yashov* is based on an inverted root.

6. There are two roots for the word strive, *yod, resh, bet*, and *resh, yod, bet*. The same might apply to the Hebrew words for abide, and return.

3. DRAW OUT ALSO THE SPEAR; AND THE BATTLE-AX, AGAINST THEM THAT PURSUE ME; SAY UNTO MY SOUL; I AM THY SALVATION.

DRAW OUT ALSO THE SPEAR. It is, as if it was You,[7] who draw out the spear.[8]

AND THE BATTLE-AX,[9] AGAINST THEM THAT PURSUE ME.[10] Close them in, so that they do not over take me,[11] when they pursue me.[12]

SAY UNTO MY SOUL: I AM THY SALVATION. For salvation[13] will come from God.

4. LET THEM BE ASHAMED AND BROUGHT TO CONFUSION THAT SEEK AFTER MY SOUL; LET THEM BE TURNED BACK AND ABASHED THAT DEVISE MY HURT.

LET THEM BE ASHAMED… LET THEM BE TURNED BACK. *Yissogu* (let them be turned back) is similar to *yikkonu*[14] (directed) (Ps. 119:5). It is a *nifal*.[15] If *yissogu* came from a word that had a *nun* as its first root letter,[16] then it would be vocalized like the word *yippelu*[17] (sink) in *They*[18] *sink into the heart of the king's enemies* (Ps. 45:6).

---

7. Not I.

8. See I.E.'s comment on the previous verse. I.E.'s interpretation negates any implication of anthropomorphism in our verse.

9. The Hebrew reads *u-segor*. *Segor* may be rendered, a weapon or close. See Radak. I.E. renders *u-segor*, and *close*.

10. I.E. renders our clause as follows: *Draw out also the spear, and close against those that pursue me.* Hence the interpretation which follows.

11. Lit., "him."

12. Literally, "him."

13. Lit., "the salvation." David's salvation.

14. From the root *kaf, vav, nun.*

15. From the root *samekh, vav, gimel.*

16. If *yissogu* (let them be turned back) came from the root *nun, samekh, gimel* then it would be vocalized like the word *yippelu*.

17. From the root *nun, peh, lamed.*

18. God's arrows.

5. LET THEM BE AS CHAFF BEFORE THE WIND, THE ANGEL OF THE LORD THRUSTING THEM.

LET THEM BE… It is possible for the wind to drive the chaff in a place where it will rest. However, if the angel drives it, then it will never find rest. It will be totally scattered and will never be found.

6. LET THEIR WAY BE DARK AND SLIPPERY; THE ANGEL OF THE LORD PURSUING THEM.

LET THEIR WAY BE DARK. When they flee, so that they do not know which way to flee.

THE ANGEL OF THE LORD PURSUING THEM. So that they will not saved. *Chalaklakkot* (slippery) comes from a doubled root.[19] It is like *secharchar*[20] (fluttereth) (Ps.38: 11) and *shecharchoret*[21] (swarthy) (Songs 1:6). *Chalaklakkot* (slippery) refers to a thick and smooth (chalak) darkness that the sense of touch can recognize.[22] Our verse is similar to *even darkness which may be felt* (ve-yamesh) (Ex. 10:21), which is akin to *as the blind gropeth* (yemashmesh)[23] in darkness (Deut. 28:29). It is totally incorrect to interpret *ve-yamesh* (be felt) as if written, *ve-ya'amesh* (and let it be very dark).[24]

7. FOR WITHOUT CAUSE HAVE THEY HID FOR ME THE PIT, EVEN THEIR NET; WITHOUT CAUSE HAVE THEY DIGGED FOR MY SOUL.

FOR WITHOUT CAUSE HAVE THEY HID FOR ME THE PIT. *Shachat* (pit) is related to the word *yasho'ach*[25] (he boweth down) (Ps. 10:10). It follows the paradigm of

---

19. Its root is *chet, lamed, kof.* However, the last two letters of this root have been doubled forming the word *challaklak.*

20. Which is formed by doubling the last two letters of the root *samekh, chet, resh.*

21. Which is formed by doubling the last two letters of the root *shin, chet, resh.*

22. I.E. renders our clause as follows: *Let their way be dark with a darkness that can be felt,* that is, may a thick cloud descend upon them. See I.E. on Ex. 10:21.

23. Lit., "feel."

24. As Rashi on Ex. 10:21 does. See I.E. on Ex. 10:21.

25. Which comes from the root *shin, vav, chet.*

rachat. Compare, *Which hath been winnowed with the shovel* (ve-rachat) (Is. 30:24). *Ra-chat* (shovel) is related to the word *ru'ach* (wind).[26]

8. LET DESTRUCTION COME UPON HIM UNAWARES; AND LET HIS NET THAT HE HATH HID CATCH HIMSELF; WITH DESTRUCTION LET HIM FALL THEREIN.

LET DESTRUCTION COME UPON HIM UNAWARES. The meaning of *tevo'ehu sho'ah lo yeda* (let destruction come upon him unawares) is, let such an evil[27] befall each one of them,[28] that all who hear of it will be astonished.[29]

AND LET HIS NET THAT HE HATH HID CATCH HIMSELF. *Tilkedo* (catch himself)[30] is similar[31] to *yikre'o* (he shall be called)[32] in *And this is the name whereby he shall be called* (yikre'o) (Jer. 23:6).

9. AND MY SOUL SHALL BE JOYFUL IN THE LORD; IT SHALL REJOICE IN HIS SALVATION.

AND MY SOUL. *Nafshi* (my soul) alludes to the soul from on high. It is referred to by the term *nefesh*[33] because it is tied to it.[34]

---

26. From the root *resh, vav, chet*. In other words the root *shin, vav, chet* gives birth to the noun *shachat* in the same way that the root *resh, vav, chet* gives birth to the noun *rachat*.

27. I.E. reads our verse as if written, *tevo'ehu ra, sh'oah lo teda* (let evil come upon him, an unknown astonishment).

28. Scripture employs the singular *upon him*, even though it speaks of David's many enemies, for the psalm speaks of each one of David's enemies.

29. I.E. interprets the word *sho'ah* (destruction) to mean astonishment. Cf. *mishta'eh* in Gen. 24:21. He reads our clause as follows: *Let an evil destruction come upon them, An unknown astonishment.* Hence his interpretation.

30. According to I.E. the meaning of *tilkedo* (catch himself) is, catch him. Thus our text should have read: *tilkedehu*, or *tilkedennu*.

31. In that Scripture uses an abbreviated pronoun, i.e. a *vav* in place of a *heh vav*, or a *nun vav*.

32. According to I.E., *yikre'o* (he shall be called) means, they shall call him. Thus Isaiah should have read: *yikrahu*.

33. According to I.E. there are three souls in the human body: a rational soul, an animating soul and a lusting soul. He believes the term *nefesh* usually refers to the "lusting" soul. See *The Secret of the Torah*, Page 96.

34. The rational soul that is in the human body is occasionally called *nefesh* because it is tied to the *nefesh* (the lusting soul) when it is in the body.

10. ALL MY BONES SHALL SAY: LORD, WHO IS LIKE UNTO THEE; WHO DELIVEREST THE POOR FROM HIM THAT IS TOO STRONG FOR HIM, YEA, THE POOR AND THE NEEDY FROM HIM THAT SPOILETH HIM?

ALL MY BONES. *My bones* allude to the body, for the bones are the foundations of the body. My bones will, as it were, speak and bear witness that there is no God but the Lord, who is able to help this poor man.[35]

11. UNRIGHTEOUS WITNESSES RISE UP; THY ASK ME OF THINGS THAT I KNOW NOT.

UNRIGHTEOUS WITNESSES RISE UP… David explains why God brought evil upon them.[36]

Let destruction come upon him unawares (v. 8), for[37] *They ask me of things that I know not.*

They ask me of things that I know not means, they ask me to give them things that I do not know of.[38] They produce only lying witnesses.[39]

12. THEY REPAY ME EVIL FOR GOOD; BEREAVEMENT IS COME TO MY SOUL.

THEY REPAY ME. The evil that they repay me is bereavement to my soul.
The word *shekohl* (bereavement) is a noun.

13. BUT AS FOR ME, WHEN THEY WERE SICK, MY CLOTHING WAS SACKCLOTH, I AFFLICTED MY SOUL WITH FASTING; AND MY PRAYER, MAY IT RETURN INTO MINE OWN BOSOM.

BUT AS FOR ME… David speaks of his goodness, namely that he wore sackcloth when they were ill.

---

35. David.

36. David's enemies.

37. Literally, "is in contrast to."

38. They invent claims. See I.E. on Ps. 37:33. Also see Radak.

39. To substantiate their claims.

Note the following: We know that whenever the word *affliction* is connected to the word *soul* the reference is to fasting. Compare, *and ye shall afflict your souls*[40] (Lev. 16:31); *And satisfy the afflicted soul*[41] (Is. 58:10); *The day for a man to afflict his soul*[42] (ibid. v. 5). This being the case: Why does scripture add *with fasting*?[43]

[The answer is:]

The *bet* of *ba-tzom* (in fasting) is vocalized with a *pattach*.[44] This indicates[45] that his friends[46] called for a fast on the very day that his[47] illness climaxed. It was thus a specific day.[48] David[49] also fasted in that day.

AND MY PRAYER, MAY IT RETURN INTO MINE OWN BOSOM. Rabbi Levi says that the *u-tefilati al cheki tashuv*[50] (and my prayer, may it return unto mine bosom) means, I offered my prayer bowed and humbled.[51]

However in my opinion the meaning of *u-tefilati al cheki tashuv* (and my prayer, may it return unto mine bosom) is similar to *And render unto our neighbors sevenfold into their bosom* (Ps. 79:12). It means; may God give me what I asked of Him in my prayer on their[52] behalf.[53]

40. The meaning of which is, and you shall fast.

41. The meaning of which is, feed those who have not eaten.

42. The meaning of which is, *the day for a man to fast.*

43. To *I afflicted my soul.*

44. A *bet* so vocalized indicates the direct object. *Ba-tzom* (with fasting) thus means, *in the fast.*

45. Lit. "The reason is."

46. The friends of the one who was ill.

47. One of David's adversaries.

48. Hence the term *ba-tzom.* I.E. explains our verse as follows: I afflicted my soul in the fast that they proclaimed.

49. Lit. "I."

50. Lit. *And my prayer returned to its bosom.* Hence the interpretation which follows.

51. Lit. *The prayer that I offered bowed and humbled.* David sat on the ground and bowed his head between his knees in prayer. His prayer was thus, as it were, poured out in his bosom

52. Lit., "on his."

53. In other words *unto mine bosom* means, to me. *And my prayer, may it return unto mine bosom* means, the good that I asked for them when I prayed, should befall me. (Radak).

14. I WENT ABOUT AS THOUGH IT HAD BEEN MY FRIEND OR MY BROTHER; I BOWED DOWN MOURNFUL, AS ONE THAT MOURNETH FOR HIS MOTHER.

I WENT ABOUT AS THOUGH IT HAD BEEN MY FRIEND OR MY BROTH-ER. *I went about* is connected to *as one that mourneth for his mother.*[54] However, it appears to me that *I went about* is connected to *mournful.* It means; *I went about mournful.*[55]

Scripture reads *koder*[56] (mournful), because it is the practice of people in mourning to dress in black.

15. BUT WHEN I HALT THEY REJOICE; AND GATHER THEMSELVES TOGETHER; THE ABJECTS GATHER THEMSELVES TOGETHER AGAINST ME, AND THOSE WHOM I KNOW NOT; THEY TEAR ME, AND CEASE NOT.

BUT WHEN I HALT THEY REJOICE. This alludes to David's illness.[57] David[58] could not stand on his feet and walk as all healthy people do. The word *tzali* (halt) is connected to the word *tzole'a* (limped) in *and he limped upon his thigh* (Gen. 33:22)."[59]

THE ABJECT GATHER THEMSELVES TOGETHER, AND THOSE WHOM I KNOW NOT. The word *nekhim* (abject) is an adjective. It is vocalized like the word *metim* (the dead). It refers to those who are of an abject spirit.[60] *Nekhim* (abject) is similar to *ge'im* (haughty).[61]

---

54. Our verse literally reads: As though it had been my friend or my brother I went about, as one that mourneth for his mother, I bowed down mournful. This interpretation explains our verse as follows: [I felt] as though it had been my friend or my brother, I went about as one that mourneth for his mother, I bowed down mournful. Filwarg.

55. This interpretation reads our verse as follows: [I felt] as though it had been my friend or my brother, I went about mournful; As one that mourneth for his mother, I bowed down. Filwarg.

56. Lit. *black* (koder).

57. Lit. "The allusion is to my illnesses."

58. David was not really lame. However, when he was ill he walked as if lame.

59. Lit. "The allusion is to David's illness. It is connected to and *he limped (tzole'a) upon his thigh* (Gen. 33:22) because he could not stand on his feet and walk as all healthy people do."

60. See Is. 66:2.

61. In that it refers to the state of a person's spirit.

Some say that *nekhim* (abject) is similar to *nekhe* (lame) in *lame of his feet* (11 Sam. 4:4). *Nekhim* (abject) is parallel to *be-tzali* (when I halt).[62]
Those whom I did not know means; I did not know that they were *unrighteous witnesses* (v. 11).
Those whom I knew and visited in their illness rejoice and gather together around me.[63] People who were inferior to them, men of abject spirit, gather to visit me.[64] They[65] gather around me even though I do not know their identity.

THEY TEAR ME. They tear my flesh. The latter is a metaphor for the evil that they speak about David. [66]

AND CEASE NOT. The word *dammu* (cease) comes from the same root as *dammam* (silent). It comes from a double root.[67] *Dammu* is similar to *tammu* (ended) in *The words of Job are ended* (Job 31:40).[68]

16. WITH THE PROFANEST MOCKERIES OF BACKBITING, THEY KNASH AT ME WITH THEIR TEETH.

WITH THE PROFANEST MOCKERIES OF BACKBITING. Some interpret *be-chanfe la'age ma'og* (with the profanest mockeries of backbiting) to mean that the wicked say things that make the owners of the cake laugh.[69] This interpretation expands on the text[70] and makes no sense.
However, in my opinion *be-chanfe la'age ma'og* (with the profanest mockeries of backbiting) means, [71] these wicked people are wicked mockers. Mocking to them is as pleasur-

---

62. In other words *nekhim* means lame. According to this interpretation our clause should rendered: *The lame (nekhim) gather themselves together against me.*

63. I.E.'s explanation of the first part of our verse.

64. When I was ill.

65. The inferior ones.

66. Lit., *"for the evil which they speak about me."*

67. Its root is *dalet, mem, mem.*

68. In that *tammu* comes from a double root *taf, mem, mem.*

69. The word *ma'og* means a cake. Cf. 1 Kings 17:12. This commentator explains *ma'og* (cake) to mean the possessor of a cake. He believes that "the owner of the cake" is a metaphor for the wealthy, those who have plenty of food. It renders our verse as follows: The evil men (be-chanfe) make the owners of the cake laugh (la'age ma'og). Compare, Rashi: "They flatter Saul so that he will give them food and drink."

70. It says more then the text says.

71. According to I.E. *be-chanfe lage ma'og* (with the profanest mockeries of backbiting) literally means, with the evil of the mockers of cake (ma'og). Hence his interpretation.

able as a cake to those who eat it. Our verse is like *Who eat My people as they eat bread* (Ps. 4:4).[72] Scripture therefore above reads: *They tear my flesh* (v. 14). This interpretation is proven by *They knash at me with their teeth* which follows.

17. LORD, HOW LONG WILT THOU LOOK ON; RESCUE MY SOUL FROM THEIR DESTRUCTIONS, MINE ONLY ONE FROM THE LIONS.

LORD, HOW LONG WILT THOU LOOK ON. And I will not see You exact my vengeance from them.

FROM THEIR DESTRUCTIONS. *Mi-sho'ehem* (from their destruction) is a noun.[73] It has the same meaning as *mi-sho'atam* (from their destruction),[74] for some nouns come in the masculine and feminine forms.
Mine only one from the lions means, from the teeth of the wicked[75] whose teeth are like the teeth of lions.

18. I WILL GIVE THEE THANKS IN THE GREAT CONGREGATION; I WILL PRAISE THEE AMONG A NUMEROUS PEOPLE.

I WILL GIVE THEE THANKS… David vowed that after being saved he would publicly give thanks to God.

19. LET NOT THEM THAT ARE WRONGFULLY MINE ENEMIES REJOICE OVER ME; NEITHER LET THEM WINK WITH THE EYE THAT HATE ME WITHOUT A CAUSE.

LET NOT THEM THAT ARE WRONGFULLY MINE ENEMIES REJOICE OVER ME. The word *sheker* (wrongfully) is connected to *oyevai* (mine *enemies*).[76] *Oyevai sheker* is similar to *sonai chinnam* (that hate me without cause).[77]

---

72. David's enemies want to destroy him with their mocking. They, as it were, want to bite into his flesh.

73. *Mi-sho'ehem* is the noun *sho'ah* with a prepositional *mem* prefixed to it and a pronoun suffixed to it.

74. Which is the word *sho'ah* plus the pronoun for *their*. The Hebrew word for destruction is *sho'ah*. *Sho'ah* is a feminine. We would thus expect our verse to read, *sho'atam* rather then *sho'ehem*.

75. Heb. *Mi-shinehem*. Lit., "from their teeth."

76. In other words *oyevai sheker* is one phrase. *Oyevai sheker* can be interpreted as, those who hate me by lying about me (see Rashi). Hence I.E.'s comment.

77. They both have one basic meaning, hating without a reason.

Yikretzu ayin (wink with the eye) means to hint by closing the edge of the eye,[78] as those who mock are wont to do.

20. FOR THEY SPEAK NOT PEACE; BUT THEY DEVISE DECEITFUL MATTERS AGAINST THEM THAT ARE QUIET IN THE LAND.

FOR… THEM THAT ARE QUIET IN THE LAND. Rabbi Moses says that *rige eretz* (them that are quiet in the land) means, the cracks in the land. It alludes to a hiding place.[79] Compare, *My skin breaks* (raga) *and is abhorrent* (Job 7:5).

21. YEA, THEY OPEN THEIR MOUTH WIDE AGAINST ME; THEY SAY, AHA, AHA, OUR EYE HATH SEEN IT.

YEA, THEY OPEN THEIR MOUTH WIDE… The term *he'ach* (aha) alludes to vengeance.[80]

22. THOU HAST SEEN, O LORD; KEEP NOT SILENCE; O LORD, BE NOT FAR FROM ME.

THOU HAST SEEN. *Thou hast seen* is in contrast to *our eye hath seen it* (v. 21). *Keep not silence* is in response to *they say aha, aha* (v. 21).

23. ROUSE THEE, AND AWAKE TO MY JUDGEMENT, EVEN UNTO MY CAUSE, MY GOD AND MY LORD.[81]

ROUSE THEE, AND AWAKE TO MY JUDGEMENT. *Ha'irah* (rouse Thee) and *ve-hakitzah* (and awake Thee) are intransitive verbs.[82]
It is also possible that *ha'irah* is transitive and means rouse Yourself. It is like the word *hillakhti* (I go) in *I go mourning* (Ps. 38:7), wherein *hillakhti* is transitive.[83]

---

78. It means to wink.

79. According to I.E., our clause should be rendered: But they devise deceitful matters against them that hide in caves and crevices.

80. It is a shout of jubilation when seeing one's enemies in trouble.

81. Our verse literally reads: *Rouse Thee, and awake to my judgment, My God and My Lord to my cause.*

82. According to this interpretation *ha'irah* (rouse Thee) and *ve-hakitzah* (and awake Thee) mean, *awaken.*

83. I.E. renders this clause as follows: *I caused myself to go in mourning.*

Elohai (my God) and *Adonai (my Lord)* are connected to *le-rivi* (unto My cause) because *ha-irah* (rouse Thee) and *va-hakitzah* (and awake Thee) are connected to *mishpati* (to my Judgment).[84] The meaning of our verse is as follows: *Rouse Thee my God to my judgment and awake My Lord to my cause.*

However, in my opinion, *Elohai va-Adonai* (My God and Lord) means, *because You are My God and You are my Lord.*[85] *Adonai* (My Lord) means, my Lord, for *Adonai* is spelled *alef, dalet [nun, yod]*.[86]

24. JUDGE ME, O LORD MY GOD, ACCORDING TO THY RIGHTEOUSNESS; AND LET THEM NOT REJOICE OVER ME.

JUDGE ME. Execute righteous judgment upon them on my behalf.[87]

25. LET THEM NOT SAY IN THEIR HEART: AHA, WE HAVE OUR DESIRE; LET THEM NOT SAY: WE HAVE SWALLOWED HIM UP.

LET THEM NOT SAY… Let their spirits not rejoice [88] and let them not praise themselves with their tongues.[89]

26. LET THEM BE ASHAMED AND ABASHED TOGETHER THAT REJOICE AT MY HURT; LET THEM BE CLOTHED WITH SHAME AND CONFUSION THAT MAGNIFY THEMSELVES AGAINST ME.

LET THEM BE ASHAMED AND ABASHED TOGETHER. This was said in contrast to *The abjects gather themselves together against me* (v. 15).
The object of *that magnify* is missing.[90] The reference is to their tongues or their words.[91]

---

84. In other words our verse is arranged verb (ha-irah ve-hakitzah) subject (Elohai va-Adonai).

85. This interpretation reads our verse as follows: *Rouse Thee, and wake to my judgment, even to my cause; because You are my God and my Lord.*

86. And means Lord. The tetragrammaton (YHVH), which is the proper name of God, is not used.

87. In other words, *Judge me* means, Execute judgment on my behalf.

88. I.E.'s interpretation of *Let them not say in their heart.*

89. I.E.'s interpretation of *Let them not say.*

90. Our clause literally reads, *that magnify against me.* I.E. suggests that the latter means, that magnify their tongues against me.

91. Lit., their word.

27. LET THEM SHOUT FOR JOY, AND BE GLAD, THAT DELIGHT IN MY RIGHTEOUSNESS; YEA, LET THEM SAY CONTINUALLY: MAGNIFIED BE THE LORD, WHO DELIGHTETH IN THE PEACE OF HIS SERVANTS.

LET THEM SHOUT FOR JOY. When those who rejoice in my troubles are put to shame then those who desire to see my righteousness will rejoice.

Magnified be the Lord is in contrast to *That magnify themselves against me* (v. 26).

28. AND MY TONGUE SHALL SPEAK OF THY RIGHEOUSNESS, AND OF THY PRAISE ALL THE DAY.

AND MY TONGUE SHALL SPEAK OF THY RIGHEOUSNESS. In contrast to them that say *Aha, aha* (v. 21).

Shall speak of Thy righteousness is in keeping with *Judge me...according to Thy righteousness* (v. 24).

All the day means, it shall always be so.[92]

---

92. In other words *all the day* means, always.

CHAPTER 36.

1. FOR THE LEADER. [A PSALM] OF DAVID THE SERVANT OF THE LORD.

David refers to himself as *the servant of the Lord* because he later speaks of those who transgress and rebel against God the revered.

2. TRANSGRESSION SPEAKETH TO THE WICKED, METHINKS[1] – THERE IS NO FEAR OF GOD BEFORE HIS EYES.[2]

SPEAKETH. The following is the meaning of our verse: I think in my heart that transgression speaks, as it were, to the wicked person and tells him, "Do not be afraid."[3] Therefore God is not before his eyes.

3. FOR IT FLATTERETH HIM IN HIS EYES, UNTIL HIS INIQUITY BE FOUND, AND HE BE HATED.

FOR IT FLATTERETH HIM. The word *hechelik* (flattereth) is related to the word *hechelikah* (maketh smooth) in *that maketh smooth her words* (Prov. 2:16). It is similar to *chalak* (smooth) in *a smooth man* (Gen. 27:11).
Transgression makes smooth in the eyes of the wicked that which is evil. It does this so that God will find the iniquity of the ungodly and hate him.
Until his iniquity be found is similar to *God hath found out the iniquity of thy servants[4]* (Gen. 44:16).[5]

---

1. Lit., "in the midst of my heart."

2. Our verse literally reads as follows: *The word of transgression to the wicked, in the midst of my heart, there is no fear of God before his eyes.* Hence I.E.'s interpretation.

3. From sin.

4. This was spoken by Joseph's brothers regarding their selling of Joseph into slavery.

5. *God hath found out the iniquity of thy servants* is not to be taken literally, for God was always cognizant

4. THE WORDS OF HIS MOUTH ARE INIQUITY AND DECEIT; HE HATH LEFT OFF TO BE WISE, TO DO GOOD.

The word *chadal* (left off) is followed by[6] a *lamed*.[7] It is similar to *va-yachdelu li-venot ha'ir* (and they left off to build the city) (Gen. 11:8).[8]

5. HE DEVISETH INIQUITY UPON HIS BED; HE SETTETH HIMSELF IN A WAY THAT IS NOT GOOD; HE ABHORRETH NOT EVIL.

HE DEVISETH INIQUITY UPON HIS BED. At night.

HE SETTETH HIMSELF. During the day. The latter is the reverse of *upon his bed*.[9]

IN A WAY THAT IS NOT GOOD. This clause refers to the violation of negative commandments.

HE ABHORRETH NOT EVIL. Scripture repeats itself.[10]

6. THY LOVINGKINDNESS, O LORD, IS IN THE HEAVENS; THY FAITHFULNESS REACHETH UNTO THE SKIES.

O LORD, IS IN THE HEAVENS. The *heh* that is missing in the word *ba-shamayim* (in the heavens)[11] in *The Lord hath established His throne in the heavens* (Ps. 103:19), is present in the word *be-ha-shamayim* (in the heavens). Hence the word *ba-shamayim* is vocalized with a *pattach*.[12]

---

of the sin that Joseph brothers committed. What it means is that God waited till now to execute punishment. The same is the case with *Until his iniquity be found*.

6. Lit., "connected to."

7. Our verse reads: *chadal le-haskil*. The usual form of "left off" is *chadal* followed by a *mem* (chadal mi...) Hence I.E.'s comment.

8. Here too *chadal* (left off) is followed by a *lamed*.

9. Which relates to the night.

10. *He abhorreth not evil* repeats *He setteth himself in a way that is not good*.

11. *Ba-shamayim* is short for *be-ha-shamayim*.

12. Unlike the *bet* in our verse which is vocalized with a *sheva*. I.E.'s point is that *ba* is short for *be-ha* (in the).

The following is the meaning of our verse: I am the servant of God. Hence I know that God's loving kindness takes in everything.[13]

Scripture reads *Thy loving kindness...is in the heavens.* It so reads, because there is nothing above the heavens that is visible to the eye.[14]

Other believe that Scripture says *Thy loving kindness...is in the heavens...*[15] because heaven is the source of righteousness and the fountain of faithfulness.

7. THY RIGHTEOUSNESS IS LIKE THE MIGHTY MOUNTAINS; THY JUDGEMENTS ARE LIKE THE GREAT DEEP; MAN AND BEAST THOU PRESERVEST, O LORD.

THY RIGHTEOUSNESS. Rabbi Moses says that the meaning of our verse is as follows: People cannot bear Your righteousness, for Your righteousness is like the mighty mountains. However, in reality its meaning is that God's righteousness is beyond comprehension. It is like the mighty and powerful mountains that no man can reach. The knowledge of God's judgments is similarly like the great obscure deep, which man cannot see.[16]

The meaning of *man and beast...* is that God will judge all sentient creatures. Our verse is similar to *at the hand of every beast will I require it* (Gen. 9:5).[17]

8. HOW PRECIOUS IS THY LOVINGKINDESS, O GOD![18] AND THE CH3ILDREN OF MEN TAKE REFUGE IN THE SHADOW OF THY WINGS.

HOW PRECIOUS. Scriptures mentions those who are superior to human beings[19] because it previously mentioned man and beast.

How precious[20] is to be read as if written twice. The latter is in keeping with Biblical style.[21] The second part of our verse is to be read as if written, how precious are the children of

---

13. Lit. "For I am the servant of God. For I know that God's loving-kindness takes in everything."

14. The sky is as far the eyes sees. Hence Scripture only speaks of the heavens and not that which is above it.

15. See Radak who comments: "In the heavens means, until the heavens." I.E. apparently interprets similarly.

16. Lit. *Similarly the knowledge of Your judgments is like the great deep which is deep and man cannot see.*

17. Which shows that God will judge animals and beast.

18. Heb. *Elohim.*

19. The angels. According to I.E. Elohim refers to angels. He reads our verse as follow: *How precious are your loving kindness O angels* i.e. how precious is the loving kindness that God has shown you.

20. Heb. *mah yakar.*

21. Lit., "as is the rule."

men[22] who take refuge in the shadow of Thy wings. Its meaning may also be, how precious is the lovingkindess which You have shown to each one of the children of men.[23]

9. THY ARE ABUNDANTLY SATISFIED WITH THE FATNESS OF THY HOUSE; AND THOU MAKES THEM DRINK OF THE RIVER OF THY PLEASURES.

The word *yirveyun* (abundantly satisfied) is similar to the word *yirbeyun* (multiply) (Deut 8:13).[24]

Thy are abundantly satisfied with the fatness of Thy house refers to those who isolate themselves in their home in order to serve God. The service of God fattens the soul and the knowledge of God gives it[25] pleasure.

River is a metaphor for that which is unending.[26]

10. FOR WITH THEE IS THE FOUNTAIN OF LIFE; IN THY LIGHT DO WE SEE LIGHT.

FOR WITH THEE IS THE FOUNTAIN OF LIFE. *The fountain of light* refers to the life of the soul from on high,[27] which does not die.

IN THY LIGHT DO WE SEE LIGHT. This alludes to the reward given in the world to come, for there is nothing in this world more precious than light. It is a substance that is incorporeal.[28]

---

22. This interpretation maintains that the second time *how precious* "appears" in the verse it does so as a plural (*mah yekarim*), for *bene adam* (the children of men) is a plural.

23. In this case the second time *how precious* appears in the clause it is in the singular (mah yakar) and refers to each one of the plural.

24. They are of similar grammatical construction. The usual plural of will be satisfied is, *yirvu. Yirveyun* is a variant form. Hence I.E. points out that we find the same with *yirbu* and *yirbeyun*.

25. Lit., them.

26. Lit. "River means, unending."

27. An alternate interpretation is, man's highest soul. In either case the reference is to man's rational soul. For the three souls in man see *The Secret of the Torah* page 96-97.

28. Hence it is used as a symbol of the reward given in the world to come.

11. O DRAW[29] THY LOVINGKINDNESS UNTO THEM THAT KNOW THEE; AND THY RIGHTEOUSNESS TO THE UPRIGHT IN HEART.

O DRAW. *Them that know Thee* refers to those of exalted status.[30]

Scripture reads, *O draw.* It so reads, because God's loving-kindness is in the heavens. The word *draw* is to be read as if written twice. Our verse is to be read as if written, and draw Thy righteousness[31] to the upright in heart. The reference is to those who have good deeds to their credit. Scripture says *O Draw Thy loving kindness to the upright,* even though they are not on the same level as those who know God.

12. LET NOT THE FOOT OF PRIDE COME WITH ME;[32] AND LET NOT THE HAND OF THE WICKED DRIVE ME AWAY.

LET NOT. *Let not the foot of pride*[33] *come with me* means, let not the foot of men of pride come to me.

The word *tevo'eni* (come with me) is similar to *yishkavennah* (lie with her) (Deut. 28:30).[34] David, as it were, says let not the proud join me in the house of God.

AND LET NOT THE HAND OF THE WICKED DRIVE ME AWAY. Our verse makes mention of the foot and the hand. Our clause means, let not the hand of the wicked drive me away from the fatness of Your house[35] to another place.

13. THERE ARE THE WORKERS OF INIQUITY FALLEN; THEY ARE THRUST DOWN, AND ARE NOT ABLE TO RISE.

THERE. Our verse means, before the workers of iniquity come to me, they will fall[36] into the place where they intended to drive me.

---

29. Translated literally. Hebrew, *meshokh*.

30. People who know God are on a very high spiritual level.

31. From heaven.

32. Translated lit. Heb. *Tevo'eni*.

33. In other words *foot of pride* is short for, foot of men of pride.

34. The word *tevo'eni* (come with me) is a compound of the words *tavo* (come) and *oti* (me). Thus *tevo'eni* literally means, come me. However, this makes no sense. Hence we must render *tevo'eni* come to me. We find the same to be the case with *yishkavennah, which* literally means " shall lie (yiskkav) her (otah)" but must be rendered "shall lie with her."

35. See verse 9.

36. I.E. renders *nafelu* (fallen) (lit. fell) as an imperfect, will fall.

Other say that it means, when the foot of pride[37] runs with the intention to come to me it will stumble, and when the hands of the wicked[38] strengthen themselves to drive me away they will be thrust down.

Dochu (they are thrust down) is similar to *dacho* (thrust) in *dacho dechitani linpol* (Thou didst thrust sore at me that I might fall)(Ps.118: 13).

The meaning of *sham* (there) is, then.[39] Compare the word *sham* in *Then*[40] (sham) *they cry, but none giveth answer* (Job 35:12).[41]

It is also possible the word *sham* alludes to the place where evildoers fell in time of yore.[42] According to this interpretation, the meaning of our verse is as follows: I know that the hand of the wicked will not drive me away, for they shall fall as their counterparts fell in times past.

---

37. Mentioned in the first part of verse 12.

38. Mentioned in the second part of verse 12.

39. The word *sham* literally means there. Hence I.E.'s comment.

40. Translated according to I.E.

41. This interpretation renders our clause as follows: *Then are the workers of iniquity fallen.*

42. In other words *sham* maintains its normal meaning.

CHAPTER 37

1. [A PSALM] OF DAVID. FRET NOT THYSELF BECAUSE OF EVIL DOERS, NEITHER BE THOU ENVIOUS AGAINST THEM THAT WORK UNRIGHTEOUSNESS.

[A PSALM] OF DAVID. FRET NOT THYSELF. Some say that the word *titchar* (fret thyself) is a *hitpa'el* and that it is related to the word *charon* (anger).[1] They say that the word *ba-mere'im* means, because of evildoers.[2] According to this interpretation,[3] *titchar* follows the paradigm of *titgar* (harass) in *harass them not* (Deut. 2:19).[4]

Others say that the word *titchar* is related to the word *tetachareh*[5] (join)[6] in *Then how canst thou join with the horses* (Jer. 12:5). This is so even though *titchar* is a *kal*.[7]

2. FOR THEY SHALL SOON WITHER LIKE THE GRASS, AND FADE AS THE GREEN HERB.

The word *chatzir* (grass) means, the greens.[8] The same applies to the word *chatzir* in *Who maketh the mountains to spring with grass* (chatzir) (Ps. 147:9), and *the leeks* (chatzir) *and the onions* (Num. 11:5).

---

1. In other words *titchar* comes from the root, *chet, resh, heh.*

2. In other words the *bet* of *ba-mere'im* means, because of. The *bet* with a *pattach* beneath it usually means, in the. Hence I.E.'s comment.

3. That *titchar* is a *hitpa'el* from the root *chet, resh, heh.*

4. *Titgar* is short for *titgareh*. Similarly, *titchar* is short for *titchareh.*

5. From the root *tav, chet, resh.*

6. Translated according to I.E. (See I.E. on verse 6). According to this interpretation our clause reads as follows: *Do not join with evildoers.*

7. And *tetachareh* is a piel.

8. Edible greens, for *chatzir* is parallel to *yerek* (herbs).

The word *yimmalu* (wither) comes from a double root.[9] This is so even though the *lamed* does not have a *dagesh* in it.[10] Compare, *he-ezah fane'ha* (an impudent face) (Prov. 7:13).[11]

4. TRUST IN THE LORD, AND DO GOOD; DWELL IN THE LAND, AND TEND[12] FAITHFULNESS.

TRUST IN THE LORD... Rabbi Moses says that our text should be interpreted as follows: Do good and trust in the Lord; tend faithfulness and dwell in the land. It is possible that what is recorded in the second part of the clause is the cause of what is in the first part. If you will do good then you will be secure;[13] and if you tend faithfulness then you will dwell in the land.[14]

However, in my opinion people are envious of those who work unrighteousness because of the wealth in which they put their trust.[15] Hence the psalmist now says, trust in the Lord[16] and do not refrain from doing good.[17]

Shekhon eretz[18] (dwell in the land) means, you will dwell upon the land all the days of your life.

AND TEND FAITHFULNESS. *U-re'eh emunah* (and tend faithfulness) is similar in meaning to *shomer emunim* (keepeth faithfulness) (Is. 26:2),[19] for a shepherd (ro'eh) keeps the sheep.[20]

---

9. Its root is *mem, lamed, lamed*.

10. To compensate for the missing *lamed*. Literally, "is missing a dagesh."

11. *He'ezah* comes from the root, *ayin zayin, zayin*. Nevertheless the *zayin* in *he'ezah* does not have a *dagesh* to compensate for the missing letter. A missing letter is usually compensated for by a *dagesh*. I.E. thus points out that there are exceptions to this rule.

12. Translated literally. Hebrew *u-re'eh*.

13. According to this interpretation the *bet* in *betach ba-Adonai* (trust in the Lord) has the meaning of, because. Hence betach *ba-Adonai* means; You will be secure because of the Lord.

14. In other words, our verse should be understood as follows: If you will do good *then* you will be secure; and if you tend faithfulness *then* you will dwell in the land.

15. Verse 1.

16. And not in wealth.

17. And do not be envious of the wicked.

18. Lit. "Dwell land." Hence I.E.'s comment.

19. Thus the meaning of *u-re'eh emunah* (and tend faithfulness) is, and keep faithfulness. *U-re'eh emunah* literally means, and feed faithfulness. Hence I.E.'s comment.

20. *Re'eh* and *ro'eh* come from the same root.

Some say that *u-re'eh emunah* means do not eat that which is stolen and acquired by oppression as evil people do.[21]

6. SO SHALT THOU DELIGHT THYSELF IN THE LORD; AND HE SHALL GIVE THEE THE PETITIONS OF THY HEART.

SO SHALT THOU DELIGHT THYSELF IN THE LORD. You will seek your needs from the Lord as a workman who looks forward for his wages.

7. COMMIT THY WAY UNTO THE LORD; TRUST ALSO IN HIM, AND HE SHALL GIVE THEE THE PETITIONS OF THY HEART.

COMMIT. The word *gol*[22] (commit) follows the paradigm of *sov*[23] (turn).[24] Our verse is similar to *Cast thy burden upon the Lord* (Ps. 55:23).
Thy way means your needs. The same is the case with the word *darko* (his way) in *A man's heart considers his way* (Prov. 16:9).[25]

6. AND HE WILL MAKE THY RIGHTEOUSNESS TO GO FORTH AS THE LIGHT, AND THY RIGHT AS THE NOONDAY.

AND HE WILL MAKE THY RIGHTEOUSNESS TO GO FORTH AS THE LIGHT. *The light* means, in public. The following is the meaning of our verse: God will fulfill your needs and exact vengeance on your behalf by the light of day, that is, in public. Your righteousness will then be seen.

7. RESIGN THYSELF UNTO THE LORD AND WAIT PATIENTLY FOR HIM; FRET NOT THYSELF BECAUSE OF HIM WHO PROSPERETH IN HIS WAY, BECAUSE OF THE MAN WHO BRINGETH WICKED DEVICES TO PASS.

RESIGN THYSELF UNTO THE LORD AND WAIT PATIENTLY FOR HIM. Some say that the word *ve-hitcholel* (and wait patiently) is related to the word *tochelet* (hope).[26]

---

21. This interpretation renders *u-re'eh emunah,* and feed faithfully.
22. From the root, *gimel, lamed, lamed.*
23. From the root *samekh, bet, bet.*
24. Both words come from double roots and are imperatives in the *kal.*
25. Translated according to I.E.
26. From the root *yod, chet, lamed.*

Others say that *ve-hitcholel* is related to the word *chel* (pain)[27] in *And pain, as of a women in travail* (Jer. 50:43).[28] The latter interpretation is correct. The *lamed* in *ve-hitcholel*[29] is doubled like the *nun* in *ve-hitbonen* (and consider) (Job. 37:14)
The word *lo* (for him) means, because of Him.[30] It is like the word *li* (of me) in *say of me: He is my brother* (Gen. 20:13).[31] *Ve-hitcholel lo* (and wait patiently for him) means, and bear the pain because of Him. Hence *titchar* (fret thyself) in *fret not thyself* comes from the word *charon* (anger).[32]
The *bet* prefixed to the word *matzli'ach* (prospereth) means, because.[33]
If we connect the word *titchar* (fret) with *tetachareh* (join) in *how canst thou join with the horses* (Jer. 12:5)[34] then the meaning of our verse is, bear the pain and resign yourself unto God and in any case do not join with them *that are given to change*[35] (Prov. 24:21).[36]

8. CEASE FROM ANGER, AND FORSAKE WRATH; FRET NOT THYSELF, IT TENDETH ONLY TO EVIL DOING.

CEASE FROM ANGER. If you are incensed because he is wealthy and you are not, do not get angry[37] and harm him.[38]
However, if we connect *titchar* (fret...thyself) with *tetachareh* (join) in *canst thou join*[39] (Jer. 12:5) then its meaning[40] is, do not join with him and show him love and goodwill when your intention is to harm him.[41]

---

27. From the root *chet, yod, lamed*.
28. According to this interpretation, our clause reads: Resign yourself unto the Lord and suffer on his account.
29. *Ve-hitcholel* is spelled with two *lameds*.
30. The word *lo* usually means, to him. Hence I.E.'s comment.
31. In this verse *li* has the meaning of *because of me*, and not *to me*, which is its usual meaning.
32. Thus our verse means, bear the pain for the sake of God; anger not yourself because of the prosperity of evil -doers.
33. Thus the meaning of *be-matzli'ach* is, because of him who prospereth.
34. See I.E. on verse 1.
35. Those who want to change God's law.
36. *That are given to change* is another way of saying, *of him ...who bringeth wicked devices to pass* (le-hara). According to this interpretation our clause means, do not contend with those who bring evil devises to pass.
37. I.E. renders *al titchar* (fret not thyself), do not get angry.
38. I.E.'s interpretation of *it tendeth only to evil things*.
39. Translated according to I.E. See note 4.
40. The meaning of the second half of our clause.
41. According to I.E. the second half of our verse should be interpreted, do not join yourself (to him), if

9. FOR EVIL-DOERS SHALL BE CUT OFF; BUT THOSE THAT WAIT FOR THE LORD, THEY SHALL INHERIT THE LAND.

FOR EVILDOERS SHALL BE CUT OFF. This means that the children of the evildoers shall be cut off.[42]

BUT THOSE THAT WAIT FOR THE LORD, THEY SHALL INHERIT THE LAND. The *yod* in *koye* (wait)[43] is in place of a *vav*.[44] *Koye* is in the *kal*.

10. AND YET A LITTLE WHILE, AND THE WICKED IS NO MORE; YEA, THOU SHALT LOOK WELL AT HIS PLACE, AND HE IS NOT.

AND YET A LITTLE WHILE. Wait a little while and your eyes shall behold the day when the above-mentioned wicked person[45] shall be cut off.

11. BUT THE HUMBLE SHALL INHERIT THE LAND, AND DELIGHT THEMSELVES IN THE ABUNDANCE OF PEACE.

BUT THE HUMBLE SHALL INHERIT THE LAND. In contrast to the wicked. When the wicked are destroyed then peace comes to the earth. This is the meaning of *the abundance of peace.*

12. THE WICKED PLOTTETH AGAINST THE RIGHTEOUS, AND GNASHETH AT HIM WITH HIS TEETH.

THE WICKED PLOTTETH AGAINST THE RIGHTEOUS. David tells the righteous, You must hate the wicked person. Do not join him in fellowship, for he designs evil plots against you. If any misfortune befalls you, he gnashes his teeth at you in order to take hold of you.[46]

---

your intention is to do evil (to him).

42. The second half of the verse speaks of the children of the righteous, for it speaks of inheriting the land. Hence I.E.'s comment.

43. This is I.E.'s reading. Our texts of the Bible have *kove*. See Fillwarg.

44. For the root of *koye* is *kof, vav. heh.*

45. The reference is to verse 9.

46. Of that which belongs to you. Hebrew, *le-ha-chazik mi-mekha.*

13. THE LORD DOTH LAUGH AT HIM; FOR HE SEETH THAT HIS DAY IS COMING.

THE LORD DOTH LAUGH AT HIM. The wicked person does not know that the Lord who knows the future laughs at him. The latter is metaphoric.[47]

14. THE WICKED HAVE OPENED THE SWORD,[48] AND HAVE BENT THEIR BOW; TO CAST DOWN THE POOR AND NEEDY, TO SLAY SUCH AS ARE UPRIGHT IN THE WAY.

THE WICKED HAVE OPENED THE SWORD. The sword is closed when it is in its sheath. Hence Scripture reads: *The wicked have opened the sword.*
Others say that *patechu* (opened) means sharpened.[49] The word *petichot* (keen-edged swords)(Ps. 55:22) is similar.
The[50] sword is taken openly,[51] the bow in a hidden place.

15. THEIR SWORD SHALL ENTER INTO THEIR OWN HEART, AND THEIR BOWS SHALL BE BROKEN.

THEIR SWORD SHALL ENTER INTO THEIR OWN HEART. The *mem*[52] of *libbam* (their own heart) refers back to the wicked, for God will punish them for their deeds.

16. BETTER IS A LITTLE THAT THE RIGHTEOUS HATH THAN THE ABUNDANCE OF MANY WICKED.

BETTER… The righteous is happy with the little wealth that he has.

THAN THE ABUNDANCE. The word *hamon* (abundance) means money. Compare, *hamon* in *nor he that loveth abundance*[53] (Ecc.5: 9) and *yehemayun* (they gather money) in *Surely for vanity they gather money* (Ps. 39:7).[54]

---

47. For God does not laugh. See I.E. on Ps. 2:4 and the notes thereto.

48. Translated literally.

49. Lit. "The opening of the sword is its sharpening."

50. Lit. "Behold, the sword is taken openly."

51. *The wicked have opened the sword* means; the wicked have taken the sword openly.

52. Which is a third person pronominal suffix meaning *their*.

53. Translated according to I.E.

54. I.E. interprets *the abundance of the wicked* as meaning, the money of many wicked.

17. FOR THE ARMS OF THE WICKED SHALL BE BROKEN; BUT THE LORD UPHOLDETH THE RIGHTEOUS.

FOR THE ARMS OF THE WICKED... Scripture mentions *the arms* because they bend the bow.

Scriptures notes that the bows of the wicked will be broken[55] and that no harm shall befall the righteous.[56] It also notes[57] that the same fate[58] will befall the arms of the wicked. *But the lord upholdeth the righteous* is in contrast to[59] *For the arms of the wicked shall be broken.*

18. THE LORD KNOWETH THE DAYS OF THEM THAT ARE WHOLE-HEARTED; AND THEIR INHERITANCE SHALL BE FOREVER.

THE LORD KNOWETH... Some say that the meaning of *knoweth the days* is, shall extend the days.[60] However, in my opinion our verse is similar to *the number of thy days I will fulfill* (Ex. 23:26).[61] God knows all of those whose days will be full.

The days of the wicked are cut short in accordance with their deeds as in *why shouldest thou die before thy time* (Ecc. 7:17). Hence the length of days depends upon their actions.

THEIR INHERITANCE. This refers to the legacy that they will leave for their children or to the inheritance and the portion that God gave them.

19. THEY SHALL NOT BE ASHAMED IN THE TIME OF EVIL; AND IN THE DAYS OF FAMINE THEY SHALL BE SATISFIED.

THEY SHALL NOT BE ASHAMED IN THE TIME OF EVIL. *In the time of evil* refers to a time of plague.[62]

---

55. Verse 15.

56. I.E.'s paraphrase of *But the Lord upholdeth the righteous.*

57. First part of our verse.

58. That befell the bows of the wicked.

59. Lit., is the reverse of.

60. Thus our clause means; the Lord shall extend the days of them that are whole hearted.

61. Hence the meaning of our clause is, the Lord shall fulfill the days of them that are whole hearted.

62. Lit. Such as in a plague.

David tells us [63] that the day set for one to die "has not come" for the one who dies in war or in famine.[64]

20. FOR THE WICKED SHALL PERISH. AND THE ENEMIES OF THE LORD SHALL BE AS THE FAT OF LAMBS - THEY SHALL PASS AWAY IN SMOKE, THEY SHALL PASS AWAY.

FOR THE WICKED SHALL PERISH. The wicked shall die in the time of evil and famine.[65]

AND THE ENEMIES OF THE LORD SHALL BE AS THE FAT OF LAMBS - THEY SHALL PASS AWAY IN SMOKE, THEY SHALL PASS AWAY. *Ki-yekar karim* means, as the fat of lambs.[66] It is similar to *im chelev karim* (with the fat of lambs) (Deut. 32:14). The reference is to the fat of plump lambs.
They shall pass way in smoke means; they shall pass away moment by moment.[67]
Others say that the meaning of *ki-yekar karim* (as the fat of lambs) is as the grass[68] of the valleys. Compare, *Kar nirchav* (large pastures)(Is. 30:23). The word *kikkar* (plain) in *kikkar ha-yarden* (the plain of the Jordan) (Gen.13: 10) is similar. The *kaf* in the word *kikkar* is doubled.[69] It is similar to the word *bavat* in *be-bavat eno* (the apple of his eye) (Zech. 2:12).[70]
According to this interpretation,[71] *in smoke* means, they shall be destroyed, as the grass of the valley is, when the one who lights the fire sets them ablaze.
The first *they shall pass away* refers to the fat of the lamb,[72] the second to the wicked. The second *kalu* (shall pass away) is penultimately accented[73] because it comes at the end of the verse.

---

63. 1 Sam. 26:10.

64. One who dies in a plague or in war dies prematurely. He does not die on the day "assigned" for him at birth. See I Sam. 26:10.

65. I.E.'s interpretation of *For the wicked shall perish*. According to I.E. *ki* (for) should here be rendered, *and*. He thus renders our clause as follows: *And the wicked shall perish*.

66. The word *yakar* means precious. Thus *ki-yekar karim* literally means the precious part of the lambs. Hence I.E.'s comment.

67. Literally, moment after moment. They will burn continuously till they are completely destroyed.

68. The precious part of the valley.

69. For the basic word is *kar*.

70. The basic word is *bat*. See Ps. 17:8. The *bet* is doubled in *bavat*.

71. That *ki-yekar karim* means, as the grass of the valleys.

72. Or to the grass of the valley.

73. Whereas the first *kalu* is ultimately accented as it usually is.

21. THE WICKED BORROWETH, AND PAYETH NOT; BUT THE RIGHTEOUS DEALETH GRACIOUSLY, AND GIVETH.

THE WICKED BORROWETH. The wicked person borrows in his time of need and does not repay his debt. The righteous man is gracious and gives money to the wicked because he has pity on him. Compare, *If thine enemy be hungry, give him bread to eat* (Prov. 25:21).

22. FOR SUCH AS ARE BLESSED OF HIM SHALL INHERIT THE LAND; AND THEY THAT ARE CURSED OF HIM SHALL BE CUT OFF.

FOR SUCH AS ARE BLESSED… Such as are blessed of the Lord shall inherit the land because *The blessing of the Lord, it maketh rich* (Prov. 10:22).

23. IT IS OF THE LORD THAT A MAN'S GOINGS ARE ESTABLISHED; AND HE DELIGHTETH IN HIS WAY.

IT IS OF THE LORD… The meaning of *mitzade* (goings) is movements.[74] The term *gever* (man) in our language refers to a wise man.[75] Compare, *go now ye that are men* (gevarim) (Ex. 10:11). The wise individual[76] will be righteous.[77] AND HE DELIGHTETH IN HIS WAY. God delights in all of his ways. Therefore the wicked will not succeed against him.[78] Our verse is to be so interpreted, even though there is no *bet* before the word *darko* (his way).[79]

24. THOUGH HE FALL, HE SHALL NOT BE UTTERLY CAST DOWN; FOR THE LORD UPHOLDETH HIS HAND.

THOUGH HE FALL, HE SHALL NOT BE UTTERLY CAST DOWN. The word *yutal* means, will be cast down. Compare, *va-hatiluni* (and cast me) in *and cast me forth into the sea.* (Jonah 1:12).[80]

---

74. *Mitzade* literally means steps. Hence I.E. comment.

75. Lit. [To a man who is] full of knowledge. I.E. comments thus, because he believes it is only the movements of a righteous person that God establishes.

76. Lit. The one who is full of knowledge.

77. Hence God will establish the movements of the wise man.

78. Lit. Therefore he will not succeed.

79. In other words *darko* is to be read as if read *u-ve-darko*. Our verse literally reads, *And He delighteth His way.* Hence I.E.'s comment.

80. The root *nun, tet, lamed* (the root of *yutal*) usually has the connotation of to lift or bear. Hence I.E.'s

Some say that *though he fall* means, though he fall in spirit.

25. I HAVE BEEN YOUNG, AND NOW AM OLD; YET I HAVE NOT SEEN THE RIGHTEOUS FORSAKEN, NOR HIS SEED BEGGING BREAD.

I HAVE BEEN YOUNG, AND NOW AM OLD. I have experienced this in my youth and in my old age.

YET I HAVE NOT SEEN THE RIGHTEOUS FORSAKEN. Totally forsaken. Compare, *for I will not forsake thee* (Gen. 28:15).[81] Now Jacob asked for bread and a garment (ibid. 20).[82]

NOR HIS SEED BEGGING BREAD. *His seed* refers to the small children that the righteous leave behind. God will not forsake them, because of the merit of their father.

26. ALL DAY LONG HE DEALETH GRACIOUSLY, AND LENDETH; AND HIS SEED IS BLESSED.

He will live well all of his days, and after his death his children will be blessed, for the meaning of *li-verakhah* (is blessed)[83] is, all who see them will bless them.

27. DEPART FROM EVIL, AND DO GOOD; AND DWELL FOR EVERMORE.

DEPART FROM EVIL. Refrain from violating the negative commandments.
AND DO GOOD. Observe the positive commandments.
AND DWELL FOR EVERMORE. *And dwell* means, and you will dwell.[84] *Be fruitful and multiply* (Gen. 1:22) and, *and die in the mount* (Deut. 32:50) are similar.[85]

---

comment.

81. Translated according to I.E.

82. Thus only one lacking food or garment is considered forsaken.

83. Lit. For a blessing.

84. *Shekhon* (dwell) is an imperative. However here it has the meaning of an imperfect.

85. The Hebrew forms of *Be fruitful and multiply* (Gen. 1:22) and, *and die in the mount* (Deut. 32:50) are in the imperative. However, they are to be interpreted as imperfects. *Be fruitful and multiply* is to be interpreted as you will be fruitful and multiply, and *die in the mount* as and you will die in the mount, for it is not in the hand of a person to determine these things. See I.E. on Gen. 1:22.

28. FOR THE LORD LOVETH JUSTICE, AND FORSAKETH NOT HIS SAINTS; THEY ARE PRESERVED FOR EVER; BUT THE SEED OF THE WICKED SHALL BE CUT OFF.

FOR THE LORD LOVETH JUSTICE… Scripture earlier noted[86] that the righteous is not forsaken. It now adds that God will never forsake him.

THEY ARE PRESERVED FOR EVER… The righteous and his seed are preserved forever. In contrast to the righteous *the seed of the wicked shall be cut off.*

29. THE RIGHTEOUS SHALL INHERIT THE LAND, AND DWELL THEREIN FOR EVER.

THE RIGHTEOUS … Scripture earlier states: *and dwell for evermore* (v. 27). It now states that the aforementioned is God's law and true statute that He established upon the earth.

30. THE MOUTH OF THE RIGHTEOUS UTTERETH WISDOM, AND HIS TONGUE SPEAKETH JUSTICE.

THE MOUTH OF THE RIGHTEOUS UTTERETH WISDOM. Scripture earlier mentioned that the righteous does acts of loving kindness and is gracious with his wealth (v. 26). It now says that the righteous person acts loving kindly in sharing his wisdom and teaching the lost.[87]

31. THE LAW OF HIS GOD IS IN HIS HEART; NONE OF HIS STEPS SLIDE.

THE LAW OF HIS GOD IS IN HIS HEART. The Psalmist tells us that the righteous is inwardly as he appears he appears outwardly.[88]

---

86. In verse 25.

87. Those who are spiritually lost.

88. Lit. For His inside is like his outside. In other words he is not a hypocrite.

32. THE WICKED WATCHETH THE RIGHTEOUS, AND SEEKETH TO SLAY HIM.

THE WICKED WATCHETH THE RIGHTEOUS... When the wicked at his end sees that he has ultimately fallen from his rich state as in *and at his end he shall be a fool* (Jer. 17:11), he envies the righteous and because of his envy seeks to kill him.

33. THE LORD WILL NOT LEAVE HIM IN HIS HAND, NOR SUFFER HIM TO BE CONDEMNED WHEN HE IS JUDGED.

THE LORD... The meaning of *nor suffer him to be condemned* is that God will demonstrate the righteousness of the righteous. Scripture says the aforementioned because when the wicked see that they in their jealous fits cannot kill the righteous, they seek to invent claims against the righteous. They claim that the righteous man owes them money[89] or that the righteous person has committed an act of violence against them.

34. WAIT FOR THE LORD, AND KEEP HIS WAY, AND HE WILL EXALT THEE TO INHERIT THE LAND; WHEN THE WICKED ARE CUT OFF, THOU SHALT SEE IT.

WAIT FOR THE LORD. Occupy yourself[90] with this[91] all your days.

AND HE WILL EXALT THEE TO INHERIT THE LAND. *Vi-yeromimekha* (and He will exalt thee)[92] can refer to God or God's way,[93] for we find the word *derekh* (way) in the masculine in our language.[94]

[WHEN THE WICKED ARE CUT OFF, THOU SHALT SEE IT.] You, like the righteous who came before you, will see the wicked destroyed.[95]

---

89. Literally, that they gave him money.

90. Lit. Its meaning is...

91. Keeping God's way.

92. Which is in the masculine.

93. *Vi-yeromimekha* can be rendered, and He will exalt thee or and it will exalt thee. Hence I.E.'s comment.

94. Hence *vi-yeromimekha* (and He will exalt thee), which is in the masculine, can refer to God's way. According to this interpretation our clause should be rendered and *it will exalt thee* i.e. God's way will exalt thee.

95. Literally, will see the wicked are cut off.

35. I HAVE SEEN THE WICKED IN GREAT POWER, AND SPREADING HIMSELF LIKE A LEAFY TREE IN ITS NATIVE SOIL.

I HAVE SEEN THE WICKED IN GREAT POWER. David says: I have seen the wicked person displaying his power so that people will fear him.

Mitareh (spreading himself) means, revealing himself,[96] doing all evil things in public. The word *ke-ezrach* (like...in its native soil) is vocalized with a *pattach*.[97] It is in the construct. The word *etz* (tree) has been omitted.[98] The word *ra'anan* (leafy tree) means moist.[99] The word *ezrach* is similar to *ezrach* (one that is born) in as *one that is born in the land* (Ex. 12:48).[100] *Ezrach* is a tree with many branches.[101] Similarly a person who has a large family is said to have many branches.

Ger (stranger) is the reverse of *ezrach*,[102] for a *ger* is like a berry (gargir) that has been cut from the tree.

The following is the meaning of our verse: I have seen the wicked powerful like a many branched tree; doing all sorts of wicked acts in public.

36. BUT ONE PASSED BY, AND, LO, HE WAS NOT; YEA I SOUGHT HIM, BUT HE COULD NOT BE FOUND.

BUT ONE PASSED BY, AND, LO, HE WAS NOT...This means that the wicked person and his wealth will quickly be destroyed.

37. MARK THE MAN OF INTEGRITY, AND BEHOLD THE UPRIGHT; FOR THERE IS A FUTURE FOR THE MAN OF PEACE.

MARK THE MAN OF INTEGRITY. Now, pay attention and observe the man of integrity and behold the man who is upright. You will always see that their end is peace.

---

96. The root of *mitareh* is *ayin, resh, heh*. This root means to reveal or uncover.

97. *Ezrach* is vocalized with a *kametz* in our texts.

98. *Ke-ezrach ra'anan* literally means, "like in its native soil leafy (or full of sap)." I.E. says that the phrase is to be read as if written, *ke-ezrach etz ra'anan*. He interprets the latter to mean *like a many-branched tree* (ke-ezrach etz) *that is moist* (ra'anan).

99. That is, full of sap.

100. I.E. renders this, *as one who is many branched in the land*.

101. Lit. *Ezrach* means with many branches.

102. The Torah contrasts the *ger* with the *ezrach*. See Ex. 12: 48-49. Hence I.E.'s elaboration on these terms.

The word *tam* (integrity) is to be read as if written twice. The last part of our verse is to be interpreted as if written, For peace is the future[103] of the man of integrity.[104]

38. BUT TRANSGRESSORS SHALL BE DESTROYED TOGETHER; THE FUTURE OF THE WICKED SHALL BE CUT OFF.

BUT TRANSGRESSORS… *Transgressors* are in contrast to *the man of integrity*[105] and *wicked* is in contrast to *the upright*.[106]

39. BUT THE SALVATION OF THE RIGHTEOUS IS OF THE LORD; HE IS THEIR STRONGHOLD IN THE TIME OF TROUBLE.

BUT THE SALVATION OF THE RIGHTEOUS … As in *The name of the Lord is a strong tower* (Prov. 18:10) in every place[107].

40. AND THE LORD HELPETH THEM, AND DELIVERETH THEM; HE DELIVERETH THEM FROM THE WICKED, AND SAVETH THEM, BECAUSE THEY HAVE TAKEN REFUGE IN HIM.

AND THE LORD HELPETH THEM. We have seen that God saved many righteous.[108] He will similarly save the righteous forever.

---

103. Or, ultimate end.

104. The last part of our verse literally reads: For end to the man of peace. I.E. believes that this should be interpreted: *For peace is the* [ultimate] *end of the men of integrity.*

105. Mentioned in verse 37.

106. Mentioned in verse 37.

107. *In every place* is I.E.'s addition to the verse. In other words the meaning of Prov. 18:10 is as follows: God is in every place a stronghold in the time of trouble.

108. In the past.

CHAPTER 38

1. A PSALM OF DAVID, TO MAKE MEMORIAL.

The latter means, a psalm of David, which is to be performed to the tune of a song that begins with the word *le-hazkir*, to make memorial.[1]

2. O LORD, REBUKE ME NOT IN THINE ANGER; CHASTEN ME IN THY WRATH.[2]

O LORD, REBUKE ME NOT IN THINE ANGER. The word *not* (al) is to be read as if written twice. Our verse is to be read as if written, Chasten me **not** in Thy wrath. *And I have the knowledge of the Holy One*[3] (Prov. 30:3)[4]; *And two captains of bands were the son of Saul*[5] (11 Sam. 4:2)[6] are similar.

3. FOR THINE ARROWS ARE GONE DEEP INTO ME, AND THY HAND IS COME DOWN UPON ME.

FOR THINE ARROWS ARE GONE DEEP INTO ME. The word *nichatu* (are gone deep) is a *nifal*. *Nichatu* is similar to *ninchatu* (are gone deep).[7] It is related to the word

---

1. See I.E. on Ps. 4:1.

2. Translated lit.

3. Translated lit.

4. This is to be read as if written, *And I **do not** (lo) have the knowledge of the Holy One,* for the word *lo* from the first part of the verse is to be read as if written twice.

5. Translated lit.

6. This is to be interpreted as if written, *And two captains of bands were captains of the son of Saul,* for the word *sare* (captains of) is to be read as if written twice.

7. *Ninchatu* is the complete form. In *nichatu* the *nun* of the root is missing. See Radak.

va-tinchat (come down)[8] in *and Thy hand is come down upon me.*[9] The reference is to the illnesses and pains that struck David like arrows.

4. THERE IS NO SOUNDNESS IN MY FLESH BECAUSE OF THY INDIGNATION; NEITHER IS THERE ANY HEALTH IN MY BONES BECAUSE OF MY SIN.

THERE IS NO SOUNDNESS IN MY FLESH. The word *metom* (soundness) is related to the word *tam* (whole, complete). It[10] means health.[11] David first mentions the immediate cause of his illness, namely God's indignation.[12] He then[13] mentions the distant cause of his illness, namely his sin.[14]

BECAUSE OF MY SIN. For You are angry with me because of my sins.

5. FOR MINE INIQUITIES ARE GONE OVER MY HEAD; AS A HEAVY BURDEN THEY ARE TOO HEAVY FOR ME.

FOR MINE INIQUITIES ARE GONE OVER MY HEAD. My iniquities were so many that they piled up heap by heap, until they grew so high that they went over my head.

6. MY WOUNDS ARE NOISOME,[15] THEY FESTER,[16] BECAUSE OF MY FOOLISHNESS.

MY WOUNDS ARE NOISOME. *Hivishu* (are noisome)[17] is intransitive. It is like the word *hivish* (rot) in *and it did not rot* (Ex. 15:24). On the other hand David might be

---

8. In the second part of our verse.

9. It comes from the same root and has a similar meaning.

10. Here.

11. I.E. renders our clause: *There is no health in my flesh.*

12. Lit., "because of Thy indignation."

13. In the second part of our verse.

14. Lit. "Behold, he mentions the immediate cause, why this came about, because of Thine indignation, and the distant cause."

15. Heb. *Hivishu.*

16. Lit. "They are noisome, they fester my wounds."

17. Lit., "stink."

the object of *hivishu*.[18] David tells of the wounds that appeared on his body. He declares that his wounds were caused by his foolishness.

7. I AM BENT AND BOWED DOWN GREATLY; I GO MOURNING[19] ALL THE DAY.

I AM BENT AND BOWED DOWN GREATLY. I am bent and bowed because I do not have the strength to stand tall, straight and upright. My face is changed as if the sun struck me all day. This is the meaning of *koder hillakhti* (I go mourning).[20]

8. FOR MY LOINS ARE FILLED WITH SHAME;[21] AND THERE IS NO SOUNDNESS IN MY FLESH.

FOR MY LOINS ARE FILLED WITH SHAME. Its meaning is that David's intestines are filled with unmentionable disgusting and shameful matter. David once again mentions that there is no soundness in his flesh. The reference is to the visible organs of his body.[22]

9. I AM BENUMBED AND SORE CRUSHED; I GROAN BY REASON OF THE MOANING OF MY HEART.

Nefugoti (I am benumbed) is related to *va-yafag* (fainted) in *And his heart fainted* (Gen. 45:26).

I GROAN.[23] I roar[24] because of my great pain. It is similar to *I make myself like unto a lion until morning* (Is. 38:13).[25]

---

18. So Filwarg, According to this interpretation our verse reads as follows: My wounds have made me odious, my wounds fester.

19. Lit. "I go black."

20. Lit. "I go black."

21. Translated according to I.E. Hebrew, *nikleh*.

22. The same clause [*there is no soundness in my flesh*] in verse 4 refers to David's inner organs.

23. Hebrew, *sha'agti*, literally I roar. Hence I.E.'s comments.

24. See note 23.

25. The meaning of which is, I groan all night. We thus see that Scripture compares a groaning individual to a roaring lion.

10. LORD, ALL MY DESIRE IS BEFORE THEE; AND MY SIGHING IS NOT HID FROM THEE.

LORD, ALL MY DESIRE IS BEFORE THEE. My desire for a chance to live is before You alone and not before physicians.

11. MY HEART FLUTTERETH,[26] MY STRENGTH FAILETH ME; AS FOR THE LIGHT OF MINE EYES, IT ALSO IS GONE FROM ME.

MY HEART FLUTTERETH. The Aramaic renders the word *saviv* (round about) by the word *secharchar* (fluttereth).[27] *Libbi secharchar* (my heart fluttereth)[28] means, my heart does not find rest.

MY STRENGTH FAILETH ME. My natural power.

MY STRENGTH FAILETH ME; AS FOR THE LIGHT OF MINE EYES, IT IS ALSO GONE FROM ME.. This is what happens to sick people.

12. MY FRIENDS AND MY COMPANIONS STAND ALOOF FROM MY PLAGUE; AND MY KINSMEN STAND AFAR OFF.

MY FRIENDS. The friends that I had.

STAND ALOOF FROM MY PLAGUE. Because my wounds reek.

13. THEY ALSO THAT SEEK AFTER MY LIFE LAY SNARES FOR ME;[29] AND THEY THAT SEEK MY HURT SPEAK CRAFTY DEVICES, AND UTTER DECEITS ALL THE DAY.

THEY ALSO THAT SEEK AFTER MY LIFE LAY SNARES FOR ME The word *nafshi* (my life) is to be read as if written twice. Our clause is to be interpreted as if written;

26. Heb. *Secharchar.*
27. See *Targum* on *Koheleth*, 12:5; *Songs* 3:2.
28. Lit., my heart is encircled i.e. my heart is encircled by trouble.
29. Lit. *They lay snares, they that seek after my life.* Hence I.E.'s comment.

They lay snares for my life, those who seek after my life.[30] Our verse is to be so interpreted because the word *nafshi* (my soul) is the object.[31]
Lay snares for me means; their words serve as snares for me.

14. BUT I AM AS A DEAF MAN, I HEAR NOT; AND I AM AS A DUMB MAN THAT OPENETH NOT HIS MOUTH.

These are bodily defects.[32]

15. YEA, I AM BECOME AS A MAN THAT HEARETH NOT, AND IN WHOSE MOUTH ARE NO ARGUMENTS.

I AM BECOME AS A MAN THAT HEARETH NOT. I choose to act as a man that does not hear what the person who speaks to him says.[33] Our clause means, I do not answer them.

16. FOR IN THEE, O LORD, DO I HOPE; THOU WILT ANSWER, O LORD MY GOD.

FOR IN THEE, O LORD, DO I HOPE. I have no hope except for You.[34]
Thou wilt answer, O Lord my God means, I will not pay attention to their words, for I rely upon You with my heart, and I address my speech to you.

17. FOR I SAID: LEST THEY REJOICE OVER ME; WHEN MY FOOT SLIPPETH, THEY MAGNIFY THEMSELVES AGAINST ME.

THEY MAGNIFY THEMSELVES AGAINST ME.[35] *They magnify* (higdilu) means, they magnify their words.[36]

---

30. Filwarg.

31. Of *va-yenakkeshu* (lay snares).

32. In this verse David compares himself to a person who is actually deaf and dumb. I. E. Comments thus to avoid redundancy, for a similar metaphor is employed in the next verse.

33. Unlike the previous verse that employs the image of one who is actually deaf, our verse employs the image of one who acts as if he is deaf.

34. You are my only hope.

35. Literally, *they magnify against me*. Hence I.E.'s comment.

36. In other words *they magnify* is short for they magnify their words. According to this interpretation our clause reads: *they magnify their words against me*.

On the other hand it is possible that the word *higdilu* (they magnify) is intransitive.[37] The meaning of *pen yismechu li*[38] is: *Lest they rejoice over me.*[39] Compare, pen *yomeru li* (that men not say of me) (Judges 9:54).[40] When David's foot slipped and he took ill, his enemies magnified themselves over him.[41]

18. FOR I AM READY TO HALT; AND MY PAIN IS CONTINUALLY BEFORE ME.

FOR I AM READY TO HALT... Our verse is similar to *But when I halt (u-vetzali) they rejoice together* (Ps. 35:15).[42] However, its correct interpretation appears to be, I am ready to halt,[43] for I will not be able to get up for many days and my pain is continually before me.

19. FOR I DO DECLARE MINE INIQUITY; I AM FULL OF CARE BECAUSE OF MY SIN.

FOR... *For I do declare* mine iniquity means, I confess my sin to people. *I am full of care*[44] means, I worry my heart.[45]

20. BUT MINE ENEMIES ARE STRONG IN HEALTH; AND THEY THAT HATE ME WRONGFULLY ARE MULTIPLIED. BUT MINE ENEMIES ARE STRONG IN HEALTH.

Some say [that our verse is connected to the preceding verse. Our texts should be read as follows:] *For I do declare mine iniquity; I am full of care because of my sins*, lest I die and *my enemies are strong in health.*

---

37. In this case our clause means; *they magnify themselves against me.*

38. Which literally means, lest they rejoice to me.

39. In other words the word *li*, which usually means to me, is here to be rendered because of me or over me.

40. Here too the word *li* is to be rendered, of me and not to me.

41. Lit. "For behold, when my foot slipped and I took ill, they magnified over me."

42. In other words our verse continues the thought of the previous verse i.e. my enemies will rejoice when I halt.

43. This interpretation takes *nakhon* literally, i.e. it means ready or prepared.

44. Heb. *Edag.*

45. *Edag* is short for *edag libbi.*

21. THEY ALSO THAT REPAY EVIL FOR GOOD ARE ADVERSARIES UNTO ME, BECAUSE I FOLLOW THE THING THAT IS GOOD.

THEY ALSO THAT REPAY EVIL FOR GOOD. David's words show this[46] to be the case, for as he notes in another psalm, David visited them when they were ill.[47]

22. FORSAKE ME NOT, O LORD; O MY GOD, BE NOT FAR FROM ME.

BE NOT FAR FROM ME. Be not far from me is in contrast to *and my kinsmen stand far off* (v. 12).

23. MAKE HASTE TO HELP ME, O LORD, MY SALVATION.

According to my opinion the latter means, make haste to help me, You O Lord who is my salvation. Compare, *Say[48] unto my soul: I am thy salvation* (Ps. 35:3). However, Rabbi Moses says that the word *chushah* (make haste) is to be read as if written twice. Our verse is to be interpreted as follows: Make haste (chushah) to help me, O Lord make haste (chushah) to my salvation.

---

46. That David's enemies repay evil for good.

47. See Ps. 35:13.

48. This is addressed to God.

CHAPTER 39

1. FOR THE LEADER, FOR JEDUTHUN. A PSALM OF DAVID.

I have previously, at the beginning of the book,[1] explained the meaning of this clause.[2] According to my opinion, there was a well-known poem at that time[3] that was composed by Jeduthun.[4] On the other hand, some one else may have composed it in praise of Jeduthan.[5] The poem opened with *For Jeduthun.*[6]

This psalm is like the one above, for it speaks of David's illness.

2. I SAID: I WILL TAKE HEED TO MY WAYS, THAT I SIN NOT WITH MY TONGUE; I WILL KEEP A CURB UPON MY MOUTH, WHILE THE WICKED IS BEFORE ME.

I said (v. 2) means, I said in my heart.

I will take heed to my ways (v. 2) means; I will take heed with regard to my nature[7] and my practice. Compare, *and art acquainted with all my ways* (Ps. 139:3). Its meaning is, I will not speak as sick people do when they are in great pain. There is thus as it were a muzzle upon my mouth. I will keep this curb in my mouth and will not remove it.

WHILE THE WICKED IS BEFORE ME. The wicked that came to visit me.[8]

---

1. See I.E.'s introduction to the book of Psalms.

2. *For Jeduthun. A psalm of David.*

3. Literally, *in* their generation. Reading: *be-doram* rather than *be-darom* (in the south) (Filwarg).

4. This psalm was to be sung according to the tune of Jeduthun's song. See I.E. on Psalm 4:1.

5. Literally, "in praise of him."

6. The psalm was to be chanted to the tune of a psalm opening with the words *For Jeduthun.* See I.E. on Ps. 4:1.

7. My impulses.

8. In my illness.

3. I WAS DUMB WITH SILENCE, I HELD MY PEACE, HAD NO COMFORT; AND MY PAIN WAS HELD IN CHECK.

I WAS DUMB WITH SILENCE, I HELD MY PEACE. From even speaking good.[9]

4. MY HEART WAXED HOT WITHIN ME; WHILE I WAS MUSING, THE FIRE KINDLED; THEN SPOKE I WITH MY TONGUE.

MY HEART WAXED HOT… My heart waxed so hot within me, that when I spoke, fire blazed out.[10]

THEN I SPOKE WITH MY TONGUE. Scripture repeats itself.[11] Or it means, this[12] is what I spoke.[13]

5. LORD, MAKE ME TO KNOW MINE END, AND THE MEASURE OF MY DAYS, WHAT IT IS; LET ME KNOW HOW SHORT-LIVED I AM.

LORD, MAKE ME TO KNOW… HOW SHORT-LIVED I AM. The word *chadel* (short-lived) is an adjective. *Ede'ah meh chadel ani* (Let me know how short lived I am) means, let me know how long I shall be among the inhabitants of the world.[14]

6. BEHOLD, THOU HAST MADE MY DAYS AS HAND-BREADTHS; AND MINE AGE IS AS NOTHING BEFORE THEE; SURELY EVERY MAN AT HIS BEST ESTATE IS ALTOGETHER VANITY. SELAH.

BEHOLD… *Tefachot* (as hand-breadths) means, a small amount. *As hand-breadths* means, as something which is measured by hand-breadths. The word *cheldi*[15] (mine age) is simi-

---

9. Consoling myself with words of hope.

10. This is obviously a metaphoric statement.

11. *Then I spoke* repeats *while I was musing.*

12. What follows in the next verse.

13. In other words, the meaning of our clause is, then I spoke the following with my tongue.

14. I.E. connects the word *chadel* to *cheled* (world). *Ede'ah meh chadel ani* literally means, let me know how "worldly" I am. Hence I.E.'s interpretation. See his comments on the next verse.

15. From the root *chet, lamed, dalet.*

lar to *chadel*[16] (short-lived) (v. 5).[17] Compare, *keves* (sheep) and *kesev* (sheep);[18] *simlah* (garment) and *salmah* (garment).[19]

SURELY EVERY MAN… ALTOGETHER VANITY. Is every man.[20] Our verse is similar in meaning to *vanity of vanities* (Ecc. 1:1).[21]

[AT HIS BEST ESTATE.] The meaning of *nitzav*[22] (estate) is, it is forever so. In other words, man's condition will never change; he will never cease from his insignificant status.

7. SURELY MAN WALKETH AS A MERE FORM;[23] SURELY FOR VANITY THEY ARE IN TURMOIL; HE HEAPETH UP RICHES, AND KNOWETH NOT WHO SHALL GATHER THEM.

SURELY MAN WALKETH AS A MERE FORM. For man's changes in his form from day to day, and from time to time. He is unlike[24] a moving river whose form remains. Others say that the word *tzelem* (form) is to be rendered, a dark valley.[25] However, in my opinion man is like a "form." When the form changes man changes.[26] The form spoken of in our verse refers to the arrangement of the planets vis a vis the upper stars.[27] This arrangement does not last for even one moment. Those who are learned in the science of Astronomy know this.

---

16. From the root *chet, dalet, lamed.*

17. They come from the same root. However, the second and third stem letters change place.

18. *Keves* and *kesev* come from the same root. However, their second and third stem letters change place.

19. *Simlah* and *salmah* are one and the same word. However, the *mem* and the *lamed* change places.

20. Our verse reads: *akh kol hevel kol adam.* This literally means, surely altogether vanity every man. I.E believes that our verse should be read as if written, *akh kol hevel hu kol adam* (surely altogether vanity **is** every man).

21. Surely all men are all vanity means, surely all men are eternally a vanity of vanities. See Radak.

22. Literally, standing.

23. Translated literally. Hebrew *tzelem.*

24. So Filwarg. The printed texts of I.E. read: He is like a moving river.

25. According to this interpretation our clause should be rendered: Surely man walks in a dark valley. See I.E. on the word *tzalmavet* (Ps. 23:4).

26. Man's life follows a heavenly pattern (form). When the pattern changes, man's fortunes change.

27. "It is because of the (changes in the alignment of the heavenly bodies) that change comes to all things born of the earth...for no two arrangements (of the heavenly bodies) will be found to be the same in myriads of millions of years." (The Secret of the Torah, p. 173).

The meaning of *yehemayun* (they are in turmoil) is, they gather money. Compare *hamon* (abundance) in *he that loveth abundance* (Ecc. 5:9).[28]

HE HEAPETH UP. He heaps up riches little by little and he doesn't know who upon his death is going to gather them all up in one moment.

8. AND NOW, LORD, WHAT WAIT I FOR? MY HOPE, IT IS IN THEE.

AND NOW, LORD… Behold, my end has come.[29] What hope do I have?[30] My only hope is in You. My hope is as follows:

9. DELIVER ME FROM ALL MY TRANSGRESSIONS; MAKE ME NOT THE REPROACH OF THE BASE.

DELIVER ME FROM ALL MY TRANSGRESSIONS. For I have become ill because of sins.[31]

10. I AM DUMB, I OPEN NOT MY MOUTH; BECAUSE THOU HAST DONE IT.

I AM DUMB. David says: *I am dumb* and I do not answer the base,[32] because he previously said: *Make me not the reproach of the base* (v. 9).

11. REMOVE THY STROKE FROM OFF ME; I AM CONSUMED BY THE BLOW OF THY HAND.

REMOVE… BY THE BLOW OF THY HAND. *Mi-tigrat yadekha* (by the blow of Thy hand) literally means, from the fear of Your hand. The reference is to God's blow.[33] Compare *va-yagar mo'av* (and Moab was sore afraid) (Num. 22:3).[34]

---

28. I.E. renders our clause: *Surely for vanity they gather up money.*

29. In other words, *And now* is short for, and now my end has come.

30. I.E. renders *mah kivviti* (what I wait for) as, what hope do I have? According to I.E., our verse should be rendered as follows: And now, Lord, what hope do I have? My hope, it is in You.

31. Hence the term *hatzileni* (deliver me).

32. Lit., "him." *And I do not answer the base* is a paraphrase of *I open not my mouth.*

33. Thus the meaning of the clause is as follows: I am consumed by the fear of the blow of Your hand.

34. *Tigrat* and *va-yagar* come from the same root.

The word *tigrat* (blow of)[35] is similar in form to the word *tikhlah* (measure) in *to every measure* (Ps. 119:96).

I will later explain that *tikhklah*[36] is similar in meaning to the word *kol*[37] (measured)[38] in *And measured...in a measure* (Is. 40:12).

12. WITH REBUKES DOST THOU CHASTEN MAN FOR INIQUITY; AND LIKE A MOTH THOU MAKEST HIS BEAUTY TO CONSUME AWAY; SURELY EVERY MAN IS VANITY. SELAH.

WITH REBUKES… *With rebukes dost Thou chasten man for iniquity* is similar to *He is chastened also with pain* (Job 33:19).[39] We know that You chasten a man for his sins with pain.

HIS BEAUTY. The beauty of his body. His beauty is[40] thus a vanity.

13. HEAR MY PRAYER, O LORD, AND GIVE EAR UNTO MY CRY; KEEP NOT SILENCE AT MY TEARS; FOR I AM A STRANGER WITH THEE, A SOJOURNER, AS ALL MY FATHERS WERE.

HEAR MY PRAYER. Note the following: The prayers and tears of the psalmist are like the medicines of a physician.

FOR I AM A STRANGER WITH THEE. As is stated in the Torah.[41]

---

35. The absolute form of which is *tigrah*. *Tigrat* is in the construct.

36. From the root *kaf, lamed, heh*.

37. From the root *kaf, vav, lamed*, or *kaf, lamed, lamed*. Filwarg.

38. Translated according to I.E.

39. *Dost Thou chasten* means, dost Thou chasten with pain.

40. Lit. "Was."

41. See Gen. 23:4: *I am a stranger… with you*. I.E. renders the aforementioned, *we are all mortal*.

14. LOOK AWAY FROM ME, THAT I MAY TAKE COMFORT, BEFORE I GO HENCE, AND BE NO MORE.

LOOK AWAY FROM ME. *Hasha me-menni* (look away from me) means, let go of me.[42] Compare *she'u* (let go) in *Let go of me* (Is. 22:4).[43] The vowel changes[44] because of the guttural.[45]

THAT I MAY TAKE COMFORT. The meaning of *ve-avligah* (that I may take comfort) is, that I may grow strong. It is a transitive verb.[46] Its meaning is, that I may strengthen myself.[47] Compare, *mavligiti* (though I would strengthen myself) (Jer. 8: 18).[48]

---

42. I.E. renders our verse as follows: Let go of me, that I may take comfort.

43. Translated according to I.E.

44. The word is vocalized *hasha*, rather then *heshe*. See next note.

45. The *ayin*. The root of *hasha* is shin, ayin, heh. *Hasha* is in the *hifil*. It is an imperative. The usual vocalization for such words when the final stem *heh* is omitted is *segol, segol*. However, *hasha* is vocalized *Kametz, pattach*. Hence I.E.'s comment.

46. See next note.

47. Thus our text should be read as if written, *va-avligah et atzmi*.

48. Translated according to I.E.

CHAPTER 40

1. FOR THE LEADER. A PSALM OF DAVID.

2. I WAITED PATIENTLY FOR THE LORD; AND HE INCLINED UNTO ME; AND HEARD MY CRY.

I WAITED PATIENTLY. The word *Kavvoh* (waited) is an irregular verb.[1] It is vocalized *with a cholam.*[2] Compare, *yassor* (chastened)[3] in *The Lord hath chastened me sore* (Ps. 118:17). AND HE INCLINED UNTO ME. Scripture reads thus because God abides in eternity[4] and is enthroned in the heavens.[5]

3. HE BROUGHT ME UP ALSO OUT OF THE TUMULTUOUS PIT,[6] OUT OF THE MIRY CLAY;[7] AND HE SET MY FEET UPON A ROCK, HE ESTABLISHED MY STEPS.[8]

HE BROUGHT ME UP… This is to be taken metaphorically, for David was[9] brought low[10] by adversity in that he was surrounded by enemies.

---

1. *Kavvoh* should have been vocalized *pattach, tzere* (kavveh). See next note.

2. Reading *al devar ha-cholam* in place of *al derekh ha-shalem.* The latter reading is impossible to explain. See Filwarg. *Kavvoh* comes from the root *kof vav, heh.* It is an infinitive in the piel. It should thus have been vocalized with a *tzere* in place of a *cholam* i.e. *kavveh.* Compare, *dabber, shabber.*

3. *Yassor* is also irregular, for it is a piel infinitive and should have been vocalized *yasser.*

4. See Isaiah 57:15.

5. See Ps. 123:1.

6. Hebrew, *mi-bor sha'on.*

7. Hebrew, *mi-tit ha-yaven.*

8. Translated according to I.E. Hebrew, *konen ashurai.*

9. Lit. "I was."

10. Hence he speaks of being in a pit.

Some say that the word *sha'on* (tumultuous) is related to the word *sho'ah* (destruction).[11] However, in reality the meaning of our verse is as follows: He brought me up out of the pit of the tumultuousness mighty waters[12] or out of the miry clay.[13]

The *heh* of *ha-yaven* (miry) is also to be prefaced to the word *tit* (clay), which comes before it.[14] Compare, *et yom ha-shevi'iy*[15] (the seventh day) (Gen. 2:3).

The word *yaven* (miry) has no cognate except for *bi-yeven metzulah* (deep mire) (Ps. 69:3). Its meaning is,[16] filthy water, thick mire.

The rock is mentioned[17] in contrast to the pit.

He established my steps means; He established my steps so that I could ascend the rock.

4. AND HE HATH PUT A NEW SONG IN MY MOUTH, EVEN PRAISE UNTO OUR GOD; MANY SHALL SEE, AND FEAR, AND SHALL TRUST IN THE LORD.

UNTO OUR GOD. Scripture employs the plural *Elohenu* (our God)[18] because it goes on to say, *Many shall see, and fear, And shall trust in the Lord.*

5. HAPPY IS THE MAN THAT HATH MADE THE LORD HIS TRUST, AND HATH NOT TURNED UNTO THE ARROGANT, NOR UNTO SUCH AS FALL AWAY[19] TREACHEROUSLY.

HAPPY IS THE MAN. Then they will say; *Happy is the man that hath the Lord his trust.*

---

11. According to this interpretation our verse reads: *He brought me up also out of the pit of destruction* (mi-bor sh'ao'n).

12. See Is. 17:13. In other words *sha'on* means, roaring (tumultuous) and is short for *she'on mayyim*.

13. According to I.E., *out of the miry clay* does not describe the pit of the tumultuous waters.

14. Thus *mi-tit ha-yaven* is to be read as if written, *me-ha-tit ha-yaven*. I.E. comments thus, because according to the rules of Hebrew grammar when an adjective has the definite article before it, the noun that it is modifying must also have the definite article before it.

15. This too is be read as if written, *et ha-yom ha-shevi'iy*. However, see I.E. on Gen. 2:3.

16. Of *yaven*.

17. Lit. "He mentions the rock."

18. Up till know David spoke of himself. Thus he now should speak of *my God* rather then employ the plural *our God*. Hence I.E.'s comments.

19. Hebrew, *sate*.

The meaning of *el rehavim* (unto the arrogant) is, to the mighty for help.[20] Compare *rahav* (the mighty) in, *that pierced the mighty* (Is. 51:9).[21]

The word *sate* (fall away) in Aramaic means, to incline.[22]

6. MANY THINGS HAST THOU DONE, O LORD MY GOD, EVEN THY WONDROUS WORKS, AND THY THOUGHTS TOWARDS US; THERE IS NONE TO BE COMPARED UNTO THEE! IF I WOULD DECLARE AND SPEAK OF THEM, THEY ARE MORE THAN CAN BE TOLD.

MANY THINGS. This is the new song.[23]

The word *rabbot* (many things) is an adjective modifying *nifle'otekha* (Thy wondrous works).[24] The word *rabbot* is similar to the word *rabbim* (many) in, *kol rabbim ammim* (so many peoples) (Ps. 89:51).[25]

Makhshevotekha means, *Thy Thoughts,* Your decrees.

The word *elenu* (towards us) means, because of us. On the other hand the word *elenu* is to be taken literally.[26]

David employs the term *elenu*[27] because he had previously used the plural *Elohenu* (our God) (v. 4).

THERE IS NONE TO BE COMPARED UNTO THEE.[28] It is impossible for any human being to set all of Your works before You.[29]

---

20. In other words the meaning of *And hath not turned unto the arrogant* is, and has not turned unto the arrogant for help.

21. Translated according to I.E.

22. According to I.E. *ve-sate khazav* (nor as such as fall away treacherously) means, nor to those who incline to treachery.

23. Mentioned in verse 4.

24. Even though the adjective precedes the noun. The latter is not the usual Hebrew syntax, for in Hebrew the noun comes before the adjective. I.E. comments thus, because our verse literally reads: *Many hast thou done, O Lord my God, Thy wondrous deeds.* I.E. believes that this should be interpreted as, many wondrous deeds hast Thou done, O Lord My God.

25. Here too the adjective (rabbim) precedes the verb (ammim).

26. It means towards us.

27. See note 18.

28. Hebrew, *En arokh elekha.*

29. This interpretation renders *arokh,* set. Thus according to this interpretation *en arokh elekha* (there is none to be compared unto Thee) literally means, *there is no setting before Thee* i.e. it is impossible for any human being to describe all of Your works when praising You.

The end of the verse[30] proves that this is its meaning.

Some say that the word *arokh* (compared) is similar to the word *ya'arokh* (be compared) in *be compared unto the Lord* (Ps. 89:7). If this is the case, then *they are more than be told* refers back to *Thy wondrous works.*[31]

7. SACRIFICE AND MEAL-OFFERING THOU HAST NO DELIGHT IN; MINE EARS HAST THOU OPENED; BURNT-OFFERING AND SIN OFFERING HAST THOU NOT REQUIRED.

SACRIFICE AND MEAL-OFFERING. Peace offerings[32] and meal-offerings in a stewing-pan[33] or on a griddle.[34] The meaning of our verse is that God intends to be good to us. His goodness is not dependent on payment.[35]

Observe, after mentioning sacrifice and meal-offering, David goes on to mention the burnt-offering and the sin-offering.

Rabbi Moses says that the word *lo* (no) in the phrase *Thou hast no delight* is to be read as if written twice.[36] *Mine ears hast Thou not (lo) opened* means, when You spoke with us on Mount Sinai, [37]You did not did command that sacrifices be offered.

However, I believe that the meaning of our clause is, You did not request a sacrifice. On the contrary *Mine ears hast Thou opened* so that I will obey Your voice.[38] Compare, *Behold, to obey is better than sacrifice* (1 Sam.15: 22).

8. THEN SAID I: LO I AM COME, WITH THE ROLE OF A BOOK, WHICH IS PRESCRIBED FOR ME.

THEN SAID I. Rabbi Marinus[39] says that David speaks on behalf of the community of Israel. He explains that *Lo, I am come with the role of a book* alludes to the words *We will do and obey* (Ex. 24:7), which our fathers uttered at Sinai. However, I believe that David spoke on his own behalf,

---

30. Which reads: *If I would speak of them, they are more than can be told.*

31. Its meaning being, *Thy wondrous deeds are more than can be told.*

32. According to I.E. *zevach* (sacrifice) refers to peace offerings.

33. Heb. *Marcheshet.* See Lev. 20:7.

34. Heb. *Machavat.* See Lev. 20:5.

35. On sacrifice.

36. In other words *Mine ears hast Thou opened* should be read as if written, *Mine ears hast Thou not (lo) opened.*

37. Lit. "You did not did command like this in my ears when You spoke with me on Mount Sinai."

38. In other words *Mine ears hast Thou opened* means, You told me to obey your voice.

39. Rabbi Jonah ibn Janach.

for when he was in distress he took a vow.[40] He commanded that it be written[41] that he would sing a new song.[42] David now comes to repay his vow.[43] The correct interpretation[44] is that the vow that David uttered was, *To do Thy will* (v. 9).[45] The latter was David's only desire.[46]

9. I DELIGHT TO DO THY WILL, O MY GOD; YEA, THY LAW IS IN MY INNERMOST PARTS.[47]

THY LAW IS IN MY INNERMOST PARTS. In my hidden parts. Our verse is similar to *eat this roll* (Ezek. 3:1).

10. I HAVE PREACHED RIGHTEOUSNESS IN THE GREAT CONGREGATION; LO, I DID NOT REFRAIN MY LIPS; O LORD, THOU KNOWEST.

I HAVE PREACHED RIGHTEOUSNESS. The word *bissarti* (I have preached) means, I gathered people[48] to deliver news to them. It can refer to good or bad news.[49] Compare, *And he that brought the tidings* (ha-mevasser) *answered* (1 Sam.4:17).[50]

11. I HAVE NOT HID THY RIGHTEOUSNESS WITHIN MY HEART;[51] I HAVE DECLARED THY FAITHFULNESS AND THY SALVATION; I HAVE NOT CONCEALED THY MERCY AND THY TRUTH FROM THE GREAT CONGREGATION.

I HAVE NOT HID THY RIGHTEOUSNESS…This is parallel to, *I have preached righteousness*. David speaks of his relationship to God's righteousness, in secret and in public.

40. To sing a new song to God. See v. 4.

41. In a scroll (a role of a book).

42. To the Lord.

43. Lit. *I have now come to pay my vow.*

44. Contrary to what I.E. just wrote.

45. V. 9 literally reads: *To do Thy will O God is my desire.*

46. Lit. "This is my only desire."(v. 9). See above note.

47. Hebrew, *memai.* Literally, in my intestines. Hence I.E.'s comment.

48. Lit. "All flesh."

49. It usually refers to good news. Hence I.E.'s comment.

50. The reference here is to bad news.

51. David did not keep the truth regarding God's righteousness to himself.

12. THOU, O LORD, WILT NOT WITHHOLD THY COMPASSIONS FROM ME; LET THY MERCY AND THY TRUTH CONTINUALLY PRESERVE ME.

LET THY MERCY AND THY TRUTH CONTINUALLY PRESERVE ME. *Thy mercy and Thy truth* which I related to a large congregation will preserve me from all enemies.

13. FOR INNUMERABLE EVILS HAVE COMPASSED ME ABOUT, MINE INIQUITIES HAVE OVERTAKEN ME, SO THAT I AM NOT ABLE TO LOOK UP; THEY ARE MORE THEN THE HAIRS OF MY HEAD, AND MY HEART HATH FORSAKEN ME.[52]

FOR… MINE INIQUITIES HAVE OVERTAKEN ME. The punishment and the evil, which come upon a person, are called iniquities (avon), because they are the cause of the evil that come upon a man.[53] Compare, *My punishment (avoni) is greater than I can bear* (Gen. 4:13); *For the iniquity (avon) of the daughter of my people is greater than the sin of Sodom* (Lam. 4:6); *there shall be no punishment (avon) happen to thee* (1 Sam. 28:10). The same applies to *Mine iniquities* (avonotai).[54]

The meaning of our verse is; my punishments have overtaken me, so that I am not able to look up. The latter is similar to *and they* (the locusts) *shall cover the face of the earth that one shall not be able to see the earth* (Ex.10: 5).[55] The meaning of our verse is, *I am not able to look up*[56] because my iniquities are beyond count.[57] On the other hand *I am not able to look up* might refer to that which the heart sees.[58] Compare, *Now Jacob saw* (Gen. 42:1).[59]

MY HEART HATH FORSAKEN ME. I am as it were left without a heart.

---

52. Translated literally.

53. I.E. renders *Mine iniquities* (avonotai) *have overtaken me* as; *My punishment* (avonotai) *has overtaken me.*

54. Its meaning is, my punishment.

55. In other words the locusts shall be so numerous that they block the sun and the earth will not be seen.

56. Hebrew, *li-re'ot* (to see).

57. David's eye has grown dim because of his many punishments.

58. In this case the meaning of the verse is; my punishments are so many that I can't think straight.

59. The meaning of which is, now Jacob perceived.

14. BE PLEASED, O LORD, TO DELIVER ME; O LORD, MAKE HASTE TO HELP ME.

BE PLEASED… MAKE HASTE TO HELP ME. *Le-ezrati chushah* (make haste to help me) means, hasten to be my help.[60] On the other hand *le-ezrati* (to help me) might be an infinitive[61] meaning to help me.

15. LET THEM BE ASHAMED AND ABASHED TOGETHER THAT SEEK AFTER MY SOUL TO SWEEP IT AWAY; LET THEM BE TURNED BACKWARD AND BROUGHT TO CONFUSION THAT DELIGHT IN MY HURT.

LET THEM BE ASHAMED… TO SWEEP IT AWAY. The word *li-sepotah* (to sweep it away) is similar in meaning to the word *tispeh* (sweep away) in *wilt Thou indeed sweep away* (Gen. 18:23).

16. LET THEM BE APPALLED BY REASON[62] OF THEIR SHAME THAT SAY UNTO ME: AHA, AHA.

LET THEM BE APPALLED… After they finish bringing shame upon me.[63] Others say that the word *ekev* (by reason of) means, in recompense for. Compare, *le-olam ekev* (for ever is the reward).[64] The word *boshtam* (their shame) is interpreted the same way[65] in both interpretations.[66]

---

60. According to this interpretation *le-ezrati* means, to my help.

61. Our texts read, an adjective. Filwarg emends to an infinitive. His emendation should be accepted.

62. Hebrew, *ekev* (end of). Hence I.E.'s interpretation.

63. I.E. renders our clause: *Let them be appalled at the end of their shaming me.*

64. Translated according to I.E. According to this interpretation, our verse should be rendered: Let them be appalled in recompense for shaming me.

65. *Their shame* is to be interpreted, *for shaming me.*

66. Of the word *ekev.*

17. LET ALL THOSE THAT SEEK THEE REJOICE AND BE GLAD IN THEE; LET SUCH AS LOVE THY SALVATION SAY CONTINUALLY: THE LORD BE MAGNIFIED.

LET ALL THOSE THAT SEEK THEE REJOICE… This is what Scripture means by *I have preached righteousness.*[67]

18. BUT, AS FOR ME, THAT AM POOR AND NEEDY; THE LORD WILL ACCOUNT IT UNTO ME, THOU ART MY HELP AND MY DELIVERER; O MY GOD, TARRY NOT.

BUT, AS FOR ME, THAT AM POOR AND NEEDY. I consider myself poor and needy and unable to stand before my enemies.

THE LORD WILL ACCOUNT IT UNTO ME.[68] The Lord will account this unto me. The reference is to the David's humility.[69] On the other hand it is possible that the word *li* (unto me) is in place of "for me."[70] Compare *lakhem*[71] (for you) in *The Lord will fight for you* (Ex. 14:14).

THOU ART MY HELP AND MY DELIVERER; O MY GOD, TARRY NOT. *Te'achar* (tarry not) is transitive. It is like the word *echeru* (tarry) in *Why tarry…* (Judges 5:28).

---

67. This is what David preached.

68. The text literally reads: *The Lord will account unto me.* Hence I.E.'s comment.

69. Our clause should be interpreted as; the Lord will account my humility unto me.

70. In other words the word *li* here means *for me* (unto me). According to this interpretation we do not have to add the word "this" in order to explain our verse.

71. Lit., *to you.*

CHAPTER 41

1. FOR THE LEADER A PSALM OF DAVID.

This psalm deals with David's illness.[1]

2. HAPPY IS HE THAT CONSIDEREETH THE POOR; THE LORD WILL DELIVER HIM IN THE DAY OF EVIL.

HAPPY IS HE THAT CONSIDEREETH THE POOR. Some say that the word *maskil* (considereth) means, to look. Compare, *mistakkel² havet* (I looked)[3] (Dan.7:8).[4] However, in reality *maskil* is related to the word *sekhel* (wisdom). The psalm speaks of a person, who when ill, sets his mind[5] to study God's work[6]. The word *dal* (poor) refers to one poor in money or to one poor in flesh, that is, to one who is ill.[7] Compare the word *dal* (leaner) in, *Why, O son of the king art thou thus becoming leaner* (dal) *from day to day?* (2 Sam. 13:4). The words *dallut* (poverty) and *re'ut* (friendship) are adjectives.[8]

Some say that the word *maskil* (considereth) is a transitive verb. Our verse refers to the one, who visits the sick, to comfort and enlighten him.[9]

The day of evil speaks of the arrangements of the heavenly bodies on the day of his birth.[10]

---

1. Lit., "his illness."

2. Both words come from the same root, *sin, kaf, lamed.*

3. Translated according to I.E.

4. According to this interpretation, our clause should be rendered: *Happy is he that looks to the poor.* The meaning of the latter is, happy is the person that visits the poor and takes care of his needs.

5. Literally, "his heart."

6. He continues to study God's work when ill or he learns a lesson from his illness.

7. According to this interpretation our verse reads: Happy is he who enlightens himself when ill.

8. In contrast to *dal* and *re'a* which are nouns.

9. According to this interpretation our clause reads: *Happy is he that enlightens* (maskil) *the poor.* He enlightens the poor by telling him that God will deliver him from his sickness.

10. I.E. believed that the arrangement of the stars at the time of a person's birth influence that individuals fate.

THE LORD WILL DELIVER HIM. The Lord alone and not the hand of any human being.

The Lord preserve him means, his[11] illness will not increase.

The sick person is afraid of death. Hence Scripture reads: *and keep him alive.*

3. THE LORD PRESERVE HIM, AND KEEP HIM ALIVE, LET HIM BE CALLED HAPPY IN THE LAND; AND DELIVER NOT THOU HIM[12] UNTO THE GREED OF HIS ENEMIES.

LET HIM BE CALLED HAPPY IN THE LAND… He will live many years beyond those of his generation and his enemies will not see their wishes come to pass.

The *tav*[13] of *tittenehu* (deliver Thou him) refers to the subject, although the subject is not mentioned in the text.[14] Compare, *Whom she bore to Levi* (Num. 25:59).[15] *Tittenehu* refers to God's word[16] or decree.[17] On the other hand the *tav*[18] might refer to God. There are many such cases in Scripture.[19]

4. THE LORD SUPPORT HIM UPON THE BED OF ILLNESS, MAYEST THOU TURN ALL HIS LYING DOWN IN HIS SICKNESS.[20]

THE LORD SUPPORT HIM UPON THE BED OF ILLNESS. The word *davvai* (illness) is a noun.[21] It means illness.[22]

---

11. Lit., "he"

12. Hebrew, *tittenehu.*

13. The *tav* prefixed to a verb can be a second person masculine future prefix, or a third person feminine prefix. *Tittenehu* can be rendered, you shall deliver him or it shall deliver him. I.E.'s first interpretation renders *tittenehu* as a third person because the first half of the verse is in the third person.

14. I.E. renders *tittenehu*, let it deliver him. He renders our clause as follows: *And let not God's decree deliver him unto the greed of his enemies.*

15. Translated lit. Here too the subject is missing and must be supplied by the reader.

16. *Imrah*, which is a feminine.

17. *Gezerah*, which is a feminine.

18. Of *tittenehu.*

19. Where the verse opens in the third person and concludes with the second person.

20. Literally, *All his bed, Thou turned, in his illness.* Hence the interpretations that follows.

21. Not an adjective. See I.E. on verse 2.

22. Literally, "it is similar to the word *madveh* (disease)." See Deut. 28:60.

The Lord supports the sick person little by little when his illness turns for the worse, or when his affairs and his concerns turn while he is on his bed. However, in reality[23] the *tav*[24] of *hafakhta* (mayest Thou turn)[25] refers to God.[26] Our clause is metaphoric.[27] Its meaning is, You God support him and turn him from side to side on his bed. In other words the sick man has no need of human help to support him.

5. AS FOR ME, I SAID: O LORD, BE GRACIOUS UNTO ME; HEAL MY SOUL; FOR I HAVE SINNED AGAINST THEE.

AS FOR ME, I SAID…Its meaning is, when I pray in my illness,[28] "O Lord be gracious unto me and heal me even though[29] I have sinned against You," my enemies say: "When shall he die".[30]

For (ki) I have sinned against Thee is similar to *for (ki) it is a stiff-necked people* (Ex. 34: 9).[31]

6. MINE ENEMIES SPEAK EVIL OF ME:[32] WHEN SHALL HE DIE, AND HIS NAME PERISH.

MINE ENEMIES SPEAK EVIL OF ME: Then[33] my enemies say of me:[34] *When shall he die.* Compare, *And pharaoh will say of the children of Israel*[35] (*li-vene yisra'el*) (Ex. 14:3).

---

23. Lit., "the correct interpretation is."

24. The second person imperfect suffix.

25. Literally, "You turned."

26. According to this interpretation *hafakhta* (You turned) refers to the illness or to the affairs of the afflicted. What the verse is saying is, You God will support the person whom You struck with illness.

27. For God does not actually turn the sick person over.

28. Lit. "I say."

29. In other words, *ki* (for) here has the meaning of *even though*; for it makes no sense to pray, heal me **because** I have sinned.

30. See I.E. on next verse.

31. Here too the word *ki* has the meaning of *even though*, for it would make no sense for Moses to say to God, "go in the midst of Israel, for *(ki)* it is a stiff-necked people." What Moses said was, "go in the midst of Israel, **even though** *(ki)* it is a stiff-necked people." See I.E. on Ex. 33:9.

32. Literally, *Mine enemies speak evil to me* (li). Hence I.E.'s comment.

33. When I pray, *O Lord be gracious unto me… (v. 5).*

34. The word *li* literally means, to me. However is here to be rendered, of me.

35. Literally, to the children of Israel. However its meaning here is, of the children of Israel.

David's enemies act the reverse of the one who considers the poor.[36] They say to people: *When shall he die?*[37]

7. AND IF ONE COME TO SEE ME, HE SPEAKETH FALSEHOOD; HIS HEART GATHERETH INIQUITY TO ITSELF; WHEN HE GOETH ABROAD, HE SPEAKETH OF IT.[38]

AND IF ONE COME TO SEE ME.[39] *To see* means to visit.

HE SPEAKETH FALSEHOOD. To me and says, "I am greatly pained that you are sick."

HE SPEAKETH.[40] He speaks an evil thing of me when he goes outside to converse with my other enemies who did not see me. He tells them, "A difficult illness is firm in him (v. 9)." The word *yatzuk* (cleaveth fast)(v. 9)[41] is similar to *yatzuk* (firm) in *His heart is as firm as a stone* (Job 42:16).

[8. ALL THAT HATE ME WHISPER TOGETHER AGAINST ME, AGAINST ME DO THEY DEVISE MY HURT:

9. AN EVIL THING CLEAVETH FAST UNTO HIM; AND NOW THAT HE LIETH, HE SHALL RISE UP NO MORE.]

10. YEA, MINE OWN FAMILIAR FRIEND, IN WHOM I TRUSTED, WHO DID EAT OF MY BREAD, HATH LIFTED UP HIS HEEL AGAINST ME.

YEA, MINE OWN FAMILIAR FRIEND... Also the one who was not my enemy, the one who did eat of my bread, namely, the one whose life I sustained has raised his heel against me.

HATH LIFTED HIS HEEL AGAINST ME. Its meaning is, he has raised the importance of his foot, for He does not visit me. He considers himself extremely exalted.

---

36. See verse 1.

37. In other words, *When shall he die...* does not refer to what they say in their minds.

38. *Of it* is not in the Hebrew text. In Hebrew the verse concludes with *he speaketh*.

39. Lit., and if (one) come to see.

40. See note 39.

41. In *devar bliya'al yatzuk bo* (an evil thing cleaveth fast in him) (v. 9).

11. BUT THOU, O LORD, BE GRACIOUS UNTO ME, AND RAISE ME UP, THAT I MAY REQUITE THEM.

BUT THOU, O LORD, BE GRACIOUS UNTO ME. This is in contrast to the words of David's enemies: *An evil thing cleaveth fast unto him* (v. 9).
And raise me up is in contrast to *He shall rise up no more* (ibid).

12. BY THIS I KNOW THAT THOU DELIGHTEST IN ME, THAT MINE ENEMY DOTH NOT SHOUT[42] OVER ME.

BY THIS. *That Mine enemy doth not shout* as they who triumph in the day of war do. Our verse is similar to *Philistia, cry aloud[43] because of me* (Ps. 60:10).

13. AND AS FOR ME, THOU UPHOLDEST ME BECAUSE OF MINE INTEGRITY, AND SETTEST ME BEFORE THY FACE FOR EVER.

AND AS FOR ME, THOU UPHOLDEST ME BECAUSE OF MINE INTEGRITY. *Be-tummi*[44] is to be rendered, because of mine integrity.[45] Some say that *tummi* (mine integrity) refers to bodily health.[46] The latter is correct.

14. BLESSED BE THE LORD, THE GOD OF ISRAEL, FROM EVERLASTING TO EVERLASTING. AMEN, AND AMEN.

BLESSED BE THE LORD. I am therefore obligated to bless God[47] at all times. This is the meaning of *From everlasting and to everlasting*.[48] I say time after time: it is true;[49] it is true. My comments on the first book of Psalms are completed. I offer my thanks to God.

---

42. Translated literally. Hebrew *yari'a*.

43. Hebrew, *hitro'a'iy*.

44. Lit., "my wholeness."

45. The *bet* usually means in. Hence I.E. points out that it here has the meaning of, because.

46. My integrity refers to the integrity of the body. I.E. renders our clause as, in my integrity You uphold. The meaning of the latter is, You uphold the integrity of my body.

47. Blessed is the Lord is to be interpreted as, I am therefore obligated to bless God.

48. *From everlasting and to everlasting* means, at all times.

49. The blessing that I utter.

BIBLIOGRAPHY

Ben-Menahem, N. *Ibn Ezra. Studies* (Hebrew), Jerusalem: 1978

Cohen, Joseph. *Haguto Ha-Filosofit Shel Rabbenu Avraham ibn Ezra*, Israel: 1996.

Goldstein, David. *The Jewish Poets of Spain.* London:1965.

Filwarg, J. Bene Reshef *[Supercommentary on Ibn Ezra's Commentaries on Scripture].* Piotrekow: 1900.

Fine Harry H., *Gems of Hebrew Verse.* Boston: 1940.

Fleisher J. L. *Avraham ibn Ezra, Kovetz Ma'amarim Al Toledotav Vi-Yitzirotav.* Tel Aviv: 1970.

Friedlander, M. *Essays on the Writings of Abraham Ibn Ezra.* London: 1877.

Friedlander, M. *The Commentary of Ibn Ezra on Isaiah.* London: 1873.

Golb, Norman. *History and Culture of the Jews of Rouen in the Middle Ages (Hebrew).* Tel Aviv: 1976

Goldstein, D. *The Jewish Poets of Spain.* Middlesex: 1965.

Gratz, Heinrich. *Divre Yeme Yisrael.* Translated by J.P. Rabinowitz. 1916

Husik, I. *A History of Mediaeval Jewish Philosophy.* Phila: 1940.

Ibn Ezra, Abraham. *Commentary on Psalms.* Mikra'ot Gedolot.

Ibn Ezra, Abraham. *Commentary on Psalms.* Mikra'ot Gedolot; Ha-Keter. Israel: 2003.

Kahana David. *Rabbi Avraham ibn Ezra.* Warsaw: 1922.

Katz, Sarah. *Fair Verses of the Jewish Adalusian Poets (Hebrew).* Jerusalem: 1997.

Klatzkin, Jacob. *Otzar Ha-Munachim Ha-Filosofiyim.* Berlin: 1928.

Kook, Abraham Yitzchak . *Orot Ha-Kodesh, Musar Ha-Kodesh Vol. 11.* Jerusalem: 1990

Krinsky, J.L. *Chumash Me-Chokeke Yehudah.* New York: 1975.

Levin, I. *Abraham Ibn Ezra Reader (Hebrew).* New York-Tel Aviv: 1985

Melammed E.Z. *Mefareshe Ha- Mikra.* Jerusalem: 1978.

Sela, Shlomo. *Abraham Ibn Ezra And the Rise of Medieval Hebrew Science.* Boston: 2003.

Schmelzer, Menahem H. *Yitzhak ibn Ezra Shirim.* New York: 1979.

Shirman, Chaim. *Ha-Shirah Ha-Ivrit Bi-Sefarad U-Ve-Provance.* Jerusalem -Tel Aviv: 1956.

Simon Uriel, *Four Approaches to the Book of Psalms: From Saadiah Gaon to Abraham ibn Ezra.* Translated By Lenn J. Schramm. New York: Press, 1991

Strickman, H. Norman. *The Secret of the Torah: A Translation of Ibn Ezra's Yesod Mora Ve-Sod Ha-Torah.* New Jersey: 1995.

Ibn Ezra's Commentary on the Pentateuch (Genesis).

Translated & Annotated by H. Norman Strickman and Arthur Silver. New York : 1988.

Ibn Ezra's Commentary on the Pentateuch (Exodus).

Translated & Annotated by H. Norman Strickman and Arthur Silver. New York:1996.

Ibn Ezra's Commentary on the Pentateuch (Leviticus).

Translated & Annotated by H. Norman Strickman and Arthur Silver. New York: 2004.

Ibn Ezra's Commentary on the Pentateuch (Numbers).

Translated & Annotated by H. Norman Strickman and Arthur Silver. New York: 1999.

Ibn Ezra's Commentary on the Pentateuch (Deuteronomy).

Translated & Annotated by H. Norman Strickman and Arthur Silver. New York: 2001,

Menorah Press, New York. 1999.

Waxman Meyer, *A History of Jewish Literature, Vol. 1.* (New Jersey, 1960).

Wilinsky, M. *Sefer Ha-Rikmah Le-Rabbenu Ibn Janah, Be-Targumo Shel Rabbenu Yehudah Ibn Tibbon,*

Jerusalem: 1964.

INDEX OF NAMES

INDEX OF BIBLICAL SOURCES

21:13-16	243
22:49	169
23:26	54
24:14	140
28:10	300
28:15	155

2 Samuel

1:23	115
2:22	125
4:2	282
4:4	257
5:8	213
6:10	71
7:1	216
13:4	303
14:2	181
15:18	250
19:28	110
20:1	146
23:2	14
76:27	231

1 Kings

1:24	184
2:2	190
8:61	177
13:2	14
19:8	47
21:13	87
22:36	119, 232

2 Kings

3:18	133
3:19	211
11:1	28
12:11	39, 136, 215
24:15	28

Isaiah

1:30	33
2:2	244
2:4	186

2:16	152
3:25	103, 171
6:4	20
8:7	126
8:22	180
9:4	127
12:6	167
13:8	126
13:10	146
16:7	90
19:6	146
19:10	97
20:5	97
21:8	96
22:4	294
22:7	38
23:11	196
25:11	57
26:2	100, 269
30:15	180, 181
30:23	275
30:24	69, 253
30:28	179
32:6	36
38:5	56
38:13	284
40:4	225
40:12	293
42:24	83
43:21	83
45:2	209
48:14	236
50:9	57
51:9	297
53:8	206
55:3	215
55:6	231
57:20	18
58:10	255
63:17	16
64:10	166
66:7	69

Jeremiah

2:24	136, 188
5:13	87

8:6	181
8:18	294
9:7	50
10:18	162, 164
10:20	125
11:19	236
12:5	268, 271
15:19	103
17:3	217
17:9	85
17:11	279
20:7	126
21:3	37
23:6	253
23:10	134
25:32	27
30:10	17
31:8	27
31:15	52
31:18	188
39:12	241
42:10	250
46:27	17
50:17	92
50:41	27
50:43	89, 271

Ezekiel

2:8	103
3:1	299
6:6	53
9:8	56
13:18	75
19:4	83
19:8	70
24:3	171
25:15	203
28:17	172
29:14	175
31:10	80
32:2	169
37:25	17
39:26	228
47:12	21
47:13	115

Hosea

2:4	48
13:3	22
14:1	249

Amos

1:5	115
1:8	115
4:1	170
6:6	116
6:8	184

Obadiah

1:10	101

Jonah

1:5	21
1:12	276
2:5	55
2:8	34, 205

Micah

1:16	169
2:12	140

Habakkuk

1:2	16
1:3	93
1:16	52, 101
2:20	211
3:1	16

Zephaniah

3:3	92

Haggai

1:6	168

LaVergne, TN USA
05 November 2009

163236LV00001B/36/P